. . .
h
n

Fair
story
nbers
rry

parts
es of
enter

man
rs'

MY SONG
A MEMOIR
HARRY BELAFONTE
with MICHAEL SCHNAYERSON

CANONGATE
Edinburgh · London

First published in Great Britain in 2012 by Canongate Books Ltd,
14 High Street, Edinburgh EH1 1TE

www.canongate.tv

1

First published in the United States of America in 2011 by Alfred A. Knopf,
a division of Random House, Inc, New York

British Library Cataloguing-in-Publication Data
A catalogue record for this book is available on
request from the British Library

ISBN 978 0 85786 586 1

Printed and bound in Great Britain by
CPI Group (UK) Ltd, Croydon CR0 4YY

To Melvine Love
(my mother)

PART ONE

1

The phone rang late in the evening in my New York apartment. It was the night of August 4, 1964. A night of grief and anger for all of us in the civil rights movement, but especially those in Mississippi. "We've got a crisis on our hands down here," the young man on the line said. "We need help."

At the start of that fateful summer, hundreds of volunteers, most of them students, many of them white, all of them knowing how dangerous the work would be, had come down from northern universities to register black voters and support rural blacks in pursuit of their civil rights. They were fanning out along the front lines of a civil rights war, unarmed in a state of seething segregationists.

Mississippi's police stood ready at the slightest pretext to beat them bloody and throw them in jail. The Ku Klux Klan might well do worse. That day, we all learned just how much worse. The bodies of three volunteers, missing since June 21, had been found in a shallow grave near Philadelphia, Mississippi. Michael Schwerner, James Chaney, and Andrew Goodman—two of them white, one black—had been arrested on an alleged traffic violation, briefly jailed, then allowed to drive off, after dark, into a KKK ambush. All three had been beaten, then shot. Chaney, the black volunteer, had been tortured and mutilated.

I'd helped raise a lot of the money to launch Mississippi Freedom Summer. I'd called all the top entertainers I knew—Frank Sinatra, Lena Horne, Henry Fonda, Marlon Brando, Joan Baez, the Kingston Trio, Dick Gregory, and more—to ask that they give money directly or participate in benefit concerts. That money bought a lot of gas and cars, housing and food. But now more was needed. A lot more.

The original plan had called for students to do two-week shifts, then go home and be replaced by others. With the ominous disappearance of Schwerner, Chaney, and Goodman, every shift had insisted on staying. Now that the bodies had been found, all those volunteers voted to stay not just through summer, but into the fall as well. "It's good they're staying," explained Jim Forman, the young man who called me that night. Jim was the de facto head of the Student Nonviolent Coordinating Committee (SNCC), one of several civil rights groups down there. "Because if they leave now, or even at the end of August, the Klan will say it intimidated them into going, and the press will play it that way. And if they all stay, we can get thousands of more voters registered. The problem is we don't have the resources to keep them all here."

"What do you need?" I asked.

"At least fifty thousand dollars."

I told him I'd get it, one way or the other. "How soon do you need it?"

"We're going to burn through the rest of our budget in seventy-two hours."

Before he rang off, Forman told me one other thing. "This could get really ugly," he said quietly. "I'm hearing a lot of people say enough is enough, the hell with nonviolence. They're taking up guns. I'm worried they're going to take matters into their own hands."

I had to think hard about where that money might come from, and how I might get it to Greenwood, Mississippi. I could tap my own savings for the whole $50,000—I'd written a check to SNCC for an amount not much smaller than that in its early days to help establish it, and others since then. For me it was "anything goes," but I owed it to my family to keep us financially safe. Paul Robeson, the extraordinary actor, singer, and activist whose path I'd tried to follow my whole adult life, had given so much money to social causes that he'd left himself vulnerable to his enemies, chief among them the federal government, a formidable force led by J. Edgar Hoover and the Federal Bureau of Investigation, when he was blacklisted as a communist in the late 1940s. With Senator Joseph McCarthy riding shotgun, the federal government had cowed Carnegie Hall and other American venues into not hiring him, then seized his passport so that he couldn't earn a living performing abroad. Eventually Paul ran through his savings and slid into a deep place of sadness. I never forgot that. Somehow, I'd have to raise most of this money from others. In two days, maybe three. Then there was the matter of how that money would get to Mississippi. I couldn't just wire it and have a black civil rights activist go to the local Western Union office to ask for his $50,000, please. He'd be dead before he drove a mile away. So would a white college volunteer. As for banks, those fine institutions owned and operated by Mississippi's white power elite? No way.

The money would have to be brought down in cash. And unless I could come up with some brighter idea, I'd have to take it down myself.

My wife, Julie, started pulling together a New York fundraiser at our West End Avenue apartment. I flew to Chicago. Irv Kupcinet, as powerful a columnist in his city as Walter Winchell was in New York, gathered dozens of guests at his home on a day or two's notice. White guests, bearing checkbooks. Why did I, as a black performer, have such sway with Irv and his friends? Our friendship traced back to my club-circuit days as a young troubadour in the early fifties, but our personal history was just one part of it. Without quite knowing how I did it, I had some power to reach a hand across the racial divide. That, I knew, had as much to do with the moment as with me. Galvanized by the shocking news of the volunteers' murders, Irv's guests thrust cash and checks at me—$35,000 worth—as if I was the personal emissary of the civil rights movement. Which in a way, in that place and on that evening, I was. After making a trip to Montreal, I had another $20,000.

When I got back to New York, Julie and I took in $15,000 more from our own apartment fundraiser. Time was running out: I'd hoped to raise $100,000, but $70,000 would have to do. I felt pretty good about that sum of money. I felt even better now that I had a sidekick for the trip: my pal from our days together as struggling actors in Harlem, Sidney Poitier.

Sidney and I were like brothers. Born within eight days of each other, we shared the same West Indian heritage, and the same burning desire to break out of grinding poverty. Incredibly, both of us had achieved our dreams as entertainers. Sidney was the top black actor in Hollywood. I'd found my first successes as a singer, but had gone on to my own share of Broadway and Hollywood triumphs. We were, to put it simply, the two top black male entertainers in the world. Like brothers, we were also fiercely competitive, and had our differences, both political and personal. For starters, Sidney was a lot more cautious than I was. "What kind of protection are you going to have?" he asked warily when I asked him to come.

"I talked to Bobby about it," I said. Robert F. Kennedy was still serving, after his brother's assassination, as U.S. Attorney General under President Johnson. He'd directed me to Burke Marshall, head of the Justice Department's civil rights division. Both understood the risk I was taking. In Mississippi's vicious climate, the chances of a Klansman taking a potshot at me were actually pretty high. Knocking off that rich Negro singer from New York who thought he knew what was best for the South? Ten points! Marshall heard me out on the phone, and took down my itinerary. I conveyed all this to Sidney, maybe presuming a bit more from my conversation with Marshall than I should have. "Marshall's on it," I told him. "That means federal security every step of the way."

"Every step of the way," Sidney echoed.

"Right," I said. "Besides, it'll be harder for them to knock off two black stars than one. Strength in numbers, man."

"Okay," Sidney said grimly. "But after this, Harry?"

"Yeah?"

"Never call me again."

I knew Sidney well enough to know he meant it—at least at that moment. Of course I chose to view his fury as a joke and laughed it off, but I laughed alone. Unaccompanied, and not making much conversation, the two of us boarded a plane in Newark, New Jersey, bound for Jackson, Mississippi. I'd deposited the fundraiser checks and replaced them with cash, so we had $70,000 in small bills stuffed into a black doctor's bag. In that long-ago time, no one asked us what we were carrying. A flight attendant just waved us aboard.

Our flight to Jackson was the evening's last one into the main airport. We found Jim Forman and two other SNCC volunteers waiting for us, but otherwise the terminal sat virtually deserted. The only sign of local authority we saw was a black maintenance man pushing a broom. Sidney shot me an angry glance. "That's our federal security?"

"Probably an FBI agent in disguise," I told him. Sidney didn't so much as chuckle.

The volunteers led us out into the heavy, humid Mississippi night and over to a private strip beside the airport where a little Cessna was waiting. The pilot, who was white, greeted us most soberly, with a deep southern accent. As we piled in, I stole another look at him. Was he a Klansman, leading us into a trap? He sure seemed to fit the role.

My fears deepened as the tiny plane flew toward Greenwood. It was a bumpy ride. The pilot seemed unconcerned. We took every pitch of the plane as the beginning of the end.

Finally we landed on a dirt runway beside a shack that constituted Greenwood's airport. The pilot taxied past it, and then back, let us out, and took off immediately. What did he know that we didn't? I looked around, struck as much by the darkness as by the heat. I'd never seen a night as black as this. A poem called "The Creation," by James Weldon Johnson, came back to me.

> . . . far as the eye of God could see
> Darkness covered everything,
> Blacker than a hundred midnights
> Down in a cypress swamp.

Two more SNCC volunteers were waiting for us, with two cars, to take us into town. Sidney and I slid into the back of one, with Jim Forman in the passenger seat and a young SNCCer named Willie Blue in the driver's seat; the rest got into the second car. Both cars had been sanded to a dull finish so they wouldn't shine at night. A good precaution, but not good enough: As Willie and the other driver started their engines, a long row of headlights flashed on at the far end of the dark airfield. "That must be the federal agents," I said to Sidney. But we could see that the pairs of headlights were at different heights, and they blazed with differing degrees of brightness. Willie Blue dashed my hopes. "Agents, my ass," he muttered. "That's the Klan."

Instead of driving away from the row of headlights, in the direction of the main road to town, Willie and the other driver started moving at full speed toward them. We got close enough to see the dim outlines of three or four old pickup trucks. Then, as if at some prearranged signal, Willie and the other driver veered off to the side, taking a rough, alternative route to the road that led to town. The pickups fell in line behind us.

"Why aren't you driving faster?" I shouted. Willie was keeping right to the forty-mile-an-hour speed limit. "Faster, man!"

"No," Willie shouted back. "That's exactly what they want us to do.

They got a state trooper up there waiting in his car with the headlights off, ready to arrest us for speeding. He takes us to the station, lets us out in an hour, and even more of the Klan be waiting for us. That's how they work. That's how those boys got killed."

From behind us, the first pickup truck sped up and started to pass us. Through the rear window, we could see it had a two-by-four across its grille—a makeshift battering ram—and no license plate. Willie swerved into the middle of the two-lane road to keep the pickup from pulling alongside. Now the pickup started ramming the back of our car. "We can't let him pull up beside us," Willie shouted. "They'll shoot."

Willie switched on his walkie-talkie and radioed the SNCC office in Greenwood. From the other walkie-talkie I heard a crackling voice: "We're on our way."

The pickup truck kept ramming our car, but Willie stayed doggedly to the center of the road, edging left every time the truck tried to pull up. Finally, after two or three terrifying minutes that seemed like forever, I looked down the road to see a convoy of cars coming toward us from Greenwood. "That's them," Willie said. The SNCC brigade to the rescue. My heart was still pounding, but I started to breathe again.

As the convoy approached, the pickup trucks slowed, and their headlights retreated. That was when we heard the shots, a dozen or more. Whether the Klansmen were firing at us or shooting up in the air, we couldn't tell. No one was hit, and no bullets pierced our cars. When we turned off the main road, secure now among the SNCC fleet, we looked back to see the pickups rolling off down the main road, with more gunfire as they went.

The convoy led us into Greenwood, and beyond, to an Elks hall, where hundreds of volunteers were gathered. They had spent the day in heated debate, tense and tired, over what their next moves should be. Most of their options depended on us. When Sidney and I walked in, screams of joy went up from the crowd. Sidney and I had heard a lot of applause in our day, but never anything like those cheers. After weeks of lonely, scary fieldwork, these volunteers were wrung out and in despair. To have two of the biggest black stars in the world walk in to show solidarity with them—that meant a lot to them, and to us.

The crowd took up a freedom song, and then another—the spirituals that had given these brave volunteers comfort and encouragement day after day. Finally Sidney spoke. "I am thirty-seven years old," he told the crowd. "I have been a lonely man all my life . . . because I have not found love . . . but this room is overflowing with it." Then Sidney turned to me. I let a pause fall over the room, then sang out, "Day-o . . ." The crowd picked it up with a roar. The "Banana Boat Song" was my musical signature, but more than that, it was a cry from the heart of poor workers, a cry of weariness mingled with hope, both of which those volunteers felt profoundly that night. *"Day-o, Day-o / Daylight come an' me wan' go home"* had also been turned into a civil rights anthem—*"Freedom, freedom, freedom come an' it won't be long."* When the crowd had sung both versions, I held up the black satchel I'd brought, upturned it on the table in front of me, and let the bundles of cash cascade out, to delirious shouts.

As Sidney had said, we felt a lot of love in that barn. Outside it, though, Ku Klux Klanners sat in idling cars; we could hardly keep them out of Greenwood. That day planes had flown overhead, dropping KKK leaflets that urged Mississippians not to let the niggers steal their rights. Late that night, after a dinner of chicken and spareribs, Sidney and I were escorted to the house where we were to sleep, with armed guards patrolling outside. Our bedroom had one double bed—not too big a double bed, either—shoved up against a wall under a window. Sidney blanched.

"Look, I'll take the inside, okay?" I told him, meaning the side by the wall. I meant it as a concession: I'd be the one scrunched in by my snoring bedmate.

Sidney gave me a suspicious look. "Yeah, but if someone sticks a gun through that window and shoots, I'll be more apt to get hit."

He was only half joking.

"Okay, okay, I'll take the outside," I said.

Sidney thought about that. If I was willing to take the outside, maybe it was the better side after all. "No, I'll take the outside," he said. "If you do get shot, I'd hate to have to climb over your dead ass to get to the door."

In bed with the light out, we talked for a while. I told Sidney some of my ghost stories. Finally I fell into a ragged sleep, only to be awakened, in the pitch darkness, by a strange rasping sound. I reached over to nudge Sidney awake. The other side of the bed was empty. The rasping sound was louder. "Sidney?"

"Yes," he rasped.

"What the fuck are you doing?"

"Push-ups," Sidney said. "I can't sleep. And when those mother-fuckers come for us, I want to be sure I'm ready."

Often in the days after I got home to my wife and children, I asked myself why I had taken on the civil rights movement as my personal crusade. I knew the reason I'd gotten involved in general—any black American with a pulse and a conscience had done that by the summer of 1964, at least to the extent of writing the occasional check. A lot of white Americans had, too. All of us sensed this was a point at which history simply had to turn. We couldn't tolerate more lynchings and beatings. We couldn't abide more "whites-only" signs on the hotels and restaurants and gas stations and water fountains and bus stations of the segregated South. We couldn't let black Americans be treated as slaves in all but name anymore. This we knew. But why did I feel so personally offended, sitting in my twenty-one-room apartment on West End Avenue, when I saw news pictures of student protesters beaten by truncheon-wielding state police and bitten by police attack dogs? What deep wellspring of anger did those images bring up, and why had I felt so angry, for so long, about so many other related issues of freedom, and democracy, and equality, as if the perpetrators of these grave indignities—from the president to the FBI to the military to the man in the street—had set out to do *me* wrong? And why, when I also cared so much about making a success of myself as an actor and singer, had I jeopardized—in some ways damaged—a career trajectory that had made me, at thirty, the world's first so-called black matinee idol?

My mother had a lot to do with it. To a lesser degree my father, but he was in there. I also knew that from childhood, I'd occupied a lonely place, not just between West Indian and American culture, but between black and white. And in both the actual worlds I'd balanced between as a kid—Kingston and Harlem—I was as poor as poor could be. I was definitely angry about *that*.

Long after I'd immersed myself in the civil rights movement, I would still be trying to understand that anger and make it melt away. With Martin Luther King, Jr., to guide me, I would embrace nonviolence—not just as an organizing tactic, but as a way of life. Half a century of Freudian analysis would help, too. But as I began to set down the story of my life, I would still be piecing the parts together. I know more now than when I started this book. I see the little boy I was, in all his complexities, angry and hurt, almost always alone. Yet why this little boy, among all others, should use his anger to push himself up, make a name for himself, and then make it his mission to smash racial barriers and injustice with such grim determination, I'm not sure I can say.

Perhaps, in the end, where your anger comes from is less important than what you do with it.

2

I was born into poverty, grew up in poverty, and for a long time poverty was all I thought I'd know. It defined me; in the depths of my soul I think it defines me still. I felt not just angry but somewhat afraid, and vulnerable. All of this my mother felt, too, from the moment she stepped off a steamer called the *Cananova* onto Ellis Island on July 20, 1926. But at first, she also felt hope.

My mother, Melvine Love, was a true Jamaican beauty of twenty-one, with dark eyes, high cheekbones, and a trim figure she held so straight that no one ever failed to note her sense of pride and purpose. She was one of thirteen children born to a farming family up in the mountains of St. Ann Parish, on the island's north coast, her café au lait skin the telltale sign of her interracial roots. Her father was a black sharecropper, her mother the white daughter of a Scottish father who'd come to Jamaica to oversee a plantation for an absentee owner. It was a common story in the islands. So were large families, with not all the children necessarily born of the same two parents. A few of my mother's siblings probably had different fathers, and darker or lighter skin to show for it; I'm fairly sure my grandfather had a few offspring sprinkled among the surrounding hills. Millie, as my mother was known, was one of the ten children of her family who survived childhood. Jamaica held nothing for them but a hardscrabble farming life, so four of Millie's siblings had already come to New York; two were waiting for her in the reception area. My aunt Liz was dressed in a fancy hat and tightly tailored wool suit. The suit was meant to impress, and it did. With her was my uncle Castel, who probably looked like her driver; in fact, he had a car he operated as a taxi, taking Harlem fares no self-respecting white cabbie would touch—they never came to Harlem.

As a girl who'd grown up in a two-room shack in rural Jamaica, Millie was awed by the jostling crowds and honking automobiles around her when she took her first steps in Manhattan, clinging to Liz's arm. Awed and overwhelmed. But there was no going back. If she had any doubts, Millie had only to remember why she'd come. With her mother's help, she'd learned how to read and write on a slate board, and dared to imagine she might become an educated woman. At eight years old, she'd proudly shown the slate to her father, her heart filled with great expectations. "Fine, that's all you need," her father had said. "Now, in the mornings, you can teach your younger brother to do as good as you, and in the afternoons you can lend a hand in the fields." What craziness was she thinking—an education? Years later, I would marvel at the perfect curves and strokes of my mother's penmanship, all that remained of her girlish dreams.

Millie's first taxi ride took her to 145th Street and Seventh Avenue, in Harlem's West Indian community. Liz's apartment was in one of the better buildings on the block. When she led her younger sister inside, a neighbor called out a cheery greeting, "Hello, Miz Hines." Millie gave her a curious look, but said nothing as they passed upstairs to a taste-fully decorated six-room apartment with four bedrooms. "It's beauti-ful," Millie managed to say. "Does everybody in New York live like this?" Liz explained she had tenants for three of the four bedrooms; they helped with the rent. She'd made one of the bedrooms available for Millie, which was, as Liz hardly needed to add, a financial sacrifice. Millie could stay there, Liz said, until she got something going. From the way Liz laughed when she said it, even Millie realized what she meant: *Until you find a man.*

Millie was the newest member of an immigrant group within a larger immigrant group. A white New Yorker in 1926 might see no distinction between Harlem's American and Caribbean blacks, except for the islanders' lilting accents. But the differences were profound. American blacks bore the burden of two hundred years of pre–Civil War slavery and postwar segregation. Most had lived in poverty so long they'd lost all hope. They still fought to escape its pain and indig-nities, but they'd learned how to accommodate them. The islanders in Harlem in the early twentieth century weren't like that. They were first-generation immigrants, fired with ambition to better their lots. Their ancestors had been slaves in conditions often more brutal than those in the American South—worked to death like mules—but precisely because of that, they'd staged more rebellions and escapes; they didn't have the choice of groveling for slightly better treatment, as some slaves in the American South did. In part because of those rebellions, by the mid-nineteenth century Spain, France, and England were forced to abolish slavery in their colonies. Though they went on to train a skillful class of civil servants as overseers for their absentee landowners, that was not enough to contain the islanders' rebellious spirit. So independence had been doled out, bit by bit, until, by the mid-1920s, blacks on the islands could even aspire to be landowners, lawyers, or doctors. On most of the islands, they also composed the majority. Most were still poor, but they had pride and ambition.

A lot of those who made their way to Harlem came first to the Gulfport area in Mississippi, drawn by promises of steady work that turned into a new kind of slavery: indentured servitude. Contractors whisked these people off to the interior, where they found themselves cutting sugarcane, picking cotton, and living in crude barracks, earning only enough to fall into debt at the company store. The toughest and most determined of them had escaped—no less runaway slaves than their forebears in the islands—to head up north.

As a result, Harlem's West Indians were going to let nothing stop them from making their way. Not for them the institutional, dead-end poverty of American blacks. For their part, American blacks called the islanders the "Jews" of their community. It was a knock tinged with anti-Semitism, but there was more than a little truth to it. Like the Jews who'd colonized other pockets of Harlem, the islanders prized education, both in itself and as a means of escaping poverty. Like Jews, their aspirations were high. And like some American Jews of the 1920s, if they couldn't succeed within the law, they'd succeed outside it. Many islanders in those Prohibition days were rumrunners, working routes from the West Indies up along the East Coast. In Harlem, they ran the numbers games. Millie must have learned that early on, because Liz ran a numbers operation with her part-time boyfriend, Jimmy Hines.

A few West Indians had invented the numbers game not long before, brought it to Harlem, and by the mid-1920s made it a hugely profitable—and illegal—syndicate. The idea was brilliantly simple.

People bet on what the last three digits would be that day for any of various publicly toted-up figures. The stock market's closing price would do fine. So would the U.S. Treasury balance. The most popular was the total of what winning horses paid that afternoon at one of the tracks. All these totals were more than three digits when the cents as well as the dollars were included, so the last three digits—the most random ones—were those that bettors tried to guess. If the total for what a slate of winning horses paid that day was $264.64, the "full number" would be 464. Guessing all three in order was so unlikely that the odds were a thousand to one. But you could bet on a single digit or double digits, too—what the first number would be, say, or the first two—for a far more modest return.

As a numbers operator, Liz had her own bank, which meant she took in the bets from blocks around. Every morning, her runners would fan out through the neighborhood, knocking on every door. "What are you playing today, Mrs. Davis?" "Oh, give me three-forty-one for twenty-five cents." It cost so little to play that almost everyone did. And everyone had a "dream book" dictionary, with numbers written in beside telltale words. So Mrs. Davis might be betting on 341 because she'd had a dream about fire the night before—and there, by the definition of *fire* in her dream book, were the numerals 341. At the end of the day, someone always won, and the bankers, like Liz, always paid out—that was what kept the game going. That, and an absolutely scrupulous honesty on the part of the bankers: Any runner caught pocketing bets would pay a terrible price. Honesty was what kept Mrs. Davis and her neighbors betting; nothing could interfere with that process. Of course, there was a lot left over, too, which was why Liz had such a nice apartment and such finely tailored clothes.

Liz couldn't run a numbers game by herself. She needed a partner with muscle and political clout. For that, she had Jimmy Hines, who, to Millie's shock, wasn't an islander at all: He was an Irish politician, a Tammany Hall boss in the corrupt administration of Mayor Jimmy Walker. Hines was charming and ruthless. He'd started in his father's stable, ingratiating himself with the city's political machine by shoeing the city's police and fire horses. Soon he'd become a district captain. By 1926, he had his hands in all sorts of pies. The numbers operation he ran with Liz was just one of them: He was extracting another $30,000 a year in protection money from the other numbers bosses by bribing the local police to stay away. Hines had a wife and three sons downtown. But for his uptown rounds, he had Liz.

Almost every Sunday night, Jimmy and "Miz Hines" threw a bois-terous dinner. Politicians mixed freely with numbers bosses and various underworld types to eat Liz's Caribbean food. One regular was Dutch Schultz, the so-called Beer Baron, who controlled the Prohibition beer business in Harlem; another was Schultz's partner at the time, Lucky Luciano. In the mid-twenties, the white gangsters viewed the numbers game with scorn; to them it was nickels and dimes compared to the rackets they were running. That would change with the Depression, and the end of Prohibition. For now the gangsters socialized cheerfully with the numbers operators they met at Miz Hines's, and graciously supplied the liquor. The more the liquor flowed, the looser everyone got. In that spirit, at one of the Sunday dinners, Liz introduced Millie to an eligible bachelor named Harold Bellanfanti.

Harold was Jamaican and, like Millie, the child of a mixed-race union. His mother was a black Jamaican, his father a white Dutch Jew who'd drifted over to the islands after chasing gold and diamonds, with no luck at all, in the newly formed colonies of West Africa. Harold had grown up just as poor as Millie, but he was making a career for himself as a cook, sometimes in New York restaurants, more often on United Fruit Company boats—banana boats—between New York and various Caribbean and South American ports.

By the second or third Sunday dinner, Liz was nudging her younger sister to take Harold on as a boyfriend. He was, after all, quite a looker. She even encouraged Millie to use the little bedroom down the hall to consummate the romance. Not long after that, my mother got preg-nant with me. I don't know that her pregnancy was the only reason she married Harold; she also wanted to escape Liz's world, and even without a child on the way, she would have seen Harold as her best opportunity, her quickest way out.

Whatever role love played in the process, it was pushed aside, soon enough, by the daily hardships and humiliations of being inescapably poor.

Millie knew one thing: She didn't want a job in Liz and Hines's num-bers racket. Her values were much too different for that. So on most days, with or without morning sickness, she made her way over to Park Avenue and Ninety-seventh Street. There she stood with a loose-knit group of other women, hoping to be chosen by the white folk who made the daring drive north, across the divide of Ninety-sixth Street, to find their domestic servants.

Ninety-seventh Street was where the Park Avenue train tracks emerged from their subterranean tunnel, turning the wide street of white-gloved doorman buildings into one of tenements shadowed by the tracks overhead, with gloomy stone arches at each intersection. The women gathered under one of those arches. Later, when I was old enough, I'd wait there with my mother. She would sit me off to the side, perhaps with one or two other children, where she could keep an eye on me. She didn't want me close, because then the people driving by wouldn't hire her. When she did get chosen, she'd ask the white woman in the car if it was all right for me to come, too. If her new employer grudgingly agreed, I'd slide into the backseat with her. If the woman shook her head no, I'd be passed off to my aunt Mabel, who'd come down to the arches, too, or to one of our many other friends from the community.

Millie could clean and iron and sew. She was also a terrific cook, which got her jobs for fancy Saturday-night dinner parties. Usually those evenings went well. But one time, I remember going with her to cook for a rich Jewish family on Central Park West. While she sweated in the kitchen, I sat in the pantry. Somehow, one of the entrees got burned. The hostess swept through the swinging door into the kitchen, stormed up to my mother, and slapped her in the face. Thank God my aunt Mabel had come with her that night. Seeing the rage in my mother's face, Mabel threw her arms around her and kept her from going for the butcher knife that lay nearby. The evening was over: My mother left furious and humiliated, and I left quite terrified.

All that was later. While Millie was pregnant with me, she worked right up until the day her water broke—she had no choice. It happened on one of her Upper East Side day jobs. The closest hospital was Lying-In Hospital in the Jewish section of the East Side, so that's where I was born, on March 1, 1927, as Harold George Bellanfanti, Jr.

The twenties were still roaring south of Ninety-sixth Street on the Upper East Side, but up in Caribbean Harlem, to which Millie soon returned with me, the Depression had come early. Or, more accurately, never left. The apartments that Millie and Harold lived in after I was born were shared by four or five families: one in each bedroom, usually with a bathroom down the hall shared by all. Some of my earliest memories are of the perpetual smells of Caribbean food cooking. Not just ours but our neighbors'. Usually the families shared the kitchen as well as the bathroom, and cooked their meals in shifts, though the poorest of the poor rented rooms with no kitchen privileges—all you had was a room to sleep in.

Grim as these arrangements were, they fostered a real generosity among the tenants. Leftovers were passed along; meals were shared. *"Listen, Millie, I left some ackee and saltfish, I don't want it to spoil, so use it, darling"*—said, of course, in the West Indian lilt that made such offers all the sweeter. Food went bad fast, even in the iceboxes cooled by a big dripping block of ice. But more than practicality prompted these gestures. Poor people help one another; they always have. As I would see growing up, theirs is a world of shared vulnerabilities, of understanding, and of sympathy that the rich can never know. I never forgot the camaraderie of poverty, and never stopped feeling I was a member of that tribe. Years later, when I'd talk to the black waiters at the Palmer House in Chicago, or to a proud, poor farmer in Senegal, I wouldn't just be saying hello. It always felt more like I was checking in.

One of my other earliest memories is of my father yelling and the absolute terror that went along with it. Almost certainly he was drunk when I heard him. Almost certainly there was blood on his hands, and on the bedsheets, as the yelling always led to the violence he brutally visited on my mother. But all I sensed as an infant was a terrible claustrophobic closet of fear.

I was eighteen months old when my mother took me to Jamaica for the first time. In New York, Millie had more than enough relatives to babysit me while she went to work. But Harold was gone more and more often as an onboard cook, and Millie simply couldn't keep caring for me on her own during a grueling day. Grudgingly, Harold took us along on one of his banana boat trips to Jamaica and deposited me in the warm embrace of my grandmother Jane, on the porch of the two-room mountain shack where my mother had been raised.

Millie's father—the stern one who'd turned her out in the fields— had died by now, and nearly all the children were grown and gone. I can't swear that any of my memories of Jane are from that first year I lived with her, but I can say that my first memories of her are her warm and comforting voice, and the wonderful smells of food as she cooked at the stone stove outside. I slept on a tiny bed, on a mattress stuffed with soft grass and swatches of discarded cloth. When I opened my eyes I saw rough-wood beams and calico curtains waving at the open windows. Outside were cultivated fields, as far as I could see. On the porch sat Jane—my white grandmother, whose skin I never noticed as any color other than what it should be—eternally darning clothes for one grandchild or another.

One day I sat watching her work, and as my curiosity grew, I decided to investigate the sewing basket beside her rocking chair. I took out a pair of scissors, and then a rag, and began cutting. I came to the edge of the fabric, which had a thick border, hard to cut. Frustrated, I started pulling up at it with the scissors. Finally I cut through—and one of the scissor points stuck me in the right eye.

I screamed, and my grandmother leaped up in horror to see my eye bleeding. Outside of cleaning the eye and putting a patch on, there wasn't anything she could do that day; we were up in the mountains, far from medical help. I remember Jane's endless grief, and hand-wringing, and guilt, but it was all for naught. I had essentially blinded myself. From that day on, I would see only flashes of light in that eye, flashes that diminished over time as the ocular muscles deteriorated, until at last I saw nothing at all.

Later, when I had such terrible problems learning to read, I assumed the blind eye was to blame. Not for some decades would I come to realize that I was almost certainly dyslexic, and that all my anger and frustration at doing so poorly in school, and my dropping out halfway through ninth grade, had more to do with that disability than my self-inflicted wound that long-ago day on my grandmother's porch.

My mother came to snatch me as soon as she heard about the scissors, though it took a while; she had to come by banana boat. Back in Harlem, she'd moved to a new apartment, and soon would move again. There were lots of apartments. Sometimes my mother fled because she couldn't pay the rent, sometimes because my father had made her life a living hell. And sometimes she swept me off into the maze of other immigrants' homes because she'd heard the immigration agents might be on her trail. My uncle Castel, in addition to owning a livery cab, had a moving truck and moved all the Caribbeans on the run to their new places of momentary anonymity. It was a very profitable business. He'd come with two other guys in the middle of the night, pack us up, and we'd be gone, on to the next place.

The agents were on Millie's trail because she had long since over-stayed her visa. Both she and Harold were illegal immigrants. Harold at least had working papers that let him go from job to job, but technically he was illegal, too. Neither of my parents would be legal until they divorced and married U.S. citizens—in my mother's case, not until I was seventeen.

This meant that throughout my childhood we lived an underground life, as criminals of a sort, on the run. We had almost no family pictures, because no one would permit him- or herself to be photographed. When I was old enough to play outside, my mother taught me never, ever to speak to strangers. On weekends, she and a girlfriend would go off on domestic jobs, and I would be left alone in the apartment—I couldn't have been more than four years old—but only after she'd made me promise, on fear of death, not to answer the door no matter who knocked. More than once, when my mother feared the jig might be up, she changed her name and bought forged papers. Bellanfanti became Belanfonte, and then, after another variation or two, Belafonte.

We shook the agents, but poverty always found us wherever we landed. Often my mother would bring me dinner and say she'd been fed on the job. I knew she hadn't. The bare necessities were food and rent and coal; even clothes were a luxury. Winter was hell. By the time I went to school, my mother had come to the conclusion that there was no deal she could make with God or the Devil to ease the sting of poverty. The best she could hope for was to instill strong goals and values in me—and later, my younger brother, Dennis—and push us to excel. It was the classic immigrant story.

And yet she didn't quite buy into it. Somehow, no matter how much I triumphed later as a singer and actor, my mother could never bask in my success. She just kept working, set on elevating herself above her station, but growing ever more bitter as she stayed where she was, stubbornly reluctant to accept any of the luxuries I tried to confer on her.

In one effort to pull herself up, my mother forged a friendship with a Jewish tailor whose shop she passed on the way to that Park Avenue gathering place for domestics. The tailor taught her how to sew and mend clothes, skills that helped her earn a little extra money. He sold clothes, too. One day, Millie noticed that some of his clothes had been in his window so long that the sun had bleached the fabric in certain spots. So these were damaged goods, yes? Well, yes, the tailor admitted. But could they be dyed a different color and made to look new? Certainly, the tailor said, if anyone wanted to do the job. Millie did. She negotiated a good price with the tailor, who told her what packet of dye to use. Back in her apartment, Millie filled a tin tub with hot water, mixed the dye in, and dipped the clothes in until they became one new color—dark blue. Invariably the process was successful. Either my mother sold the clothes or, if they failed to sell, she gave them to me. Before long, I had a fine wardrobe of little boy's suits—nearly all of them blue. In one of our few family pictures, I'm wearing a blue-dyed tie; my mother is in fancy clothes borrowed from one of her more kindly employers. That tailor gave me my first sense of kinship with Jews, which would deepen over time. But for all that entrepreneurship, and all that blue dye, my mother stayed just as poor as she'd been before.

Years later, I told that story, and others about my mother, to a psychiatrist, who asked if I could arrange for him to meet her. I did. Afterward he told me that Millie was one of the most remarkable people he'd ever met. How clever she was in how she met life and overcame her challenges, he said, what a genius for survival she had. And somehow, though the struggle made her hard, she never let go of a certain innate sweetness—the sweetness of her youthful hopes. She would tell my brother and me stories, and listen to us talk, and help us with our homework. Always she told us to be aware of the decisions we were making, and to be sure they helped us extricate ourselves from the hard life we'd been dealt. Raising ourselves from poverty wasn't enough, she would add. We would have to help others.

Limited as her means were, my mother was determined to give me a nice present for my fourth Christmas. She did: It was a secondhand tricycle.

All morning I waited eagerly for my father to take me out so I could ride it. Finally, at midday, we left our apartment and walked over to a park at 145th Street and St. Nicholas Avenue—today the site of a housing project. From there I could look down a hill and see the Polo Grounds, where the New York Giants played. "Don't ever ride away on your own," my father instructed me. "Always have a grown-up with you."

I remember the view, and the walkway that sloped down from where we were. My father got to talking to someone as I waited for him to guide me down. As he kept talking, he seemed to forget that he'd been holding the handlebar to keep the tricycle from rolling. He started gesturing with both hands to his friend. Suddenly the tricycle started rolling downhill. I felt a whoosh of exhilaration in my stomach. Perhaps in those first few seconds I could have stopped, but the ride was too much fun. Then I heard my father scream my name at the top of his voice. When I looked back, I thought I was watching the giant from "Jack and the Beanstalk" chase after me. I pedaled as fast as I could to escape him. Not fast enough. At the bottom of the hill, he caught me and yanked me off the tricycle. My feet were still pedaling in the air. Then he dragged me over to some bushes, broke off a thin branch, and proceeded to beat me with it.

Again and again he beat me, until I bled through my shirt and pants. Then he stopped. The blood seemed to shock him back to his senses.

"You must never tell your mother what happened," he told me hoarsely. "Say some boys tried to steal your bike, and then they beat you up . . . and I saved you."

On the way home we passed a little corner store, the kind that used to sell candy and stationery and cigars. In the window was a white model sailboat, with beautiful white trim. I had always admired that boat. Only weeks before, I'd asked to have it for Christmas. When we got to that window, my father said into my ear, "If you don't tell your mother, I'll buy you that boat."

As soon as my mother saw me, she screamed. "Oh, my God, what happened!" She looked at my father, half sure he'd beaten me, half disbelieving that even he could do such a thing. He told her the story. She looked at me. I nodded weakly, corroborating what he'd said. Distraught, my mother filled a tub of warm water and shook in a generous portion of CN, a disinfectant of the day similar to iodine. Carefully she peeled my bloody clothes off me, sat me in the tub, and cleaned my wounds.

For days she kept up this regimen as the lash marks slowly healed. At some point, my father left, as usual, off on his next shipboard job. He gave me a knowing look as he left, and I looked away. I wanted to tell my mother what had happened. But I didn't, not then, not even after he'd left for good.

I remember many, many years later telling my psychiatrist, Peter Neubauer, this story. When I said, "Until this day I never got that boat," Peter asked if I was still expecting it. By then I'd been seeing him for some time. "Yes," I said at last, and realized how much longer I would be lying on his couch!

I often wondered later how my father could have terrorized me this way. Not just once, but many, many times. He had a cruel streak, that much was for sure. But I know my mother helped bring it out.

What a tragic, tangled-up marriage my parents had. In those small apartments, my father would grope my mother provocatively, especially when he'd just returned from a trip and the two of them had had a few drinks. She'd slap his hand, but even I could see she liked his touch. When they disappeared behind the bedroom door or a drawn makeshift curtain, I'd hear moaning, and when they appeared again, both my parents would look pleased. Sex was a powerful thing, I could see; it changed people. But not completely, and not for long. Alcohol was an integral part of it, so one thing I learned, subconsciously, was that sex wasn't about two people with real feelings communicating; it was a strange and rather alarming exercise in unreality in which both participants were drunk: a bacchanal. As the alcohol wore off, my mother would start railing at him again—for his drinking and philandering, for being an absent husband and father and not providing enough. I think she'd learned from her own father's philandering, and from his cruelty in dashing her dreams, not to trust men—any of them—very much. And when she started in on my father, she let the zingers fly. I think she castrated him, in a way, made him doubt his manhood, and that one of the ways he coped was to take out his frustrations on me—an object of his failure as a father and as a man.

Even at four and a half years old, I could see that my father's rages grew worse after my mother brought home my baby brother, Dennis. I would have to get a year or two older before I understood that it might have something to do with the fact that Dennis was much lighter skinned than any of us, very sandy haired and gray eyed. My father seemed to disapprove.

That confused me, because I understood that, to my parents and their friends, the lighter someone's skin tone, the better. In the West Indian caste system, wavy hair was better than kinky hair, and blue eyes were better than brown or black. But the differences with Dennis were too marked. Later, my mother would confide in me that my father had decided the child wasn't his own. That drove my mother into a depth of anger and hurt from which she never entirely returned. My father ought to have known that in interracial families, traits from one generation often appear two or three generations later. In the islands, the genetic mix was all the more muddled by parents' or grandparents' polygamy. A child might well have the pale blue eyes of his mother's lover—or not. If you suspected your partner was to blame, and said so, you not only risked ruining your marriage; you risked being wrong. But my father would not be swayed, and so my parents' marriage, such as it was, endured on the tenuous strength of a very thin string, which eventually snapped.

Now, when my mother went off to work on summer days or weekends, I was assigned to care for Dennis. She had no one else to help, after all. What was she to do? That, at any rate, was how I viewed the job until long afterward, when my psychiatrist held up a hand. "Let's back up a bit," he said. "You had a certain responsibility for your brother."

I nodded.

"You were always told you should take care of him, look out for him, babysit, make him dinner sometimes."

Yes, I said, that was right.

"How old were you?" the psychiatrist asked quietly.

As the realization set in, I felt like gasping for air. "Five or six," I said at last. With that, something unlocked, and the tears came flooding out. Tears of anger, disappointment, frustration. Resentment at my mother, for whom, until that point, I'd always made excuses. Anger at my brother as well, for entrapping me in this role that I had to uphold, no matter how scared I was. At five years old, I knew only that my mother was out in the world doing that grueling, soul-deadening work, and with my father gone most of the time, I was the one who had to help her, somehow, to escape or at least withstand her penury. I felt I had no right to resent my mother for the position in which I found myself, no right to complain about the responsibility that now sat on my shoulders. Above all I had to prove to her—and to myself—that I wouldn't abandon her as my father had. The worst thing she could say to me was, *"You're just like your father."* Whenever she did, I just wilted.

Now, for the first time, I felt all that five-year-old boy's fear and hurt, as if a drawer kept closed for decades had opened at last.

In that drawer was a memory, like an old black-and-white snapshot, that I'd all but forgotten. I knew the day of the week and the time: a winter Saturday, late afternoon, the sky already dark. I'd taken care of Dennis all that day while my mother worked. I was hungry and tired, but more than anything else, I wanted my mother to praise me—for being such a good older son, the man of the house. Instead, she walked slowly over to the bed of our small apartment and sat down without saying a word. In a state of great melancholy, she gazed into what seemed endless space. After a while I asked her what was the matter. As she fought back tears that would not be denied, she began to remove her hat and, as she methodically stuck her hat pin into place, said, "When you grow up, son, never ever go to bed at night knowing that there was something you could have done during the day to strike a blow against injustice and you didn't do it." She fell back into silence, leaving me to wrestle with what that simple direction meant.

It was my Rosebud—the moment that imprinted itself on me more lastingly, and meaningfully, than any other.

As my parents drifted apart, my mother grew more religious, which had direct implications for me.

Growing up in the hills of St. Ann Parish, Millie had heard her share of self-taught, self-appointed evangelical preachers, holding forth from simple shacks. They'd done nothing for her. "Too nigger-ish," my mother would sniff: all that Holy Roller stuff. But Catholicism was something else altogether. My mother loved its majesty, its incense and mystery. Father, son, and especially *holy ghost*—the ghost was her favorite. As her immigrant's dreams fell more out of reach, and her marriage evaporated, she slipped more and more into the folds of the church, and her daily reliance on Jesus grew more intense. My mother's religion became everybody's burden, especially my father's. Trying his best to be worthy of her, he became more Catholic than the Pope. When I grew too big for him to brutalize, I would on occasion utter blasphemies that truly rattled him. He would furiously finger-stab himself with three or four signs of the cross in an attempt to exempt himself from any curse that might be on the way. If these dramas took place outdoors, he would move several paces away from me to assure that God's wrath, wrapped in a bolt of lightning, would not miss its intended target.

As for me, I had no choice in the matter. Every Sunday I went with my mother to Catholic services, dressed in one of my little blue suits. I went to Catholic school, too: St. Charles Borromeo, on West 142nd Street off Seventh Avenue. The nuns rapped my knuckles hard, especially when I fared poorly at reading. I'd look in their faces for some sign of forgiveness, but saw none. They seemed to take no joy in teaching or learning. I could see that to them, their jobs in this dreadful Harlem outpost were just a trial to be endured. Every day I trudged miserably to that school, knowing that no pleasure of any kind awaited me there—only, as for the nuns, the grim victory of passing time in penance.

With my father gone so much of the time now, I needed a surrogate, and I found one in Uncle Lenny, one of my mother's many siblings. Uncle Lenny was, like Hines, a numbers boss, with his own bank. He was a huge, barrel-chested, handsome man—and very tough. No one messed with Uncle Lenny, except perhaps my mother. When he strolled into a local bar, a circle of admirers and lieutenants would gather 'round. Once, I remember, my mother sent me to the bar to find him. As I was sitting with him, a big black cop in full uniform came in and confronted him about something. An argument ensued, and suddenly Lenny reared back and cold-cocked him. One punch! I've watched sacks of yams come off ships. This cop went down harder than that. Lenny looked down at him, said to me, "Come on, boy," stepped over him, and out we went. No look back—and, unbelievably, no repercussions, probably because the cop was contesting the size of his payoff.

I loved seeing Lenny on the street and having him say, "Harry, come with me." It meant I'd get a lollipop or maybe even a nickel, and on occasion get to follow him on his numbers rounds. We'd go into the Cuban cigar stores, which almost always had numbers operations in back. But you could play the numbers at markets, too, as you bought your yams, and pawpaws, and gingerroot. Lenny's runners collected the cash and bets, but Lenny liked to pay social calls to the various merchants. *Good for business, you know, Harry.* Often we'd end up at the barbershop, where the men of the neighborhood traded gossip, and the sweet smells of aftershave and cheap cologne hung in the air. I'd curl up in one of the red leather chairs by the wall, sucking my lollipop, and take in the stories of last night's boxing match at Madison Square Garden. Joe Louis had done it again! Was there anyone that black man couldn't beat?

My mother did her best to stay out of Lenny's business, but sometimes she'd bring him a package: the day's bets from her building or block. She could hardly refuse, because almost every Sunday, Lenny gave us five or ten dollars to help us get through the week. In the 1930s, that bought a lot of groceries. When Lenny came in looking severe, we knew he was drunk. "You know how lucky you are, boy, that you got your mother?" he would say. "Don't you ever disobey her no more!" And then Lenny would start to cry. "I don't have my mother, I left her a long time ago in the islands—you should worship your mother."

Lenny did have a son, Lloyd, but he lived with his mother, from whom Lenny was estranged. Lenny always had this long, white silk handkerchief in his back pocket; he'd pull it out and snap it and blow his nose, and then stuff it back in. If he kept on like that, my mother would come over and seize him by the tie. "Get yourself together, man!" Lenny would be startled. She was the only one who could talk to him like that.

Lenny was our family godfather, but he was the first to say I shouldn't view him as a role model. "I don't want any of you to grow up like me," he'd drunkenly wail, and out would come the handkerchief again. There were plenty of others to choose from in Harlem, for most of the famous black Americans of the day lived there, rubbing shoulders with the rest of us; they certainly weren't welcome in the fancy buildings south of Ninety-sixth Street. I could see Duke Ellington, coiffed in a do-rag, shopping for groceries, and Langston Hughes at a local bar. One of my heroes was A. Philip Randolph, head of the Brotherhood of Sleeping Car Porters. Randolph had founded the union and won a bitter struggle with the Pullman Company to get better pay and hours for his seven thousand members. I may not have known the details, but I knew, from my mother, that Randolph had dared to stage a strike, and won it. He was a hero. I just loved watching him lead his troops through Harlem on parade, with their red collars and shiny buttons and red caps tilted just so. Everyone admired the porters, not just for the handsome salaries that Randolph had negotiated for them, but because they were worldly—they traveled far and wide—and because most had college degrees. They were a workingman's elite, one tier down from doctors and lawyers. I would have been thrilled to know, at age six or seven, that I'd be a sleeping-car porter one day. To learn instead that I would come to know Randolph in the heat of the civil rights movement through Martin Luther King, Jr.—that would have baffled me utterly.

Ironically, by the time the movement became a reality, Hollywood had caricatured the proud railroad porters as smiling, servile "darkies." The real ones, educated and proud, had engaged in long, late-night conversations with their passengers, black or white. Hollywood's porters catered abjectly to the white leading men and ladies whose stories they bobbed in and out of, carrying their bags and catching tips with a grateful "Thank you, suh!"

One film in particular—a short Mack Sennett silent movie—sealed the demeaning image of these proud men of service. It was the story of a rich, white adulterer getting on a Pullman train with his mistress of the week. Unbeknownst to them, the adulterer's wife boards the same train. From this moment on, it's a series of comedy routines of wife, mistress, and adulterer going in and out of staterooms, barely missing one another and causing the adulterer to narrowly avoid several heart attacks. The only person privy to the truth besides the adulterer is a groveling bug-eyed black Uncle Tom porter. As a reward for his silence and loyalty to the rich, white adulterer, the porter is tipped each time they pass each other in this supposedly comic routine. Every time this happens, the porter bows, grins, and bites the coin to make sure it is not counterfeit. So the routine goes. At the end of the trip, neither of the women is the wiser, and the adulterer is spared a tragic end for which he is eternally grateful to the porter, whom he rewards with one last tip and wink. This rather silly piece, at the dawning of Hollywood, forever changed the image of porters. A severe blow to a group of truly dignified men of color!

I had white role models, too, for West Indians admired success whatever color it came in. My mother never missed a fireside chat by President Roosevelt; both he and Eleanor were her greatest heroes. I revered them, too, never imagining that one day Mrs. Roosevelt would call me on the phone, and that our meeting would mark the start of a life-changing friendship for me. I loved almost every actor I saw on the screen, but especially the hard-boiled ones: Jimmy Cagney, George Raft, Edward G. Robinson. They were our folk heroes—working-class heroes, fighting all the forces that threatened us, too: the cops, the FBI, the banks with their snooty white tellers who'd never cut us a break, either. We'd cheer them on as they stuck a gun in those tellers' faces. They were our Robin Hoods. Take that money and run! Along with white actors, I admired white sports figures, too, like the battling boxer Jimmy Braddock. But for a black boy in the mid-1930s, all these were eclipsed by the great black god who would soon knock Braddock out—Joe Louis.

Louis lived in Detroit, but he trained for his New York fights at a camp in Lakewood, New Jersey, and that got him to Harlem a lot. "Hey, I heard Joe Louis is over on One Hundred and Twenty-fifth and Lenox," some street friend would say. "Let's see if he's still there." So we'd run over and learn he was in a restaurant having lunch, and press our noses to the glass for a glimpse of this living legend.

Lenny started promising me he'd take me to Lakewood to see the great champ train. But he had to wait until Louis's next scheduled bout at Madison Square Garden, a once- or twice-a-year occurrence.

For a few weeks before these historic spectacles, you could drive over on a Sunday and buy tickets; it was how Louis defrayed the costs of the camp. Finally, on a Sunday when my father happened to be home, Lenny came by to take us to Lakewood in his gleaming black Packard; Louis was in training across the river again at last. I had my little blue suit and blue tie on, all ready to go, but apparently I did something—I can't recall what—to offend my mother. No training-camp trip for me—my punishment was to stay at home, alone, while the others went. My father tried to plead my case, but my mother held firm. Finally, to my astonishment, he said, "Well, then I'll stay, too." He changed out of his suit, and when Millie and Lenny had gone, he took me up on the roof of the building to play marbles.

Almost seventy-five years later, I have to stop and blink back tears at the memory of his kindness that day—a rare kindness, but no less real for that. Which man was he, the one who beat me violently or the one who played marbles with me that day on the roof? Both, perhaps. Though to this day I don't really know.

When at last we got an arc-shaped RCA radio, I had a whole new gallery of heroes. The Green Hornet for one, the Lone Ranger, for another, and Amos and Andy, the white comics who sounded as black to us as they did to the rest of America. It was also through the radio that I learned I might have some musical ability. A favorite song would come on, and my mother and I would harmonize in the kitchen. That led to my mother prodding me to sing for relatives. All pretty corny stuff. I remember an old Irish tune about mothers that began, "*M is for the million things she gave me, / O means only that she's growing old, / T is for the tears she shed to save me, / H is for the heart as pure as gold . . .*" And another set to the poem "I think that I shall never see / A poem lovely as a tree." I took my voice for granted, but I know that in doing these little parlor turns, I got a lot of encouragement.

There was more music—much better music—to be found a short walk away at the Apollo Theatre. I really loved going to the Apollo on a Sunday after mass, as young as seven years old, dressed in my best blue suit, to hear Cab Calloway or Count Basie or Duke Ellington or Lucky Millinder, Billie Holiday or Ella Fitzgerald. As suffocating and interminable as mass seemed, I could endure it if I knew that a few short hours later I'd be in the real cathedral of spirituality. I heard them all at the Apollo, every last one, and somehow my mother managed to find the money to take me. Or, if she was working that day, to have my father or one of my relatives take me.

She must have started nurturing the hope that I might join that immortal pantheon, because one day I came home from school to see two men struggling up the four flights to our apartment with a rented stand-up roller piano. You could put in paper rolls and have it play itself, but you could also play it as a proper piano. To learn how, my mother informed me, I would enroll in Miss Shepherd's classes for fifty cents a lesson.

Miss Shepherd was a spinster, with a high-collared blouse and long dress, who kept her hair up in a bun and wore pince-nez glasses, and gave lessons to support herself and her mother. She was considered the best music instructor for blocks around. Also the strictest. Every time I made a mistake playing scales, she'd rap me across the fingers with a ruler, as hard as the nuns did. It was torture. Finally I started cutting her classes and hanging out on the street, playing marbles for purees with a few of the neighborhood toughs. To my horror, my mother happened to walk by and see me. Grimly, she hauled me off to Miss Shepherd's to learn what was going on. The truth was that I hadn't been in class for weeks. "Do you know what I had to do for all those lessons at fifty cents a lesson, Harry?"

For the first time but not the last, I'd crushed her expectations for me, and the immigrant dream she'd had, to sacrifice herself for her children's betterment, was crumbling, maybe already shattered.

That week, my mother got rid of the piano. "You're on your own now," she said. And I was.

3

For all that my mother and father and Uncle Lenny tried to teach me, by the age of seven I'd become a difficult child. I gave back as good as I got, not just at home but on the way to school, where I passed a daily gauntlet of young Irish and Italians who liked nothing better than to pick a fight with a black kid on his own. School was P.S. 186 on 145th Street, a five-story redbrick building between Broadway and Amsterdam Avenue, where most of the students were white—which led to more fighting. I walked the halls ready to explode if another student so much as bumped me accidentally as he went by. And that happened a lot.

To these fisticuffs, my mother had strong but contradictory reactions. Once, when I was in elementary school, she bought me a second-hand white shirt required for a class play. I was keenly aware of the sacrifices my mother made to give me the simplest things; that shirt meant a lot to me. The night before the play, I lay in bed listening to *Amos 'n' Andy* and watching as she mended it and sewed on a needed button. The next day I felt really spiffy, and the play went well. That afternoon on the way home, however, I was set upon by a group of boys who cruelly taunted me. I was enraged, but not wanting anything to happen to my new shirt, I ignored them. Emboldened, they started shoving and then punching me. I took flight and ran several blocks to escape them. As fate would have it, I literally ran into my mother in front of our house. She demanded to know what was going on. As I told her, I watched her eyes narrow and her anger take hold. She marched me back to the scene to look for my tormentors. When we found them, she grabbed my books and jacket and said, "Go do what you got to do!" I was nonplussed. She pushed me in the direction of the biggest bully in the crowd. In a choked voice, she whispered, "Get him!" Elated by her encouragement, I proceeded to stomp the guy. When I got through, there was more than just a bloody nose. I couldn't believe it when the others started scampering away. I turned and saw my mother smiling. Filling up with tears, I grabbed her around the waist in the biggest hug I'd ever given her. "Thanks for the help, Ma," I said. She hugged me back. "Sometimes," she told me, "there's more to life than the shirt on your back."

After school, I roamed the neighborhood freely—too freely. One day I was playing in the streets and got hit by a car. I woke up in Harlem Hospital to find my leg broken, hanging in traction in a waist-high cast. My mother blamed my father, as usual. "If only he was an honorable man and held the home together." But she also blamed herself, as she had when I stuck my eye with the scissors.

The medicines I was given in the hospital left me thirsty all the time, and my lips were soon badly chapped. If I sucked them in a certain way, I found, it helped produce saliva. By the time I went home, I'd made such a habit of it that my lower lip on one side swelled up in a large lump. But now I couldn't *stop* sucking it. My mother tried everything. She put tape on the lump; I pulled the tape off. She coated it with bitters or hot sauce; I kept sucking till the bad taste was gone. Finally she recruited my father.

"Boy, if you suck that lip again you'll regret it," my father warned. But I did. And so came the punishment to fit this latest crime. First my father pushed me onto my bed and locked me between his very strong legs. Then he held me by the chin with one hand. With the other, he held his cigar out and blew the ash off it. Its burning red ember glowed brightly. "You want to suck your lip?" The ember came closer to the lump on my lip. "You want to suck it?" Again the ember came closer, an inch each time. Just as it was about to burn me—I could feel its heat—he moved it away. Then he flogged me with his belt.

Better, my mother declared, to send this truant back to Jamaica; at least I wouldn't get hit by a car there. While Dennis stayed with my mother in Harlem, I went down with my father on a United Fruit Company boat. When I wasn't confined to his cabin, I was in the ship's kitchen, watching him serve up three meals a day for the captain and crew. I saw a new side of him on that trip. He was the head chef, ordering the scullery cooks around with great dispatch. Much as I feared and hated him, for the first time I admired him, too.

The mountain village my grandmother Jane lived in was called Aboukir, I now learned. Her wood-framed house stood on stilts, built into the hillside, with a roof of patchwork pieces of zinc and wood salvaged from construction projects in nearby Ocho Rios. There was no electricity; at dusk, Jane lit the oil lamps. No plumbing, either; the outhouse was in back. On her small plot of land, Jane grew plantains, yams, passion fruit, okra, callaloo, and ackee, a local fruit that you boiled (and boiled). Her relatives and grown children lived the same way. Everyone had a small cottage and an acre or two of land, on former plantations now broken up and parceled out. The colonial era was still just receding, and the islanders remembered all too well what life had been like before they owned their own land. They cherished those plots with all the passion and pride of a Lord Mountbatten surveying his large estate.

All the warmth and love I'd felt as an infant from my grandmother I felt more keenly now. I adored her in return. Jane Love was matriarch to a large clan of children, grandchildren, and various other relatives, all of whose clothes she continued to mend, but I felt she carved out a special place for me. Perhaps part of it was that I was the one from far away. Perhaps she saw that I was troubled, and so tended to my every need with that much more concern. Perhaps her guilt at the scissors accident made her that much more solicitous. All I know is that never was a surname more appropriate, and more deserved, than hers.

My relationship with her had a strong and particular effect. For the rest of my life, I would feel an unusual sense of ease in moving between races and classes—an ease that would help me as an entertainer, later as an activist, too, mediating between Martin Luther King and his southern Baptist followers on the one hand, and the Irish, patrician Kennedy clan on the other. I think that traces to the fact that Jane, who was as white and blue-eyed as a person can be, so enveloped me with love. "Where's me Harry?" I can still hear her say. "Where's me sweet boy Harry?"

Almost every day, several of her flock would come by for dinner, both because they, too, loved Jane, and because Jane was a formidable cook. She had only her outdoor wood-burning stove, hand-hewn from local stones. And she didn't have that much to work with; of the fruits and vegetables she harvested, only some were in season at any given time. For meat she mainly had chicken. But that she had year-round. Jane raised all the chickens she could manage, and then some; if we could have hatched more chickens by sleeping on eggs, she would have had us do that. While chicken was on the menu almost every night, no two dishes tasted the same, so clever was Jane with her spices, and the ways she varied her other ingredients, and by her choice to roast or boil or fry the chicken that night. Happily sated at the end of the evening, her guests wandered off on dark paths to their own cottages, and one by one their own oil lamps winked on in the surrounding hills.

In the mornings I walked on my own to a one-room schoolhouse, where I struggled, with little success and a lot of resentment, to read. Afterward, Jane might send me on an errand to the next village. *"Go to Mrs. Richards and tell her we need some yams, and don't dilly-dally . . ."* On the hilly paths from one village to another, I'd pass huge concrete tanks, open-topped, some aboveground, some below. The rain that collected in these tanks was our only source of drinking water. Zinc funnels protruded from the tanks to sluice the water into our bottles and barrels; to me they looked like giant arms, about to scoop me up, and I gave them a wide berth. My fear was soundly based. Sometimes people fell in, and if the water was low in the tank, they couldn't climb out. They might drown—and once in a while did—if they weren't discovered and rescued by rope.

The nearest market was Brown's Town, to which the villagers brought their harvested goods by donkey and cart. When their carts were full, they carried more on their heads, wrapped in colorful bandannas. If I was lucky, I'd be asked to go with one of my uncles, either to walk behind or, as a special treat, to ride on the donkey. (*"Don't crush the banana!"*) Sometimes I was lucky enough to hitch a ride on one of the few trucks in the region. (*"Hey, mon, you want a fender ride?"*) I'd hop on the fender and hold on to the window frame, and we'd roll down the dirt roads, inevitably passing a group of bauxite workers headed home, their faces red from bauxite dust.

The larger market, especially for bananas, was Ocho Rios, with its deepwater pier, where the United Fruit Company boats loaded up. Bananas, sugarcane, mangoes, oranges—all these were shipped, after being tallied and paid for by the UFC tallyman. *"Come, Mr. tally man, tally me banana, / Daylight come and me wan' go home."* Not by chance did that song become my signature; I knew of what I was singing.

Once the men were paid, I'd follow them through the streets of Ocho Rios as they shopped for the enamel pots or the store-bought rockers their wives had asked for. They might also stop at the local pub and grab a few shots, and sometimes come home very drunk, their trucks bumping along the roads as their headlights swept the fields. Perched on the fender, I felt the cool night breeze on my face and pretended I was hanging on for dear life.

When school was out, my father took me back to New York on one of his banana boat runs. I was eight now, old enough to get into new kinds of trouble.

That summer, in our latest multiple-family apartment, I befriended a girl named Eleanor, who shared my interest in playing doctor. The scene is as clear to me today as it was then, a stark stage set in my mind. At stage left, the kitchen. At stage right, the bedroom. At center stage, connecting the rooms, a little pantry where canned goods are stored. A young boy and girl are fumbling with each other's buttons in the bedroom. The boy's mother is cooking in the kitchen. Usually the thick curtain between the bedroom and pantry is kept closed. Today, perhaps hearing her son in the bedroom and wanting to tell him something without moving out of the kitchen, the mother slides the curtain aside. The children freeze. The girl flees upstage. Mother and son trade horrified looks. Finally the mother speaks. "This one I'm saving for your father."

Absent as he usually was, my father, unfortunately, was home that week. For a day or two he said nothing, and I dared to think I might escape whatever terrible new form of punishment I was due. Then, on Sunday, just as I'd finished dressing for church, my father pulled me into the bathroom. I saw that the tub was filled with hot water: scalding, steaming water. "You know what this is for?"

I didn't answer.

"Get out of your clothes."

Slowly I undressed. I couldn't believe he was going to put me into that tub. I started crying, and he whacked me across the face. By the time I'd gotten down to my underwear, I stopped crying. I'd come to terms with pure terror. I was ready to step in. Or perhaps my mind had shut down.

Just before I stepped in, my father yanked me away from the tub. Once again he flogged me with his belt, so badly that my mother had to intervene. I blamed him, but I blamed her, too. She hadn't known what the punishment would be. But she must have known it would be extreme.

From Aunt Liz and Uncle Lenny, I'd nurtured a keen curiosity about numbers, as in *the* numbers. I could feel the excitement that playing the numbers stirred in the poor and the desperate, which was to say almost everyone in my world. The numbers had such power—to pay the rent, to restore marital harmony, to buy happiness, for a short while at least. And so perhaps it was inevitable that I would be drawn, one day, to a game of three-card monte in the street. In my pocket I had ten dollars my aunt Liz had given me to pass on to my mother for groceries. All I knew, after watching the three-card-monte dealer, was that I might multiply that bill if I took the chance. So I did, and suddenly the ten dollars was gone.

Panicked, I went back to my aunt's apartment, because there, I knew, I would find more money—lots of money. The beds in the bedrooms down the hall were covered with packets of money about to be brought by runners to the lucky winners. I snuck into one of the bedrooms and slipped a ten-dollar bill from one of the packets. Surely Aunt Liz would never miss the money, much less accuse me of taking it. But she did. Hawkeyed businesswoman that she was, she discovered the shortfall that day, ticked off the possible suspects, and came to the clear conclusion that the culprit was me. She couldn't call my mother—we had no phone—but the next time she saw her, she told her so. My mother reacted with righteous indignation. "How dare you accuse my son?" she snapped back. In the background I listened, sick with guilt, incapable of admitting what I'd done, until the talk became so heated that my mother told her sister what to do with herself . . . after which they did not speak again for the longest time. And I, burning with shame, had to pretend, for the rest of her life, that Aunt Liz had done me wrong.

I learned from that day not to steal my gambling funds, but I didn't learn not to gamble. All through my youth I would play for marbles, using cigar boxes for our game of choice. The dealer, so to speak, would cut three little Roman arches in one side of the box, and set the box in the gutter down a slope in the street. The game was to let your marble find its way into one of those holes from five or ten feet away. If it went into one hole, that was a one-puree payoff: The other pint-size gamblers had to give you a puree marble for the one you'd gotten in the one-puree arch. If you got your marble in the two-puree hole, better for you, and the three-puree hole, better yet. But if your marble didn't roll through any of those holes, then you lost it.

I played for purees in the street, and I bet on flipped cards—heads or tails—but after that incident with Aunt Liz, I always kept to my limit, as a child, as a teenager in the navy, even afterward, when I came back to Harlem and played poker, sometimes for pretty serious stakes. Not until I got to Vegas would I be so drawn to the lure and adrenaline of the big, big win that I'd start playing beyond my limit, and keep playing, until I had to stop—for keeps.

It was time, my mother decided, to take her children home—home to Jamaica for a good long stretch, away from the dangers we faced in Harlem, away from its temptations, too. Dennis and I would attend a proper British-style school, and my mother would get some kind of work. She brought a trunk for herself, along with ours, and promised she'd stay. I was nine, Dennis was five, the year was 1936. For none of us did things turn out as hoped.

We rented a tiny one-room house in Kingston, not far from one of my aunts, and for two or three weeks, my mother searched for work. Only there wasn't any. One day I saw her, silent and defeated, her mouth set in a line, packing her clothes back into her trunk. I didn't ask what she was doing, or why. I knew.

That day, my mother enrolled me in the Morris-Knibb Preparatory School, which took in boarding students. That part of the plan, at least, worked out. The school started with fifth grade. Dennis was too young, so my mother would take him to an elementary school—humbler and less expensive than Morris-Knibb, because that was all my mother could afford—and have him board with a local family. I would see him every two weeks, my mother explained, for movies and ice cream. At least I'd had both of my parents, some of the time, until I was nine. Dennis would never get over the anger and loneliness he felt at being abandoned, or so he felt, at five, by both parents. It would haunt him, and grind him down, until he died of a heart attack at forty-four. And when he did, our mother would weep, racked by guilt for leaving him on his own those many years ago.

When we got to Morris-Knibb, I begged my mother to change her mind and take us both back north. I didn't care how small the next apartment in Harlem might be. I didn't mind how much babysitting I'd have to do. I just wanted to be with her. She told me to buck up— "*Get yourself together, boy!*" She helped me find the room where I'd be bunking, and put my clothes in my little cubby. All too soon we were back outside by the waiting taxi, and she was giving me a hug and saying good-bye. I watched the taxi roll off, and the school gates close behind it. Finally I ran at the gate, devastated, and put my face through the bars, howling with grief and fear. But the taxi never came back.

My new teachers brought me back to the classroom and sat me at my desk. I wept and wept. I couldn't eat that night; I didn't take a proper meal for days. Then one morning I woke up and found myself completely self-reliant. My mother had abandoned me; nothing could change that fact. I would never again look to my mother for love. I was now a world of one. I was the only one I could trust, the only person who cared about me in this bleakly institutional place. I would have to protect myself by doing whatever it took to keep these new authority figures from zeroing in on me. I would resist all that they told me I should believe.

Mary Morris-Knibb was a prominent figure in Kingston who would soon become the first Jamaican woman elected to a political post. Like most islanders, she adopted the British way of life, and modeled her school accordingly. We learned British history and etiquette, took on British accents, read British newspapers and accepted their editorial opinions, followed soccer and cricket, and swelled with pride at being a part of the British Empire, especially when viewing such movies as *The Charge of the Light Brigade,* even though we were among the many conquered nations of Britain's empire. The only thing British we didn't like was being oppressed.

I was an exception in one regard: I hated cricket. This was not the way to ingratiate myself with my new classmates and teachers. Soon enough I became known as the hard case in school—it didn't take much—and the inevitable caning followed, for some minor infraction I can't recall, as there were so many. I lay down on my stomach, and four upperclassmen held my arms and legs while the principal gave me five or more lashes across the bottom. I might have cried, but I never became the subservient little student the caning was meant to produce.

Eventually I was told to board elsewhere; the teachers didn't want to see any more of me than necessary. So I went to live at Mrs. Shirley's, where three other boys boarded as well. All four of us had bunks in the same room. For this, and for feeding me, my mother sent Mrs. Shirley a stipend each week. Whatever she paid, it was too much. One night not too long after my arrival, I woke up covered in bites. "Must be mosquitoes," Mrs. Shirley declared over breakfast the next morning. "No, ma'am, I don't think so. I think some bugs in the bed." Mrs. Shirley slapped me. "No bugs in my bed!" I stormed back to the bedroom and stripped my bunk in rage, while she stood frozen behind me. There, around each button of the mattress, were hundreds of bedbug eggs. Embarrassed, Mrs. Shirley told me it was time for me to leave.

Over the next four years, various relatives and friends of relatives took me in—not for love, but for money. Meager as my mother's earnings were up north, a small sliver of them bought a lot of room and board in Jamaica, where an American dime had the value of a dollar. The household I remember best was that of my mother's sister Geraldine, whose skin was almost Tahitian in tone. Aunt Gerry, or Aunt G, as I called her, had upped the already high social standing her light skin conferred by marrying a pink-faced Scotsman named Eric Pigou (*pig-ew*). In the Pigous' capacious house at 17A Connolly Avenue in Kingston, I learned just how rigid Jamaica's racial stratification could be.

Mr. Pigou was the postmaster, or so I remember; perhaps he was one of two or three. Either way, he earned a good enough salary to maintain a two-story wood-frame house with a tennis court and highly manicured lawn and garden. The Pigous had three children, two girls and a boy—Phyllis, Violet, and David—all of them as white as their father. In addition, there was Annette, or Nettie, an adopted child, or "ward," as she was described to me, some six or seven years older than I. Because she was adopted, and because her skin was mulatto, Nettie lived in the back of the Pigous' house, in a small downstairs bedroom by the back staircase. That's where I lived, too, in a bedroom next to Nettie's. The Pigous' children were in upstairs bedrooms, much larger than Nettie's and mine. When company came, Nettie and I were forbidden to make an appearance, and ate in the kitchen with the servants while the Pigous and their guests took their dinner in the dining room. The Pigous didn't want their friends to know that there could possibly be dark-skinned next of kin living in the house; it would have tainted their reputation. Eventually, I would learn the Pigous had a deeper secret to keep. Nettie was Gerry's daughter by another man. Whether Mr. Pigou knew this and let Gerry keep Nettie under his roof, or didn't and simply believed Nettie was a ward, I never knew.

If no guests were invited, Nettie and I did join the others in the dining room. In truth, we preferred the kitchen, for the Pigous dined with excruciating formality, their backs ramrod straight, every aspect of culinary etiquette strictly observed. We knew the precise moment to pick up our serviettes, shake them once, and place them on our laps.

We tipped the outward side of our spoons into the soup just so, moved the spoon outward, then drank from the heel of the spoon. And so it went from soup to nuts. The Pigous made stilted dinner conversation in high-British accents—I can still see Mr. Pigou turning his spectacled gaze to me and saying, *"My dear boy, that is not what one does at the table"*—as properly as any English lord or lady at high tea. Was it really just a generation ago that Aunt Gerry's parents had shaken off the yoke of indentured servitude, only to seize all the trappings and affectations of their overseers? So it was. And in less than twenty years, strangers who met me would assume I was a highborn college graduate, so ingrained were these bits of culture the Pigous and Mrs. Morris-Knibb had appropriated from the British, and passed on, in their stern way, to me.

Outside the Pigous' proper household lay a very different world. On Kingston's busy streets, peddlers sang their goods for sale. "Guava jelly, guava cheese . . . yellow yam, yellow yam, come get your yellow yam!" The fishmongers were the best; they had a new song for whatever their catch of the day was. At the wharf, mento bands would sing to the endless stream of tourists disembarking from cruise ships. Even politicians sang to gather crowds before delivering their speeches. A politician named Simpson had an artificial leg made of cork that buffered the stump against the wooden peg. *"Cork Foot Simpson the Vagabon' / if I catch you I chop off de other one"* was the verse written and sung by the opposition candidate. Simpson won the contest, and on the night of his victory rally he responded by singing his victory rebuttal.

All this music I took in, along with my first snatches of classical music as I passed a big hillside house, its large front lawn set off by an imposing gate. Whoever lived in that house listened to the BBC all day, or so it seemed. The British announcer spoke through crackling static that dramatically heightened the distance his broadcast traveled. I scampered up a Bombay mango tree that hovered over the road at the edge of the property and perched in the comfort of its crisscrossed branches. Those great orchestral waves of the London Philharmonic wafted to where I sat, endlessly sucking on the nectar of one of several sun-ripened fruits easily reached from my nesting place. I listened to Beethoven being played by a conductor whose very name bespoke British pomp and majesty: *Sir Thomas Beecham.*

Despite that, I was lonelier now in Jamaica than I'd ever been in Harlem. To the Pigous I was a boarder—a dark-skinned boarder. In Nettie I had someone to share my lowly status, but the difference in our ages made us housemates more than friends. The older Pigou children had lives of their own; so did the other students at the Morris-Knibb Preparatory School, most of whom lived at home, and who regarded me, rightly, as a loner, best avoided. Alienated and hurt, I grew more rebellious, until Mrs. Morris-Knibb suggested to my mother I might be happier at another school, and so began a series of short stints at schools whose names I just dimly remember: Mico, Wolmer's Boys' School, Half Way Tree. Decades later, when Michael Manley, the prime minister of Jamaica, awarded me a doctorate from the University of the West Indies, I would tell him I was surely the only recipient of this honor who had the distinction of attending every school in Kingston.

I did have one passion, and for a while, I felt sure I'd make it my profession one day. Every morning at five o'clock, I'd sneak out of the Pigous' house and scurry over to the Kingston racecourse to see my cousin Charlie Gossen, the island's best jockey, put his horses through their paces. Charlie's mother was Liz, my numbers-boss aunt. On Jamaica, he was famous, the greatest jockey of his day. He let me assist in mucking out the stables and grooming his horses, and eventually he taught me to ride. We both felt I had promise, until, to my mortification, I had a growth spurt that just wouldn't quit. Charlie told me sympathetically—looking up at me—that I'd have to find a new ambition.

At last, in the winter of 1940, my mother came back for my brother and me. Perhaps I imagined that she just couldn't bear to be separated from us anymore. In fact, the war had more to do with it. The Nazis were marching through Europe, conquering one country after another; the latest to fall was France. My mother was not alone in fearing England would be next, and that the British Crown's colonies might be put under Nazi rule before she could rescue her sons.

Both Dennis and I were ecstatic to be reunited with our mother, and our joy wasn't diminished in the least by seeing that her newest apartment, on 114th Street and Manhattan Avenue, was her smallest yet: a single room partitioned into two, with a common toilet down the hall. The three of us slept on one side of the curtain my mother had made to divide the space; on the other side was a kitchenette and dining area. My parents were legally separated. As they were good and obedient Catholics, divorce seemed out of the question. My father, I was told, had taken up with a German woman named Edith. My mother was single, but she did have a friend in the janitor of the building, a very light-skinned black man named William Wright. From the way he and my mother chatted on a daily basis, I don't think it would have surprised me to learn that they had a romance. Before long, Bill Wright would become my stepfather.

Despite whatever sparks this new friendship was generating, my mother was determined to move out of her tiny room in Bill Wright's building to a larger apartment more appropriate for the three of us, and not just any would do. She wanted to live in a clean, well-kept complex at 130th and Amsterdam Avenue. The only catch was that blacks weren't allowed. That didn't stop my mother. To the rental agent, she presented herself as Spanish. Not Hispanic, from Puerto Rico or south of the border, but from Spain, by way of the West Indies. This, and twenty dollars, helped secure our new home. But now Dennis and I were Spanish, too.

So began my "passing" period. On the building's front stoop the first day I hung out there, I got razzed by the Greek and Irish kids who lived in the complex. "Hey, you're a nigger," they said in amazement.

"No, I'm not," I said. "I'm not a nigger."

"You sure look like one."

"I'm not."

"You have hair like one."

"Unless you've been caught in a fire like I was, shut your fucking face." Attitude won that day. During the brief silence that followed, I stared them down, knowing that when you don't have truth on your side, attitude is your best friend.

I stuck to my story—the name Belafonte helped flavor the dish, too—and they bought it. They soon nicknamed me "Frenchy," since I told them that my grandfather on my father's side came from Martinique and that my family had come originally from Europe. For the first time, I belonged—by not being black.

As Frenchy, I ranked above the few black students, in this largely Irish and Greek neighborhood, who attended P.S. 43, the local public junior high school. In the lunchroom, I sat with my new white pals. After school, I joined them for pickup games of stickball or basketball, and because of my moves, I invariably got chosen first. But this new camaraderie went only so far. I was accepted, but only as a visitor. I wasn't a member of their tribe. When they had parties, I wasn't invited. And I knew better than to try to date any of the white girls. I could chat them up in the corridors between classes, but had I asked any one of them out to the movies, I would have been met by a look of genuine astonishment, followed by one deceitful nervous excuse after another.

So I was a misfit, adrift somewhere between white and black, New York and the West Indies. The only thing I clearly was was poor. That, as much as my dubious skin tone and kinky hair, limited my social options. To any son or daughter of middle-class parents—from butchers to firemen to construction workers—I was of a lesser order, below which there might not *be* any other orders: the son of a single woman who worked as a maid.

It was a lonely time, of alienation and racial confusion, only made worse by my mother's relentless efforts at monitoring me, which she soon gave up, now that I was a teenager. One thing she would not yield on, though, was having me accompany her to one political gathering after another.

She was frustrated by her failure, through the Depression, to better her lot, and her political views, always strongly held, had grown only more strident and bitter. One of her heroes was Marcus Garvey, the black nationalist, who was born in my mother's own St. Ann Parish in Jamaica. Garvey had formed the United Negro Improvement Association (UNIA) with the bold vision of uniting blacks around the world and reconnecting them with their African roots. He'd gone so far as to promote a new African homeland in Liberia, with new colleges and industries, to knit the entire black diaspora together, as the state of Israel would for Jews a generation later. A young J. Edgar Hoover, head of the "anti-radical" division of what would become the U.S. Federal Bureau of Investigation, had managed to get him deported in the year of my birth. At about the time I returned from Jamaica, Garvey died. But his image, and his dream, lived on. To me, Garvey was just a portly black man in a silly admiral's hat, but to my mother, who went to meetings in Harlem held by his followers, he was a beacon of hope. Later I would realize that, in his own way, Garvey was a founder of the civil rights movement, and my mother's admiration for him had a lasting influence on me.

At some point, my mother would marry Bill Wright. She had little choice, since she was pregnant with my brother Raymond, soon to be followed, a year later, by my sister, Shirley. Bill was a gentle man— quite a change from my father—and both Dennis and I liked him just fine. Bill had one flaw: He was an alcoholic. But he also had one saving grace. Unlike my father, he had no capacity for violence. I wasn't particularly close to Raymond and Shirley, since I was so much older than they. (In later life, Shirley and I grew extremely close, once I rescued her from the Catholic Church.) I was happy for my mother; it was only she who seemed incapable of enjoying this new state of affairs. Ground down by poverty, she'd lost the capacity for happiness, if she'd ever had it. As loving as her new husband was, she seemed destined to remain a tortured character, seeking her only solace in church.

The surprise was my father. By the time I was fourteen, he'd become a different man. I could see that on Friday afternoons, when I took the subway down to lower Manhattan to pick up the weekly child-support money that a court had ordered him to pay my mother.

My father still worked as a cook, but a landlocked one now, overseeing the basement kitchen of a busy downtown restaurant on Union Square. There wasn't much time for conversation—he was too busy barking orders to the men under him. But for all the stress of his job, he seemed much more relaxed. Even handing over the envelope with the child-support money didn't ruin his mood. On the first of those visits, he introduced me to Edith, a solidly built waitress with very strong features—far from the beauty my mother was, but cheerful and kind, with a heavy New York accent. She was soon to be my father's new wife.

After they married, I would visit them occasionally in the Bronx, where they lived in a neighborhood thick with Edith's relatives, all of whom, to my further surprise, thought the world of Edith's new husband. They could see, as I could, that he doted on her. When she asked him to do some small task, he did it with alacrity. When she voiced opinions at the dinner table, he listened and nodded; when she made jokes, he laughed. Who *was* this impostor? And what had they done with my father? For surely this was not the man who'd bristled at the smallest request my mother made, and beaten her bloody, and then beaten me, too. Yet he was, and that was the mystery for me. Why had this plain, strong German woman charmed my father when my sweet, loving, eternally right mother had not? I knew my mother's nagging must have had a lot to do with it, and more than that, her deeply rooted certainty that men were feckless creatures destined to fail her. For my father, perhaps, that had become a self-fulfilling prophecy. But also, I realized later, it was because both were alcoholics. Poverty, youth, and alcohol: It was a toxic combination, made more so by the fears involved in being illegal immigrants on the run.

At fourteen, I had no citizenship worries. I might be poor, but at least I'd been born on U.S. soil. It was just everything else I had to worry about, starting with who I was. By the time I started ninth grade at George Washington High School, my passing period had ended, not due to any dramatic turn of events, just the inexorable drift toward kinship with black students rather than white ones. Now the question was not which group to join, but which gang. The Midtown Midgets? The Scorpions? The Sharks? The Spiders? All of them fought with rocks, with knives, with chains, with brass knuckles and zip guns—anything they could get their hands on. Some were black and some were Hispanic, and I could go either way, but I didn't want any of them. The constant awareness of race—and the daily challenges to fight based on race—only left me more alienated than ever. Schoolwork frustrated me, too. I still had so much trouble reading that I began to fear I might fail every one of my high school courses. I got through the first semester of ninth grade, but dropped out the next.

My mother was devastated when I told her my plan. I can remember exactly how her face fell at this latest disappointment in her life, the most crushing yet. I had failed her by skipping out on my piano lessons, and now I'd failed her by dropping out of high school. She let me know it every day. I would never feel worse about myself than in the year or so that followed. Both to earn money and to be away from her, I did a number of odd jobs. I delivered groceries and moved produce from the cellar to the display floor for a local market. I worked a bit in the garment district, carting racks of clothes. I worked for an adopted uncle from the Caribbean named Vincent Newby, who ran a tailor shop. I delivered clothes for him, and learned to work the pressing machine. Ah, now I was moving up! I was a presser! Perhaps, with luck, I'd eventually even have my own little tailor shop. I couldn't imagine anything better. I could imagine a whole lot worse.

One day, to escape these worries, I slipped into a showing of the new Humphrey Bogart movie *Sahara*. I'd gone in for Bogie, but I became transfixed by a black actor named Rex Ingram. Ingram played the part of a Sudanese soldier who'd fallen in with a group of Allied soldiers lost from their various regiments in North Africa. The story followed this motley crew across the Libyan desert until it encountered a German regiment. At one point in the story, Ingram gave chase to and tackled a Nazi officer and pushed the guy's face into the sand. The camera zoomed in for a searing image of Ingram's black hand, suffocating the Nazi soldier in the desert sand as the Germans riddled him with bullets. To me, Ingram's scene of revenge was galvanizing. I'd never seen a film that showed a black character so heroic. Yes! I thought. This was the war for me!

Shortly after my seventeenth birthday—March 1, 1944—I told my mother I wanted to enlist in the U.S. Navy. A lot of other seventeen-year-olds were signing up, too; they just needed a parent's written permission. It was a patriotic time, with the United States now fully involved in both theaters of World War II and the tide just beginning to turn for the Allies. To me, the navy seemed the best by far of the military branches; sailors never had to tramp through mud like army soldiers, they never got shot out of planes, and they got to go to sea, which I knew I liked from my trips to and from Jamaica.

My mother sat silently in the living room as I packed, and barely stirred herself to see me to the door. I told her I'd be back with lots of stories, and then I was gone. I had no idea what the future held, and certainly not an inkling that it might, in some circuitous way, lead me to a microphone and a stage.

4

I'd boarded a train for Chicago, journeying to the U.S. Navy's largest training center, north of the city on Lake Michigan. Only later would I realize I'd embarked at the same time on another kind of journey. My days of passing as "Frenchy" were behind me. But as a New York–born son of West Indian immigrants, I had no idea how I fit into the mainstream of mid-twentieth-century American Negroes. And for all I'd experienced of urban poverty, I hadn't yet felt the sting of segregation. The plight of southern Negroes was some distant problem, like that of Haile Selassie's ragtag Ethiopians mowed down by the mechanized divisions of Italy's Fascist army. Selassie was another of the black political leaders and causes my mother had embraced. I didn't yet realize that southern poverty and prejudice affected me as a black man in America and simply as an American.

That realization came with my arrival at Naval Station Great Lakes, where I was put in an all-black camp, Robert Smalls, one of perhaps ten—the others all white—in this vast U.S. Navy complex. No surprise there: In 1944, all the armed forces were segregated. What astonished me was the sheer range of American blacks around me. I met rural southerners, farmers mostly, who spoke in such a deep, dense drawl that at times I needed a translator. A group of northern intellectuals seemed no less exotic to me. But I felt more drawn to them. At least I could understand what they were saying, and their political bull sessions intrigued me. The ongoing debate was whether or not Negroes should be in the war at all. Until recently, they'd been allowed to serve only as mess attendants, munitions loaders, and stevedores; they still had almost no chance to rise in the ranks. Some felt that if black companies fought with courage, racial prejudice in America would ebb, ushering in a postwar era of new opportunities. Others scoffed at that idea. The cynics, without exception, were draftees, dragged into the war against their will. So cutting were they about the black enlistees that I started adding years to my age and saying I, too, was a draftee. When I dared to ask questions, though, I showed how naïve I was. "Where did this Chihuahua come from?" one of the intellectuals asked. As if throwing bones to a dog, they tossed me political pamphlets, and I began to read.

The name W.E.B. Du Bois came up a lot in those pamphlets. I learned that as an educator and intellectual, Du Bois had helped found the National Association for the Advancement of Colored People in 1909 to fight racial violence and discrimination. I was fascinated to read that he and my mother's hero, Marcus Garvey, had become bitter rivals, Du Bois advocating integration, Garvey pushing for separatism. Du Bois, the first black student at Harvard ever to attain a Ph.D., envisioned a black elite class reaching the highest levels of politics, Wall Street, and academia with sheer brainpower: a "talented tenth," he called it. Garvey's appeal was to the working class; to him, Du Bois was a snob.

Along with the pamphlets, my new barracks-mates passed on Du Bois's latest book, *Dusk of Dawn*, about African-Americans' quest for freedom. As I devoured it and other books they let me leaf through, I noticed how often he footnoted other scholars and their works. One name came up more often than any of the others. Determined to impress those black intellectuals, I took the train into Chicago on my next leave and sought out the public library. My dog tags were all I needed to borrow books; servicemen could take them back to base and put them in a return bin there.

"Yes, how can I help you?"

The woman at the information desk appeared to be in her early sixties, with peppery hair, a ruddy complexion, and lovely big blue eyes. She might have been Mr. Pigou's sister. When I showed her the list of books I wanted, she blanched. I'd written down close to a dozen titles. "That's just too many," she said gently.

"I'll make it easy, ma'am," I said. "Just give me everything you got by Ibid."

She gave me a look. "There's no such writer," she said.

"Are you sure?" I bristled.

"No, I'm not sure," she replied.

"Would you be so kind as to check it out?" I countered.

She paused and made a not-too-subtle display of visually noting the number of people standing behind me.

"I'd like to find out before the war's over," I said with attitude.

The librarian bowed her head and went back to the card file. She brought back the drawer marked IA–IC. "Look for yourself," she said. "There's no 'Ibid' in here."

Incensed, I shot off a few more zingers and watched her shoulders sag. Before she could reply, I stormed out. Back at the base, I told my mates what had happened. To my mortification, they started howling with laughter. Finally they explained the enormity of my blunder. After an author listed a book as one of his sources, if he mentioned the book again, instead of giving the full title, he could just write *"Ibid."* "It's just a little literary shorthand," one man said. I got it. That poor librarian!

On my next leave, I went back to the library in Chicago, but the little old lady was gone. She'd been a volunteer, I learned. I guess I'd cured her of that. I'd crushed her spirit with my angry rants. I hung around the area for her that day, but to no avail. From then on, whenever I saw someone from behind who looked like her—not just in Chicago, but anywhere I was—I'd speed up my walk and give her a sidelong glance, hoping at last I'd have the chance to apologize. But I never found her.

Toward the end of basic training, the navy's newest recruits were given an I.Q. test. To my surprise, I did far better than my scholastic record suggested I should. I showed a special aptitude for organization, which qualified me for training as a navy storekeeper: an overseer of supplies. Off I went with a trainload of other black would-be storekeepers to Hampton, Virginia. We settled into makeshift barracks on the campus of Hampton Institute, a college founded in 1868 on the site of an antebellum plantation to train former slaves as teachers. The college now offered a standard liberal arts education, but all its students were still black. Few were happy to see us. The presence of U.S. sailors, they felt, tainted Hampton's academic atmosphere. The school's administration no doubt agreed, but Hampton was getting a lot in return for hosting us "gobs." For starters, the navy had built an Olympic-sized pool and a sports complex on campus that both students and sailors could use, plus multiple barracks, classroom facilities, and other structures that enhanced the school's image.

The fall term hadn't quite started in late August 1944 when we arrived on campus and marched smartly across the green, our duffels on our shoulders, our hats at just the right angle, our eyes straight ahead. Somehow, in our peripheral vision, all of us managed to notice the gorgeous coed, a senior, addressing a group of freshmen on a gentle slope. The freshmen had fanned out in a semicircle around her. She stood a few steps uphill, facing them—and us. The coed had a perfect figure and a lovely café au lait complexion. Even her hair was perfect. "Always marry a woman with good hair," my mother had told me. Good hair meant straight hair. This coed had straight, glossy hair, and it was shoulder-length! As soon as I set eyes on her, I was in love. I vowed then and there to marry her. Only later would I learn that she was the leader of the anti-sailors contingent on campus.

It took me quite a while to get a first date with Frances Marguerite Byrd. Dating *anyone* was a challenge; sailors stayed in a special area fenced off from students, and our superior officers made it clear that relationships with coeds were strictly forbidden.

My next glimpse of her, like my first, was from afar. I attended a college football game—Hampton was on the black-college circuit—and peered down from the stands at a Chevrolet convertible rolling slowly along the track around the field. Perched on the folded-back ragtop, waving to the crowd, was the Hampton Institute beauty queen. Same girl! I probably learned her name that day, but I would have to wait for a campus social to meet her.

The socials were sanctioned with some reluctance, out of a grudging patriotic spirit that barely outweighed the administration's wish to keep sailors and students apart. A navy band played all the standards, and I knew this was my chance to shine: I'd learned a lot of dance steps back in junior high school, and somehow, despite my lack of money, I'd amassed quite a stack of records, which I brought with me to parties, thus assuring my popularity. The records were at home, but I still had the moves. That night, I managed to score a dance with Marguerite.

"You better be nice to me," I said to her as the song came to an end. "Why?"

"Because I might just end up marrying you."

Marguerite was shocked. "Why? Has the world run out of other men?" she declared. But beneath her scowl, I thought I detected the barest trace of a smile.

From then on, I just kept after her. I'd hang out at her dorm after she came back from classes. I was never threatening, only humorous, and little by little she began to thaw. One day I found her outside her dorm in a circle of friends, one shoe hanging off her heel as she balanced it, unconsciously, on her toes. I saw my chance and snatched the shoe. I thought she'd demand it back, but she just stormed back into her dorm, one foot shod, the other stockinged. So I kept it. Now, every time she saw me, she asked when she'd get her shoe back. I said she'd get it when she went out on a date with me. Finally, she gave in.

I'd met one challenge with Marguerite, only to realize, on our date, that I was up against another. She came from a family of high achievers. She herself planned to earn graduate degrees and become a child psychologist. Her four siblings either were or were becoming teachers of one sort or another. Her family lived in a house—not an apartment—in northwest Washington, D.C.

"So what does your father do?" I finally asked.

"He's in the real estate business."

"The real estate business," I echoed. "And what does he do in the real estate business?"

"He works for a top real estate firm."

"And what does he do for that top real estate firm?"

"He handles the money."

This was yet another group of American Negroes foreign to me: the segregated middle class. In Washington, the Byrds had no choice but to live in a Negro neighborhood, send their children to Negro schools and colleges, take taxis designated for Negroes, and ride in the back of the bus. But they didn't mind any of that. Their neighborhood, from what Marguerite told me, was clean and well kept, the streets lined with handsome houses, many of them the fraternities and faculty housing of nearby Howard University, which infused the neighborhood with an ivy-and-brick, white-columned campus gentility. The public schools might not be quite as good as the white schools, but teachers and students shared the same strong drive to better themselves through education, and they did. Most important, in abiding by all the strictures of segregation, the Byrds and their neighbors communicated minimally with whites, and so felt almost none of the sting of racism that poor southern Negroes did on a daily basis. The Byrds lived in a bubble, but within it, from what I could tell, they were shaping their own version of the American dream.

I was way outmatched—socially, economically, educationally—and I knew it. So I did the only thing I could think to do: I lied. Shamelessly, I told Marguerite I'd been chosen for a special team trained personally by Admiral Nimitz, so secret we had no idea what mission we'd be assigned to. Something with submarines, I said vaguely, something that would put us behind enemy lines, exposing us to grave and constant danger. I didn't so much win her over as wear her out; and to a degree she was attracted by my storytelling, exaggerated though it might be. What crazy stories would that crazy boy from New York come up with next?

As I realized how conservative her values were, I challenged her on racial issues, and our dates became debates. Our running argument was about whether, as Negroes, we should fight racism wherever we saw it, never accepting our status as second-class citizens (my view), or settle for the bourgeois comforts of a segregated black society and hope for the best (her view). Segregation hadn't stopped Marguerite from working toward the career of her choice, so it just didn't faze her, and she wasn't the least bit angry about it. For those less fortunate, she took the long view: The Negro's position in American society had improved a lot already, and was getting better with time. Marguerite was a serious student of black history and culture, and while she never cooled my own growing anger at racism, she did expose me to a lot of good books. As I struggled through them, I began to feel I might acquire an education after all.

I felt bad about misleading Marguerite, so by our fourth or fifth date, I thought I might risk revealing that my mission had been changed to handing out sweatshirts and skivvies to sailors. To soften her up for that, I gave her a gold locket. To my surprise, she accepted it. Then disaster struck.

I couldn't have imagined that volunteering to give blood would land me in a military prison, but it did. In the town of Hampton, a woman had lost so much blood from giving birth that her life was in jeopardy. An SOS went out to all naval personnel for type-O donors. I qualified, and went to the hospital with four or five other sailors. Only two of us, it turned out, had blood types that exactly matched the need. We rolled up our sleeves, but after a short time the other sailor's blood stopped flowing freely. Desperate, the nurses asked if I would give more than the usual limit. I did.

I came back to the base feeling awfully woozy—too woozy for the nighttime guard duty to which I had been assigned. I explained my situation to the officer in charge, and asked if I could switch nights with someone. The officer, who was a dyed-in-the-wool redneck cracker, seemed to take special pleasure in informing me that I was at fault for giving blood when I knew I had guard duty. A sailor's commitment to his duties was absolute! Off I went, blearily, to my post. I had a feeling he'd come by to check on me two or three hours into my shift, and I was right. "Sleeping on guard duty!" he shouted as he jumped out of his jeep. "That's a punishable crime!"

I said I wasn't exactly sleeping, just trying to hold it together.

"Sleeping on guard duty! I hereby order you to appear at captain's mast!" Captain's mast was a navy judicial panel.

"Why don't you go fuck yourself," I said with sudden fury, and reared back to punch him.

The officer's driver subdued me—I wasn't much of a challenge, barely able to keep my eyes open—and the pair of them promptly arrested me for attacking an officer. I drew a two-week sentence at Portsmouth Naval Prison, and found myself walking the yard amid a number of other imprisoned servicemen. The servicemen, black and white, wore rough denim uniforms with a big P on the back. In another part of the camp lounged a larger group of German prisoners of war. No prison-issue wear for them. They sported their own uniforms and fur-collared leather bombardier jackets. They ate separately from us, and got better food. Unlike us, they had no prison duties, at least none that I could see. Their daytime hours were all spent in the recreation area. We were told they were just being treated in accordance with the articles of war. We didn't believe that for a minute. Here were Nazis who'd done all they could to kill American soldiers. Yet they were white, and we were black. The injustice of this sickened me.

I came back to my barracks a notorious figure. Unfortunately, Marguerite had heard the news, too. Even when I explained the whole story, I could sense her wondering why she'd spent time with a sailor, and such a headstrong one at that. None of her other suitors had to worry about being thrown in the brig. They were big men on campus, with job prospects and money to spend.

Before I could ease those doubts, I got my orders to board a troop train bound for some undisclosed location. Marguerite kept my locket and gave me a little hug good-bye. I wasn't sure I'd ever see her again.

Rolling westward, we guessed our destination easily enough: Camp Shoemaker, the vast "Fleet City" in the San Francisco Bay Area, where up to twenty thousand sailors at a time prepared to head off to war in the Pacific theater. We assumed we'd be assigned to various warships as storekeepers, then steam off to south China or Iwo Jima. Instead, we arrived to learn we'd be staying right there, in the part of the fleet city called Port Chicago. We wouldn't be storekeepers at all. We would be loading live munitions onto merchant ships and other warships, which, like hungry animals, devoured all the bombs fed to them. Not only was this menial work, it was incredibly dangerous, the more so because none of us had had any training for it. We knew exactly why we'd been chosen. This was scut work for the lowliest and most expendable sailors in the U.S. Navy: the black ones.

Not long before, on July 17, 1944, a vast explosion had rocked Port Chicago. Live munitions being loaded onto a merchant ship had detonated, causing a terrible chain reaction that killed 320 sailors and injured 390 more. Two-thirds of those sailors were black. In its aftermath, 258 black sailors at Port Chicago had refused to move any more munitions. As we arrived on the scene, with mangled structures and debris still in evidence, those sailors were being court-martialed, 50 of them sentenced to long terms for mutiny.

Those sentences would be commuted after the war, but the sailors would remain dishonorably discharged, deprived of their pensions, barred from any civil service jobs—all because they'd dared to stand up to blatant institutional racism. We didn't know that at the time. Nor could we know that the political reverberations of the Port Chicago disaster would help lead to desegregation of all the armed forces in 1948. We just wanted to get as far from Port Chicago as we could, as soon as possible. A day or two later came wonderful news: We were off the hook. The navy had filled its quota of black munitions loaders without us. Back east we rolled on another train, to another undisclosed location, like a newsreel in reverse. This time we emerged on the New Jersey coast, at the navy's Weapons Station Earle, just south of Staten Island. We'd still be storekeepers for munitions loaders, and still be handling live ammunition ourselves. But at least the New Jersey base hadn't blown up as yet. And it was close to Asbury Park, with its boardwalk and beach.

For me, any fears of the job at hand were more than offset by the joy of being stationed just hours away from Marguerite, who had now graduated from Hampton and was living at home. On my first leave, I took a train to Washington, barely able to contain my excitement. When I emerged from Union Station, I had a taste of blatant, south-of-the-Mason-Dixon-Line segregation: I had to wait on the colored-only line for a "colored taxi." Whites waited at the front of the station; the colored-only line was off to the side, in the station's shabbiest part. As I would learn, "colored only" was always off to the shabby side, whether it pertained to a public bathroom, a movie theater entrance, drinking fountain, or roadside motel. The absurdity of this "colored-only" taxi line was that it didn't even keep whites and blacks from sharing the same facilities. There wasn't any difference between the taxis that came to the whites-only line and those that served the colored-only line—except perhaps that white taxi drivers could decide whether they wanted to pick up black passengers or not. Even if the passengers were U.S. servicemen risking their lives to protect the nation.

The Byrds lived at 501 T Street—a very nice address, the black driver confirmed en route, in the heart of Washington's black community. The block was tree-lined and pretty—no kids on the sidewalk shooting marbles here, only riding bicycles—and yet a faint suspicion stirred in my mind as I got out. The Byrds lived in a nice house, but it was a two-family house. Marguerite's father might handle the money, but not perhaps *that* much money. I might have a chance after all.

Marguerite's mother opened the door, greeted me cordially, and gave my crisp white sailor's suit an approving look. "Wait a minute," she said. "I'll get her."

Marguerite looked more beautiful than ever. She seemed pleased to see me, but kept her distance. Before long, she would warn me that she was dating someone new—a "Jodi," as we called draft-age civilians who'd wangled deferments. Jodis tended to be college students with 4F medical classifications—not qualified for military service thanks to allergies or psoriasis, homosexuality or just a psychiatrist willing to deem them demented—or they'd found work in the war industry. One way or another, they'd kept themselves out of the war itself. Over the next months, every time I proposed coming down from New Jersey on leave, Marguerite informed me she was dating some other Jodi. She still kept my locket, though, which I took as a sign of hope.

I passed the last months of the war in New Jersey, wheeling live munitions from bunkers to trucks, then driving down to the docks to unload them onto cargo vessels. They didn't explode; that was enough for me. On our leave days, we'd head into Manhattan in groups of two or three, pick up dates through friends, and then go over to the jazz clubs. One night, I took a gorgeous girl named Dorothy Newby to the Copacabana to see the Ink Spots. I couldn't wait to impress her with a table and a bottle of Champagne on ice. But when our turn came to go in, the big white guy at the door had us stand aside while he ushered in the next couple, and the next couple after that. "What's going on?" I asked him finally. But I knew what was going on before he told me.

"No more seats, buddy."

"How come all these other people are getting in?"

"They got reservations."

I looked again at the long line of white people waiting and then at the bouncer. I wouldn't attract many supporters once I took on this son of a bitch. Dorothy, fearful of what was to come, grabbed my arm and urged me to leave. The humiliation for us was severe, but the white cop standing by watching the incident seemed less than sympathetic to my plight, and he convinced me with his smirk that a black sailor on his night's arrest sheet would suit him just fine. Our night was destroyed, and all I could do was slink off with my date, humiliated and my rage in check. Little did I know that I would one day have my payback with the Copacabana.

My eighteen-month hitch ended December 3, 1945. I could have reenlisted—I had no better prospects—but I'd had enough of military service: not just the numbing routine and the mortal risks with munitions but the all-too-frequent incidents of prejudice that kept me in an almost constant state of simmering rage. All but broke, I made my way back to Harlem to live with my mother and her new husband, Bill Wright, my little brother, Dennis, and my two new half siblings, Raymond and Shirley, in their latest apartment, on Amsterdam Avenue. My stepfather, always kind, took me on as an assistant janitor at the buildings he serviced. I mopped halls, stoked furnaces, and made small repairs. Almost immediately, I sank into a funk much deeper than any I'd ever known. Whatever dangers there were in the military, and whatever racism I faced, I knew it was all temporary. As far as I could tell, janitorial work was what I'd be doing for the rest of my life, and I knew I could never settle for that.

One day in January 1946, a tenant in the building asked me to hang her venetian blinds. When I managed that modest task, she gave me, as a tip, two tickets to a play at the American Negro Theatre. She was an actress, she explained; she and her boyfriend were in the play; perhaps I'd like it. I'd never heard of the "ANT," as she called it, but I was curious. I had no money for the dinner that a date would have required, so I went on my own that night to the Elks Lodge on 126th Street off Lenox Avenue, where the ANT staged its productions. It was the first play I'd ever attended.

Ushered to my seat, I turned to look at the forty or fifty people in semidarkness around me. They were talking in whispers. In any venue I'd known for entertainment—the Apollo Theatre, vaudeville, and movie houses—a different mood prevailed. There was always some kind of noise or laughter. This place was hushed, like a Catholic church.

When the curtain rose and the actors appeared, so poised and confident, they radiated a power that felt spiritual to me. The play, titled *Home Is the Hunter*, by Samuel Kootz, was freshly written, about returning black servicemen trying to establish postwar lives in Harlem. I knew these characters. I knew the problems they were talking about. That play didn't just speak to me. It mesmerized me. This was a whole new world—an exhilarating world. And there onstage, among the other actors, were my tenants, Clarice Taylor and Maxwell Glanville. Outside the theater, I was just their janitor, but here in the darkness, I felt a kinship with them. Maybe I could be part of this, somehow, not as an actor but just . . . a helper of some kind.

When the play ended and the houselights came up, I stayed riveted to my seat until everyone else had gotten up to go. Finally I ventured toward the stage, where audience members were greeting actors they knew. Shyly, I told Max and Clarice how much I'd enjoyed the play. As others came up to say hello, I noticed the stagehands emerging from backstage to strike the set; this was the last night of the play's short run. I saw they could use help, so I went up to move braces and scaffolding. They just assumed I was a stagehand, too, so I kept working for an hour or more, until it was done.

That night, I was too excited to sleep. I kept tossing and turning, thinking, How do I get possession of this? How do I find a way to make the theater and these people a part of my life?

The next day I knocked on Clarice and Maxwell's door to tell them again how much I'd enjoyed their performance. And did they, perhaps, need a volunteer to help move furniture over there at the ANT? Clarice laughed. She said, "Did I hear you say 'volunteer,' Harry?"

"Yes, ma'am."

She said, "Come with me the day after tomorrow. I'll introduce you to our department of historic treasures."

The ANT had started up in 1940 as a community repertory theater in the basement of a Harlem public library called the Schomburg, to create plays, as W.E.B. Du Bois had urged, "by, for, about, and near" black audiences. The few black roles on or off Broadway were slaves, maids, or butlers, for the most part, with a few gangsters and prostitutes (*Porgy and Bess*), one jealous Moor (*Othello*), and one reprehensible tyrant (*The Emperor Jones*). The ANT was meant to redress that. It was a collective of sorts; the acronym indicated that everyone would pitch in together, like worker ants—black ants! Already, its founders' ideals had faded somewhat, after a play called *Anna Lucasta* had gone from the ANT to Broadway and made stars of its cast, most notably Hilda Simms, who rode it all the way to London. The rest of the ANT's troupe was left back in Harlem, hoping for a similar break that never quite came.

The ANT would fold in 1949 amid a lot of hard feelings. But it still had some juice in January 1946, and a few more careers to launch. Clarice Taylor, for one, would star in *The Wiz* on Broadway, and on television as Bill Cosby's mother, Anna Huxtable, in *The Cosby Show*. Max Glanville would stage-manage and direct many New York productions, and eventually act in movies (*Cotton Comes to Harlem, Desirée*) and television dramas (*The Iceman Cometh*). A third member of the ANT would go on to a pretty good run as an actor after losing his West Indian accent—and I don't mean me, though this other fellow and I had a lot in common. Both Sidney Poitier and I were skinny, brooding, and vulnerable within our hard shells of self-protection, and each was about as unlikely as the other to become a future star.

Sidney was so quiet, so monosyllabic, that I didn't even realize at first he was from the West Indies. One day we found ourselves together under the stage, in a dank, musky place—this is what Clarice called "our department of historic treasures"—digging through old trunks for costumes. Sidney didn't say a word. I'd known guys like that before; I grew up with them—they were the outside-the-law crowd, with a lot to hide. When the silence stretched on, I finally stopped rooting through the costumes and asked him straight up, "Sidney, have you ever served time?"

He glowered at me with silent fury. Wow! Whatever I'd touched with my little gibe was clearly reverberating. "Where'd you get that?" he said at last.

"I didn't get it from anywhere."

"So what's your point?"

I stared at this brooding mass for a moment and just dropped the subject.

Partly I'd sensed it might be true; partly I was trying to find out who he was. In fact, Sidney *had* been to prison—three times! All three were just overnight stays for petty crimes as a youth: raiding a cornfield in Nassau, for one. But these were deep, humiliating secrets for him, and he was appalled to think they'd somehow gotten around.

That got us off to a rocky start. Not for a while would I learn how uncannily similar our backgrounds were. Like me, Sidney had been born in the United States—in Miami, Florida—but spent much of his childhood in the islands, in his case the very remote Cat Island, in the Bahamas, where his parents lived. Like me, he'd grown up between two cultures, an angry misfit. Like me, he'd joined the service as soon as he could—for him it was the army—and been assigned to a black company. His own military experience had been rougher than mine. Mercilessly teased for his West Indian accent, he'd almost suffered a nervous breakdown. Like me, he'd come to New York City when he mustered out and taken menial jobs to survive. When I met him, Sidney was working hard to lose his accent—he seemed to think if he didn't talk at all, it might go away—but he faced a much bigger challenge. He was tone-deaf. Even the stage directors at the ANT assumed that any black actor worth his salt knew how to sing and dance. Sidney couldn't do either.

Once Sidney and I got past that rough introduction, we started hanging out together. This was more than a casual new acquaintance for me. Sidney was my first friend—my first friend in life. As a child I'd moved from place to place too often to make lasting friendships. In the navy I'd generally kept to myself; if I socialized with other sailors, it was only in the most superficial way. This was different. Sidney and I were soul mates—separated at birth, or so it seemed. Our setbacks and hurts, hopes and ambitions were so parallel that each of us knew what the other would say—about almost anything.

Of course, we were both so desperately poor that our main topic of conversation was get-rich-quick schemes. Sidney had a plan to market a Caribbean conch extract said to be an aphrodisiac. Or maybe it had bodybuilding ingredients. Whatever its promise, the plan didn't go far when we realized we'd need capital to produce it. Then we decided to be a stand-up-comedy team—Belafonte and Poitier. For weeks we feverishly wrote routines, rehearsing them on my rooftop, until we realized they weren't funny. But we grew close—very close—as we realized not only how much we had in common, but how much fun we had hanging out together. We started going to the theater once or twice a week, splitting the cost of a single ticket. One of us would go in for the first half, come out at intermission and pass the stub, along with a plot summary, to the other. We saw some theater that way, and agreed that seeing half of each play taught us more than not seeing a play at all.

In those early months of 1946, Sidney seemed no more likely to be an actor than a comic or conch entrepreneur. He'd failed in his first audition for the ANT, losing out on a three-month trial with the troupe. In desperation he'd pleaded to be allowed to work as a janitor at the theater—anything to feel he was at least associated with something he wanted to do—and won his three-month trial that way. Now it was coming to an end, and the ANT's director, Osceola Archer, was disinclined to give him another trial period. Sidney told me he felt Osceola was racist. She was very Indian-looking, with long, black, thick hair and rather light skin. Sidney felt strongly that she liked me more than him because my skin was quite a bit lighter than his. I never saw any evidence of this, and thought Sidney was just oversensitive and vulnerable. But what made him that way, more than anything else, was the darkness of his skin. He felt isolated by it, cut off not just from white society, but many black people, too.

Both to Sidney's shock and to mine, Osceola asked me to fill a role in the ANT's revival of a comedy called *On Strivers' Row*. I hadn't sought it out; unlike Sidney, I hadn't even wanted to act. I just liked being around the theater, with all these exuberant characters, doing manual work: being backstage, burning my hands on ropes, handling hot bulbs, building and breaking down sets. When Osceola first asked me to read for a role, I refused. "No, no, you won't get me into that," I said. I hadn't imagined I could be an actor. Certainly I didn't have the chops yet even to try. But Osceola kept after me, telling me I was the right type, and the rest of the cast began giving me the "group muscle," making me feel I was letting the whole organization down. By the time they got through all that, I was in the play.

Anyone in Harlem knew the subject of that play from its title: Strivers' Row was an enclave of elegant town houses on West 138th and West 139th streets, between Seventh and Eighth avenues, where Harlem's black elite lived. The play, by Abram Hill, one of the ANT's founders, mocked the strivers' social pretensions, which came out in full force when their teenage children brought social undesirables home. I played one of the children, such a small role that I felt less like an actor than a stagehand with a couple of lines. But I must have shown some promise, because right after that, I landed a larger role in a play called *The Days of Our Youth*, a college drama by Frank Gabrielson. Sidney was about to leave the company—his three-month trial was up, and Osceola had told him it wouldn't be extended, with or without janitorial duties. But as a parting gesture, she cast him as my understudy. Sidney, of course, thought it was a last swipe on her part not to give him the role and make *me* the understudy.

As I read through the play, I began to sweat with dread. This character of mine had a lot of lines! How could I possibly remember them all? I went back to Osceola and asked her to let me off the hook. This had gone far enough. I wasn't an actor. I'd just ruin the production. Osceola shook her head with a smile. Everyone felt this way at first, she said. I'd get over it. Besides, I thought, did I really want to surrender this moment in the spotlights . . . to Sidney?

I got through opening night pretty well, and by the second night, I couldn't wait for the show to start. My euphoria ended with a phone call hours before a special performance of the play that Osceola had scheduled for an audience of one: James Light, director of the original Broadway production of *Days of Our Youth*. On the phone was the guy I'd lined up to take over my evening janitorial duties back at my stepfather's building. Something had come up; he couldn't make it. I tried everything—even offering him more than a buck and a half!— but he wouldn't budge. I hung up in despair. As much as I wanted to perform for the prestigious Mr. Light, I couldn't blow off the 8:00 p.m. garbage run. Every night I had to be in the basement right on time to operate the dumbwaiter that brought the garbage down. I'd ring the buzzer for each floor, the tenant on that floor would ring back, and when he'd filled the dumbwaiter, I'd bring it down with that floor's garbage. If no one was there to work the dumbwaiter, the garbage would stink by morning, the tenants would be furious—and I'd be out of a job I couldn't afford to lose. Crestfallen, I told Osceola that I had no choice but to miss the special performance. And so Sidney got his chance.

Mr. Light, as it turned out, liked what he saw in Sidney Poitier. The fact was, he'd come to the ANT specifically in search of black actors to round out his Broadway cast of *Lysistrata,* by Aristophanes. It would be an all-black production. Sidney's first piece of luck was in being chosen by Mr. Light for that Broadway show. His second was more extraordinary. Although the play got dreadful reviews after it opened on October 17, 1946, and closed after four performances, a Hollywood agent attended one of them. He was seeking a black actor for a leading role in a new movie! And from that came Sidney's Hollywood break, in the crackling Joseph L. Mankiewicz film *No Way Out,* as a hospital resident forced to deal with two racist brothers, one of them played by Richard Widmark, wounded in their latest bank robbery.

When the movie came out in 1950, I sat through it with such strong, conflicting feelings: awe, pride, envy, and despair. There was my fellow actor, playing the role I could have had if only I hadn't had to work as a janitor that fateful night! Mercifully, by the time the film appeared, I'd had a break of my own. But for years after that, I couldn't help tweaking Sidney every time I saw another interview in which he spoke of his rise from oblivion to stardom. I knew what his success was really based on, I'd tell him. The demands of garbage!

I did get to perform in *Days of Our Youth* for the rest of the play's brief run, which led another ANT director, Charles Sebree, to give me my first lead role, in July 1946, as a young Irish radical in an ANT production of *Juno and the Paycock,* by the Irish playwright Sean O'Casey. That the play was about white characters, written by a white playwright, bothered us not at all. We easily identified with the Irish peasants resisting their British oppressors; we knew exactly how it felt to live in a society where those in power deprived the conquered of their civil rights. The catch, and it was a big one for me, was that the play was written in brogue. I took the play home and struggled painfully, with my poor reading skills, to master every syllable of my part. I nursed my fears by reminding myself I had only one *really* long speech, and did my best with the brogue by inventing my own West Indian version of it. (The other actors pretty much followed suit.) Then, on that first night, as I felt the audience respond to my opening lines, I couldn't wait to tear into it. Why did I only have *one* long speech? At the end, as all of us took our bows, I felt, for the first time in my life, part of something grand and wonderful. I'd never felt so happy. All I wanted was more.

One night before the curtain went up on *Juno,* word went around that Paul Robeson was in the audience. This was astonishing. We were so moved that he was there. What was he doing in our humble Harlem theater? Robeson was the American theater's black god, a star of such Promethean talent that he truly had no equal. That had first become clear in his college days at Rutgers, when, as the only black student on campus, he lettered in every sport, made Phi Beta Kappa, and was named valedictorian of his class of 1919. Playing professional football after that was just a throwaway for him. By the mid-twenties he was starring in every major play that had a black lead character, from Eugene O'Neill's *The Emperor Jones* and *All God's Chillun Got Wings* to Shakespeare's *Othello*. With his remarkable basso-profundo singing voice, Robeson had immortalized the song "Ol' Man River" in *Show Boat*, and embarked on a parallel career as a performer of folk songs and spirituals.

Initially Robeson had felt that as an artist he should avoid any political involvement. But on a tour in Wales at the end of a performance to a sold-out audience, as he left the theater through the back-stage alley in the height of winter, he saw a small group of Welsh miners on strike, standing there with their voices raised in song, trying to raise money for their needy families. Robeson, caught up in the moment, joined the singing with full force. Later, he referred to the story as the quintessential moment in the politicizing of his art. The next day he visited the miners in their homes, and from that moment on never turned his back on needy workers wherever in the world he found them.

By the outbreak of the Spanish Civil War in 1936, Robeson had begun speaking out against Generalissimo Francisco Franco and his Fascist takeover of Spain. When Hitler and Mussolini joined forces with Franco, Robeson raised money for the Abraham Lincoln Brigade, an American unit that joined the international volunteer army to defend Spain's threatened democracy. He also made headlines by going personally to Madrid; during the destructive bombing of the city by Hitler's Luftwaffe, he stood in the middle of the terror and sang to the liberation forces. In this time of global depression, Robeson felt a powerful bond with the oppressed in all countries. That had led him to embrace the Russian proletariat and the ideals of socialism.

Throughout World War II, Robeson had given benefits for the American war effort. He'd also begun to speak out against racial injustice in the United States. His strong words to baseball club owners were helping lead the way for Jackie Robinson to break the sport's color barrier. He'd demanded that President Truman investigate the wave of postwar lynchings in the South that began when southern black servicemen returned home expecting respect, only to stir Klansmen to murderous fury.

With awe and admiration, I followed everything Robeson said and did. To be such a consummate artist and at the same time speak out against injustice—there could be no higher platform than the one to which he'd ascended. I couldn't imagine what the great Paul Robeson would think of my Irish brogue, but I would find out.

We came out after the show to see an even larger man than I'd expected. He grinned at us and said that he couldn't wait to tell Sean O'Casey, one of his closest friends, what we black actors were doing with his play in New York. Our *Juno* was a fine production, Robeson told us. Everyone had done well. But what he really admired was our decision, as a black repertory company, to take on this play in the first place: a play of great dramatic power, hard to sustain onstage, and created by a white playwright about white characters. Robeson strongly supported the ANT's mission of nurturing black playwrights and producing their work. But the sad truth, he said, was that few great black plays were yet to be found. And so while we should do our share of works by Zora Neale Hurston, Langston Hughes, and a very small handful of others, we should also take on plays by white playwrights that dramatized social issues important to us all, from John Steinbeck and Clifford Odets to George Bernard Shaw. There was so much our theater could do to help teach people about those issues; we must do all we could to help it grow.

We listened in amazement, too thrilled to respond. What I remember, more than anything Robeson said, was the love he radiated, and the profound responsibility he felt, as an actor, to use his platform as a bully pulpit. I had no expectation that my acting on a basement stage in Harlem would lead me anywhere. But I knew I'd found my role model, and that I'd never look at theater the same way again. My mother had told me to wake up every morning and know how I'd wage the fight against injustice. That night, Paul Robeson gave me my epiphany: It would guide me for the rest of my life.

I had neither the confidence nor the cash in this period to pursue Marguerite. This was especially frustrating because after graduating from Hampton and living at home for a while, she'd landed a job in New York. She would be working at the Bethany Day Nursery, a highly regarded child development center in the East Thirties, and living in the teachers' dormitory beside the school, while she applied to New York University to pursue a graduate degree in education. I visited her as soon as she settled in. She seemed happy to see me, but I could tell she regarded me more as an exotic friend than a romantic prospect. My newfound passion for acting genuinely alarmed her. How would acting pay the rent? What kind of insanity was this? Her doubts only strengthened my resolve.

Along with hoping to rise socially in Marguerite's eyes, I wanted to do something that gave my life meaning, and being in the arts made sense. Downtown, I'd heard, a German émigré director had established the most exciting theater workshop in New York, as part of the New School for Social Research. Everyone at the ANT was talking about it. Best of all, the G.I. Bill would cover my tuition. Marguerite really flipped at that. How could I think of squandering my G.I. Bill money on . . . acting classes?

Undeterred, I went down for an interview. Yes, I could join the Dramatic Workshop, as it was called, and yes, the school would accept payment through the G.I. Bill—assuming I was a high school graduate and had the diploma to prove it. I started pleading my case. How could the New School let a technicality like that keep out such a talented actor, a veteran of so many productions on the venerable stage of the American Negro Theatre? I could save my breath, my interviewer explained; I would have to make a formal appeal to the workshop's board. At the appointed time, I arrived to find four judges waiting for me. The most intense one had pink skin, a shock of white hair, and penetrating eyes. He spoke with a German accent, and had a stern Prussian manner. That was the German director I'd heard about, the one who'd founded the workshop: Erwin Piscator. He was the one I had to please. I knew he had strong socialist views, so I played up my plight as a victim of society, forced to leave school in order to work. It was a rather melodramatic picture I painted, with the truth stretched a bit. But it worked.

Perhaps, to be honest, the board liked the idea of adding an American Negro or two. The school had none in the beginning, and as I soon realized on my first day, I was the only one in my class. I introduced myself to my fellow students, and they introduced themselves to me. *Walter Matthau, Bea Arthur, Elaine Stritch, Wally Cox, Rod Steiger, Marlon Brando.* Also, one Bernie Schwartz, later known as Tony Curtis. The names meant no more to me than mine did to them.

The one name that stood out was Piscator's. He was a giant of twentieth-century German theater, whose brutal experiences in World War I as a draftee in the German infantry had shaped his artistic vision. After the war, he'd joined the Dadaist movement, staging plays that embraced the Dadaists' message of nonsense and formlessness as the only response to war's absurdities. When he'd sensed Dada's limits, he'd moved to Berlin to start a proletarian theater, staging plays by Maksim Gorky, among others, that played in workers' halls and granted free admission to the unemployed. The plays dramatized political issues of the day, with bold new visual elements that addressed his audience directly: relevant facts flashed on a small side screen, for example, as the actors spoke their lines, or war footage shown behind them. Because these devices were like a Greek chorus, filling the audience in, Piscator and Bertolt Brecht called their approach "epic theater." Hitler's rise drove Piscator to Moscow as a political refugee; Stalin's rule of terror led him to flee again, this time to Paris. In 1939, with Hitler's invasion of France imminent, Piscator needed yet another political haven, and found one at the New School. And so began one of the most exciting and influential experiments in American theater.

The great director didn't hold acting classes. He gave lectures, which I attended, but I saw him up close only when he hurried past me in the halls. I knew not to break his stride with small talk; if you had something to say to Mr. Piscator, it had better be important. Yet the workshop bristled with his energy and sense of mission, and all of us were inspired by it. Drama was serious; it was a tool to speak truth to power, to change society and, especially, to show the folly of war. There was no light fare or screwball comedy at the Dramatic Workshop. And no stars, at least not in theory. We were all workers of equal standing in Piscator's dramatic collective. In that spirit, we learned not just acting but stage design and set-building, lighting, directing, and playwriting. I might be an actor in one production, but then up on the catwalk, manning lights, in the next. Some of our plays we wrote as collective efforts. But Piscator's reputation also brought us new plays by world-class writers. Jean-Paul Sartre let the workshop stage the first U.S. production of *The Flies* while I was there, and he came to the opening. Robert Penn Warren gave us his first stage adaption of *All the King's Men*, his Pulitzer Prize–winning novel. Inspired, I read these and every other play that Piscator mentioned, and all the classics I could get my hands on. In those first months at the Dramatic Workshop, I felt my whole world opening up.

Almost as soon as I enrolled in the workshop, I moved down to the Village. My mother, like Marguerite, was horrified I'd blown my G.I. Bill money on drama school, and my living with her and her new family in a cramped Harlem apartment had put us all on edge. The ANT director Charles Sebree invited me to share his Bleecker Street apartment for free until I found a place of my own. His generosity came at a price, I soon learned; Charles was gay, and had hopes that I might move from the living room to the bedroom. That got awkward. As soon as I could, I found a better setup through another ANT colleague, a songwriter named Alan Greene. Alan and a fellow songwriter shared a large basement apartment in the Eighties off Central Park West. They were both harmonica players and had a pretty good act. They proposed that I pay just $9.50 a month, quite a bit less than a third of the rent, and make up the difference by serving as the group's cook and cleanup man. For that, I still needed a part-time job, so I found one back in the garment district, pushing racks of clothes.

Both of my new roommates were white, and cooking and cleaning up for them might have made me feel like some black retainer. But it didn't. For the first time in my life, I felt no racial distance. Always with white people, I'd had my guard up, waiting for the next racist slight, unconscious though it might well be: the white woman in the elevator, tensing as I got on and pulling her handbag tighter under her arm; or the white guy in a suit and tie talking in what he thought was black lingo, to show how liberal he was. Here there was none of that. Alan and his roommate were free of prejudice and, by no coincidence, passionately left wing in their politics.

All over postwar Manhattan, but especially on the West Side and down in the Village, everyone was talking politics. Socialism, communism, Progressivism—the fault lines among these were never very clear, at least not to me in 1947, for everyone seemed to share the same idealistic goals. At parties, cheap wine and booze fueled long bull sessions on how to achieve a classless society, not just in America but around the world. Writers from John Steinbeck to Ernest Hemingway, playwrights from Arthur Miller to Clifford Odets, even poets like Dylan Thomas—all were writing, and speaking publicly, about how to reshape capitalism, and Russia, still our ally in victory against Hitler, seemed to be leading the way. Race issues were very much in the mix of all this: In whatever brand of utopia was being promoted, there would be a full embrace of racial equality and civil rights for all. I went to lectures at the Jefferson School on Sixth Avenue, which openly billed itself as an institute of Marxist thought affiliated with the American Communist party. At one, I remember, journalist I. F. Stone spoke. There were lectures, too, at union halls, where young leftists mixed with hard-core laborers. Socialists and communists alike embraced the working class as the bedrock of a new political order. They railed at the federal government for its strike-busting laws, and vowed to overturn them. I liked the spirit of brotherhood that those meetings nurtured. But I never signed on as a member of the American Socialist or Communist party, or even viewed myself as a fellow traveler, as the jargon of the day had it. Perhaps the notion of joining anything held me back. The only group with a political agenda I'd joined was the U.S. Navy, and I was thrilled to be out of that.

For fun, I often hung out with Tony Curtis. He lived in the Bronx with his family; why live downtown, he'd say, when he could live uptown for free? And who cared if they still greeted him up there as Bernie Schwartz? Tony knew just how talented he was, and how handsome—pretty more than handsome—and he didn't need to live in the Village to prove himself. We went to a lot of parties together. Occasionally we went with Elaine Stritch, who swore more colorfully than any sailor I'd known, and Bea Arthur, who'd start matching wits with Elaine until the two of them had everyone in uncontrollable laughter. They were a gorgeous, sexy, vibrant pair, Bea the blunt Jewish comic, Elaine the diva. Walter Matthau, who lived in Hell's Kitchen, was wonderful company, too, though even then he cared a lot more about betting on horses than going to parties. I can remember one time, distinctly, when two or three jowly-looking types in raincoats came to visit him at school because he owed them money.

The classmate we all wanted to be with more than any other, though, was Marlon Brando. By the fall of 1947, Brando had made a name for himself as a stage actor, mostly for his brooding portrait of a troubled veteran in Maxwell Anderson's *Truckline Café*, which had gotten him notice as "Broadway's Most Promising Actor." He'd gone on to co-star with Katharine Cornell in her latest production of George Bernard Shaw's *Candida*, and then to star with Paul Muni in an unabashedly political play, *A Flag Is Born*, advocating the creation of a new Jewish state in Palestine. Now he'd landed the lead in a new play called *A Streetcar Named Desire*. He'd never attended classes very much at the

Dramatic Workshop, and with *Streetcar* in rehearsals, he came to even fewer.

But whether he showed up in class or not, Marlon had a huge impact on us. All of us, without quite realizing it, began acting with a Brando-like intensity. When he did come to class, he always seemed brimming with emotion, and we never knew which way he'd go, joyful or sullen. Afterward, I'd sometimes catch a ride with him on his motorcycle, wrapping my arms around his sweater and hanging on for dear life as he roared down the Village streets with his cycling soul mate, Wally Cox—all of us bareheaded, of course (no one wore a helmet back then, at least no one remotely cool). I was on the verge of buying a bike of my own and becoming part of this cult when I stepped back and thought harder about it. My instinct for survival turned out to be stronger than my desire for peer approval.

Soon after we met, Marlon and I discovered that both of us came from alcoholic families. That was a powerful bond. We talked about our fathers, and what their drinking had done to us; we understood each other's internal vocabulary. We also realized, right from the start, that we both liked women a lot. Which was also to say, we liked a lot of women. I think our alcoholic families had something to do with that; we were always in search of more approval and love. To be honest, we knew we cut the mustard. We didn't have to do much looking for women. They came looking for us.

Before long, Marlon and I were doing a fair amount of double-dating. I'd never met a white man who so thoroughly embraced black culture. He loved going with me to jazz clubs. I tended to chat with the black musicians between sets, and I could bring Marlon into those circles. Soon, of course, he'd need no help from me, but at that particular point, before *Streetcar* opened, I was a way in for him. What Marlon loved even more than black musicians was black women. My God! He'd found a whole bevy of beautiful ones at the Katherine Dunham Dance Company, and eagerly enrolled in Dunham's dance and drumming classes. He was passionate about drumming—Chano Pozo, the great Cuban drummer, was one of his idols. I'm sure he bedded some of his fellow drumming students, but he focused on a lead dancer named Julie Robinson. I didn't know that at the time, but I did see Julie when she came, with a couple of other Dunham dancers, to give a performance at the New School. She was so lithe and sexy, I was instantly smitten. But I didn't actually meet her. I certainly had no idea that I'd end up marrying her one day.

Marlon was a prankster; if he saw you napping, he'd tie your shoe-laces together. We did that to each other, more than once. But as a friend, he was bedrock loyal. Not long after our respective careers took us to Hollywood, I hooked up with him to go to a black after-hours joint in L.A. While we were there, the place got raided. Suddenly customers were being pushed up against the wall at gunpoint, frisked and handcuffed, and led off to paddy wagons. Marlon was a rising star—thanks to *Streetcar*, which had also come out as a movie by then—and the police recognized him. They took him aside and quietly told him to ease out the back door. "I've got a friend with me," he said, pointing to me. I wasn't famous yet; no one recognized me. "Look," said a policeman with some irritation to Marlon, "you're lucky we're letting you out on your own." Marlon shook his head. "No, I'm sorry—I can't leave without him." Finally, in exasperation, the police let both of us go.

From Marguerite, at this time, came bad news. She was dating a black reporter from *The New York Times*, and the romance was getting serious. Though she enjoyed our friendship, and wanted to keep seeing me, she also wanted to give me back my locket. I was still supporting myself by pushing racks of clothes in the garment district, so my own career trajectory—and marital prospects—looked pretty flat. But I hadn't given up hope of changing that with some breakthrough role, then dazzling Marguerite into matrimony. So I was relieved not to see an engagement ring on her finger. I've still got running room, I thought.

I had an unexpected ally in the Bethany Day Nursery's director, a tall, very Ivy Leaguish woman named Mrs. Bears. She turned out to be as politically progressive as I was. She nodded approvingly, pursing her lips as I told her about union meetings I'd gone to lately, and what I planned to do to support Henry Wallace in his presidential campaign for the new Progressive party. I could see Marguerite struggling to grasp that her new boss agreed with my crazy political views.

Somehow, in filling me in on all her siblings' latest degrees earned and honors won and job offers received, Marguerite let slip a little detail about her father that floored me. Mr. Byrd was still handling all the money for that fancy real estate law firm. Only his job wasn't quite what she'd implied. He was the law firm's handyman. The janitor! He kept the place in order! Every Friday, as one of his duties, he carried the week's checks in a big bag to the bank, deposited them, and brought back the deposit slip. That was the money he "handled."

Here was another lesson for me in what it meant to be black in America—in what lay at the heart of the outwardly comfortable black middle class. The *segregated* black middle class, with all its own social delineations. To be accepted by that middle class of lawyers and doctors and accountants, Mr. Byrd had to act as if he was already there. And his children, consciously or not, had to burnish his image with all *their* friends—which was to say: lie. Not everything Marguerite told me about her family was exaggerated. Her father had put his five children through college; even if scholarship money had helped, that was quite an achievement. And he did maintain the house at 501 T Street. But he was not, in any true sense of the phrase, the one who handled the money.

The New School had two theaters for its productions—a large, former Yiddish theater on East Houston Street we called the Rooftop, and a smaller but better equipped uptown theater on Eighth Avenue at Forty-eighth Street, where the most ambitious of our plays were staged. Marguerite came to see me perform at both, though she remained baffled by where this acting might lead me. Of the two, I preferred the uptown theater, so much so that if I didn't have an acting role in an uptown production, I'd volunteer to do props or lighting there. I still liked the manual work. Even more, I liked heading over after the last curtain call to the Royal Roost, one of the best New York jazz clubs ever. Marguerite had almost no interest in jazz, so when I went to the Roost, I was on my own.

Swells took tables and ordered expensive drinks. I stayed by the bar in back, behind a glass divider, where, for fifty cents, I could buy a bottle of beer and stand as long as I wanted, hearing all the greats, from Charlie Parker to Ella Fitzgerald, from Miles Davis to Lester Young. I got to know the waiters well enough that on a slow night, they'd let me move to a table up front. The best jazz in the world for fifty cents! I was in heaven. And then, little by little, I began hanging out with the musicians between sets, getting them a beer or just being a good listener. They talked about everything: the struggle with tough times, local or world politics, issues of race, and, of course, Joe Louis's latest fight, and how Jackie Robinson would do in his early days with the Brooklyn Dodgers. But mostly they talked about the music and musicians they knew, and the trouble that this one or that one was in, with drugs, or a woman, or both.

I loved them all, but a special favorite was Lester Young, the great tenor saxophonist whom Billie Holiday had named the "Pres," for both his brilliant playing and his absolute cool. Here's how cool Lester was: He'd invented the word! It was part of a private language he shared only with his bandmates and close friends. A "molly trolley" was a rehearsal, "bread" was money for a gig ("Does the bread smell good?" he'd say), and a player's keys, or his fingers, were his "people." Lester had played with Fletcher Henderson, Andy Kirk, and Count Basie. He'd backed Nat King Cole as well as Billie Holiday. Recently he'd started touring with Norman Granz's ever-changing Jazz at the Philharmonic ensemble—it had started at the Philharmonic but kept the name when Granz took it on the road—but between those dates he'd occasionally play the Roost with a backup band that included, at various times, Charlie Parker, Miles Davis, and pianist Al Haig. By 1948, a lot of jazz buffs, including me, considered him the greatest saxophonist in the world.

Lester kept to a tight circle. An outsider might turn out to be a narcotics detective—a "Bob Crosby," in Lester's private language—which Lester and his bandmates had reason to fear, as I would come to learn, given the amount of cocaine they consumed offstage. Even if not, chances were a stranger wouldn't be cool. So I wasn't entirely sure if Lester was accepting me, or challenging me, when he turned to me one night between sets and said, "What is it, exactly, that you do?"

I told him I was a student. A drama student.

"What in drama do you study?"

Acting, I told him.

He paused for a moment, perhaps giving safe passage to his most recent snort of cocaine, then said, "And how do you do that?"

I'd never been asked that question, and to this day I cannot answer it. I told him I didn't know, but it must work, because we were putting on pretty good plays.

"How do you know they're good?"

"Well, Lester," I said, "why don't you come on by and see for yourself?"

So Lester, his sidemen, and the club's young promoter and booking agent, Monte Kay, came to the Forty-eighth Street theater one night to see our production of John Steinbeck's *Of Mice and Men*. I played the Troubadour. There is, of course, no character named the Troubadour in *Of Mice and Men*. The director had invented this mystical figure to appear between scenes, singing snatches of Woody Guthrie and Leadbelly tunes to evoke the story's time and place, and to give the stagehands time to change sets. I never would have had the nerve to present myself onstage as a singer. But as the Troubadour, I was an actor, singing in character. That made all the difference for me.

The jazzmen stayed till the end, and had a lot of nice things to say when I walked back to the Roost with them for a celebratory drink. Now, at least, they knew what I did. That was enough for me. I couldn't have imagined they'd think enough of my singing to make a suggestion that would change my life.

The workshop roles kept coming, but by early 1948, the euphoria I'd felt in joining this great collective had ebbed. It was supposed to help launch me as an actor, but I'd gotten nowhere in landing even a small part in any off-Broadway play, or lining up an agent. My classmates were all making headway, getting breaks; they had a lot to talk about when they got together. As a black actor, I was out of the loop, and so I spent less and less time socializing with them. The loneliness I'd felt so keenly in my youth, that bitter sense of not belonging, came back in full force, and nothing Marguerite could say would ease the anger it brought. I'd rant about how few parts there were for black actors in this racist white society. I'd rail at racist white politics: Blacks were getting lynched in the South, and Strom Thurmond, avowed segregationist, was running for president! The smallest thing would set me off. Riding on the subway with her, I'd point to the advertisements overhead for various beauty products. Why were all those models white, when so many of the riders on the subway were black?

The bleaker my acting prospects looked, the more I threw myself into political organizing. At various union halls, I helped put on agit-prop plays—taking a union crisis and dramatizing it, so the rank and file would be inspired to rally for better wages and working conditions. With my two roommates, I went during the summer break to a beautiful union retreat in Pennsylvania called Beaver Lodge, and helped the entertainment staff stage plays and sing-alongs. Time has blurred those events in my mind, but I remember sharing stages with Pete Seeger, Lee Hays, Josh White, and others, all protesting inequality and injustice. The war had been fought for democracy, yet all around us, the system we'd fought for and won kept failing us. The federal government suppressed strikes and censored free speech. It viewed its own citizens as traitors for espousing "undemocratic" political views. Most abominably, it did nothing to stop the scores of beatings and lynchings down South, many of returning black servicemen who'd gotten the "uppity" notion that they, too, had fought a war for democracy. I well remember one of the first victims, Isaac Woodard, a decorated black soldier from South Carolina who, in February 1946, boarded a Greyhound bus and got into an argument with the white driver. At the next stop, the driver reported him to the local police. Although he had a chest full of medals, the police dragged him off the bus and gouged out both his eyes. He would come to speak at rallies, his concave eye sockets a terrible testimony to what prejudice could do. In the postwar South, thousands more were savaged or killed without record or retribution.

Paul Robeson spoke and sang at some of those rallies. He was the star draw, and I was an usher. But I did approach him to tell him I'd been in that play at the ANT, and to say I'd read his last speech, and how much I'd admired it. He came to recognize me, and to flash that great grin when he saw me. "Oh, Harry—you're here. Good to see you."

Only in retrospect did I realize how much my politicking began to burden the friendships I had with my fellow workshop actors. I was walking around with too much of a conscience, always busy making people feel responsible and guilty if they didn't get as caught up in social issues as I was. They liked me, probably more than I knew, but in the end, I was a bit too much for them. In truth, some of my indignation had less to do with the issues or my parents or poverty than it did with the fact that my classmates had begun to get work—parts in real plays, not just school productions. I was getting nothing at all.

One day that winter, my luck took a turn for the better at last. I got a call from Osceola Archer, the director from the ANT who'd cast me in my first roles. She was planning an off-Broadway production of *Sojourner Truth*, about the Negro abolitionist who became an early icon of civil rights. She wanted me to play Sojourner's son. For me, this was huge. Erwin Piscator's productions were, in a sense, off-Broadway, too. But they got staged and were financed by an academic institution; they weren't competing commercially. *Sojourner Truth* would open at the 92nd Street Y, hardly the Palace or the Winter Garden. But officially and formally, it would be an off-Broadway production—my first. Best of all, I'd be playing opposite Muriel Smith, one of the New York theater's rising stars. Smith had won a lot of attention for her fourteen-month run in *Carmen Jones,* the all-black Broadway, Oscar Hammerstein version of the Bizet opera *Carmen.* Her reputation as a singer secure, she hoped that playing Sojourner would establish her as a dramatic actor, too, and lead to more Broadway plays. That it didn't may have been, at least in some small part, my fault.

Opening night—April 20, 1948—went off without a hitch. The problem came at the start of the next day's matinee. In the show, Muriel Smith's co-star played a white woman whose son was my character's friend. The two of us were like Huck Finn and Tom Sawyer, always getting into mischief. As the play opened, we were being chased across the stage by cops, and were then supposed to jump through a basement window, only to land, to our surprise, in a secret abolitionists' meeting. My friend jumped first. At this matinee, when he did, his pants ripped right up the backside, revealing that he was wearing no underwear. To see him put a hand back to try to cover his white behind struck me as hilarious—so funny that I started laughing at him, and kept laughing throughout the scene, no matter how many of my fellow actors gave me furious sidelong looks. Muriel Smith was the angriest of them all. This was her play, her vehicle, and I was making a mockery of it. She didn't talk to me again, not the rest of that day, as we put on our third and last performance at the 92nd Street Y, nor when we staged the production up at the American Negro Theatre the next month.

That uptown performance brought two consolations. One was that Eleanor Roosevelt came to see the play, since it was written by her friend Katherine Garrison Biddle. In her "My Day" column that week, Mrs. Roosevelt praised Muriel Smith's "beautiful voice" and called her "a really fine actress," easing my guilty conscience somewhat. "Many of the men impressed me also," she added, which I took as my first critical praise in print. Even more important, Marguerite came to the Harlem performance.

Something clicked for Marguerite as she watched me onstage that May night. When she came up to me afterward, she gave me a big, soulful hug. After the show, we strolled over to the East River Drive and walked along the promenade, the bridge lights twinkling above and below us. On a whim, I pushed her toward the railing and threatened to throw her into the current if she didn't agree to marry me. After shrieking a bit, she did. We set a date of June 18.

Over the next few weeks, I worried Marguerite might change her mind. But when I came to pick her up during her lunch break at Bethany Day Nursery on June 18, there she was, still game for getting hitched to an aspiring black actor whose prospects seemed only slightly less meager than before his off-Broadway debut. She'd even found a wedding dress to wear. Mrs. Bears—her boss and my supporter—came down to City Hall with us, along with several of the teachers, to serve as witnesses, and an aunt of Marguerite's from Jersey City showed up to represent the Byrds. Marguerite had broken the news to her parents the night before, and they'd done little to hide their horror at her rash move. No one from my family attended. Why would they? My mother disapproved of my getting married so young—but then, for that matter, she disapproved of me in every particular. My stepfather, Bill Wright, wouldn't have come on his own without her, and their children were about four and six years old. My father didn't disapprove of me, exactly; we just had no communication, now that Millie had remarried and he no longer had to supply child support on a weekly basis. As for my younger brother, Dennis, his main feeling toward me was resentment—for being the brother who wasn't there, and out on my own. I don't recall feeling sorry for myself about any of this. It just was what it was.

For our honeymoon, Marguerite and I went down to Beaver Lodge, the union lodge in Pennsylvania where my roommates and I had entertained workers that winter and spring. The organizers put on the Ritz for us, in part because I'd agreed to stay on for the summer as one of their paid entertainment staff. After ten blissful days, Marguerite went back to Manhattan and her job at Bethany Day Nursery. Often, in the next months, the seventy-five dollars she earned each week at Bethany would be all that stood between us and destitution. I was twenty-one. Professionally, I was a black actor whose G.I. Bill money for classes had just run out. And now a *married* black out-of-work actor. At summer's end, I would have to find an apartment for the two of us and a job to pay the rent. And whatever job it was, it would have to be something better than pushing clothes racks in the garment district, because by August, Marguerite was pregnant.

5

I remember a cold rain that night in January 1949, and a brisk wind that I tried to block with the collar of my navy peacoat. As I reached the Royal Roost, Pee Wee Marquette, the midget who stood outside in an admiral's suit luring passersby in with his steady patter, mangled my name as usual. "Harry Bella Buddha! How are ya, Mister Harry?"

I hesitated. Marguerite was right: Whiling away these winter nights at the Roost just kept me from facing my new responsibilities as a husband and soon-to-be father. But the streets were frigid, inside was warm, and the Roost was the one place in my life that felt like home. As I opened the door, a slow, smooth, perfect tenor sax solo pulled me in. How could I *not* go in when Lester Young and his band were playing?

I'd had a tough few months. With the end of my G.I. Bill money, I'd had to withdraw from classes at the New School's Dramatic Workshop. My off-Broadway break in *Sojourner Truth* hadn't led to more roles. I was still pushing clothes racks in the garment district—now full-time, for forty dollars a week. And for the moment, at least, I couldn't see what difference my activism had made. Despite all those rallies and agitprop plays and sing-alongs, Henry Wallace's presidential bid had gone nowhere, blacks were still being lynched in the segregated South, and the country seemed no closer to a classless society than before.

Through these months, I thought hard about giving up acting. I knew Marguerite wanted me to put my life on a proper track at last: a high school equivalency diploma, college, a real job. Her parents made no bones about telling her she'd made a big mistake marrying me. They'd assumed she'd marry some upstanding black graduate student—or at least that *New York Times* reporter—and so had she. Instead, she'd gotten snared by a kid who was pretty slick and fast on his feet, a kid who was fun to be around, a curious creature who elicited her sympathy as much as her love. In our courtship, I'd played on that sympathy to reel her in. And now that she was carrying our child, I felt a heavy burden not to fail as a provider. My parents' voices echoed in my mind, engaged in those same old bitter battles. "Why can't you earn a decent living, Harry?" "I do what I can." "It's not enough!" "You ask too much." "I only ask you to be a responsible husband and father!" Above all, I wanted not to fail in Marguerite's eyes, as my father had in Millie's.

That night at the Roost, the waiters let me sit up front, and when the set ended, Lester and his bandmates came over. "How're your feelings?" Lester asked. He always put it that way. In the months since he'd come to hear me play the Troubadour in *Of Mice and Men,* we'd gotten pretty close. One night I'd told him about my two weeks in Portsmouth Naval Prison, and he'd told me his own, far more horrifying story. As a draftee in Alabama, Lester had been arrested for possessing marijuana and barbiturates. When the authorities had learned he had a white girlfriend, they added miscegenation to the rap. In Alabama, miscegenation was defined by law as interracial sex, with or without matrimony. Lester had sat out the rest of the war in a military prison, an experience that traumatized him and would partly account for his nervous breakdown some years later.

"My feelings aren't doing so well," I admitted, and told him just how bleak my prospects were.

"Well, why don't you ask Monte to give you a gig?" one of Lester's sidemen asked. "Something to tide you over."

Monte was Monte Kay, the Royal Roost's new young manager.

"I'm not a singer," I said. "What you saw me do was acting. It just happened to involve singing."

"Talk to Monte," another of the sidemen said.

To my astonishment, Monte didn't need persuading; he liked what he'd heard at the Forty-eighth Street theater, too. Monte was about my age, an olive-skinned Sephardic Jew who loved jazz and hoped his gig at the Roost would lead to managing his own clientele of singers and players. He'd come pretty far already: Though the mob owned the Roost (as it did nearly every significant nightclub in the country), Monte had the power to book any acts he liked. If he heard some kid in St. Louis could blow a horn, Monte would fly down to check him out. "How about singing in the intermissions?" he suggested to me. "We could try it for a couple of weeks and see how it goes."

"But I don't have a repertoire," I responded.

"Well, you can sing," Monte said. "And it's easy enough to work up enough songs for an intermission."

Monte went to Al Haig, Lester's pianist, the one white guy in Lester Young's band, a regular player with Dizzy Gillespie, Charlie Parker, and Miles Davis. Al said he'd be happy to oblige.

"Don't worry," Monte said to me. "We'll pay you, too—scale. Seventy bucks per week."

Seventy dollars! To sing!

That week, Al and I worked up a few standards, starting with "Pennies from Heaven." My roommate Alan Greene contributed a song he'd written called "Lean on Me." I threw in an original, too—the only song I'd written—from a Dramatic Workshop musicale at the Houston Street theater. The revue, called *Middleman, What Now?*, had focused on soldiers returning from the war and trying to fit into postwar society; the students had contributed songs or vignettes, as they liked. My song, "Recognition," was about the struggles of trying to make it as a black veteran in white America.

> *I'm known as a roamer*
> *Wandering roun' from town to town*
> *Tryin' hard to find a corner*
> *Where I can lay my weary head down.*

I ended by singing, *"I'm gonna put my shoulder to the wheel of freedom and help it roll along."*

For my big night, I went out and bought a blue suit—secondhand but very sharp. Marguerite was impressed I'd be earning seventy dollars, though not impressed enough to come down and hear me. If acting was a dubious profession, in her eyes, singing was just a lark.

I sat quaking through Lester's first set that next Tuesday night, my mouth dry, my palms sweaty. When it came to an end, and all the players except Al melted away, I almost bolted. Before I could make a move, Pee Wee Marquette popped up onstage, his admiral's hat at a rakish slant. Monte had brought him down from the street to do the honors. "Ladies and gentlemen, the Royal Roost is pleased to introduce a new discovery, Harry Bella Buddha!"

Al gave me a little nod and a smile and played a little flourish as I walked across the stage in a stupor. And then something very odd happened, something I remember as vividly today as when it happened more than sixty years ago.

Tommy Potter came out onstage with us, picked up his bass, and started playing along. I looked at him, surprised and confused. He gave me a nod and a smile.

Then Max Roach glided out and slid behind his drum set.

And finally Charlie Parker emerged from backstage and picked up his sax.

Al Haig, Tommy Potter, Max Roach . . . and Charlie Parker!

I couldn't believe it. Four of the world's greatest jazz musicians had just volunteered to be the backup band for a twenty-one-year-old singer no one had ever heard of, making his debut in a nightclub intermission. They hadn't decided to sit in because they thought I had the greatest scat going, or some new way of phrasing. They came out because they liked this kid who came to the club a lot, and wanted to give him a send-off.

Al launched into "Pennies from Heaven" in E flat. But if anyone had told Charlie about the sixteen-bar intro, he'd forgotten. As I was about to open my mouth, Charlie raised his sax high and tore into a riff. I stood there nodding along, both thrilled and terrified, my count completely blown. I couldn't even tell where the intro began. Finally Al gave me a nod, and I just plunged in.

The Roost had a good crowd that night, and I got a nice hand for "Pennies." With each of the next four songs, the applause grew louder. At the end, I got a solid ovation, and when I dared at last to look over at Monte, he was sitting off to the side with a Cheshire cat grin, as if he'd known exactly what the crowd's reaction would be all along.

Whatever I said to thank the players that night, it wasn't enough. I could never repay them, not then or later, for this amazing act of generosity. Just by coming onstage and picking up their instruments, they'd validated; the crowd knew that that kind of heat wouldn't get up to play for some flunky. And so the din of conversation had died, the drunks had stopped flagging their waiters for more drinks, and everyone, out of sheer curiosity, just listened. And I'd had my chance. All I could do was be alert, in years to come, for opportunities to help some talented unknown the way those guys had helped me, and to hope, when those opportunities came, as they did, that in some small way I was passing that karma on.

Monte extended my gig by a week, and then another, and another: twenty-two weeks in all. I sang two or three intermissions each night, my repertoire expanding as I went. Al Haig was my only backup now, but he was more than enough; thanks to that all-star sendoff the first night, I'd made my mark. With packed rooms cheering me on, Monte even upped my pay, to $200 a week. It was breathtaking. I went from being a nobody who didn't think he could sing to walking onstage at Carnegie Hall, one night that spring, to accept a plaque from the *Pittsburgh Courier*, an African-American newspaper, as the most promising new singer in the country.

I had a voice the crowd liked, and a look. "The Gob with a Throb," as one nightlife columnist dubbed me. But I could have sung those songs in a hundred other jazz joints around the country and gone nowhere. The Roost wasn't just another joint. In the winter of 1949, it was the epicenter of jazz, a birthplace of bebop, its nightly torrent of hot licks broadcast live around the country from a glassed-in booth in the back of the club by radio's premier jazz DJ, Symphony Sid. And it was Symphony Sid, as much as Monte Kay, who helped launch me.

"This is your man Symphony, Symphony the Sid, your all-night, all-frantic one . . ." Symphony Sid, born Sidney Tarnopol on the Lower East Side, had become the "dean of jazz," a white hipster who introduced black jazz stars to mass radio audiences. He had a regular show on WJZ, which Lester Young promoted in his song "Jumpin with Symphony Sid" (*"The dial is all set right close to eighty . . ."*). But in a collaboration with Monte, he often broadcast live from the Roost. That first week of my intermission gig, Sid presided from his booth in back, telling his fans to listen. "Down here at the Royal Roost, a lot of exciting stuff going on, we got an exciting singer here, Harry Belafonte. Now this is a great story, folks. . . . One week ago he was in the garment district pushing a rack of clothes. Now he's packin' 'em in at the Roost! It's a Cinderella story, is what it is, which is why we call him . . . the Cinderella Gentleman!"

That first week, Monte and Symphony Sid became my co-managers, and the Roost's publicist, Virginia Wicks, became my publicist. Until I made some serious money, Monte and Sid would help me for free; Vir-

ginia was the only one I had to pay, for working the phones to bring
the jazz critics in, and for planting a mention here and there. What I
needed, Monte and Sid agreed, was a record, right away. Monte had the
moxie to make that happen.

Overnight, he formed Roost Records, rented a studio, and hired a
few sidemen. These were none other than Machito and His Orchestra,
the hottest Latin band in America. During the recording of one of the
cuts—"Lean on Me"—the trumpeter Howard McGhee and tenor saxophonist Brew Moore stepped to the mikes for two remarkable solos.
The B side was the song that I had written—"Recognition."

The copy Monte gave to Symphony Sid was probably still hot from
the pressing. "Listen to this, my fellow hipsters," Sid crooned that
night to his radio audience, "the Cinderella Gentleman, Harry Belafonte, has gone and made a record." Fortunately, Sid's arrest for marijuana possession had just that month ended in a mistrial. Instead of
doing a short term in the pen, he stayed right there in his glass booth at
the Roost, and with his steady plugging, the record sold ten thousand
copies in New York City alone. At that rate, Monte told me excitedly,
we could sell a million copies around the country. Except that Roost
Records had no distribution, only Monte and Virginia going around on
their own to New York record stores.

The news did reach Edgecombe Avenue, Harlem's most elite address,
where Paul Robeson lived with his wife, Eslanda. On one of my nights
off from the Roost, the Robesons invited me and Marguerite to dinner.
They lived on that part of Edgecombe Avenue called Sugar Hill—the
nicest part of a very nice neighborhood—in an apartment filled with
framed pictures, some of Robeson onstage, others signed from black
leaders around the world. Eight or ten guests were gathered, including
John Oliver Killens, who would soon publish his deeply moving novel
Youngblood, about a black family in Georgia at the turn of the century;
Langston Hughes, the poet I'd spied glimpses of on Harlem streets; and
none other than Dr. W.E.B. Du Bois, who laughed indulgently when I
told him the story of going to the Chicago public library to seek out the
great "Ibid" he'd referenced in so many of his footnotes.

Over dinner, at a long table set off by two huge silver candelabras,
the conversation crackled with hot political talk. Robeson was about to
go to Paris for the Soviet-sponsored World Peace Congress, a controversial move now that the Cold War had begun. I remember a couple
of his guests arguing about the wisdom of his going, and I remember
going back to Sugar Hill for dinner upon his return, after he'd uttered

the words that brought the full force of the federal government down upon his head.

Robeson had angered a lot of America by declaring, in Paris, that in the event of a full-blown conflict between the two superpowers, it would be "unthinkable that American Negroes would go to war on behalf of those who have oppressed us for generations [by which he meant the United States] . . . against a country which in one generation has raised our people to the full dignity of mankind [by which he meant the Soviet Union]." I remember him saying his quote had been taken out of context. But he didn't disown the sentiment.

At that long table, Robeson and his guests debated only which civil rights blacks should hold out for before once again joining a war to fight for white America—not whether or not they should hold out. The previous July, President Truman had formally desegregated the entire U.S. military by executive order, and to the black bourgeois— like Marguerite's family—that was a grand step forward. In his deep, commanding voice at the head of the table, Robeson dismissed Truman's move as a bone thrown to black northern voters for the 1948 presidential election. For all anyone knew, it may have provided the critical votes in Truman's upset victory over Wallace and Dewey. But what was Truman doing for blacks now that he'd won reelection? Nothing, as far as Robeson could see. Not until the South's last COLORED ONLY sign was banished, the last school desegregated, and every black allowed to vote in free and fair elections should blacks begin to feel patriotic again. At Robeson's table, we all agreed that Truman was as cynical a politician as we'd seen, and that only mass protests would push him to do more for civil rights.

Late that August, Robeson traveled up to Peekskill, New York, to headline one of those protests: a benefit concert for the Civil Rights Congress, an alliance of labor and Negro groups condemned by the Truman administration as a communist front. As Robeson approached the rally site by car, he and his hosts could see locals beating early arrivals with baseball bats, and a cross burning on a nearby hill. Robeson tried to get out of the car to confront the mob, but his hosts restrained him. The concert was rescheduled for some days later. This time, I was one of the roughly twenty thousand people who came to hear Robeson perform, along with Pete Seeger and Woody Guthrie. The labor unions had organized a tight cordon of security around the crowd, and the angry locals were kept at bay. But as the concertgoers left, they had to drive through a miles-long gauntlet of jeering counterprotesters, shouting, "Go back to Russia, you niggers," and spewing their venom just as harshly at the "white niggers" who'd attended. Some concertgoers were pulled from their cars and beaten as the police stood by. As an unknown, I would suffer no consequences for appearing at that Peekskill rally, but Robeson would soon be forced to surrender his passport under the McCarran Act, and spend most of the 1950s hounded by the FBI.

Everyone at those dinners on Sugar Hill was a socialist to some degree or other—at least in the fuzzy sense of wanting the United States to become racially, as well as economically, egalitarian. Everyone, that is, but Marguerite, who sat quietly, knowing her own views would appall the others. After the first couple of dinners, she never again joined me. She'd give me an arch look when the invitations came, and tell me to enjoy myself, as if I were off for a poker night with the boys.

Marguerite was still living at the Bethany Day Nursery's dormitory, where Mrs. Bears, my staunch supporter, let me stay as well, despite the prohibition on overnight guests. But clearly, with Marguerite's swelling belly, that would have to change. Early that spring, Marguerite moved down to her family's home in Washington so she could give birth at Adams Private Hospital, the same segregated black hospital where her mother had had her. Up in Harlem, I embarked on a dogged search for the perfect apartment for the three of us. I wanted a park or river view, at least four rooms, and a rent we could afford. I never did find that apartment. But by the time Adrienne Michelle was born, on May 27, 1949, I'd settled on a fourth-floor walk-up at 501 West 156th Street. It offered three rooms instead of four, but a reasonable rent at fifty-five dollars a month, and proximity to my mother's latest apartment, which for some reason seemed a plus; despite her constant carping, I thought now that I was married with a place of my own and a glimmer of a career, we might forge a new bond. I wouldn't have dared rent an apartment on my new, uncertain income as a nightclub singer, but with Marguerite's steady seventy-five dollars a week, we could afford it. I spent my daytime hours getting the place furnished and ready for Marguerite's return in June. With her came an unexpected guest—her mother—holding Adrienne Michelle with a protective glare, to take up residence as our full-time nanny. I called her Mrs. Byrd, and neither then, nor later, did it occur to either of us that I might address her by her first name. Mimi was one formidable mother-in-law.

I can't say I much enjoyed Mimi's presence in the apartment, but I saw the need. By the time Adrienne was born, I'd gone from the Roost to a number of out-of-town clubs, like Chicago's Black Orchid and Philadelphia's Rendez-Vous Room—a quickening blur of club dates in eastern cities large and small that made me a part-time father at best.

I wore a fancy suit now, and a pencil-line mustache, as I stood stiffly in the spotlight, my hands folded over my abdomen as if I had a stomachache. My repertoire had grown, though at Monte and Virginia's insistence, I was tilting more toward pop than jazz. My new managers had noted I drew a lot more women than men, and had me crooning love songs that tugged at their heartstrings. I sang standards like "Skylark," "Lover," "Stardust," and "The Nearness of You." Afterward, I stayed up drinking with the musicians, wondering how a onetime gig at the Roost, meant only as a stopgap until I found work as an actor, had turned into a full-time job.

I felt like a fraud. I'd never had singing lessons. I hadn't taken enough piano lessons from Miss Shepherd even to learn how to read music. I might be a natural, as Monte and Virginia kept telling me, but I sure didn't sing standards as well as Billy Eckstine or Nat King Cole or Frank Sinatra. The proof was in the plastic. On July 19, 1949, I had my first big-time recording date, the first of two for Capitol Records that Monte wangled for me. I made two 78 RPM singles, one with "How Green Was My Valley" and "Deep as the River," the other with "They Didn't Believe in Me" and "Close Your Eyes." All were classic Tin Pan Alley ballads, better done by others, as my lackluster sales showed. On December 20, 1949, I recorded four more: "Farewell to Arms," "Whispering," "I Still Get a Thrill," and "Sometimes I Feel Like a Motherless Child." None of these singles took the world by storm, either.

By then the Roost had closed; its owners had failed to come to terms with their landlord on a new lease. But the party had just moved to a new space a couple of blocks north, to Broadway near Fifty-second Street. Same great jazz players, same friendly waiters, just a new name: Birdland, in honor of the Bird himself, Charlie Parker. Lester Young wrote a "Birdland" song, and played it on the club's opening night. Charlie, of course, helped inaugurate the place and Monte Kay became its manager; I was part of the opening bill. Shortly after Birdland opened, Monte booked me into a new club across the street called Bop

City. There I was part of a "History of Jazz" show, singing songs from Dixieland to bebop in a clean-cut quartet. (One of my fellow singers was Brock Peters, later to play the black man accused of rape in the movie version of *To Kill a Mockingbird*.) I felt proud to be there, but somewhat out of place: less a singer than an actor acting like one.

For better or worse, Erwin Piscator and his Dramatic Workshop had made a mark on me I couldn't—and didn't want to—erase. I'd plunged into a world of heavy academic study, read too much of Shakespeare and Aristophanes, Ibsen and Sartre, taken in too much of Piscator's passion for theater as a noble art and social mission. Suddenly I had a new life singing ballads that struck me as silly at best. *"Will you love me by the moonlight, on the shivery waters of the Baccalatta?"* I knew other singers didn't care about the lyrics, but somehow I did. Singing words I didn't believe in, I felt . . . inauthentic. I'd crossed a line I shouldn't have crossed. I'd drifted out of my realm.

During this time, between club dates, I scoured the acting trades and auditioned. Not for black parts—aside from butlers and manservants, there were none to be had—but white ones I thought *could* be black. "Look," I'd say to the white casting director, "this is just the white girl's friend, he's not a love interest; why can't he be black?" I never won that case, not once, but I kept trying, and now that I had money to spare, I took more Dramatic Workshop courses when I could. I landed one role in a production of *The Petrified Forest*, by Robert Sherwood, because I pushed hard for it—and because the character was black. Even Piscator, it turned out, wouldn't cast me in white parts.

When I played a New York club, my white Dramatic Workshop pals would come to hear me, and, ironically, marvel between sets at what they saw as my great success. Tony Curtis would come, and Walter Matthau, Marlon Brando, and Rod Steiger. To them, I was the guy with the steady gig, halfway to stardom. One of my most loyal new fans was Henry Fonda, who'd first heard me at the Roost and now followed me from club to club. He was a great jazz buff, and later a strong civil rights supporter who always answered my calls for help for the cause.

What I got from these club dates, along with applause, was much-needed bread. By the spring of 1950, when I sang a number of weeks at New York's Café Society, I was earning more than $350 a week—big money at that time for anyone, but especially a former janitor's assistant. Monte and Sid were kind enough to forgo any commission—they told me they'd start taking cuts when I played the Copacabana—so aside from taxes, I still had only to pay Virginia for feeding items to the press. I had money to help support Marguerite and Adrienne. I even had money saved, for the first time in my life—enough, I began to suggest to Monte, that maybe I could take an extended break from singing and give acting a make-it-or-break-it try. After all, I'd just recorded three more singles—for Jubilee Records—and they'd gone no further than the ones for Capitol. Shouldn't we face reality?

At that, Monte would groan and give me his pep talk yet again. Look at how far you've come, he'd say. Each season, you are playing bigger clubs. "These are the building blocks," he'd say. "Each is better than the last. This is how you play the game. If you want to make it, you play the game."

One day in the fall of 1950, Monte called me in great excitement. The next building block had just fallen into place: I had a two-week gig at Martha Raye's Five O'Clock Club in Miami, for $500 a week. This was moving up, all right. But as I pointed out to Monte, it also meant heading down deep into the segregated South—a first for me. "Oh, come on," Monte said. "It's Miami! Land of the Jews! You'll be fine."

In my nearly two years as a jazz/pop singer, I'd ventured as far west as Chicago, but no farther south than Pittsburgh. I'd sensed discrimination at almost every stop, but never overtly. The maître d' would nod when I asked for a table, then lead me back to one across from the kitchen's swinging doors even when other tables were free. The hotel desk clerk would look startled when I checked in, and fuss with his reservation book, and somehow, against all odds, I'd end up, again, on the top floor in one of the narrow, low-ceilinged rooms once set aside for live-in maids. But that was kid stuff compared to what I encountered when I got off the plane in Miami.

Martha Raye, the famously foul-mouthed comedienne, had lent her name to the Five O'Clock Club, in the heart of Miami Beach, on Twentieth and Collins. Its success owed at least as much to its policy of drinks on the house at five o'clock as to the twenty-four-hour bookies upstairs. When I arrived, the manager cheerfully handed me a number of passes and explained the drill. I would be staying in a fairly cheap motel on the black side of town. One pass was for the taxi driver to take me there—the black taxi driver, since white taxi drivers wouldn't pick me up and it was against the law for coloreds to hail them. Another was for the driver to take me back. I'd need a third pass to travel after curfew—actually a police card—and a fourth to perform at the Five O'Clock Club, just as I would, the manager helpfully explained, at any white cabaret.

Miami's "Harlem of the South" had a black business district along Avenue G, lined with wood-framed food stalls offering sweet-potato pies, barbecued chicken and ribs, and hot fish sandwiches. At night, zoot-suited dandies and their dates, in fancy silk dresses, promenaded between clubs like Harlem Square and Rockland Palace, where black entertainers like Billie Holiday and Bessie Smith held forth. For me, the sting of segregation was so strong here, so close at hand, that none of Colored Town's sights held any charm for me. In the small room shown to me, I unpacked my bags, wondering how I'd ever get through a week here, much less two.

That night I took my passes with me back to the Five O'Clock Club—curfew, the driver told me, was at nine o'clock, though of course only colored residents had to observe it—and came onstage determined not to betray any of my churning emotions. The crowd—all white, mostly women—applauded heartily, and more than one woman at the front tables gave me a wink. As long as I was onstage, crooning love songs, I had a certain power over them. But when the lights came up, I was just another colored man hotfooting it back to Colored Town—or else. And God forbid I stop to chat outside the club with any of my new white female fans. That could end in jail, or worse.

After the second or third night's performance, the manager came back to tell me he wanted me for another week. "No thanks," I told him.

He looked at me in stupefaction. "Harry, what're you talking about? You're making five bills a week here. What, the money's not good enough? You want another fifty? Okay, fine."

I shook my head. "Nope," I said. "It's not the money." I told him one week in the segregated South was enough for me.

Later that night, in my room in Colored Town, I realized I'd had enough of the whole thing: of singing mushy lyrics I didn't believe in, of being a lounge lizard for lonely women. The next day I called Monte to tell him my career as a pop singer had come to an end. No more club dates, no more singing about moons in June. For almost two years since that fateful night at the Roost, I'd made the best of my big chance, and I knew that Monte had done everything he could to help me along, but the simple truth was that I'd taken a wrong turn. I still had time to go back to New York and throw myself into acting once again. I might well fail, but I would set my course by Paul Robeson, and do what mattered, both onstage and off, whether I succeeded or not.

6

Back on West 156th Street, I broke the news of my latest career change with no small amount of guilt. I didn't want Marguerite to be the breadwinner; I wanted her to pursue her studies without worrying about money. I just couldn't do it as a moon-in-June crooner anymore, and I sure didn't want to do it as a businessman or real estate sharpie. Nor did I want to stop working for causes I cared passionately about.

Marguerite had a different perspective. Wary as she was of having a pop singer as a husband, she'd come to enjoy the good and steady cash my club dates brought in. And she had no interest in living again with an out-of-work actor, even one with some jingle saved up. She thought a suit-and-tie job was exactly what I needed, now that I'd outgrown my childish stage dreams. As for my causes, Marguerite saw them as mere distractions. "You want to save the world—how about saving yourself?" she'd say. "How can you keep struggling for all these causes that take you away from your child—and me?" I didn't intend, with my politicking, to put space between Marguerite and me. But that was the result.

I did appreciate that the less I saw of my ever-present mother-in-law, Mrs. Byrd, and the less she saw of me, the better. In her eyes, I was a dangerous bohemian, a no-account without a high school diploma, and the friends I brought by were worse—especially the white ones. Her deepest resentment she reserved for Virginia Wicks, my publicist, who happened to be a tall, very pretty Scandinavian blonde.

One night soon after my return from Miami, I brought Virginia back to the apartment to give her a parcel she needed. She'd started a fan club for me, and to help that along, I'd signed a stack of glossy head shots she could send out. Adrienne was asleep in her crib, in the first bedroom off the hall. Marguerite was asleep, too. But not Mrs. Byrd. I got Virginia the photos, saw her to the door, and gave her a sociable peck on the cheek. When I came back down the hall to the kitchen, Mrs. Byrd was waiting for me. She slapped me with her full force and fury, clearly hoping to take my head off. Then, without a word, she turned on her heel and strode down to her room. I stood there in shock, my face stinging, my ears ringing. By now I knew her well enough to know that she wasn't just angry at what she perceived as flirting on the part of her son-in-law. She was at least as angry because Virginia was white. It was neither the first nor last time I encountered racism in blacks toward whites just as strong and implacable as its reverse.

I could have demanded, the next day, that Mrs. Byrd pack her bags and go back to Washington, but with Marguerite still working at the Bethany Day Nursery, we needed her to help care for Adrienne. I'm not sure my mother-in-law would have left even if we did ask her: She wasn't going to leave her daughter in the hands of a dropout she held in such low esteem. She was on guard! I was the one who would have to change. I needed to make myself scarce, to find a new place where I could meet friends and hang out between auditions. Also, perhaps, a place to earn money. That very week, I came up with an idea over drinks with two of my best friends.

I'd known Bill Attaway since my days at the American Negro Theatre. He was a writer, a bit older than I, very smart and political, who'd written a play called *Carnival* that got produced, and two novels that got published—proletarian literature, the critics called it. *Blood on the Forge*, the more successful of the two, told a story of southern blacks drawn north to work at a Pittsburgh steel mill, only to be exploited in a new way there. Bill had drawn a lot of his material from his two years as a hobo, knocking around in the early 1930s. He still had more he wanted to do as a writer—and he would, soon enough. But in January 1951, he and I and a mutual friend of ours, a black actor named Ferman Phillips, who'd appeared with me in *Sojourner Truth*, hit on a humbler way for the three of us to make a buck while pursuing our artistic interests—by opening a hamburger joint in Greenwich Village.

I thought Marguerite would appreciate all the angles here. Starting a business, making money, getting me out of the house. In fact, she saw it as a comedown from the club circuit, and a baffling one at that. Perhaps it was, but for three artistically minded black men, open-ing a joint was one of the few ways—maybe the only way—we could make steady pay and pursue our careers without taking menial jobs in the white world. It even put us in charge of our own gig, rarer still for black men of any age. Sidney Poitier was thinking along the same lines; his place, in Harlem, would be called Ribs in the Ruff.

I was the only one of the three of us with any money, so I bank-rolled the scheme with about $2,000—nearly all I had. We found a tiny place for rent on the east side of Seventh Avenue, just below the junc-ture of Grove and West Fourth streets, Christopher and Waverly. We put a grill in the window, built a narrow counter with about ten stools, and added a few small tables against the far wall. We kept it open all day and much of the night, alternating in eight-hour shifts. One of the three of us would work the grill in the front window, flipping bur-gers and browning the potatoes and onions. Another would man the counter and tables, while the third went off, exhausted, to sleep. Aside from a kitchen man to peel the potatoes and chop the onions, we were the whole staff. We could have called our new place Harry's Hash Joint or Bill's Burger Grill, but no—the name had to be more literary than that. Bill was the one who came up with "the Sage." It was a double entendre, indicating both wisdom and the spice, though financially, the Sage was anything but a wise move, and I'm not sure we ever used sage in our short-order cooking.

Artists, actors, and writers in the Village found us right away. For them, the Sage became a little nest, a refuge where you could strum your guitar at a back table and write lyrics over a long cup of coffee, while two guys from the labor movement argued the finer points of socialism at the counter. Maybe the food wasn't that good. But the talk was, and so was the ambience—like that saloon in William Saroyan's *The Time of Your Life.* And the girls! Pretty soon, we had a regular chorus of them, stopping in to flirt with one or another of the Mighty Three. Ferman, especially, cultivated as many new female fans as any man could handle.

Before long, all these beautiful girls draped over the counter began to cause some resentment among the Italians who ran most of the other coffeehouses and restaurants in the neighborhood. We started hearing mutters, and caught some dirty looks. When a posse came in to announce we needed "protection," we got a little worried. Bill was the one who defused the situation. In his knocking-around days, he'd worked as a seaman, and a lot of the sailors he'd come to know were

Italian. A number of them now lived in the city, working waterfront jobs or waiting to ship out. A half dozen or so joined him for dinner one night at one of the key establishments in Little Italy, within sight of a don or two who witnessed the Italians treating Bill as one of their own. They nodded, gave their blessing, and the "protection" threats melted away.

To dispel any lingering tension, Bill proposed a basketball game at the courts on Sixth Avenue at West Third Street: Little Italy's best against the Sage short-order men. The three of us were pretty serious pickup players; to round out our team, we put the word out in Harlem, and recruited two other guys whom we presented as our cooks. Both were just a tad short of pro. By game day, word had gone around, and half of Little Italy came out to watch. The Sage Five romped, but everyone had such fun that it became a weekly ritual. In between, even the Italians started coming by the Sage for coffee—and to try their luck with the girls.

The Sage was always hopping. It just didn't make money. Any customer with a hard-luck story ate for free, or got his dinner with a promise to pay later, and only rarely did. Others who did pay but turned out to have lousy politics—railing at socialism or defending anti-communists—we'd basically shoo out the door. We had no sense of how to run the Sage as a business. We didn't even know what the word *wholesale* meant; we bought all our groceries at the A&P down the street. Soon enough, the debt side of the ledger began to outweigh the profits.

To meet the next month's rent, we started fanning out to Saturday night poker games to make up the shortfall, each of us sitting in on a different game to maximize our prospects. That worked pretty well . . . until it didn't. Desperate, we asked some of our customers for loans. We gravitated toward ladies who had a crush on one or another of us. They had button-down day jobs—one worked as a fact-checker at *Time* magazine—but they let their hair down at night. I'm loath to call it pimping, because there wasn't any quid pro quo; they just helped us meet our monthly credit crises, and we always paid them back—eventually. But we did play on their heartstrings and, perhaps even more, on their liberal proclivities; they were, with few exceptions, white. For that matter, the whole Village scene was mostly white, except for the three outposts where blacks were part of the mix: the Village Vanguard, Café Society, and now us.

However dire our finances, we'd take Sundays off, to play basketball at the local YMCA or, in warm weather, to play baseball with a crowd of actors and musicians at the fields near the Seventy-ninth Street Boat Basin in Riverside Park. Along with Attaway and Phillips, one of my closest friends from that time was Tony Scott, the great jazz clarinetist. Tony had discovered the Sage early on, and among the pretty girls who hung out at the counter he found his future first wife. After the Sunday games, he and Fran would have us all down to Tony's loft on Jones Street. We'd get a conga drummer and a piano player, and Tony would take out his clarinet. I didn't sing—this was strictly bebop jazz riffing—but as the spliffs went around, we all talked and talked: art, politics, life . . .

In those marathon talkfests, we always circled back to racial issues. Now that the Progressive party had fallen apart, we anguished over how best to fight segregation. Passions ran pretty high; one night they ran right over the top. Tony, who was white, was playing with a Latino conga drummer—I think his name was Lopez. When it came time for Lopez to solo, he just took off, playing with such inspiration that all of us stopped talking. Tony was riveted, too. Instead of coming back in with his clarinet, he just sat there, tears rolling down his face. Puzzled, the drummer stopped playing. "Look at what you just played," Tony burst out, and with that he stretched out a hand to include me. "What would have happened if you hadn't been slaves . . . just think what you all could have done. . . . Lopez, what do you think would have happened?"

Lopez thought about that. "You'd be playing the drums," he said, "and I'd be playing the clarinet."

When he wasn't wallowing in racial guilt, we all agreed, Tony was the best clarinetist in the world. I still think that. He'd played with Count Basie, Duke Ellington, Sarah Vaughan, and Billie Holiday, among many others. Later, he would play backup for me, too, and be the band's conductor, as well as my musical arranger on my first big breakthrough albums. By the end of the decade, though, Tony would move to Italy—both of his parents had come from Sicily; the family name was Sciacca—and perform mostly in Europe from then on. The move would be good for his music, exposing him to African and Far Eastern influences, even turning him into a New Age pioneer, but it would end his marriage to Fran. And when it did, she would marry . . . Bill Attaway! In those still-bohemian Greenwich Village days, that was about par for the course. All of us stayed close, and Bill, too, came to play an important, recurring role in my career—many roles, really—beginning, in that year of The Sage, by helping me forge a new identity, this time as a folksinger.

All through the winter and spring of 1951, I went to acting classes at the Dramatic Workshop, paying for them out of my last savings now. I took classes at the Actors Studio, too; the actress Shelley Winters became a good friend that way. But when I went on auditions, I struck out again and again. "Nothing we're doing has any Negro roles," each casting director would tell me. "If we do *The Hasty Heart*, though, we'll give you a call." *The Hasty Heart* was a wartime play about wounded Allied soldiers in a Burmese hospital, one of whom, known as Blossom, was an African who had about two lines.

I knew I had a better shot with singing; I just couldn't stand the thought of going back to those mushy pop standards. What did excite me was folk music: raw, gritty, American songs of hope, heartbreak—and protest. Pete Seeger had galvanized me at those political sing-alongs for Henry Wallace. He'd started a movement called People's Songs to force social change through folk songs—a mind-blowing idea for me. Songs weren't just entertainment. They could move people to action. They had political *power*. People's Songs had hooked up with the unions; at the top of their agenda was using folk music to fight racism. Woody Guthrie, Burl Ives, Josh White, and Tom Glazer were just some of the folksingers who'd joined People's Songs. That had a powerful appeal for me.

Paul Robeson, too, had turned to folk music as a tool for social change. I'd heard him sing southern spirituals in that unforgettable basso profundo. But I'd also heard him sing folk songs from Wales, after establishing his bond of solidarity with the Welsh coal miners, and Russian folk songs, from his trips to Moscow, before his passport was seized by the U.S. government for "un-American" activities. Along with Pete Seeger, he made me think I might find, in folk music, a way to fuse my passions for politics and art.

The Village Vanguard was just down the street from the Sage, so I'd go down to hear Woody there, and Leadbelly, the two men whose songs gave me my glory moment in *Of Mice and Men* at the Dramatic Workshop, and Josh White. At that time, the Vanguard was a folk place; only later would it become famous for jazz. The lyric power of the songs they sang mesmerized me. *"Tol' da captin ma hans was col' / Said damn yo' hans boy let da wheelin' roll."* What Tin Pan Alley tune could compete with that? Often at the Sage, a customer would take out his guitar and, urged on by me, launch into one of those powerful folk songs; I'd supply harmony, and before long, others would join in.

> *John Henry said to his captain:*
> *"Oh a man ain't nothin' but a man,*
> *An' before I let that steam drill beat me down,*
> *I'll die with my hammer in my hand."*

I got a lot of positive words for those renditions, and I started harboring the hope that I might land a gig at one of the folk clubs nearby—if not at the Vanguard, then one of the others.

There was just one problem. I hadn't hung out in the Dust Bowl with Woody Guthrie, or played banjo around hobo campfires. I wasn't from the American South, like Leadbelly; I couldn't play a six-string guitar, much less a twelve-string, as he did. I'd never done the field-work that inspired field hollers; I'd never been on a chain gang, from which some of the most powerful folk songs had come. I wasn't even a full-fledged Jamaican, or a black from Harlem with full Afro-American roots. All of this mattered, deeply, in the burgeoning folk movement of the early 1950s, because authenticity was what the songs were about, and an inauthentic singer, which was what I appeared to be, had no right to sing them.

Bill Attaway, a serious student of folk music and its traditions from his hobo days, did a lot to help me put those fears aside. He introduced me to Tony Schwartz, a great collector of folk music, who'd gathered hundreds of black folk songs from the American South, the Caribbean, and Africa. (One of his great finds was the African song "Wimoweh," which he introduced to Pete Seeger; later it would be reconfigured as the *Lion King* song.) With Bill's encouragement, I also started going down to the Library of Congress in Washington, D.C., to delve into the thousands of folk songs compiled by Alan Lomax.

Everyone in the folk movement knew about Lomax. A folk-music historian, he'd spent decades collecting songs on his travels, recording local artists in obscure roadhouses and scribbling lyrics in notebooks, then typing them up for the library's Folkways series. It was a family effort—Alan's brothers and father helped, too—but Alan was the main force. Lomax wasn't quite the saintly figure he was portrayed as;

on more than one occasion, he insisted his name be included on the copyright for folk songs he'd only recorded, not written, and profited accordingly. The Weavers, with Pete Seeger, were about to have a huge hit with Leadbelly's "Goodnight, Irene," and Lomax, who'd brought the song to light but played no part in writing it, demanded copyright co-credit, taking significant royalties from Leadbelly's impoverished family when the song became a hit. Nevertheless, thanks to Lomax, the Library of Congress now had an astonishing repository of songs from all over. I would come back from Washington, D.C., with dozens at a time, and spend my spare hours working on arrangements and fine-tuning the lyrics with a guitarist and Sage regular named Craig Work. Craig would come up with the chords, and together we'd test out our versions after hours for a throng of regulars who enjoyed them almost as much as they did the free late-night fare.

One customer who listened was a small-time theater producer named Jack Rollins. Later generations would know him as the co-producer, with Charles H. Joffe, of nearly all of Woody Allen's films, perhaps also as the manager of various well-known comics (Elaine May and Mike Nichols, Robert Klein) and television personalities (Dick Cavett and David Letterman). When I met him at the Sage, though, he was a thirty-five-year-old in search of a manager's career. We found him a fairly anxious, uptight guy, and pretty humorless for an agent who would come to represent comics. But he saw how eagerly I was taking up folk music, and when he mentioned he knew Max Gordon, I listened. Max was the founder and manager of the Village Vanguard. Jack felt sure he could get me an audition with Max.

To prepare, we started rehearsing in a small studio above the Lyceum Theatre on West Forty-fifth Street that Jack rented for us. Later, Jack would say he taught me how to move onstage and make contact with audiences, and how to fine-tune my phrasing and diction. "I took him and his folk music, tied them up with a pretty pink ribbon, and made a commercial package of them," he would tell one interviewer. That's not the way I remember it; from my years of acting classes, and from my jazz/pop days, I thought I had those bases pretty well covered. But Jack did encourage me to change from those suits I'd worn as a pop singer to a fitted shirt (unbuttoning a critical button or two), tight pants, and a heavy-buckled sailor's belt. Most important, he did know Max Gordon. Unfortunately, as it turned out, Max knew me, too. "Forget it," he said when Jack first suggested he audition me for the Vanguard. "I heard him as a pop singer and he doesn't have it. So what am I supposed to do with him?"

While Jack retired to his customary table at the Sage to restrategize, I took my songs on the road: not for money or fame, but for social causes. Henry Wallace's loss in 1948 had only strengthened my resolve to make a difference on issues that infuriated me. Thanks to the Taft-Hartley Act of 1947, unions' rights to strike were shamefully curbed; I sang in protest against that. Everyone's rights, not just union members', were under siege in the deepening Cold War. Already, the Smith Act gave the federal government the power to jail or deport any alien accused of treason—no trial needed. But the McCarran Act of 1950 went further; now the government had carte blanche to prosecute or expel even U.S. citizens deemed "subversive" by J. Edgar Hoover's FBI. I sang out against that, too.

To me, a most appalling miscarriage of justice was the arrest and indictment of one of my heroes, W.E.B. Du Bois.

By 1951, Du Bois had lived many lives as an intellectual and civil rights activist. He'd feuded bitterly with the NAACP, resigned from it, and rejoined it, only to be kicked out in 1948. Through these postwar years, he'd drawn ever closer to Paul Robeson, working with him on the Council of African Affairs, an anti-colonialist organization whose roots, in a way, lay back with Marcus Garvey and his vision of a post-colonial black Liberia. In 1950, at the age of eighty-two, Du Bois had run for U.S. Senator from New York on the American Labor party ticket and managed to win some two hundred thousand votes—mine among them. If nothing else, his campaign had kicked sand in the face of the federal government. Now the government had kicked back. The U.S. Justice Department seized on Du Bois's call for outlawing atomic weapons, declaring it Soviet propaganda, and demanded that he and the members of his Peace Information Center register as "agents of a foreign principal" under the Smith Act. When Du Bois refused, he was indicted by a grand jury, arrested, and put on trial.

At rallies and sing-alongs, I helped raise money for Du Bois's defense, because the NAACP, and almost every other member of the black elite, had cut him loose, and contributed nothing. That was a lesson I wouldn't forget: how coldly and firmly the black establishment could excommunicate one of its own. On the opening day of the trial, those of us who came to show our support were stunned to see the elderly Du Bois pulled roughly from a paddy wagon in handcuffs, ankle cuffs, and chains like a prisoner on a southern chain gang. The authorities had done everything possible to denigrate and humiliate this frail figure. Fortunately, the effort backfired when news pictures of Du Bois in chains flashed around the world. Albert Einstein joined an international network of outraged intellectuals in protesting the arrest; this threw the U.S. State Department into confusion. The government had not understood the level of great respect Dr. Du Bois attracted. Within days, the judge threw out the charges.

If the Sage had survived, I might have kept on singing folk songs for fun and social protest as I awaited my big acting break. But it didn't. A routine check by Con Edison revealed we'd been burning as much gas as the Waldorf-Astoria's kitchen. Our monthly bills would be far higher now that the meter had been read, and to assure we paid those bills, Con Ed wanted a $500 deposit. That was big money in 1951. Soon after, the IRS weighed in on the subject of back unemployment-insurance taxes—a brand-new concept to us. To our surprise, we owed them. Overwhelmed, we started looking for a buyer. Eight months into our restaurant careers, we hardly expected to sell for a profit. But we did insist that a buyer at least cover our debts—including the loans outstanding from our sympathetic angels. As soon as we found one who agreed to those terms, we handed over the lease.

The Sage had given all of us a lot of fun, but it had soaked up all my savings, much to Marguerite's alarm. So when Jack Rollins suggested we plead my case once more with Max Gordon, I was all in.

Max was a short fellow with a monklike tonsure and the gruff, blunt manner of a little Napoleon. Jack convinced him I had a whole new act—new songs, new outfit, new stage persona (all, of course, thanks to Jack, as Jack saw it). "Okay," Max said, "two songs. That's it." My audition would serve as an opening act for the jazz and blues singer Maxine Sullivan: My only accompaniment would be Craig Work. In a picture in *DownBeat* published a few weeks after our Vanguard debut, Craig and I make a sweet, smiling duo, still not quite able to grasp the scope of our success.

I felt humbled and more than a little nervous, on that night in October 1951, to walk out onto the Vanguard's tiny stage, to be standing on the same boards that Leadbelly, Josh White, and Woody Guthrie, among others, had worn smooth before me. Happily, Tony Scott and his soon-to-be wife had worked hard to pack the room with friends, sending out hundreds of postcards in advance of the show, and I felt the warmth of the crowd as soon as the spotlight hit me.

I knew encore applause when I heard it, and I heard it at the end of my two songs. Grinning at each other, Craig and I came back to do one more. This time, when we left the stage, Max Gordon was waiting with a very severe look in the minuscule back space outside his cellar office. "When I tell you two songs," he said, "I mean two songs!" I knew instantly that we were in full-throttle negotiation for the gig. Max didn't waste words: If our act had failed to impress him, he wouldn't have emerged from his office at all. And Jack wouldn't be standing beside him with as happy a look as one could hope for.

Max signed me up to a standard two-week engagement at $70 a week. In that sense, I was right back where I'd started at the Royal Roost. Only the vibe this time was even better. I opened on October 26, 1951, as one of several acts. By the second week, there were lines around the block, Max had extended my contract, and my pay was up to $225. I was hot! One indication of how crazy it got was the write-up on me each week by Rogers E. M. Whitaker, the witty writer for *The New Yorker* magazine's "Goings on About Town." The first week, he announced, a bit dismissively, "Harry Belafonte, now a folk minstrel, making his debut in his new calling." The next week he noted, with more respect, "Harry Belafonte in his new role as folk singer." The next week: "A new and better Harry Belafonte, singing folk songs from everywhere." The week after that: "Harry Belafonte has turned folk singer, a very good idea indeed." And by early December: "One of the season's catches—Harry Belafonte!"

What I suspected was that audiences liked not only my voice and my presence, but also the global range of the material, from the American chain-gang songs like "Tol' My Captain," "Jerry," "Another Man Done Gone" to "Oh No, John," an English ballad, to "Merci Bon Dieu," a Haitian folk song, to the American ballad "Shenandoah," and back to "Mo Mary," an Irish standard, even "Hava Nageela," the Hebrew anthem. Different voices, but a shared humanity; this was my platform, my authenticity, my politics. My song.

Those two weeks stretched to more than three months. That cramped little basement room was packed every night. One night I saw a familiar, broad-shouldered figure looking up at me from a table near the stage; Paul Robeson had come to check me out. When the set ended, he came to congratulate me, nearly filling the backstage space with his formidable presence. He asked me where I'd found my songs, and I told him about going to the Library of Congress. "Oh— the Alan Lomax stuff," he said, nodding. I confided that for all the applause out there, I still wasn't sure I had any right to be singing these songs; that whole question of authenticity still haunted me. Paul put one of his ham-size hands on my shoulder. "You're on a big path," he said. "Get them to sing your song, and they'll want to know who you are."

Max Gordon agreed. From the Vanguard, he moved me uptown, without a break, to the Blue Angel, the fancier after-theater club on East Fifty-fifth Street that he owned with a tall, French, very gay partner named Herbert Jacoby. Jacoby manned the front door with a rapier-like wit. "I'm Richard Townsend," a pushy customer would say. "I have a reservation." Jacoby would look coolly down his nose at the man. "You're Richard Townsend?" Yes, the man would say, yes! Jacoby would nod. "My condolences." At first, Elsa Lanchester headlined the bill, but as one month at the Blue Angel stretched to two, Max and Herbert made me the draw. By now, I had a record deal—and my first Hollywood screen test. All that in these short few months.

On April 3, 1952, the day after my last show at the Blue Angel, I made my first 78 RPM single for RCA Victor, at a New York recording studio, backed by an eighteen-piece orchestra. My contract was small; RCA committed to a few singles, and one album, with almost no money up front. At two and a half cents per song for each record sold, I'd have to sell a hundred thousand copies of a two-sided single record to net $5,000! But I could choose my songs from my growing repertoire of international folk songs. I might even get to include a composition or two of my own. This was heady stuff.

For my first single, I chose the folk classic "A Rovin'" and a new folk ballad called "Chimney Smoke"—both of them crowd-pleasers in my act. I waited for that single to shoot to the top, but I waited in vain; it sold far fewer copies than my debut on Roost Records three years before.

On my next trip to the studio, I tried a new tack: calypso. The sound and rhythm of calypso were imprinted on me from my years in Jamaica, and at the Library of Congress I'd found all sorts of great calypso songs—some traditional, some new. If I could lay claim to any kind of music, surely calypso was it. A song called "Man Smart (Woman Smarter)" had wowed the club crowds with its West Indian feminist message, and soon audiences were singing along with every calypso song I added to my repertoire. But on vinyl, with a protest song called "Did You Hear About Jerry" on the B side, it went nowhere.

When I did no better on a third single with two of the folk songs my new audiences loved best—"Scarlet Ribbons" and "Shenandoah"— I started wondering if maybe the record business wasn't for me, or I for it. My live act worked as well as it did, I knew, because I *acted* it. When I tore into a song like "John Henry" onstage, I was an actor as much as a singer—an actor who happened to sing—using my whole body to convey the song's power. How could a record capture that?

Gratefully, I plunged into a tour of top out-of-town clubs to do more of what I did best. The one I remember most vividly is the Chase Hotel in St. Louis. Missouri was a redneck state, and the Chase was its capital's imperial white hotel. Blacks weren't even allowed in to see my show. I was supposed to be grateful the hotel gave me a room; apparently, that was a first. In fact, it was a fairly small room that the hotel had me share with my new guitarist, Millard Thomas. Soon after our gig at the Vanguard, Craig Work had been drafted and sent off to Korea; he would come back from the Korean War to a high-achieving career as a NASA engineer. Craig had put me on to one of his music students. Millard was a fine guitarist and an easygoing guy who would work with me for years. He did have a few vices, however—cigarettes, alcohol, and a spliff when he could get them—and they could lead to consequences.

Late in the afternoon, Millard set a bath running and smoked a cig-arette as he waited for the tub to fill; Millard smoked a lot. I lay down to take a nap. I awoke to the smell of smoke. The room was ablaze! Millard had fallen asleep, too, and his cigarette had lit his sheets on fire. When I leaped up to try to douse the fire with my bedcovers, I found myself standing in three inches of water; the tub had overflowed. I just pulled Millard's sheets to the floor and drowned the fire. How glori-ously convenient.

"Damn it, Millard," I said. "Here we are the first niggers in the hotel, and we not only burn down the man's house but turn it into a goddamn Noah's Ark." We called the black desk clerk downstairs, and he swung into action. In three or four minutes, black maids and housemen were opening windows, changing the linens, and mopping up water. Our presence, not only as the hotel's first black room guests but as its star headliner, was a source of such pride and importance to the black staff that they let us know they'd do anything to keep this disgrace from being discovered by our white overseers. By the time Millard and I came back from our performance that night, the only trace of our debacle was the slightest hint of cigarette smoke, mingling with the strong scent of air freshener in our little room.

When Millard and I got home to New York, it was to a rousing return engagement at the Village Vanguard. "Belafonte has emerged as one of the outstanding practitioners in the folk singing field . . . causing something of a sensation," *Variety* declared. "If the customers had their way, the tall, handsome lad would be vocalizing all night."

Even if I never had a hit record, I knew I was on the map now.

The screen test was for a small role in an MGM movie to be called *Bright Road,* the story of a troubled student in a southern black school and the teacher who reached out to help him. One reason I landed the test was that Hollywood had so few black actors my age. There were plenty of old ones to play butlers and chauffeurs, but the young ones, like me, stayed in New York, not even bothering to try our luck in the movies. Sidney Poitier was an exception, his star rising fast, but for that very reason, he hadn't even been asked to read for the role; it was too small for him.

In its own modest way, *Bright Road* would break a color barrier. The story didn't explore racial issues; it just told a human story with characters who happened to be black. A West Indian teacher named Mary Elizabeth Vroman had written the story on which the script was based. My luck held when I read scenes with the actress whom MGM had cast as the teacher. No one could mistake the chemistry between us. In very short order, I got the part, and so I had the chance to observe, at close range, the actress Dorothy Dandridge, a future legend, in her first starring role.

When I flew out west for the film's nineteen-day shoot in August 1952, I had a place to stay; Shelley Winters had called her boyfriend, actor Farley Granger, who offered me the guest room of his Coldwater Canyon home. Farley had had a great triumph the year before, starring in Alfred Hitchcock's *Strangers on a Train.* Unfortunately, it would mark his career peak; a rift with Samuel Goldwyn, and two or three box-office bombs, would hurt him badly. I found him a sweet, gracious fellow, though somewhat depressed. In fact, he'd struggled with his sexuality, and sometime after his romance with Winters would acknowledge he was bisexual, taking a male partner for the last half of his life. Decorous as he was, he made no overtures to me. During that brief stay at his house, though, I did have a very unnerving experience.

One night after dinner, I went walking up Coldwater Canyon. Within minutes, a police car pulled up. I was told, in no uncertain terms, to put my hands on the car and spread my legs. "Why you out here walking, boy?" one of the cops demanded.

I said I was out in L.A. making a movie for MGM.

The other cop said, "So, you're a movie star?"

"Well, I wouldn't call it that."

"What kind of crazy-ass story is this nigger telling?" one of the cops said to the other.

The cops ordered me into the car, took me down to the Beverly Hills police station, and charged me with illegal loitering. When I asked to make a phone call, the police just laughed. In due time, they told me, in due time. Two hours later, Farley became alarmed enough to call the police and report my disappearance. When he learned where I was, he called someone at MGM, who must have called MGM's lawyers, because suddenly the presiding officers came in looking very embarrassed and released me. Most of L.A.'s cops in that postwar era, I later learned, were former U.S. military who'd enjoyed their training time in California so much that they'd come back to the area to live and had joined the city's growing police force. A lot of them had come from the South, and their ingrained prejudice had been deepened by their war years in the Pacific theater, where the prevailing ethos was that the only good Asians were dead ones. They felt the same way about blacks.

Bright Road was made on the quick and cheap on MGM's lot by Gerald Mayer, a nephew of studio chief Louis B. Mayer. Apparently Louis didn't want anyone assuming Gerald was getting an easy ride; he forced him to direct so many B movies that Gerald had become known as MGM's "Keeper of the B's," and *Bright Road* was one of them. For me, at age twenty-five, *Bright Road* was just a fun first stab at acting in films. For Dorothy Dandridge, who was then twenty-nine, it meant much more.

In her childhood, Dorothy had toured the country as one of the three singing Dandridge sisters (though only one was her sister; the other was a stand-in). As a teenager, she'd won a few small movie roles—one in the Marx Brothers' *A Day at the Races*—and shown enormous promise. Then, at twenty, she'd married Harold Nicholas, of the dancing Nicholas Brothers, and put her career on hold. Now the stormy nine-year marriage had ended, and Dorothy badly wanted the stardom she felt she'd deferred.

Dorothy and I felt a strong mutual attraction, no question about that. But during rehearsals, it became clear that no matter what our feelings might be, a romance between us wasn't going to happen. Dorothy's marriage had ended the year before, the latest in a line of abusive relationships for her. She knew how fragile she was. What she needed now was stability—meaning no men, if she could help it, and a fierce focus on getting her career back on track. Already she'd reestablished herself as a singer, with a sold-out gig at La Vie En Rose. Now she wanted to conquer Hollywood. And to take up with me, four years her junior, would lead to nothing but a lot of negative publicity.

A romance with Dorothy was the last thing I needed, either—my marriage was teetering a bit as Marguerite's and my political differences grew, though I couldn't imagine divorce—so I backed off with some relief, if not also keen regrets. In our few scenes together in *Bright Road*, that hint of unconsummated desire is all too real, made more so by Dorothy's powerful screen presence. Here was a stunningly gorgeous black woman appearing before the camera not as a maid or a slave but as a teacher! Most of America had never seen a black woman, aside from Lena Horne, look both so beautiful and so dignified.

As our short, low-budget shoot progressed, I think both of us realized we could help each other. I was the one who'd studied acting seriously; as a hardworking child performer, Dorothy hadn't had the luxury. From my New School days, I had some cardinal rules of acting to impart. What Dorothy had over me, though, were those years of on-the-road experience. She was a singer, a hoofer, an all-around crowd-pleaser. She'd even done nickelodeon moviettes. All this imbued her with a certain bedrock confidence in her natural abilities, a confidence I didn't yet feel.

At the same time, as movie actors, both of us were learning on the job. "Find your light, Mr. Belafonte," the assistant director would say.

"Uh, what do you mean? There's a lot of lights up there."

The A.D. would explain how I had to turn my face to a certain light to heighten the contrast between my eye sockets and my cheeks for the camera. When I shot Dorothy a sidelong glance, it was obvious that she had learned that rule already. She never missed her light.

With romance off the table, Dorothy and I spent our time off-set talking about how it felt to be black actors in a white world. Despite her great beauty and talent, Dorothy's chances of jumping from this first starring role to another were slim. Those roles just didn't exist, any more than black male leads did for me. *Bright Road* might mark our mutual screen debuts, but we sensed its soft little story wouldn't get us anywhere. All too soon, we'd be out-of-work actors—black actors—again.

Since I was out on the West Coast already, Jack Rollins lined me up, after *Bright Road*, with my first Las Vegas gig—at the Thunderbird, a fairly new resort right on the Strip. The Thunderbird was a big-name joint: I would be opening for Henny Youngman, the well-known king of the one-liners. This was a big move up for me, and I felt pretty excited when I saw my name under his on the marquee, topped by a huge, neon-encrusted thunderbird, blowing smoke from below its beak.

Proudly, Millard Thomas and I strode through the reception area, with its heavily southwestern decor, and presented ourselves at the front desk, along with our other—white—band members, including Tony Scott, who'd brought Fran. The desk clerk looked confused. When we said who we were, he called over a security guard. The person we needed to see, the guard explained sternly, was in an office we could reach by a back door. In the future, Millard and I were not to come through the front door. The hotel was off-limits to us—except, of course, during our shows, but even then, we'd get to the stage by a back door, and leave immediately afterward the same way.

At the office to which the two of us were led, we learned we'd be staying at a motel some miles away. A "colored" motel. Where was Jack Rollins to scream bloody murder and sort this out? Back in New York, unavoidably detained, he'd informed me, by a case of severe hemorrhoids. I was mad, though in truth there was nothing he could have done; in 1952, Jim Crow was as prevalent in Vegas as it was in the Deep South.

A taxi took Millard and me far from the Strip to the black section of town, and left us standing with our bags in front of a filthy fleabag motel. The woman behind the front desk was drunk. Weaving a bit, she showed us to a room that smelled of dog urine. "What's wrong with it?" the woman said when she saw our expressions. "It was good enough for Pearl Bailey's dog—it's good enough for you." Actually, I told her, no, it wasn't. But the evening was well under way by then, so reluctantly and resentfully, we decided to stay one night. From my ratty bed, I put in a call to my uncle Lenny in New York. "I don't know if you have any juice this far west," I said, "but let me tell you what just happened." Lenny got a little agitated, and said he'd make a call.

The next morning, I dragged Millard back to the Thunderbird, where I demanded to speak to the VP in charge of talent booking. I told him I had some problems with how we'd been treated. "I'd like to either cancel this booking or buy it out," I told him. The VP, a big bruiser of a guy, gave me a hard-boiled look. "You have a contract here," he said slowly, "and you're going to play it. The only way you're going to leave Vegas and *not* play it is in a box."

I wanted to laugh—it was such B-movie talk. But the VP wasn't smiling. Would he call on some mob goons to kill me? Maybe not, but they sure might beat us up. I didn't have the presence of mind to figure the other options. I saw no choice but to head back to that filthy motel and grit out the week as best we could.

As we stood once more in front of the Thunderbird, under the marquee that no longer filled me with joy, I heard a friendly greeting, and turned to see Pete Kameron, manager of the Weavers, Pete Seeger's group. Was I glad to see a friendly face. Pete said he'd flown up from L.A. to check out my act—to see, as he put it, where folk music was headed. I told him that at the moment, folk music was headed back to Colored Town and a very bad motel. Pete laughed sympathetically. He knew how Vegas worked. There was, he said, one decent motel on the white side of town that would take us, and so he led us there. Nat King Cole, he told us en route, had found his own way to avoid the filthy motel in the black section when he played the Thunderbird; he'd brought a trailer that he parked out back.

Half an hour later, a limo pulled up to our new motel, and the driver came looking for us. We were instructed to check out of the motel and to bring our bags back to the Thunderbird. No apologies were made when we arrived, but we were given room keys and told to enjoy our stay compliments of the house. Lenny, it turned out, had gotten through to Shondor Birns, who basically ran Cleveland for the mob. Shondor had called the Thunderbird, and now, miracle of miracles, the management had made an exception to its policy on Negro entertainers. From that moment on, Millard and I got treated with a certain deference: Shondor was a serious player who not only had killers on his payroll but booked a lot of big acts. I was delighted, but I knew the favor would be called in. A few weeks later, I had to fly to Cleveland to play the Alhambra Tavern, Shondor's place on Euclid Avenue.

When I walked out on the Thunderbird's stage that night, I saw a sea of Stetson hats and a lot of sharp-looking women. Vegas in those days drew a very exclusive crowd of western high rollers—all white, of course. I felt I was on another planet. Nervously, I started in on a sea shanty that always worked at the Village Vanguard. *"On yonder hill there stands a maiden, / Who she is I do not know . . ."* In about three seconds, the high rollers in the front who'd looked up to hear us turned back to their women and drinks. At the end of that first show, we got barely enough applause to beat it offstage.

Pete Kameron had caught the show, and came up to my room afterward. "This isn't my town, Pete," I told him. "I don't know how to reach this crowd." What I really meant was: What the hell was wrong with these people? They had literally turned their backs on me. I was furious.

Pete let me rant awhile, then held up his hands with a smile. "Okay," he said. "Okay—they're jerks. But I have to tell you something. You lost them, Harry. They didn't lose you. Those people can be had. You just didn't get them."

I instantly understood that Pete was right. I would be forever grateful that he showed up, because the time that we spent together seeking the solution paid off. Together, we started looking at my list of songs, sifting through them, and shifting them around. We thought we found an approach.

When I walked onstage for the late show that night, I was still steaming mad. I stood at the microphone and scowled out at that sea of Stetsons. This was the loudest, drunkest crowd that I had ever seen. I grabbed the mike and at the top of my lungs screamed:

"TIMMMMBBER!"

It was the first line of a Georgia chain-gang song. Again, I screamed,

> *TIMBER, TIMBER*
> *Lord, this timber gotta roll*
> *I got to pull this timber 'fore the sun go down*
> *Get it cross that river 'fore the boss comes 'round*
> *Get it on down that dusty road*
> *Come on, Jerry, let's tow this load.*

Glasses stopped tinkling; conversations quieted. I sang with all the fury I felt, and all the frustration and grim determination that Jerry the mule surely felt too. The crowd grew silent, for in this moment all the hurt, frustration, and burden of race that I had known bonded itself into this taut knot of defiance, nuclear in its power. Millard had never played better. He hung with every note and bent with me on every verse. In the end, even the waitresses stopped in their tracks and the maître d' stopped seating guests.

From then on, I made that opening my signature. The brisk walk to the mike, the stern expression, no word of greeting. And then *bam*—into that fierce first song of social protest, either "Jerry" or perhaps "John Henry." I'd hold that mood through the second song, probably the third, still with no word of greeting, definitely no smile. By now I would feel the crowd growing tense. When at last I switched to an upbeat song—and flashed them a first grin—I could hear the collective sigh as they settled back in their seats with a truly physical sense of relief. For the rest of the act, I could be as light and jokey as I wanted to be. They were mine.

On my third day in Vegas, still simmering from the way Millard and I had been treated, I saw a way to exact a little revenge. Late that morning, I put on my bathing suit, slung a towel over my shoulder, and knocked on Tony and Fran Scott's door.

"How about a swim?" I asked them.

They looked at each other and grinned. They knew exactly what I was proposing. "Why not?"

As we walked out to the oval-shaped pool, all eyes were on us. I let Tony and Fran settle on a couple of pool chairs and walked alone, slowly, to the diving board at the far end. As I did, the half dozen or so swimmers—all white, of course—began climbing out with furtive looks over their shoulders. The white sunbathers on pool chairs just stared. So did a number of heavyset white men on balconies above, who seemed to appear at the same time as if the word had gone out telepathically: *nigger at the pool.* Like the sunbathers, they just stared as I walked to the end of the diving board and for a long moment tested its flex. Then I dove in.

Incredibly, the water did not turn black. I did a couple of laps, swimming slowly, and then climbed up the deep-end ladder. As I did, a boy of about twelve approached me. He gave me a long, inscrutable look. I gazed back with a bit of a smile. Finally he spoke.

"Mr. Belafonte," he said, "may I get your autograph?" And from his pocket he took out a pad and pen.

With that, other kids began coming over, too, followed by their camera-wielding parents. "Mr. Belafonte, can I get a picture of you with my children?" As I signed the autographs and posed for the cameras, I snuck a look up at the balconies. One by one, the heavyset men were vanishing, in silence. The fans around me were responding to my new fame as a Vegas entertainer, not to the fact that I'd just become the first black ever to swim in the Thunderbird's pool. That they'd already decided my swim was insignificant—*that* was its significance. And that no one from the front desk came out to stop me, or mentioned it for the rest of my stay—that was my private act of revenge against their bullheaded prejudice. Not just to break their Jim Crow rules, but to take it a step further, to make *them* change as well.

Each next stage of my success, I was starting to see, came with its own new barriers of color. And the pain and anger I felt when I ran up against those barriers never lessened—never lessened at all. Years later, when the Thunderbird reached the end of its commercial life and was detonated in front of a crowd with seven hundred pounds of explosives, I thought: I would have loved to press that button.

7

Tony Scott threw a wonderful party that Christmas at his loft on Jones Street. He had his flute out—Tony played it as well as he did the clarinet—and with someone else at the stand-up piano, Marlon Brando and I slapped away at the congas, one drum for each of us. We played with a lot of soul, if not as much skill as we would have liked.

I loved being back among my downtown friends, a world away from Las Vegas. I loved their keen wit, their hipness, their sense of fun. Yet I appreciated what Vegas had done for me, too. Days after my return, I had played a big, cavernous room out in Queens called the Boulevard, where no one felt obliged to be polite. As I walked onstage, true to form, everyone kept talking, so I reached into my attitude bag and put my new Vegas thing into motion. *"Timmmmbbber."* *Billboard,* in its review of the show, declared I was becoming "the top folk singer in the business . . . the huge mob rocked with him with such zest that it took on an almost hysterical frenzy."

There was a lot to be happy about, and almost everyone at Tony's party was happy for me, except perhaps one guest: Marguerite. The whole scene put her off. Too much smoke, too many downtown bohemian types—losers in Marguerite's book. She looked down on the show business crowd, and, even more painfully for me, she had little regard for my choice of intellectual company—Robeson, Du Bois, Killens; anything to do with the left brought out her discontent. I didn't know where to take our relationship. At one point during Tony's party,

I looked up from my conga drum to seek her out, and saw her sitting by a window, alone. When I looked up again, she was gone.

For some time to come, Marguerite and I would keep trying to resuscitate our marriage, but more out of guilt than anything else, at least on my part. I was no longer the lost and confused young man, and Marguerite didn't know what to do with the more self-assured public figure I was becoming. Always opposites, we'd now become opposites apart, and both of us, I think, sensed that the more touring I did from now on, the better.

In a blur of club dates around the country the next year, one that stands out in memory was a return engagement at the Black Orchid in Chicago in March 1953—not so much because of the venue as because I followed Josh White. More than one critic had pronounced me "the new Josh White," which doubtless irked him as much as it did me. Josh had a powerful repertoire, his songs were beautifully styled, and, most important, he had more of that stuff I kept trying to stir up for myself: *authenticity*. He'd grown up in the segregated South. He'd played with Leadbelly and shared a Broadway stage with Paul Robeson. With Josh's songs still echoing in the Black Orchid's supper club room, I gave it all I had, and Chicago gave all that and more back to me, its critics declaring that I had a force and style all my own.

And yet for all the praise heaped on me, the "authenticity" issue kept popping up, and I felt I had to put it to rest. That same month, I became the first black to play the Cocoanut Grove in Los Angeles. The owner was a rabid anti-communist, with a son who worked for Senator Joe McCarthy. How did I get and keep the gig, considering our very different politics? The power of the jingle! "West coast audiences have been packing the big Cocoanut Grove," *Time* magazine reported, "and have accepted Harry Belafonte, 26, as a folk singer to be ranked with Josh White and Burl Ives." I was playing even larger venues, too, open-air amphitheaters like Lewisohn Stadium (capacity 27,000) in upper Manhattan and the Carter Barron in Washington, D.C., to crowds of four thousand a night. I was challenging the whole concept of what a folksinger could be and do. Potshots were inevitable. *DownBeat*'s was typical: "Belafonte is synthetic in folk singing," one of its critics wrote. "His roots are not in regional soil, as . . . Leadbelly's [are] in Texas. Belafonte is a native New Yorker, the possessor of a not-large but extremely flexible voice and a flair for theatre . . . a guy who collaborates with others to revamp different folk tunes."

So according to *DownBeat*, no one could sing songs that weren't from his home state! Recklessly breaking this law, I took another stab at a calypso song that spring, recording "Matilda," about an unfaithful woman. It would become one of my best known.

At about this time, John Murray Anderson came to hear me at the Village Vanguard and announced he wanted me to star in his latest Broadway revue. I jumped at the chance. The Canadian-born Anderson was a legend. He'd started in vaudeville, gone on to produce the *Ziegfeld Follies* along with Billy Rose's revues, done movies, and even overseen the Ringling Brothers circus. An effervescent figure, always just in from Paris and making an entrance with two or three theatrical grand dames, Anderson had an air of infallibility about him. "I've selected you to be in my revue. That means you're with the best there is!" He called it *John Murray Anderson's Almanac,* and I was thrilled to be in it.

In typical revue fashion, *Almanac* had only the sketchiest of story lines to justify its songs and dance numbers when it bowed December 10, 1953, at the Imperial Theatre. I sang three songs: "Acorn in the Meadow," by the show's musical directors, Richard Adler and Jerry Ross; "Hold 'Em Joe," an old calypso song; and one that Millard and I had written together, "Mark Twain," about the Mississippi riverboat captains whose custom of gauging the depths with weighted lines had given Samuel Clemens his pen name. A seasoned cast, including Polly Bergen, Hermione Gingold, Billy De Wolfe, and Orson Bean, did the rest. But I got more than my share of notice. Brooks Atkinson in *The New York Times* singled out my performance of "Mark Twain," declaring that my "expository style as a singer and actor makes it the *Almanac's* high point in theatrical artistry." The *New York Post* noted that "Mark Twain" routinely stopped the show. I went on to earn a Tony Award as Best Featured Actor in a Musical for *Almanac,* a dream come true.

It was in *Almanac,* though, that I first began straining my voice. In these long-ago days, no one in Broadway shows was miked, and to be heard in the back rows over the orchestra in the pit, you had to project your voice with a lot of power. Classically trained singers knew how to do that from their diaphragms. I didn't. I just sang as loudly as I could—from my larynx and throat. Pretty soon I strained my vocal cords so badly I lost my voice altogether.

By then, I'd struck up a friendship with Yul Brynner, starring in *The King and I* across the street at the St. James Theatre. Yul had problems with laryngitis, too, worse than mine after three years of playing the King of Siam six nights and eight shows a week. When he heard my news, he told me to head straight over to the one guy who could fix me up for that night: Dr. Max Jacobson. So I did. Jacobson proved to be a dashing-looking German, with a skier's body, a nice accent, and a fancy shirt with one or two buttons unbuttoned and the cuffs rolled up. No doctor's smock for him. He strapped me down, tilted the examining table so my feet were higher than my head, injected me with the contents of two or three syringes, and had me lie that way for a few minutes so the drugs would filter up faster. After a few minutes he straightened the table, slapped me on the back, and said, "Knock 'em dead." That night I gave my best performance ever.

I went back to Dr. Jacobson a few more times during *Almanac*'s run—not on any regular basis, just when I knew I was about to lose my voice again. His drugs worked every time, but they scared the hell out of me. I knew they were uppers. And while Yul got them every week and seemed just fine, I knew they weren't for me.

I stopped going at the end of *Almanac*'s run, and almost forgot about the strangely debonair Dr. Jacobson until one night six years later, when I got a call from Bobby Kennedy in Puerto Rico, where I was working. "What do you know about this guy Max Jacobson?" I told him of my experience, and warned him to be careful. "Why're you asking?" I said. That was when I learned that Jacobson was treating President Kennedy, giving him injections as needed for his back pain and exhaustion. Soon Dr. Feelgood, as he came to be known, would be treating everyone from Marilyn Monroe to Truman Capote with the same potent mix of dangerous drugs. I was just grateful I'd had the good sense to stop going. But the throat problems that robbed me of my voice would haunt me again and again, up to the day I stepped away from the world of performing.

Along with critics' reviews, *Almanac* brought scrutiny of a different, disturbing kind. On Broadway and in Hollywood, the witch hunt for communists had reached a fever pitch. Jack Gilford, a wonderful comic I'd shared bills with at the Village Vanguard and Blue Angel, went overnight from a circuit regular to unemployable. One day his phone stopped ringing; he got no more film or TV work for ten years. It was the same for Zero Mostel, the brilliant comic actor whom I'd also shared bills with: suddenly blacklisted, all but unemployed for most of the 1950s. Both went before the House Un-American Activities Committee; both invoked the Fifth Amendment, refusing to name names. Both were, to me and many in the rest of the entertainment industry, heroes. But they, along with so many others, paid a heavy price.

I'd come to prominence too late to be included in "Red Channels," a report issued by the red-baiting publication *Counterattack*, with its list of 151 entertainers said to be communists, or to be called before the House Un-American Activities Committee in its first investigations. But in January 1954, with *Almanac* packing the house every night, the editors of *Counterattack* accused me of being a "Communist fronter." My crimes: entertaining for a union that had ties to the American Communist party; singing for a nonprofit group called the Committee for the Negro in the Arts that accepted funding from the Communist party; sharing a "Freedom Rally" stage with Paul Robeson and other leftists. With that, columnists Walter Winchell and Dorothy Kilgallen took up the cry. Suddenly my whole career seemed to hang in the balance.

If someone other than Michael Grace had backed *Almanac*, I might have had to relinquish my role. But Grace, whose Irish family had made a fortune in shipping, told the editors of *Counterattack* to buzz off. The editors threatened to picket the show, but nothing came of that, and the show went on. In retaliation, they claimed a victory of sorts in their next issue. They falsely wrote, "Belafonte has since approached *Counterattack* to clarify his stand." The editors reported that I'd denied entertaining for the union but admitted other "transgressions." That was an outrageous smear. I approached Michael Grace and asked him for assistance. He gave me the benefit of legal counsel, and they confronted *Counterattack*. "As far as *Counterattack* can determine," the editors primly concluded in a later article, "Belafonte has not supported any fronts since that time."

Still, I was now a suspicious character, tainted by the mutterings of these self-appointed judges, who were, in fact, former FBI agents. Or, in the case of *Aware*, another such publication that questioned my credentials, American Legionnaires from upstate New York who worked as butchers. It was a scary time, in which the slightest whisper of communist sympathies hung in the troubled air. In Hollywood, loyalty lists were going around. I'd been asked to sign one before filming *Bright Road*, attesting that I was not, nor—as the boilerplate had it—ever had been, a member of the Communist party. Jack Rollins wanted me to sign. Instead, I'd drawn up a letter of my own, saying what I wanted to say—namely, that I'd never done more than exercise my rights of free speech to express my views on political issues. Apparently, that had satisfied the studio, but these public inferences seemed harder to expunge. Winning the Tony, I felt sure, would inoculate me against any more of these slurs. Instead, it did the opposite.

By now, Ed Sullivan had established a new tradition: The Tony Award winners went on his Sunday-night television show to perform. The musicals were his big prize. He got an extravagant crowd-pleaser for free, since the musicals' producers transported their sets from Broadway to the Sullivan show's stage. The actors got to promote their shows, and stirred additional excitement by sitting in the audience when they weren't performing. And America got to sample the new season's shows and decide what they hoped to see on their next trip to New York. Unfortunately, my Broadway agent informed me, I would not be joining the program. I was blacklisted.

Jack was still my manager, mostly for club gigs, but as my star had risen, he'd seemed more and more out of his league, so I'd turned to Freddie Fields, the well-known MCA agent, to handle Hollywood and Broadway work. It was to his New York office that I went to declare that whoever had put me on the blacklist was wrong. Fields listened soberly. Then he pulled open a desk drawer that contained some special phone. He dialed, waited a second, and said, "Harry Belafonte." After a moment, he hung up and slid the phone drawer shut. "You're on the list," he confirmed quietly. He said he'd work on it, and I left. Later that day, Fields called with more news. "Ed Sullivan wants to see you," he said. "That's all I know about it."

All-powerful as Sullivan was in the new age of television, going to see him was like paying a visit to the Wizard of Oz. At Delmonico's, the Park Avenue hotel where he lived, an elevator man took me up, the two of us riding in silence. I had the sense I wasn't the first entertainer to make this trip; Sullivan was known to be closely allied with Ted Kirkpatrick, the editor of *Counterattack,* and to vet prospective television guests with him. Sullivan opened his own door and welcomed me affably, almost a different person from the old stone face he projected on Sunday nights.

"I see we have a problem here," Sullivan began when we were seated in his sunken living room, "and I'm just trying to find a way to fix it. It's my understanding that you are caught up in a political net, but . . . there are some serious allegations."

"What are they?" I asked.

Sullivan opened a dossier and started reading down a list of progressive rallies and events I'd attended over the last several years. Then he handed it to me. "How do you respond to all of these?"

This was a crucible for me. A decision had to be made, a decision that would follow me for the rest of my days. "Mr. Sullivan," I said, "not only are all the allegations on your list as you have described them, but there are many more that haven't been included." I took a deep breath. "But let's not talk about that. Let's talk about what the list really is—and who I am."

With that, I told Sullivan a bit about my background, what growing up poor and black in Harlem was like, how I'd enlisted in the navy to serve my country, only to be segregated during that service, and how I'd begun to see that all over the country, black men were being abused by racist forces. "Seems to me that if you'd come from Ireland," I told the TV host with Irish roots, "and awakened each day to find another Irishman hanged, and you had no power to stop those killings, you'd speak out in every way you could." Sullivan nodded solemnly, but said nothing.

"I'm not a communist," I went on. "But I don't need to admit that. And if someone else were to ask me, I'd just say it's none of your business. I don't think the onus is on me—I think it's on you, to explain why you feel you need to judge in this cruel and unfair way the artists you have on your show. As for me, I have a choice: stop speaking out against racism and other issues I feel strongly about, which I won't do, or accept the consequences. I'm prepared to do that."

He nodded. "Hmm, thank you for coming," he said. And I left.

That afternoon my agent called again. "You're on the Sullivan show," he said.

So I performed after all, and my appearance did give me a boost. But in these treacherous times, going on the show made me an object of new suspicions—from my friends and colleagues. What had I done, blacklist victims wondered, to make myself acceptable to Ed Sullivan? Obviously I must have signed whatever loyalty statement he'd put in front of me, and confessed whatever sins I was accused of, to be cleansed of the communist taint. Maybe I'd even named names.

One day not long after, I went uptown with Bill Attaway to Sidney Poitier's new restaurant, Ribs in the Ruff. At the counter, as we walked in, sat a black actor/singer I knew. When he saw me, he shot me what seemed a dirty look. As Bill and I slid into a small booth, the guy kept glaring at me, until finally he slammed the counter, picked up a knife, and came at me. "You son of a bitch," he shouted. Bill and Sidney blocked him, but they couldn't stop his tirade. "For thirty pieces of silver you fucking sold us out."

I hadn't realized, until that moment, how devastating the effects of the blacklist had been in the black community. In all the literature I've read since then about that terrible time, no account has focused on the disproportionate number of black artists accused of communist sympathies, starting with Paul Robeson, W.E.B. Du Bois, Langston Hughes, and Canada Lee, but including virtually all members of the American Negro Theatre, the Committee for the Negro in the Arts, and more. This was no coincidence—far from it. The witch hunters were racists, working two campaigns as one. And how naturally, how inexorably, those campaigns fitted together! After all, hadn't Stalin said that blacks and whites were equal? And hadn't Robeson welcomed those words? So didn't that make all blacks, by definition, communists? It certainly left nearly all black artists blacklisted. As for the few exempted, they had to contend with a taint just as hard to erase: the suspicions of their friends and colleagues that they'd ratted to save their careers. The only mitigating factor was that as common practice Hollywood hired so few of them, most didn't even know they were blacklisted.

I was grateful, in a way, to that actor at Ribs in the Ruff. At least he'd hurled his doubts right at me, giving me a chance to say, in no uncertain terms, that I hadn't sold anyone out, hadn't named any names, hadn't acknowledged any "crimes," and hadn't signed any loyalty oaths. But how to defend against those who nursed their suspicions in silence? For guidance on that, I paid a visit to Robeson. He smiled when I told him the Ribs in the Ruff story and admitted that he, too, had wondered what I'd done to sanitize myself for the Sullivan show. "So you can put my doubts to rest," he said, "and maybe even those of that actor. But you can't defend yourself to each and every person. All you can do is follow your truth, know who you are, and get on with it."

That was easy enough to do with colleagues, harder when the taint of suspicion seeped into my home.

Not long before *Almanac* opened, I'd moved my family out of West 156th Street and into a real house. True, it was a two-family attached house in East Elmhurst, a working-class neighborhood in Queens within earshot of LaGuardia Airport. But it stood on a clean, leafy, safe street where Adrienne could play and make friends. White friends, for East Elmhurst was, in fact, a white neighborhood. We'd picked it because it lay outside the city and seemed less restricted than other neighborhoods we could afford. Which was to say that when I'd offered to buy the house, the white owner had sold it to me. When we moved in—the first black family on the block—I fixed up the basement as a playroom for Adrienne, complete with play kitchen, and put a swing set in the backyard. Soon all the neighborhood kids were coming over to play. One day after they left, Adrienne solemnly told her mother we had to move. Why? Marguerite asked. "Because there are niggeroos moving into the neighborhood!"

That was all the prejudice we encountered. But one day in early 1954, while I was out of town, Marguerite opened the door to two badge-flashing agents of the FBI. Stunned, she ushered them in, and listened, with her mother beside her, as the agents explained they were investigating me because of my associations with known communists, people whose mission was to overthrow the government of the United States. Who, exactly, had Marguerite and her mother seen in my company, and what, exactly, had we discussed?

Thoroughly rattled, Marguerite said it was no secret that I knew Paul Robeson and Dr. Du Bois, but other than that, she had no idea who they might mean. As soon as the agents departed, Marguerite called me in hysterical tears. I tried to explain that the visit was obviously just a fishing expedition; if the agents had been on the trail of any particular suspects, they would have asked about them. But Marguerite couldn't seem to take that in. If I was on the FBI's list, there must be some reason. Surely, agents of the federal government would not spend such time and resources tracking a folksinger if there wasn't something to the story. The point of the visit, I felt sure, was to scare us and sow distrust between us, and in that, the agents succeeded. Marguerite never quite trusted me again.

Marguerite was right about one thing: The federal government was certainly tracking me. Not long after the agents' visit, I was auditing a lecture at the Dramatic Workshop downtown when a Miss Scotti of the House Un-American Activities Committee approached me. She was wearing, rather incongruously for a government lawyer, a stylish hat and veil. In an empty classroom, she made her pitch. "We have reason to believe that you're being used by elements in this country that do not have any concern for the welfare of our nation," she said in a soothing, sympathetic voice. "We're sure you're not one of those elements, but we do fear you're being used. And we'd like to help you."

"In what way," I asked, "am I being used?"

Miss Scotti took out a list of meetings where I'd been spotted—pretty much the same list Ed Sullivan had handed me. But there was a new transgression. "We know," she said, "that you objected fiercely to the Rosenberg sentence."

I felt the sickening sensation that so many before me in the blacklist era had felt: the realization a friend had betrayed me. *Dotts Johnson.*

The previous June, I'd been downtown doing the rounds—visiting publishing companies to get the rights to songs, putting my act together—when a fellow black actor waved to me from the wheel of his fancy new car. Dotts Johnson had made a name for himself in Italy after the war, getting cast in one of Roberto Rossellini's neo-realist films, *Paisan*, as a black G.I. chasing a street urchin in Naples who steals his shoes. Back in the States, he'd acquired another *t* in his name and landed a small role in Sidney Poitier's breakout film, *No Way Out*. He and Sidney had grown so close that Dotts served as Sidney's best man at his wedding in April 1951. For a while there, Sidney's new Hollywood fame had put a little distance between the two of us, though before long, Sidney had gone back to working as a dishwasher; that was how bleak the prospects were for a black movie actor in the early 1950s. Perhaps not coincidentally, our close friendship had resumed.

Dotts offered me a ride uptown, and I slid in. It was a balmy day, so he rolled down the windows. As we set off, breaking news came over the radio: The U.S. Supreme Court had just vacated Justice William O. Douglas's stay of execution for Julius and Ethel Rosenberg. They would be executed later that day: June 19, 1953. In a rage, I pounded the passenger door. Some days later, I ran into Dotts again. "You and your goddamn politics," he said. What did he mean, I asked. "You hit my car door so hard that the window cracked, and I have to go get it fixed." Whatever the repair cost was, it was a lot, so I told him I'd pay him in bits and pieces. And I did, but clearly he hadn't forgotten the incident.

"We'd just like you to be a friendly witness," Miss Scotti suggested.

I told her I refused to be a friendly witness or any other kind. As soon as I could, I sought out Robeson again and told him the story. "Are you really sure it was him?" Robeson asked.

"We were the only ones in the car."

"Yeah," Robeson said after a pause, "but how do you know he didn't go to a poker game and say, 'That goddamn Belafonte wrecked my car in his anger over the Rosenbergs,' and then others heard it and passed it on?"

I admitted I couldn't be sure.

"Anyway, if he did rat on you, do you think he'd tell you? And if he didn't, why would you want to put it out there that he did?"

Robeson was right; I'd never know what had happened, not for sure. So I never confronted Dotts, and, as it turned out, I was never called before the House Un-American Activities Committee. Perhaps I'd scared off Miss Scotti. Or perhaps she'd been on a freelance mission, seeing what fish she could catch on her own. With that strangely fancy hat and veil, who knew?

If Dotts did name names, he certainly didn't help his career by doing it. From then until he died in 1986, Dotts Johnson had exactly one more role in a feature film—a forgotten thriller called *The Grissom Gang* in 1971—and a small one at that.

In the spring of 1954, with *Almanac* still playing to sellout crowds on Broadway, RCA rushed to capitalize on my success with my first long-playing album, titling it *"Mark Twain" and Other Folk Favorites*, highlighting the showstopper that had won me my Tony Award. Wielding my new clout, I told the label's executives I wanted to try a new approach. Most of my singles had been saturated in lush orchestrations that I felt overwhelmed the songs. I knew that was the style of the times, but I wanted a more bare-bones accompaniment. I also wanted the songs to be more international, a real expression of what "folk music" meant to me. So I chose numbers that ranged from "Tol' My Captain," a chain-gang song popularized by Josh White, to a sixteenth-century British hunting song called "The Fox," to a Caribbean song, "Kalenda Rock," about the sometimes deadly tradition of stick fighting, during Carnival, that had originated in Africa. The whole album was so eclectic—and so un-formulaic—that it caught the fancy of critics and audiences alike. It didn't go through the roof, but it did sell respectably, and that boded well. Two years later, when my next albums generated much bigger numbers, eager new fans would snatch up *Mark Twain*, too, and it would enjoy a whole new, even better, run.

Almanac brought another big dividend that spring—my first leading-man film role. Otto Preminger, the Austro-Hungarian-born Broadway and Hollywood director known as much for his hot temper and bald head as his films, came to hear me, and told me backstage afterward that he wanted me for the male lead in his film version of *Carmen*, which would be called *Carmen Jones*.

A decade before, Oscar Hammerstein II had done the hard work, updating Georges Bizet's nineteenth-century French comic opera for Broadway with a World War II setting and an all-black cast. But Preminger was taking on a considerable challenge, too. In Hollywood, all-black-cast movies were viewed as sure money-losers, after a brief vogue for them in 1943 with *Cabin in the Sky* and *Stormy Weather*, both of which had earned praise but no profits. Preminger, one very scrappy guy, was raring to prove that wisdom wrong. He'd just taken on the Breen Office—Hollywood's exercise in self-censorship—by distributing his risqué comedy *The Moon Is Blue* without a Breen seal of approval, and it was doing well at the box office anyway. Making money from a first all-black film was his next mission, he told me, and with a glint in his eye, he added that he was matching me up against the perfect co-star: Dorothy Dandridge.

Rehearsals began June 3, 1954, on the Twentieth Century–Fox lot. By then, Preminger had broken it to us that the Bizet family was taking a hard line on rights. We could use Hammerstein's lyrics and the World War II setting, but nothing of *Carmen*'s operatic structure or score could be changed. The problem was that none of us had operatic ranges. So for the singing, Preminger informed us, Fox's studio chief Darryl Zanuck insisted that all of us lip-synch our songs and have bona fide opera singers supply the voices. Marilyn Horne would do Dorothy's part; a singer named LeVern Hutcherson would do mine.

I can see LeVern in my mind's eye now, a strong, proud man with a beautiful voice. And I can see him as I found him, a decade or so later, at a late-night restaurant called Reuben's, on the East Side, where I'd gone after a performance at the Copa to get one of their outrageously large sandwiches. Before taking a table, I went downstairs to the men's room, and did a double-take when the men's room attendant handed me a towel.

"LeVern?"

He nodded with a sheepish smile.

"How's it going?" I asked him.

He shook his head. "Not well," he said softly. "It hasn't gone well."

I felt awful about that. Not in a there-but-for-the-grace-of-God-go-I way, for in truth, I had gifts that I knew would keep me working, at least in some club or other, as long as I could sing. All LeVern had *was* his voice. Aside from a few opera buffs, no one knew his face or, for that matter, his name. But would a white opera singer have gone from *Carmen* in Hollywood to working in a washroom? Not likely. LeVern was a sad reminder that for too many black performers, destitution was no more than a few paychecks away.

The news about lip-synching appalled and embarrassed us, but we knew there was nothing Preminger could do about it. Only his sheer will and stubbornness had pushed Zanuck into doing the film at all— that, and agreeing to forfeit his pay if the film bombed. He really was leading with his heart on this one. Inspired, we threw ourselves into rehearsals with a zeal I've never seen in a cast before or since: not just Dorothy and me, but Pearl Bailey, Diahann Carroll, and the rest.

I was thrilled, of course, to be working with Dorothy Dandridge again. I was thrilled just to see her. I went to her Hollywood house to work on our scenes; we went out to dinner, came back to her place, and kissed passionately on the doorstep. But it went no further. She was ready for a new relationship, she said, but it would only be with a man who'd go the distance with her. I told her how empty my marriage had become—and it had. Love had left the room some time ago; mainly now I felt a sense of grim obligation to Marguerite, and heaps of guilt. If I left her, I'd be letting her down, abandoning Adrienne, proving Mrs. Byrd right in all the doubts she loved to voice about me. But since I *was* still married, my protestations to Dorothy fell a bit flat.

What I wanted from Dorothy was more than a quick fling—I really did adore her—but less, in truth, than full commitment. I couldn't leave Marguerite, not right then, not when she'd announced, a few months back, that she was pregnant again. When I'd recovered from my shock at that news—and I *was* shocked—I'd thought: Good! Maybe a second child will pull us together as parents, if not as lovers. Maybe this perfect little family of four will be enough to curb my restlessness and dissatisfaction. I did wonder if Marguerite had gotten pregnant on purpose, but it seemed pointless to ask. If she had, she probably wouldn't have admitted it. More likely, she hadn't. Marguerite had a full-fledged career as a child psychologist; the last thing she needed was the added distraction of a second child. For a few months, I'd made myself believe that Marguerite's pregnancy had pulled me into our marriage again. But by the time I went to L.A. to do *Carmen Jones*, I knew that wasn't the case, and courted Dorothy with a not-very-clear conscience. All to no avail.

It was during one of these fruitless nights out that I learned Dorothy, too, was racked by guilt. Her marriage had produced one daughter, Harolyn, with severe mental disabilities, whom Dorothy gave up early to a foster home. Over her second drink, or her third, Dorothy talked of how beautiful and sweet Harolyn was—she called her Lyn—and of how one day, when Dorothy had made enough money from movies, she'd bring Lyn home to live with her with round-the-clock help. Dorothy's later tragic death from an overdose of prescription pills—accidental, but coming amid deep depression and despair—would have as much to do with the guilt she felt about her daughter as with the uphill climb she faced in trying to be a black leading actress in a world where there simply weren't any.

What I didn't know was that Dorothy had just taken a new lover. And despite her claims that she wanted someone who was available and ready to commit himself to her, the man she'd chosen was married.

He was, in fact, Otto Preminger.

At the time Dorothy had read for *Carmen Jones*, the two hardly knew each other. Preminger had called Dorothy to audition for a supporting role, figuring from her prim-and-proper look in *Bright Road* that she wouldn't be right as the sultry Carmen. Dorothy had donned a wig, low-cut blouse, and short skirt to make a very different impression, and Otto had been won over. Almost as soon as he gave her the leading role, however, Dorothy began to have misgivings. Maybe Carmen was *too* sultry for her; maybe it would hurt her career. Now Otto was the supplicant. He asked to come to her apartment and plead his case, and when he did, she made him his favorite dinner of cold steak and cucumbers. Once he'd persuaded her to take the leading role, he talked her into taking him to her bedroom—and one of the great Hollywood affairs of the day began. Because he was married, and Dorothy had her career to protect, the two kept their romance a tightly guarded secret. On set, they betrayed no special interest in each other. Preminger spent no more time directing Dorothy than he did anyone else; any warmth he expressed was just to soothe a temperamental diva. Off-set, Dorothy stayed utterly mum. Even the flirting she still engaged in with me was, I think, part of the act. Had she stopped, I might have suspected she had someone else. So even as I drove back after my dinners with her, wondering what I still needed to say or do to win her at last, she was doubtless on the phone to Otto, saying the coast was clear.

But if the secret eluded me, I did understand the subtext. Dorothy needed a special protector, someone with enough power in Hollywood to help pull her up, as a black actress, into the pantheon of white leading ladies. Staunch liberal that he was, with his passion for civil rights, Preminger was probably the best candidate she could have found, and their romance, eventually quite public, would last four years. But even he couldn't fix the essential problem. A Lana Turner or Elizabeth Taylor could be matched onscreen with any number of leading men, and land a dozen more top films before her luster started to fade. Dorothy's choice of co-stars was far more limited. She had me . . . and Sidney. She and I would do one more film together after *Carmen Jones*, but that was that; a leading lady couldn't be paired more than three times with the same leading man. With Sidney she'd do *Porgy and Bess*. But then she'd be relegated to the worst kind of typecasting—playing slave girls romanced by their masters, and the like—and her downward spiral would accelerate.

In retrospect, *Carmen Jones* was Dorothy's high point. For both of us, it was an intensely emotional acting experience. Otto had just ten or eleven days to shoot the whole film—that was how pinched his budget was. (My fee as the male star was, I distinctly remember, $18,000.) There was hardly a reshoot; we just went from scene to scene, from lust to betrayal and back, all while trying to stay in our roles through the songs, as we gamely lip-synched. By the time we got to the story's dramatic climax, in which I strangle Carmen, I'd floated into some zone of raw emotion I'd never felt before. "We'll do it with a boom shot," Otto instructed me. "As the camera pulls back, you turn around, Carmen comes in, you grab her, we come in closer, and as you start to choke her, you bend forward out of frame."

Okay, I thought, simple enough.

Since this was the payoff scene, we practiced it a couple of times without the cameras rolling. Then came "Action," and in I swung— into action. I remember turning to Dorothy with an expression of passionate revulsion and rage, and reaching for her neck with my hands.

"Cut! Cut!" Otto shouted, clearly very annoyed. I looked up to see him on top of the boom-shot crane. "Mr. Belafonte," he said in his thick German accent, "when you choke the leading lady in the movies, you do not put wrinkles in her neck."

Passionate but not out of control, furious but not homicidal— somehow, I got the balance right on the next take. And there it is still, on celluloid, my most dramatic moment as a Hollywood actor.

What I'd told Dorothy about my marriage was the truth. By now, Marguerite and I had both abandoned any hope that we could maintain our vows to each other. We'd always been in different worlds; those worlds had just drifted ever farther apart. Marguerite was a serious academic, soon to earn a Ph.D. in psychology. I played Vegas and made movies in Hollywood. She didn't get my friends, I didn't get hers, and, as for Mrs. Byrd, we were hardly on speaking terms, though she continued to live with us—an excruciating experience for everyone. Why not divorce, then? One reason, for Marguerite, was her newfound Catholicism. The very fact that she'd joined the Church struck me as odd; she knew how much I resented my Catholic education, and how fiercely I'd rejected the Church. Was this, to use a phrase I would come to know in therapy, a passive-aggressive move on her part? Whether it was or not, the Church's views on divorce were all too clear.

For Marguerite, the material world exerted its own allure. I was pulling in real money now. It was all pretty much a blur, and still is, but in the magazine profiles that had begun to appear—*Life* for one, *Ebony* for another—I was said to be on track to earn $350,000 a year in 1954. That was some serious jingle—almost $3 million today. Certainly it made me one of the two or three highest-paid black entertainers in America, along with Sidney and Sammy Davis, Jr. That money bought new cars and clothes, and a lot of respect. Marguerite liked her new status, not just as my wife but as the most prosperous daughter in her family. That was, as her father would say, a lot of money to handle.

As for me, I had three reasons to stay in the game. One was Adrienne, second was Marguerite's pregnancy with Shari, and, perhaps the most compelling of all, my horror at the thought of becoming my father—abandoning my marital responsibilities, as he had done. Turning into a deadbeat. The more appealing the idea of divorce became, the more I resisted it, my own Catholic guilt pulling me back in.

And then, with these thoughts churning in my mind, and Dorothy sweetly but firmly pushing me away, I got a call from Marlon Brando that changed my life.

I was spending my days on the Twentieth Century–Fox set of *Carmen Jones* as a G.I. Joe, lip-synching in a military barracks. Marlon was on another Fox set, playing Napoleon Bonaparte in *Desirée*, against a backdrop of extravagant ballrooms. "You gotta do me a favor," Marlon said. "This girl I've been dating just got here from Italy, but I can't break away until dinner. Take her to lunch at the commissary and then we'll all hook up later."

Sure, I told Marlon, I was happy to help out. That day, the choreographer for *Desirée*, Stephen Papich, brought her over to our set. I was on a soundstage, lip-synching to LeVern Hutcherson's gorgeously operatic voice, when the choreographer slid a tall rolling door aside. I saw a slim figure in silhouette, backlit by the sun so she appeared to glow. When we approached each other, I saw she had a perfect dancer's body, with a dancer's poise, bobbed dark hair, shoe-button eyes, and a dazzling smile, almost too big for her face. I had a vague but pleasing memory of Julie Robinson as that Katherine Dunham dancer who'd performed at the New School several years before. She was even more gorgeous than I remembered. "Julie Robinson," she said. "How nice of you to volunteer for foster care."

Over lunch at the Fox commissary, Julie sorted out a number of misperceptions for me. First, she was New York born and bred. She'd been in Europe touring with a trio of Katherine Dunham dancers, a subset of the larger New York–based modern dance troupe. She'd met Marlon in New York, when he'd taken dance lessons at the company— ostensibly because he loved the sensual, drum-beating African and Cuban music that Dunham favored for her dance pieces, but also because he liked meeting all those dark beauties; anyone who knew Marlon well knew he had, as we put it, a touch of "jungle fever." I had one other misperception about her that I didn't think to ask about, and she didn't think to explain. I assumed she was black, or if not that, Hispanic. Weren't all the Dunham dancers black? Julie's skin tone was more olive than café au lait, but anyone in the West Indies would have pegged her as a mixed-blood beauty with black roots. With that same skin tone, though, as I would come to see, Julie looked Italian in Italy, Russian in Russia, and Cuban in Cuba. In fact, she was the Katherine Dunham troupe's one white dancer: Her lineage was Russian. Not for months would I discover that truth.

With no hesitation or embarrassment, Julie told me she'd come to L.A. to settle her romance with Marlon one way or the other. She didn't want to be one of the birds in his flock. If he wanted her, he would have to commit. Later that day, he gave her his answer: He wanted his freedom. And yes, he told me when I called him to ask, by all means, take her out. So I took Julie to a club in Santa Monica to hear a singer we both liked, Josephine Premice, a tall, black calypsonian with Haitian roots whom I'd met at the Vanguard but who had also danced, for a time, with Katherine Dunham. That was the way it was with Julie right from the start—we knew the same singers and actors, we loved the same plays and movies and books, and we shared the same politics. She revered Robeson as much as I did! She in some ways knew more about African and African-American culture than I did, having attended the

Little Red School House, probably Manhattan's—and the country's—most progressive private school. Those experiences had inoculated her against racial prejudice, and I, with my island background of mixed-blood unions, felt as easy around her as she did around me. We could have talked all night. When I dropped her off, kissing her good night, I felt both exhilarated and anxious. This was the kind of connection that could end a marriage, especially one as much on the rocks as mine.

I'd rented a place up on Appian Way in Beverly Hills for *Carmen Jones*, and it was here that Julie and I began meeting. Later, Julie would say that the intellectual attraction drew us together as much as the sex. That was true. Julie's parents were classic left-wing Jewish immigrants from Russia. They weren't just progressive; they were deeply committed Marxists. Julie was a voracious reader; she was fascinated by Mexico, and spoke fluent Spanish, which jibed with my own curiosity about Latin culture. Early on, we drove down to Mexico for our first bullfight. When we got back to L.A., I invited her to move in while she looked for a place of her own; and she basically just stayed. Eventually she had to go back to Italy to resume her dance commitments there; she had a contract to tour with Walter Chiari, the dashing Italian movie star whose musical revue was taking that country by storm. Still, we wrote each other almost every day. By then, I had no doubt that I'd found the woman with whom I wanted to spend the rest of my life. In my letters, I told her as much.

I played a return engagement at the Cocoanut Grove that August when *Carmen Jones* finished filming, and once again, the place was packed. I had it all now: top club money and billing; the movie due out in October; and a second child on the way. What more could a man want? The right mate, perhaps.

Shari's arrival on September 22, 1954, was indeed a joyous occasion. Within days, though, Marguerite chanced upon my stash of letters from Julie, and read them through. They only confirmed what she'd suspected, but with their discovery, a line was drawn; now it was only a matter of when, not if, we'd divorce.

8

Carmen Jones was just what Otto Preminger had hoped it would be: a true sensation. Dorothy Dandridge was on the cover of *Life* magazine the week it opened, dressed as Carmen, and long lines formed at movie theaters in New York and Los Angeles. Dorothy impressed the critics, certainly more than I did. Bosley Crowther in *The New York Times* admired her "slinky, hip-swinging" sex appeal; he found me "an oddly static symbol of masculine lust, lost in a vortex of confusion." Overall, he called *Carmen Jones* "a crazy mixed-up film," and that I had to agree with, if only because of the lip-synching, which made it painful to watch. But it had a lot of passion, it stirred talk and excitement, and Preminger won his gamble. *Carmen Jones* became the first black film to make serious money, not just in the United States but in Europe, where it played nearly a year in London and Berlin. Henry Louis Gates, Jr., the well-known professor and writer, remembers it as electrifying for him and his whole community of young black friends, both for its story and for its cultural significance. It also won a Golden Globe award for Best Picture (Musical or Comedy), and for Dorothy, an Oscar nomination for Best Actress. That made her the first African-American so honored. Grace Kelly would win that year for *The Country Girl*, but Dorothy seemed to be, for that moment at least, where she'd always wanted to be: in the pantheon of Hollywood's leading ladies. I, on the other hand, found myself traveling across America on a Greyhound bus.

I'd signed on to co-star in a traveling musical revue called *3 for*

Tonight, in part because it promised to be a real greasepaint-and-glory, old-style theater tour. But it also intrigued me that the tour would wind its way through the heart of Dixie. On May 17, 1954, the U.S. Supreme Court had issued its historic *Brown v. Board of Education* ruling, making integration the law of the land in public schools and colleges. With southern governors vowing to resist it, the stage was set for the civil rights movement. I wanted to put my songs before southern white audiences so set on segregation. I wanted them to have a close look at me as I used my art to challenge their social theories. Perhaps yet another reason for going on the road was getting away from home and Marguerite's mother.

3 for Tonight had come to me by chance, as so much else had and would. Early that year, while I was in *Almanac*, an interesting character named Paul Gregory had wandered in at intermission to catch the second act. Gregory was a manager and producer with one client: British actor Charles Laughton. The two had teamed up to stage a number of Broadway shows. Their latest, *The Caine Mutiny Court-Martial*, directed by Laughton and starring Henry Fonda, was in rehearsals up the street at the Plymouth Theatre, and Gregory peeked into *Almanac* to calm his pre-opening-night nerves. He liked what he heard, and soon brought Laughton to hear me as well. Laughton liked what he saw. The plan they concocted, after coming back to hear me several times in *Almanac*, was to put me in their next theatrical venture— their inspired way of combating the dreaded new threat of television.

All over the country now, Americans were gathering nightly in front of the boob tube, which drove Hollywood crazy. The entire Hollywood star system was under siege. The studios did everything they could to stave off this box-office cancer. The question was how to get folks back into theaters, especially outside New York. Gregory and Laughton had come up with the notion of all-star dramatic readings and speaking tours. For their first experiment, they'd persuaded Charles Boyer, Agnes Moorehead, and Sir Cedric Hardwicke to team up with Laughton in black tie for a reading of *Don Juan in Hell*, act three, scene two, of George Bernard Shaw's *Man and Superman*. A lone figure would walk out on the bare stage as the curtain rose and say, "Good evening, my name is Charles Boyer." Then, in sequence, each actor introduced himself in the same way—the last being Laughton, who said, "Shall we begin?" The audience would gasp with delight; Boyer and the others were big stars, especially in the hinterlands. The troupe barnstormed around the country and made a bundle. Not the least of its appeals was that the show cost almost nothing to produce: no sets, no music, just four music stands for the four great stars. *The Caine Mutiny Court-Martial* had followed the same route to Broadway, and now the canny impresarios wanted to try their first bare-stage musical. Already, they had Marge and Gower Champion, the dazzlingly handsome husband-and-wife dance pair often compared to Ginger Rogers and Fred Astaire. They wanted me to complete their *3 for Tonight* trio.

Like most revues, *3 for Tonight* had a very loose story, a kind of apple-pie history of America with an *Our Town* sort of narrator, lots of unrelated songs, and about thirty wooden stools as our only props. But Gregory and Laughton had tapped some top production talent to put it all together. Robert Wells, who'd written "The Christmas Song" with Mel Tormé (*"Chestnuts roasting on an open fire . . ."*), wrote lyrics for many of the songs; Walter Schumann and Nathan Scott, later famous for the *Dragnet* theme, did much of the music; a young Blake Edwards, of future *Pink Panther* fame, assisted; and Laughton himself directed until we hit the road, when Gower Champion took over. Of the songs I sang, my favorite was "Scarlet Ribbons." Though not a hit when I first recorded it, the song would go on to be one of my most loved, and it helped me wend my way into the hearts of white America.

We opened on October 28, 1954, in the leafy college town of Claremont, just east of L.A., the very same night *Carmen Jones* opened on movie screens on both coasts. The audience gave us a standing ovation. No one seemed to care that a white couple and a black man were singing and dancing together, and that in the final number, the white woman and black man held hands. But Gregory had lined us up for fifty-seven cities in all, and the route would take us east through Texas and most of the Deep South.

From their previous tours, Gregory and Laughton had learned to book university auditoriums: They were easier to get for one- or two-night stands than commercial theaters, and were often the only games in town. One early stop was at the University of Utah, where an eager theater student named George C. Scott insisted on joining us after the show. That boy could drink! None of us could keep up. Nor did we try very hard.

The Jim Crow treatment started right at the Texas state line. White-only bathrooms at the gas stations, white-only restaurants, nice hotels for the rest of the troupe, colored-only motels for Millard Thomas and me. Gregory had promised we wouldn't play segregated towns, and that the cast would lodge together at every stop. But Gregory just lied, knowing that once I was on the road under contract, I couldn't back out. Neither he nor Laughton was with us for the ride. We were on our own, the Champions and me, along with Millard and the other musicians and singers. All of us were in the Greyhound, with a truck behind us carrying the instruments and all those stools. When we pulled into our next destination and the hotel said whites only, what were we supposed to do? The answer was to avoid hotels altogether if we could. Millard and I took to calling ahead to Negro community leaders to help us with our accommodations. Some offered their homes, and their hospitality was gratefully accepted.

The worst racial incidents came after Christmas. A confusing Christmas, to say the least, brightened by tiny Shari and five-year-old Adrienne, but with their parents so awkward in each other's presence that I actually felt relieved to be heading back down to the segregated South. Until, that is, our merry troupe reached Spartanburg, South Carolina.

The Ku Klux Klan was a force throughout the South, but Spartanburg was one of its hotbeds. When 3 *for Tonight* posters went up around town, showing its three stars together, the angry mutterings began. By the day of our performance, word had gotten around that the mixed-race cast didn't just appear onstage together, but danced a finale—and took their bows—holding hands. We went on anyway. Halfway through the show, the mayor came backstage to tell us the Klan was on its way over, whether to burn down the theater or shoot it up, he couldn't say. With local police keeping watch out front, we finished our numbers. Then, instead of filing out a stage door with the backup singers and musicians, Millard and I slipped out a back door, into a waiting police cruiser, and sped to a small airstrip, where a private plane, arranged for by a local promoter, was waiting to whisk us off to the campus of the University of North Carolina. The Klan never did materialize, but the fear we felt onstage, imagining they'd show up, was very real.

Who knew, in those Jim Crow situations, how much danger we were really in? All I know is that the hatred radiated like southern summer heat. Toward the end of our tour, our bus stopped at a Greyhound station outside of Richmond, Virginia, and I went off groggily to relieve myself, not noticing the WHITE ONLY sign on the bathroom door. As I unzipped my fly in front of a urinal, I heard a low, hate-filled voice behind me. "You let go one drop, you're a dead nigger." I turned to see a Virginia state trooper, standing there with his hand on his holstered gun. I can't remember another time when I had the rush of emotions I experienced then. Fortunately, my urine had more sense than I did; it retreated. And I followed it. Zipped up my fly and walked out. The rage I felt, and the embarrassment, and indignity, linger in my memory as clearly as if it were yesterday.

That night, I walked onstage in Richmond as if nothing had happened. I grinned out at that crowd in the darkness, did my best to entertain, and took my customary hand-holding bows with Marge and Gower. Afterward, we went to a reception at the home of a black newspaper editor, in whose guest bedroom I'd be staying that night.

"Congratulations," the editor told me. "You sure made history in Richmond tonight."

"Why?" I asked.

"You danced with a white woman, and held her hand in a segregated house—and nothing happened."

3 for Tonight was due to open on Broadway in April 1955, which gave me time to tuck in a club date that meant a lot to me—at New York's Copacabana. With manager Jules Podell acting as the front man for Frank Costello, one of the kings of the underworld, this most prestigious joint in New York, which for years had had a vicious racist policy, was now seeking to hire me. On the club circuit at the time, the Copa was unique—the very tip of the top. Frank Sinatra and Dean Martin played the Copa; Lena Horne and Billy Eckstine and Nat King Cole played the Copa; even Edith Piaf played the Copa. I knew that my debut at the Copa would be a validation; the Copa carried a lot of juice. It would be another sign, if one were needed, that I had arrived. But I also had a private, very personal reason to take that stage. I imagined seeing that doorman's face again. And wondered if he would even remember the black sailor he'd barred from the club in 1944. The sailor who was now the top banana inside. There's a certain mental and emotional glue associated with incidents of discrimination: You remember the faces, years after they've forgotten yours. That doorman was long gone, it turned out.

I was now signed to one of the most powerful theatrical agencies in the world—MCA. Its CEO was a man named Lew Wasserman, who, as powerful as he was then, would go on to heights not attained by anyone else in his day. For many years he was the most powerful man in the entertainment business. Lew had taken a personal liking to me, and, although many seedy and hard-edged stories were told about Lew, I made a lot of room for him. I liked him in my space. He would, in later years as the head of Universal Pictures and other institutions, be most generous each time I called on him for significant financial support for hard-to-fund causes. We even shared our experiences as members of the board of the Peace Corps appointed by President John Kennedy. It was Lew who personally guided the negotiations of my Copacabana adventure.

We carved out our space on East Sixtieth Street in Manhattan, with Millard Thomas beside me on guitar. Tony Scott pulled together an orchestra of great players, many of whom were from my Royal Roost and Birdland Rolodex. With Tony conducting, the music grooved every set, but I always had to be ready for some prank or surprise. Sometimes in the middle of his clarinet solo, Tony would stick the instrument up his nose and try to blow it! Or put a part of it in his ear and treat it like a telephone. He'd come out onstage with the top half of his tuxedo on, but not the pants. He stayed pretty well behaved at the Copa, compared to other joints we played, but I never knew what each night would bring. The audience loved him. I could count on the tables being filled. Even so, the Copa was always a challenge. Morey Amsterdam, the comedian, was the other headliner, and as zany and brilliant as he was, at many a show he'd struggle to be heard. I had better luck: I stunned them into silence with "Jerry," and by the time Tony and the band got to songs like "Angelina," "Man Smart (Woman Smarter)," or our Basie-style version of "On Top of Old Smokey," then "Hava Nageela," with the audience sing-along and a long wrap-up of "Matilda," folk singing went to another zone and I was its happy landlord.

Before the end of my run at the Copa, MCA informed me that Podell was looking for a new deal. The club wanted a long-term commitment. "What are the numbers?" I asked. Dave Baumgarden, the MCA agent of record at the time, replied, "How high the moon?" I smiled. I liked the melody, but I finally told Podell the answer was no. He was shocked. He said somewhat threateningly, "Greed could be troublesome." I pointed out that it wasn't about money. The money would never be big enough. It was about a night during the war in 1944 when a Negro man in uniform with his lady were robbed of their dignity. That moment could never be made right.

On the closing night of our performance, Podell, in a drunken fury, went to the back of the club and opened the doors to the kitchen and service area. He ran a mop handle along the dish rack, smashing every plate and cup and all the glasses in his reach and overturning pots and pans and skillets. Everything he could find. In the turmoil, customers headed for the door as security personnel got him under control. All because I had said no. It was a sad moment. The confrontation never really satisfied anything; there was no sense of justice or reward. In later years, I found myself, from time to time, thinking back on what had transpired and wondering what I should have done differently. Certainly, had Martin Luther King been in my life then, it might have been another scenario.

3 for Tonight opened April 16, 1955, at the Plymouth Theatre, to sold-out crowds and glowing reviews. In fact, they were almost too glowing. "Producer Paul Gregory doesn't need three for tonight so long as he's got Harry Belafonte for tonight," declared Walter Kerr in the *New York Herald Tribune*. That put a little chill in my relations with the Champions, no question about it. "Why is Harry Belafonte so magnificent in *3 for Tonight*?" Brooks Atkinson asked in *The New York Times*. "Because he represents the fanaticism of the dedicated artist. Eliminating himself, he concentrates on the songs with fiery intensity. . . . Mr. Belafonte never makes a mistake in taste or showmanship, for he is all artist and a rousing performer." Kerr had gone even further in the *Herald Tribune*. He said that opening night was one of those rare occasions when a major entertainer "unforgettably announces his existence."

As far as I could tell, the only person not delighted in that opening-night audience was my mother. I'd coaxed her into coming—no easy job, given her muttering that she wasn't the sort of woman who went to Broadway plays, and didn't want to accept the free tickets I was offering for her and my stepfather, Bill Wright, and their two children. Finally she'd come—alone, using just one ticket so as not to be any more in my debt than necessary. After the last thunderous ovation, she'd let herself be led backstage, and when I'd changed into street clothes, she consented to walk with me out the stage door, past the autograph-seekers, up the block to a corner coffee shop. "The people really love you," she observed.

It was a wonderful show, I replied.

"But just think if you'd taken to your music studies with Mrs. Shepherd," she said sternly in her still-soft Jamaican accent. "You'd have sounded as good as Mario Lanza."

This was a time of rising stardom for me—a first album out and more to come, my first big club dates on either coast, a leading role in a Hollywood hit, a starring role in one Broadway revue that had led to another. Yet deep down, I felt confused and, all too often, unhappy. My dying marriage accounted for much of this, and Julie, my new hope for happiness, was still in Italy with dance obligations. But my despair—and, really, it was that—had deeper, tangled roots. As if I needed reminding in my mother's remarks, my childhood had left me with emotional needs that perhaps no one could fill. My racial identity confused me still; I was black, yes, but West Indian, playing to white audiences— a cultural hybrid, in between. Success was confusing, too. Stardom had come so quickly; was it me those audiences were applauding, or some stage double named Harry Belafonte? And if it was the latter, how long could I keep up the act? As if all these weren't worries enough, that home visit from the FBI haunted me. Clearly, my government was tracking me—possibly my every move—because my liberal political views struck J. Edgar Hoover as subversive. This was enough to make anyone feel not just depressed, but paranoid.

In search of answers, I started seeing a New York psychotherapist, as often as five times a week when I was in town. I hoped I'd embarked on a useful journey of self-discovery. Instead, as I would later learn, I'd stumbled into the start of a dark political thriller, my own version of *The Manchurian Candidate.*

Back in the summer of 1954, I'd gone up for a weekend gig to the Lake Tarleton Club, a WASPy resort set in the White Mountains of New Hampshire. I sang in the evenings; during the day, guests could listen to various speakers between rounds of golf or sets of tennis. I had the days free, so I wandered in to hear the remarks of a New York psychotherapist named Janet Alterman Kennedy. Psychotherapy, especially Freudian analysis, had been embraced by most of the artists I knew; talk of blocks and breakthroughs was as much in the air at Greenwich Village parties as politics and cigarette smoke. I was under a huge amount of stress by then, and Janet spoke with an empathy and insight I found quite moving. She also mentioned that she treated a lot of Negro patients: Janet was white, so that intrigued me.

That evening, she came to hear me perform and wandered backstage afterward. With her was her husband, Jay Richard Kennedy, who told me with soulful eyes how powerfully my rendition of "John Henry" had struck him, as both a devotee of folk music and an Irish bard of sorts. Kennedy was a stockbroker as well as an author, he explained; he had a speaker's slot to discuss his new best-selling novel, an inside-Hollywood tale called *Prince Bart*.

I'd forgotten all about the Kennedys until they showed up backstage at one of the first New York performances of *3 for Tonight*. They gushed with praise, not just in general terms—by now, I was pretty impervious to that—but in a thoughtful way that put *3 for Tonight* into perspective as a race-barrier-breaking production. Over drinks at an after-theater haunt, Jay Richard told stories of riding the railroads as a hobo in his youth, of working as a longshoreman, wrangler, brick-layer, and farmer. He'd even had a go of it as a nightclub singer, he said, before reinventing himself as a novelist and screenwriter. There was no questioning his success; in addition to *Prince Bart*, he'd written the screenplay for *I'll Cry Tomorrow,* a film just out about singer Lillian Roth's long struggle with alcoholism. Along the way, he said, he'd espoused the same left-wing political ideals that I had, and joined similar groups, though in Chicago, not New York. As for Janet, she was affiliated with the psychiatric clinic at Columbia Presbyterian Hospital, where she had a practice that served a largely black, working-class community. I needed someone I could talk to—about everything—and Janet seemed so wise and empathetic. I asked her if she would give me a consultation. Janet said she'd be delighted. She soon became my analyst.

In our first sessions, Janet explained the basic principles of analysis. She kept pounding on trust and transference, how a patient digs deeper and deeper into his past until the therapist becomes for him a stand-in for the loved ones or authority figures that have had such an imprint on his life. Soon I was dredging up those painful memories of my mother and father, telling her everything and weeping on her couch. The connection grew stronger when we saw each other socially, which was more and more often. If any of my friends suggested to me at the time that socializing with your therapist was not what Freud had had in mind, I must have waved them off.

Janet had broken one cardinal rule of analysis; she was about to break another. But she did have years of experience, and where she led me was clearly where I had to go: from my parents . . . to Marguerite . . . to the casual flings I'd begun to have whenever I went on the road. I didn't need to seek out these lovers, I explained; they came to me, before or after my shows, making their hopes all too clear. But why, Janet asked, did I never say no? And what in these trysts was I hoping to find? I laughed. Wasn't the answer obvious? Sex with new partners? Yet as I recounted one after another of these brief relationships, I realized all had left me deeply disappointed. Why? All roads, of course, led back to my mother. I'd tried so hard to please her, hoping I could do enough, hoping that at last she'd love me unconditionally. I'd failed, then reenacted this hopeless drama with Marguerite, only to fall short in her eyes, too. Just as I'd become a success, Marguerite had pulled away—scared by my politics, sure the FBI must be right to think I was a communist conspirator. Neither my mother nor Marguerite, in other words, had loved me unconditionally. With this pattern set, I'd ventured off to seek that absolute, unconditional love in each next intimacy. As soon as I sensed my next lover wasn't capable of it, I'd start backing off. Often I'd see that my stardom was what had drawn them to me. They had no idea who I was beneath my stage persona; they hadn't even thought to look. That was all I needed in order to leave.

Most of these women, I acknowledged to Janet, were white. At the venues I played, almost everyone was white—not many blacks could afford the freight—so I'd fooled myself into thinking there wasn't anything notable about this. In fact, the taboo of mixed-race romance intrigued me, as it did so many. On a deeper level, my sexual desire for white women was linked, I began to see, with that underlying anger that never quite went away. The white world had done its best to deny me every chance. What better way, now that I'd triumphed despite it, to exact my revenge? What irked white men more than anything else? Seeing white women choose black men over them!

None of these casual lovers ever felt that anger emanating from me. Nor were any made to feel a target of racial revenge. I was never unkind. If anything, they felt sorry for me, at how trapped I seemed to be by my turbulent emotions. The more sensitive among them sensed my doubts, and asked what they could do to dispel them. To which I would say, quite honestly, "I don't know." And then I'd retreat—it was always I who backed off first. Over time, analysis would help me understand that pattern, how those deep, subconscious yearnings and fears manifested themselves. By then, Janet Kennedy—and Jay Richard Kennedy—would be long gone from my life.

All that digging soon brought me to my anxieties about money. No matter how much of it came my way, I felt I might lose it all and be dirt poor again. I started griping about Jack Rollins, my manager ever since that breakthrough audition at the Village Vanguard in late 1951. At the start of that ride, Jack had been a great help and a great comfort. He believed in me, he gave me good advice, he'd gotten me the Vanguard and the clubs that followed. But as I'd risen into the big leagues, Jack had panicked. Vegas was a mystery to him. So was Hollywood. He was basically in over his head. That was why I'd signed on with Freddie Fields of MCA, with Lew Wasserman at the company's helm, to handle my movie and television work. I'd kept Jack on for clubs, but now that I was getting booked in rooms like the Cocoanut Grove, he was outmatched on that front, too. Janet listened, and then made a suggestion. Her husband, in addition to stock-picking and writing, handled the finances of some of Hollywood's best-known actors of the day: Richard Conte, for one, Gene Kelly and Robert Ryan and others. Why not see if he could help me, too?

One day that May, I went down to Jay's Wall Street office to discuss the idea. The office was very impressive. Jay worked on his own, but he clearly had lots of contacts in high places. Framed pictures on the walls showed a factory in the Midwest that had made ball bearings for the armed forces during World War II. Jay said he'd run that factory. He'd even advised President Roosevelt directly, and come to know members of his cabinet. Though he also admitted, with a chuckle, that before the war his biggest customer had been the mob, which used his ball bearings for slot machines. Jay seemed to have a finger in every pot—Washington, Wall Street, Hollywood, Vegas—and that, he said, gave him enormous power to protect me from my fear of losing all my money as quickly as I'd earned it. Eagerly, I put him in charge of my finances, and gave him power of attorney.

The Kennedys lived at 25 Beekman Place, in an apartment spacious enough for Janet to have her office there. Somehow, my therapy sessions always seemed to be scheduled at the end of the day. We would emerge to find Jay mixing drinks for the three of us. Stay for dinner, the Kennedys would urge, and so I would. Sometimes one of Jay's friends or clients, just in from Hollywood, would be there; I remember Gene Kelly one night, director Anthony Mann another. More often, though, it was just the three of us, and in those cozy, familylike evenings, the transference—for that's what it surely was—became so powerful and transformational that I began regarding the Kennedys as my surrogate parents. Before I even recognized it, in some strange and insidious way, I was calling them Mom and Dad.

Soon, with a little coaxing from Jay and Janet, I made Jay not just my financial adviser, but my personal manager as well, displacing Jack Rollins. Rollins was furious. To anyone who would listen, including gossip columnists, he began spewing an angry story of treachery and betrayal on my part. Without him, he'd say, I would have gone nowhere, yet now I'd cut him loose. The Kennedys, he felt, were as much to blame as me. They'd poisoned my mind. That summer, he filed a $150,000 breach-of-contract suit against both Kennedys, accusing them of turning me against him and signing me on as a client while my contract with Rollins was still in effect. The suit was groundless; my contract with Rollins had expired. Yet there was, I have to admit in retrospect, some truth in what he'd charged. The Kennedys found fertile ground to move Jack out of my life, and not until another year had passed would I discover why they'd done it.

Not long after 3 for Tonight bowed, I got a call from one Claude Philippe, a Frenchman who'd come over to work for the Waldorf-Astoria Hotel. Claude wanted to have me do a late show at the Waldorf after I got offstage each night. When I heard that, I had to laugh. "Claude," I said, "you must have just come from France."

Everyone in the entertainment world knew the Waldorf had a Jim Crow policy: no black entertainers allowed. You could play in the orchestra if you were black, or maybe work as a substitute waiter, but not take the stage. Lena Horne, Ethel Waters, Duke Ellington, Nat King Cole—none of the major black stars had played the Waldorf, not once. The strict keeper of this policy was Muriel Abbott, a powerful executive in Conrad Hilton's hotel empire, which included the Waldorf in New York and the Palmer House in Chicago. "But, Harry," Philippe explained, "Muriel eez in Chicago . . . et nous sommes ici."

Abbott booked all the acts for the Waldorf's fabled Empire Room in New York from her Palmer House office in Chicago. But Claude, as the hotel's new vice president of food and beverage, had authority over the rest of the hotel's dining spaces, including the Starlight Roof, which had been used simply as a banquet room. Claude's plan was to turn the Starlight Roof into a new supper club. And for its debut, he had a daring idea: He said he'd book a regular act for the early show, then slide me in for the late show. Audiences would feel they were getting something special, columnists would write it up as news, the Waldorf would make money, and an important color barrier would be broken, which for Claude, God bless him, was as much a reason to do this as it was for me.

Claude kept the show a secret until the week before I opened, on June 1, 1955. Then he took out major ads in all the papers. Now, in addition to cabaret singer Felicia Sanders, the Starlight was offering . . . me. Abbott was furious, but she knew the Frenchman had outfoxed her; she couldn't stop the show without causing a scandal. What she could and did do, even after the show was a hit, was start lobbying her superiors to have Claude fired. But with several months left on his contract, Claude took his revenge by hiring all the service staff of color he could: blacks, Hispanics, Asians. And these were union jobs—no one, not even Muriel Abbott, could fire those new waiters without cause.

At the next quarterly accounting, Conrad Hilton's bookkeepers noted something very unusual: Room service revenues had gone up 30 percent. Those new waiters, knowing how lucky they were to land those jobs, had hustled that room-service food up to the rooms piping hot, and guests had ordered that much more. The Starlight Roof's revenues had gone way up, too. Somewhere in corporate offices above Muriel Abbott's little preserve, decisions were made. Claude was kept on, and, despite Abbott's indignation, I was booked that September into the Empire Room downstairs, and then, directly from there, into the Empire Room at the Palmer House—the first of what would be years of engagements at both. It had taken a secretly liberal Frenchman to test the Waldorf's color barrier, but what broke it was the jingle. In the end, profit always trumps prejudice.

Claude was right about the columnists; they did take note of the Starlight Roof show, none more flatteringly than Dorothy Kilgallen of Hearst's *New York Journal-American*. On her nighttime beat, Kilgallen was both powerful and feared. Just when you thought her column was all fluff, she'd come in with some zinger. She'd taken on Frank Sinatra more than once. Back when I was in *Almanac* and drawing the heat of those "Red Channels" editors, she'd piled on by implying that Marlon Brando and I were gay and had had trysts on Fire Island! I'd responded as I had with Ed Sullivan, by meeting with her face-to-face, at her Upper East Side apartment. "Does it mean nothing to you that you've reported something completely untrue?" I asked her. "And that this miscarriage of truth has confused and upset my family? But beyond that, what makes you write nasty slurs about someone you haven't even met?" We cleared the air soon enough, and to Kilgallen's credit, she didn't hold a grudge. Far from it—she invited me to write a guest column for her that June, the first of several, about my experiences of doing 3 for Tonight in the South. Later, when she became a regular on What's My Line?, I went on as the celebrity guest one time, and she guessed who I was. "That's my love, Harry!" she exclaimed. So we were cool.

My co-stars in 3 for Tonight, it turned out, were the ones displeased with me. All through our national tour, the Champions and I had gotten on wonderfully well. Those warm feelings had cooled a bit after the New York critics singled me out. But then a misunderstanding had arisen for which Paul Gregory was squarely to blame. Fearing the play might not last long on Broadway, Gregory had made a deal with CBS to buy it as a television special—it was to air June 22—and advised my agent that he could go ahead and quietly book me into a high-paying Las Vegas gig after that. When, to Gregory's surprise, 3 for Tonight became a solid Broadway hit, the Champions thought they had a long-time run on their hands. They were appalled—and angry—to learn that the play would have to close because I had prior commitments. In those days, you didn't do that. You didn't leave a play for some selfish reason and go book a gig that would pay you more money while putting the play and the careers of fellow artists in jeopardy. So there was this undercurrent of fierce anger, which Gower finally explained to me. I sat them down to tell them exactly what Gregory had told me, and when I did, the whole company severed relations with *him*. Marge and Gower and I stayed friends, but not without some distance for a while.

Fortunately, the TV special helped ease those bruised feelings. It was a huge hit—"one of the most exciting and beguiling evenings of the season," as The New York Times put it. So was our one-night finale, the next week, at the Greek Theatre, the open-air amphitheater in Los Angeles that held nearly four thousand people and was sold out. With that last performance, we had, in a sense, come full circle with 3 for Tonight, performing just a few miles from the Claremont theater where we'd started the previous fall. Despite its Jim Crow moments, I had nothing but gratitude for the experience. 3 for Tonight had been more than a cheerful song-and-dance revue. It had put us—the Champions, me, our backup singers and musicians—on a town-by-town tour in the grand old theatrical tradition, rolling across the heartland in our Greyhound bus, taking in the whole patchwork of America at a time when its regions were so much more distinctive from one another than they are today. It was an experience I'd always treasure, and never have again.

Unquestionably, too, the relentless pace of that tour made us stronger as performers. I felt readier to sing in larger venues—ready now, too, to absorb whatever further success fate chose to heap on me. As for the Champions, they would go from triumph to triumph—from starring in a television sitcom about themselves to Gower's string of Broadway hit musicals as director and choreographer (*Bye Bye Birdie; Carnival!; Hello, Dolly; I Do! I Do!*) before the long dry spell of flops that devastated him and ended their marriage. And then, in one of Broadway's most poignant true-life stories, Gower would try for musical success one more time with a show called *42nd Street*, only to die of cancer on opening night, August 25, 1980, thus deprived of seeing the musical go on to a fabled run as one of the best-loved Broadway hits ever. On her own, Marge would establish a new career as a prominent dance teacher in New York, where she still lives, dancing every day, vigorous, fit, and as beautiful as ever—at ninety-two.

This time, when I came to Vegas, I rode right by the Thunderbird— noting that it looked a little shabbier than it had three years before— and went on to the new Riviera.

The Riviera had just opened in April, with Liberace as its inaugural act. Its Miami backers were mobbed up, of course, though they included Harpo and Gummo Marx at the outset. To their credit, the owners hadn't wanted the Riviera to look like the other eight gambling resorts on the Strip. No glorified motor-court design for them. Instead, they made the Riviera Las Vegas's first high-rise resort, with a ten-thousand-square-foot casino. In so doing, they brought on the start of a new and far more glamorous era: the glory days of Vegas.

For the next decade or so, Frank Sinatra and the rest of the Rat Pack played the Sands (which acquired a tower of its own). But the Riviera was my place—until Caesars Palace went up and all of us decamped there—and I made sure I played it on my terms. Mr. Belafonte and his accompanist would be guaranteed a suite of their choice at the Riviera, my contract stated. They would be guaranteed access at all times to any and all public spaces at the resort, including the outdoor pool. They would in no way be discriminated against by any staff member of the hotel. On and on the contract went, until Millard Thomas started to laugh. *"During Mr. Belafonte's stay at the Riviera, no cloud shall pass over his head . . ."* Damn right! I hadn't forgotten my treatment at the Thunderbird, not one aspect of it. Nothing like that would ever happen again.

I was on a roll now, booked into one top-tier joint after another with hardly a break. After the Riviera, I came back down to L.A. to play the Cocoanut Grove, staying, when I did, as a houseguest of Richard and Ruth Conte at their Coldwater Canyon home. The rest of Jay Richard Kennedy's clients came around, too—Charlie Chaplin and Robert Ryan and director Tony Mann—all singing Kennedy's praises. In a year or so, when I learned what Kennedy's game really was, they would be furious with me for exposing him.

Then it was on to the Venetian Room in San Francisco's Fairmont Hotel, where I broke Lena Horne's attendance record; back to the Waldorf's Empire Room in New York, where I broke Frank Sinatra's attendance record; and on to the Palmer House in Chicago, where 1,100 guests were turned away from my sold-out opening show. I was thrilled. But baffled. What combination of good luck and timing had lifted me up like this? How long would it be before that upward draft subsided and let me down?

By now, I had Muriel Abbott on my side—she could read the numbers as well as anyone—but not, initially, the Chicago Empire Room's maître d' and manager, Fritz Hagner. On that sold-out opening night in Chicago, I got the call in my suite that the show was due to start; the tables were filled and the orchestra was waiting for me. So I strolled through the hotel's regal lobby and headed up the great staircase that led into the Empire Room. Hagner saw me approaching. Apparently he didn't recognize me. "Where are you going?" he demanded. I realized he had no idea who I was.

"Into the club," I said casually, indicating the velvet-framed doorway behind him.

"No, you're not," Hagner snapped.

Hagner was speaking in code, but it was clear to both of us what he meant. No blacks allowed. At least, no black paying customers. Inside, I could hear the band playing my thirty-two-bar intro. What could I do with this moment? I wondered.

Without another word, I strolled back down the stairs and sat on one of the tufted velvet sofas in the lobby. Up in the ballroom, the band played that thirty-two-bar intro again and again. Several minutes passed; then, out of the corner of my eye, I saw Muriel Abbott rush frantically past, on up the stairs. Tensely she conferred with Hagner. Where was the star act? Hagner shrugged. Then she turned and saw me down on the tufted sofa. She rushed over to me, astounded. "You're on—don't you know that?"

"Yeah, I know," I said. "But that ass won't let me in."

Muriel just wilted. Even she was mortified. She led me up the stairs herself. If looks could have killed, she would have finished off Hagner right there. Nodding coolly, I glided past him and went in to do my show. I didn't have any trouble from him again.

One night during that run, though, I did have a table of hecklers. Chicago was a big cattle town; this was a table of good ole boy cowboys in ten-gallon hats. They started by heckling the black waiters, who had to wear foppish Louis XIV–style uniforms with red jackets and white tufted shirts, pantaloons, and gold-buckled black shoes. "Hey, boy," they addressed the waiters. "More Champagne, boy." Then they started in on me. "Sing 'Melancholy Baby,'" one of them drunkenly shouted out. I looked for some posse of bouncers to come hustle this guy out, but no one materialized; at about $1,000 per table in front, you could buy yourself a lot of indulgence from the management. Instead, I caught the eye of the top waiter. He held up his hand as if to say, "I'll take care of this."

Next thing I knew, the unruly table was being served a free round of drinks. The head waiter stood beside the worst of them—the "Melancholy Baby" guy—as if awaiting his next command. In about a minute, the big cowboy slumped over, out cold. The waiters had slipped him a Mickey. With the greatest solicitude, a group of those uniformed waiters carried the drugged cowboy out of the room. For years afterward, whenever I played the Empire Room in Chicago, black waiters would sidle up to me and ask with a grin, "Remember that night with 'Melancholy Baby'?"

To my tour of top venues, I added one more that December that had special resonance for me. For the first time since I'd played Martha Raye's Five O'Clock Club, exactly five years before, I went back to Miami. Miami was still a Jim Crow town with Negro curfews, but the entertainment scene had changed considerably. Fashionable hotels had black entertainers as a matter of course, and provided sanctuaries of Jim Crow–free treatment. At the new Eden Roc, I inaugurated the Café Pompeii, and overnight put it on the club-circuit map.

I was rehearsing in the hotel's new theater—setting my lighting cues, working with the band—when a familiar figure emerged from the darkness of the outer orchestra. A cigarette holder dangled from one hand; the other held a half-empty martini glass. He might have been a cruise-ship director, with his ascot and double-breasted blazer. He was, in fact, America's best-loved comic, Jackie Gleason. The Eden Roc had promised him more than top money to be its reigning act. He would be the hotel's theatrical czar, deciding which other comics and acts would be hired, and weighing in with advice as needed. Gleason toddled up to the foot of the stage and cleared his throat. He had some advice for me: I should start out with the June Taylor Dancers, he told me, because they were his dancers and they were damned good. They would become the club's signature.

As he spoke, I looked at him as if he were a Martian. I said nothing in reply. Finally he stopped and glared. "You get it?" he said. By now it was clear to everyone onstage that the Eden Roc's theatrical czar was sozzled. That, I would learn, was his normal state. "Actually, no," I said coolly, "I don't get it. We'll do our act our way, thanks." Gleason was furious, but there wasn't anything he could do. The hotel wasn't going to fire me. For starters, I had a play-or-pay contract. And the last thing the new Eden Roc needed was a nationwide story that it had fired a top black American entertainer—at the say-so of Jackie Gleason. What I couldn't figure out about Gleason was: Where was the guy we all loved in *The Honeymooners*? Where was Ralph Kramden?

Overnight, Cafe Pompeii became a glittering new fixture on the national nightclub circuit, and I took to coming back every December for a one- or two-week engagement. I'd just checked in the following year—1956—when I got a call from a local publicist asking if I might consider singing the national anthem in a few days' time at the annual North-South All-Star football game. The game was being sponsored by the Shriners, the national fraternity of good fellows who all just happened to be white.

"The Shriners?" I echoed.

Yes, the publicist said. I'd heard that right. The Shriners would be thrilled if I agreed to sing.

Okay, I said. I'm in.

The next day, the publicist called back. He was terribly embarrassed, but there'd been a mix-up. Another singer had been asked to sing first; no one had let the publicist know. He was so sorry for the confusion.

I had a pretty good hunch that the only mix-up was one of race: The publicist had acted on his own, then proudly gone to the Shriners with his coup, only to learn that the Shriners didn't want a black man singing the national anthem at their football game. I told the publicist as much, and then I said, "Either you get that mix-up sorted out, or this story's going to find its way to the press."

Somehow, the mix-up got unmixed, and I sang at the start of the game to a packed stadium. I made sure, when I did, that I was standing beside the American flag to which everyone was paying respect. That way, when the Shriners rode by afterward, they had no choice but to salute the flag—and me.

Home in the new year of 1956 was a grim and dreary place. I'd acknowledged that the writer of those letters from Italy was still in my life, and if I didn't come right out and say that Julie had begun flying over to join me now and again on the road, Marguerite had to suspect as much, given how often I was gone. I don't think Marguerite still loved me, any more than I loved her, but she did enjoy her new social status as Mrs. Harry Belafonte. Pictures of us together accompanied profiles of me in *Look, Ebony, The Saturday Evening Post.* Even Marguerite's mother could see that this onetime no-account had made something astounding of himself. Not just a singer and actor, but a rising black star. And not just a rising black star, but one with a mission: to tear down racial barriers wherever he saw them. Marguerite admired that. She felt no more a part of my world than she had before; she rarely felt at ease with any of my friends. But she knew she was on the victory train, with money and fame coming in, and she wasn't in a rush to get off at the next station.

Day by day now, that train was picking up speed. A new and slightly alarming title was about to be coined for me: *America's Negro matinee idol.* Duke Ellington and Cab Calloway were the great jazz bandleaders; Sammy Davis, Jr., had emerged as the ultimate entertainer; and Sidney, my friendly rival, was Hollywood's first black leading man. But I stood now on a platform all my own. Nat King Cole and Billy Eckstine were matinee idols, too, both hugely popular crooners and show-biz smooth. I wasn't like that. I let my passions show. And my audiences, who were nearly all white, and mostly female, responded. In some instances with more than casual reserve.

I thought a lot about why that was, of course. I knew now, in a way I certainly hadn't as a child, or even as a teenager, that I was blessed with good looks. And for white audiences, I carried a reassuring presence, enhanced by my Caribbean diction. Black, but . . . not *too* black.

Years later, in a *New Yorker* profile of me, the professor and author Henry Louis Gates, Jr., would write, "Brown up Tab Hunter and you could hardly tell him from Harry Belafonte." Just as important, perhaps more so, I was a black entertainer who engaged the crowd without reference to color at all. In its own subliminal way, that sent a powerful message. No shucking and jiving here, no ole black Sam. Everything about the way I comported myself onstage made clear that I assumed my audiences and I were equals. So they reacted in kind. Which freed the women to regard me the way they did their white matinee idols, as a singer they could fantasize about getting to know—at least on their island vacations.

A decade or more before—certainly before the war—even northern audiences would have bridled at a black entertainer who acted like that. *Uppity* was the word that would have formed in their minds, even if they didn't quite say it. No longer. All over America, but especially in New York and California, a new generation was rising up against prejudice and segregation, and my timing, not just personally but historically, was fortuitous. Folk songs were anthems of the dispossessed, rallying cries for justice, and when white audiences listened to this black singer bring them to life, they were doing more than enjoying the tunes, or the way I sang them, or even the sex appeal I brought to the mix. If you liked Harry Belafonte, you were making a political statement, and that felt good, the way it felt good to listen to Paul Robeson, and hear what he had to say. If you were a white Belafonte fan, you felt even better. You were connecting with your better angels, reaching across the racial divide. Consciously or not, you were casting your vote for equality, and for a phrase about to hit the mainstream: *civil rights.*

9

One day in the spring of 1956, I picked up the phone to hear a courtly southern voice. "You don't know me, Mr. Belafonte, but my name is Martin Luther King, Jr."

I took a beat. "Oh, I know you," I said. "Everybody knows you."

Four months into the Montgomery, Alabama, bus boycott, King was doing better than he could have imagined—but not well enough. Back in December he had been a promising but little-known preacher at the Dexter Avenue Baptist Church, all of twenty-six, newly married with a baby, when Rosa Parks entered history by refusing to give up her bus seat to a white rider. In part because he was too new to Montgomery to have any political enemies, he'd found himself elected head of the group running the bus boycott, the Montgomery Improvement Association. Overnight, his brilliance as an orator had electrified the city and helped keep the boycott alive. Since then, his home had been bombed, he'd been arrested—twice—and he'd become a national figure. Meanwhile, the boycott wore on. It wouldn't end until December, after the U.S. Supreme Court affirmed that segregation on Montgomery's buses was unconstitutional. King needed to keep the boycotters' spirits up, and he needed money. For that, he was coming up to New York on a fundraising swing. Would I meet him, he asked, at the Abyssinian Baptist Church in Harlem, after he spoke to a gathering of fellow clergy he was hoping to recruit for his mission?

I came, but not without misgivings. The leading Negro ministers I'd known had abandoned Du Bois and Robeson in their hours of need.

Certainly I knew that whatever King wanted from me would probably involve writing a check. Still, I was most curious to meet this new prophet. No one else quite like him had appeared in my lifetime, with the exception of Gandhi. Would he live up to the hype? He did. His sermon from the pulpit of that Harlem church rocked me. This King, whoever he was, was most impressive. He might be young—two years younger than I was—but he was fully loaded and ready. At no time in his sermon did he attack the congregation or the church. Yet he made very clear that his northern brethren were failing to do their part. What does the scripture tell us to do, he asked, when we're denied justice? And, given what it tells us, he said, what do we do when a preacher in my position is accused of being a provocateur rather than a defender of the righteous word? *You do more than you're doing right now* was the unmistakable message.

When I met him afterward in a reception room, I was struck by his sense of calm. He stood surrounded by at least two hundred well-wishers, yet he seemed unaffected by the crowd, at peace with himself, as if he were standing alone. Finally he broke through the greeters and came over to me. He was shorter and stockier than I'd expected. I felt an unmistakable edge of excitement meeting him. "I'm so delighted you were able to find the time to meet," he said, looking up at me. "I can't tell you what it will mean to me and the movement if I can even just make you aware of what we're trying to do."

King motioned me to follow him downstairs. The church basement was used as a Sunday-school classroom; it had a blackboard and folding table and a dozen or so straight-backed wooden chairs. We pulled chairs up to the table, and a photographer took a few pictures. Then King gently ushered the photographer out and closed the door behind him, and it was just the two of us.

We got right into a very easy place. I made him feel comfortable; he certainly fascinated me. Above all I was taken by his humility. It wasn't false humility; I knew the difference. Nor was it humility in the service of charm. This man was both determined to do what he saw as his mission—and truly overwhelmed by it. "I need your help," he told me more than once. "I have no idea where this movement is going."

I asked King why he'd gotten involved in the first place. In his soft, fervent voice, he began to talk about the poor, and his deep commitment to alleviating their plight. But he didn't just talk—he listened, too. Our conversation was so intense—so very intense—that I had no idea, when we stood up, that three hours had passed. All I knew was that here was the real deal, a leader both inspired and daunted by the burden he'd taken on. "I'm called upon to do things I cannot do," he said, "and yet I cannot dismiss the calling. So how do I do this?"

I said I'd help him any way I could. And for the next twelve years, that's what I did. I started by making my own contributions to the Montgomery Improvement Association—sums that paid for gas for the cars that took bus-boycotters to work every day, and food for those who'd lost their jobs. I wasn't the only one writing significant checks, but I was a member of a fairly select club. At the same time, I started organizing house parties to raise sums from larger groups. Would the boycott have endured without that money? I can't answer that. But I'm proud of the fact that I definitely played a part in keeping it going. And not long after the boycott, I produced a fundraising concert at Madison Square Garden to keep the Montgomery Improvement Association afloat. I sang, and so did my Vegas compatriot Frank Sinatra.

I gave a lot, but I got a lot back. I'd worked hard for various causes, but in a scattershot way. Everything Martin did, I saw, served a higher purpose: to bring change by nonviolence, using the methods espoused by Mahatma Gandhi. That fascinated me. I felt him pulling me up to that higher plane of social protest. I wasn't nonviolent by nature—or if I was, growing up on Harlem's streets had knocked it out of me—so for some time, I would view nonviolence more as a shrewd organizing tactic than anything else. As I got to know Martin better, and saw nonviolence put to the test, I would come to appreciate its spiritual and emotional value. I'd find I wanted to live by those values myself, both to help the movement and to wash away my personal anger. For Martin, the tenets of nonviolence aligned with his deep religious faith—and that I would struggle with, for, unlike Martin, I questioned the honesty of the church and the existence of God. We'd talk a lot about that. But for now, a whole new chapter of social protest was opening for me, and I had Martin to thank for that.

By the time I met Martin, my career was hitting a new high; my second album, simply called *Belafonte,* was rocketing up the charts. *Mark Twain* had done fine, but by May 5, 1956, *Belafonte* reached *Billboard's* number two spot, and stayed near the top for months to come. I'd started to think that my stage act would never translate into major record sales. Happily, I was wrong.

Belafonte was a mixed bag. It had folk songs ("Scarlet Ribbons,"

"In That Great Gettin' Up Mornin'"), spirituals ("Take My Mother Home" and "Noah"), and a calypso ("Matilda," released earlier as a single), all from *3 for Tonight*. One reason the album worked as a whole was that Tony Scott, my old friend and brilliant clarinetist, sat in as musical director. But also, everything I'd done to date had come together behind that album: the Broadway revues, the top clubs around the country, the two movies—I was perceived as a triple threat. At that moment in the mid-twentieth century, with the civil rights movement just beginning and the word *Negro* not yet questioned by whites *or* blacks, being given the title of Negro matinee idol filled me with pride, even if it had started, as all such titles do, at the typewriter of some unnoticed newspaper writer in a column long forgotten. Simply put, it was my time, though I couldn't help but notice it was someone else's, too.

Just as *Belafonte* hit record stores, so did the debut album by some kid from Memphis named Elvis Presley. His first single, "Heartbreak Hotel," had already topped the charts. On that same May 5 *Billboard* album chart, his was number one to my number two. Different as our sounds were, I could see that in one way, at least, we were on parallel tracks. Elvis was interpreting one kind of black music—rhythm and blues—while I found my inspiration in black folk songs, spirituals, and calypso, and also in African music, which would one day be put under the heading of world music.

I hadn't met Elvis yet, but we'd had a bit of a run-in at the new RCA studios in midtown Manhattan. We were recording our albums down the hall from each other, and my sound engineer kept looking up in puzzlement. Though the studios were state of the art, he kept picking up a "leak": strange background noise leaking into the supposedly soundproof room. On investigation, he learned that Presley and his band were the culprits, playing louder than the studio designers had ever imagined anyone would play. I went right to the top of the food chain to complain—to George Marek, RCA's CEO. I told him these upstarts would just have to reschedule. Marek gently passed on this sentiment. Back came the word from Presley's famous manager, "Colonel" Tom Parker: Either I could become his new client or he would destroy me. There was also a nicely wrapped box of chocolates with a note that said "From your friend the Colonel." Somehow, Marek managed to smooth all the ruffled egos, and both albums got done.

For *Belafonte*'s success, and everything else I was doing, my new manager and surrogate dad, Jay Richard Kennedy, took his share of credit, and then some. Almost every day in the columns, as the album soared, I would read about new projects I was considering in partnership with him. A movie about witchcraft in Jamaica, co-starring Lena Horne, with screenplay to be written by Jay Richard Kennedy. Another about an alligator hunter in Florida who turns out to have singing talent, original story by Jay Richard Kennedy. Yet another about a young Negro clerk working for the British government, producer, Jay Richard Kennedy. All these were to follow my latest musical revue, *Sing, Man, Sing,* for which Jay Richard Kennedy had written most of the songs and served as producer.

In fairness, Kennedy wasn't entirely to blame for what became my one indisputable career bomb. I'd been fascinated by a vast photography exhibit at the Museum of Modern Art the previous year called *The Family of Man.* Photographer Edward Steichen had curated it, bringing together some five hundred pictures from around the world that dramatized the human experience, from birth and love and parenthood to poverty, war, and death. Why not try to capture that sense of human universality, I thought, in a musical revue? That was the genesis of *Sing, Man, Sing.*

My idea was to write a series of songs and interweave them with existing songs that addressed, in one way or another, man's evolution. I wanted it to be poignant *and* funny, with humorous songs drawn from prehistoric times, the Bible, Columbus sailing the mighty sea, on up to the present day. Initially I thought of enlisting Lord Burgess, the Caribbean-influenced songwriter with whom I'd just collaborated on my next, as-yet-unreleased album, *Calypso.* But somehow Jay Richard Kennedy elbowed Lord Burgess aside. I was fine with Kennedy writing scenes and songs, but when he started to oversee the dancers—including a young Alvin Ailey—I started to get nervous. And then the lighting, and the costumes, and the directing . . .

We started out on the road; initially, the reactions to *Jay Richard Kennedy Presents "Sing, Man, Sing"* were fairly positive. Not glowing, though. Definitely not glowing. By the time we reached Constitution Hall in Washington, D.C., my laryngitis was back. I could never prove that it kicked in when I got really nervous, but I sure felt like it did. The night before our New York premiere at the Brooklyn Academy of Music, I could barely speak above a whisper. When I told Jay we'd need to go with my understudy, his face turned red, and he started shouting in a strange, high-pitched voice. All these famous, influential people—his friends—were coming. How could I let them all down?

I told him I felt terrible about that. If he could find me some doctor who might help—anyone except Dr. Jacobson, with his toxic cocktails— I'd give him a try. He had Janet call around, and soon reported that she had found just the man, a specialist at Montefiore Hospital. The doctor looked at my vocal cords and grimaced. I had nodules, he said, that needed to be removed, an operation that would involve weeks of recovery.

"Come on, doc," Kennedy said. "There must be something you can do to get him onstage tomorrow night."

The doctor nodded. "There is—but it's very risky."

"Just do it!" Kennedy said.

The night of the opening, the doctor came to BAM and sprayed my vocal cords with ether. At intermission, he did it again. The ether was a quick fix that brought down the swelling, allowing me to sing. It did nothing to reduce the nodules that had caused the swelling in the first place. By singing, I was actually aggravating them. In other words, I was further damaging my vocal cords for Jay Richard Kennedy and his fancy friends. And once again, as in *Almanac*, I wasn't miked. BAM is a big place; to be heard over the orchestra, I had to push my voice as far as it would go.

All for nothing, as it turned out. For the first time in my career, the critics were unanimous in their lack of excitement. They threw a few respectful adjectives my way, but they hated *Sing, Man, Sing*. Kennedy's hope had been to go from BAM to Broadway, but after a few performances, I shut down the show, unleashing a wrath from Kennedy that not only startled me but forced me to review, with real concern, exactly where my life was going—starting with whether to keep Kennedy as my manager. With my laryngitis now much worse, I had to cancel my return engagement at the Waldorf, and instead, in the first week of June 1956, go back to Montefiore Hospital, this time for an operation to remove the nodules. As I lay recovering in a hospital bed, I knew my faith in Kennedy had been shaken. But how could I fire my surrogate father—and, if I did that, my surrogate mother, too?

I made a quick recovery—so quick that I was able to keep a June 28 concert date at Lewisohn Stadium, Harlem's huge colonnaded amphitheater, where everyone from Jack Benny to Woody Guthrie to Ella Fitzgerald had performed. The stadium—sadly gone now—was on a hill, surrounded by high-rise apartments, and when I looked out over the sellout crowd, I saw thousands more listening from their apartment windows, and every rooftop lined with people. Lewisohn had twenty-seven thousand seats, but when the standing-room-only tickets were added to the total, I broke the stadium's thirty-nine-year attendance record that night. It was the largest audience I'd ever played to, and with my voice back in form, I sang my heart out for that amazing crowd, relieved that for now I was back at the top of my game.

Following the pattern set by the previous year, I went on to perform at the Greek Theatre in L.A. in early July, the Riviera in Vegas, the Palmer House in Chicago, then back to New York at the Waldorf in September. My show, with nearly all new numbers, was called *A Night with Belafonte*. Two or three weeks at each venue, sellout crowds every night—even now, I remember just how exhilarating it was to get that acclaim night after night, to stand on those stages doing exactly what I wanted to do, two hours a show, then to walk off light-headed, the applause still ringing in my ears, so drenched in sweat that I'd have lost at least two or three pounds and be ravenously hungry. Usually now, Julie would be waiting backstage for me, and we'd go for a late dinner, staying up until my adrenaline dissipated. Over vodka on the rocks, our usual libation, we'd titillate each other with talk of marriage; the next day, Marguerite and I would discuss, in awkward, long-distance phone calls, the sorry, mundane details of divorce.

I was rarely home now. My tours were profitable—enormously so—but Marguerite knew I took as many bookings as I did to stay on the road as long as possible. The price I paid was not seeing my daughters. When Adrienne and Shari took the phone in those long-distance calls, I tried my best to sound upbeat, not to let my guilt and sorrow show until I'd said good night. When I did get home, I showered them with gifts and took them everywhere—Broadway musicals, fancy restaurants—knowing that this probably only further confused them. But I couldn't stop myself. If I loved them enough in these brief interludes, I felt, perhaps it would all balance out. Marguerite looked on with pursed lips, knowing on two levels how inadequate my efforts were—both as a mother and as a child psychologist. In the master bedroom of our East Elmhurst house, we stayed on our respective sides of the bed, talking quietly about the children until we fell asleep. Though it made me feel even guiltier, I couldn't wait to get back on the road again.

With all these concert dates, and all that applause, I felt sure I'd peaked. But then my third album, *Calypso*, became a phenomenon, an album, truly, for the history books: the first ever to sell a million copies.

Age five, with my mother and brother Dennis, 1932

First Holy Communion, 1934

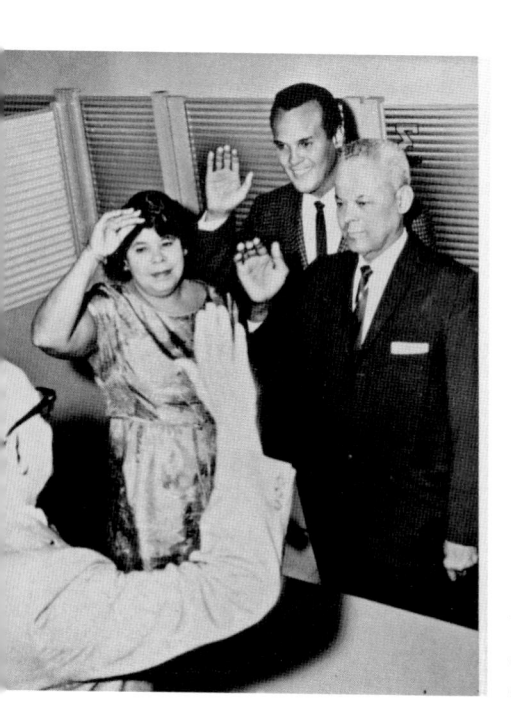

With my father, who is being sworn in as an American citizen

With my son, David,
eighteen months

The four children

With my grandmother on
her one hundredth birthda

PAUL ROBESON

CONCERTS
— OF —
Negro Music

To Harry
With warmest greetings
and sincere admiration

PAUL ROBESON
— AND —
LAWRENCE BROWN

Paul Robeson
Feb. 28
1973

Comedy Theatre
SUNDAY EVENINGS
November 14, 28
— AND —
December 5, 1926

LAWRENCE BROWN

Program

SUNDAY EVENING, NOVEMBER 14th

1. NEGRO SPIRITUALS:
   - Go Down Moses — arranged by H. T. Burleigh
   - On Ma Journey — arranged by Edward Boatner
   - Hear de Lambs a'Cryin' / Gimme Your Hand — arranged by Lawrence Brown
2. NEGRO FOLK SONGS:
   - Water Boy — arranged by Avery Robinson
   - Dere's No Hidin' Place / Sometimes I Feel Like a Motherless Chile / Little David — arranged by Lawrence Brown
3. NEGRO SPIRITUALS:
   - Lonesome Valley / Bye and Bye — arranged by H. T. Burleigh
   - Wade in de Water — arranged by Edward Boatner
   - Ezekial Saw de Wheel — arranged by Lawrence Brown
4. NEGRO SPIRITUALS:
   - Were You There? / I Want to Be Ready — arranged by H. T. Burleigh
   - Steal Away / Witness (minor version) — arranged by Lawrence Brown

VICTOR RECORDS — MASON & HAMLIN PIANO

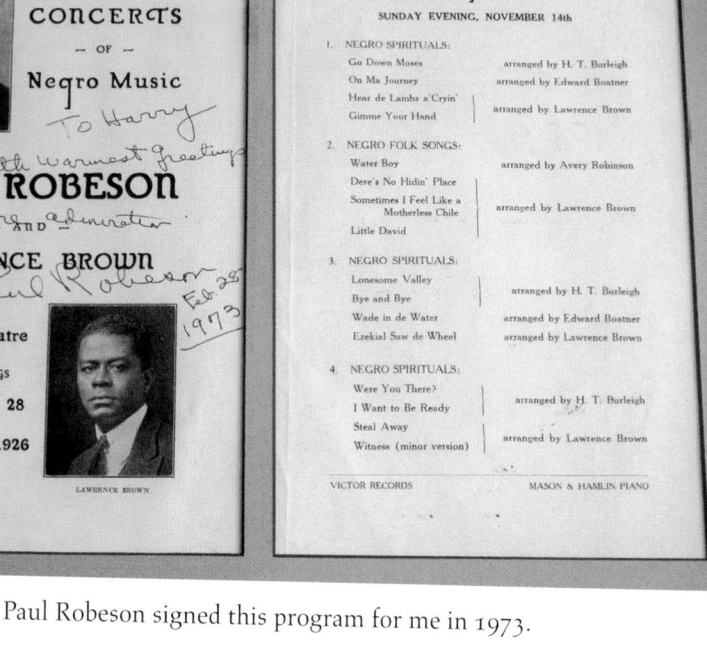

Paul Robeson signed this program for me in 1973.

An early stage performance of *The Petrified Forest,* with the Dramatic Workshop in 1944

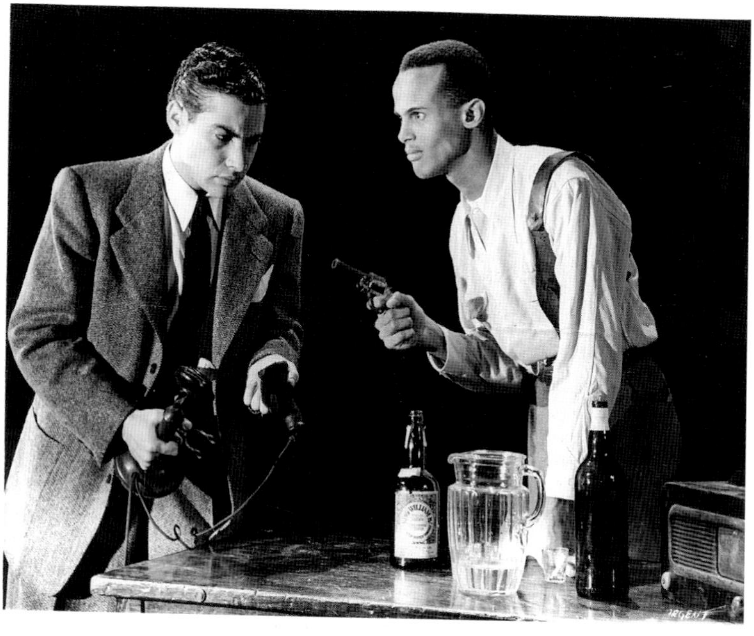

My first recording, "Lean on Me," and my first guitarist, Craig Work

With Joe Williams, Langston Hughes, and Duke Ellington on the television spec
The Strollin' Twenties

Onstage

Signing autographs for my fans

DAY O • WILL HIS LOVE BE LIKE HIS RUM?
JAMAICA FAREWELL • DOLLY DAWN

EPA-768

RCA VICTOR
A "NEW ORTHOPHONIC" HIGH FIDELITY RECORDING

HARRY BELAFONTE   CALYPSO

LIVING STEREO

RECORDED ON
RCA VICTOR
LSO-6006

BELAFONTE
AT CARNEGIE HALL
THE COMPLETE CONCERT

"MIRACLE
SURFACE"

RCA ITALIANA
45 N 0605

Cocoanut Woman

Island In The Sun

BELAFONTE

on

RCA VICTOR

LPM-3778

RCA
VICTOR

BELAFONTE

EPA 1-1505

HAITI CHERIE • LOVE, LOVE ALONE
LUCY'S DOOR • SCRATCH, SCRATCH

RCA VICTOR

BELAFONTE
SINGS OF THE
CARIBBEAN

With Joan Fontaine
in *Island in the Sun*

enes from *The World,*
e Flesh and the Devil;
lds Against Tomorrow;
d The Angel Levine

"The World, The Flesh and The Devil" 1957

"Odds Against Tomorrow" 1959

"The Angel Levine" 1969

A poster for *The World, the Flesh and the Devil*

WHICH ONE GETS
THE LAST GIRL ON
EARTH?

There are no laws...no rules. It's man-to-man with the last girl on earth at stake. A unique, spectacular drama packed with more surprises, more amazing sights than you've ever seen.

M-G-M Presents A SOL C. SIEGEL Production Starring
HARRY BELAFONTE / INGER STEVENS / MEL FERRER
THE WORLD THE FLESH AND THE DEVIL

With Sidney Poitier shooting *Buck and the Preacher*

In *Uptown Saturday Night*

With John Travolta in *White Man's Burden*

With Robert Altman

With Muhammad Ali

With Lena Horne

On the set of *Sesame Street*

Back when I'd begun to conceive my next album, no one at RCA Victor, starting with my producer, Henri René, had wanted to devote a whole album to Caribbean island songs. I did. RCA's executives worried that this kind of album would be too ethnic, too black, too out of the mainstream. I myself didn't want to be typecast as a calypso singer. I recognized that calypso was only one Caribbean style among many, and I told René that only a few of the album's songs would be actual calypso. Others would be, more broadly, mento music, from the hills of Jamaica, where men carved holes in wooden boxes and attached three or four pieces of flexible metal to them, each piece making its own note when played. Still others would be more akin to folk songs. The RCA executives were still wary, but by the time they were ready to release the album seven or eight months later, they sensed the coming trend. They had gone so far as to insist that it be called *Calypso*, over my objections. I didn't object for very long.

On my first two albums, I'd modified and updated existing folk songs. On *Calypso*, I went further. Bill Attaway, my good friend, former Sage partner, and resident musicologist, became one of my two co-writers for the album. He, in turn, told me about Lord Burgess. "You've got to meet this guy," Bill told me. "He's the black Alan Lomax—a walking library of songs from the islands."

Calypso had more than its share of newly minted royalty: kings and queens, dukes and duchesses, not to mention lords. Nearly all those titles were conferred by popular acclaim at an annual calypso contest in Trinidad. Lord Burgess was an exception: Irving Louis Burgie, born in Brooklyn to a half–West Indian family, had anointed himself. He might not have found many loyal subjects in Trinidad, but up north, no one questioned his title. It said a lot about him; he knew the culture but took a lot of liberties with it. He'd compiled all the Caribbean songs he could find—from all the islands—and had often modified the lyrics or written a new musical bridge so he could copyright them as his own. I was taking liberties with the songs myself, putting little spins on them that made them work better for my vocal range and stage act. Neither Burgess nor I was doing anything illegal in this, because the songs weren't copyrighted. Later, when my co-authors and I were forced to contest various lawsuits, we won them all. It was our interpretation of those songs that gave them value and helped make calypso internationally known, our lawyers successfully argued. Still, I would come to feel guilty about that. If there was no author of record to credit or pay, we might still have passed along a slice of our profits—somehow—to the islands whose cultures had generated those songs. The truth was, we never did. My only excuse is that no one else did, either, until Pete Seeger started the practice. I've since tried to follow his worthy example.

Soon the three of us—Attaway, Burgess, and I—were working intensely together and having a lot of fun. One of the first songs we worked up for the *Calypso* album was "Jamaica Farewell," a Lord Burgess retread of a traditional island song called "Ironbar." It would become one of my best-known, most-loved songs. Another island favorite we picked up on was "Hill and Gully Rider," better known as the "Banana Boat Song."

I'd started my next run at the Waldorf's Empire Room, and the hotel now gave me a suite whenever I played there, so it was there that Lord Burgess and Bill Attaway started bouncing new lyric ideas off each other for this old favorite. The story line in all versions was the same: After a night spent loading bananas onto boats for export, the tired farmers singing the song saw daylight breaking and wanted to go home. The "Banana Boat Song" was how islanders knew it. One version recorded not long before had been called "Day De Light," another went by "Day Dah Light." The island slang "Day-o" appeared in the lyrics of one version or another, but it was buried—a throwaway line. I came up with the idea of starting our version with a dramatic a cappella "*Day-o*" that resonated. Like the opening lyric of "Jerry," it grabbed the listener and didn't let him go.

We called our version "Day-O," and made it the album's opening track, but none of us had any idea, when we recorded it, that it would be spun off as a single, much less rocket up the charts. The fact was that after I had pushed RCA into using only Caribbean songs, we found ourselves one or two songs short, so we threw in "Day-O" as filler. Still needing a track after that, we did a retread of it as "Star-O." We felt sure that our single, if we had one, would be "Matilda" or "Jamaica Farewell."

As the album started coming together, I made a first move toward taking control of my own material. Pete Kameron, the former Weavers manager who'd given me such life-changing advice after that first Vegas show at the Thunderbird, put the idea in my head. As long as I was writing, or rewriting, these songs, Pete suggested, why not publish them?

Publishing fees, Pete explained, could be the quiet big money on a solid, long-standing hit song, and there was no reason some stodgy publishing company had to get that money just for doing the paperwork. I could do it myself. So I did. It was less about money than control, because in fact I signed away 100 percent of any publishing revenues on *Calypso* to Attaway and Burgess. All I wanted was to share title credit with them, I said, to show I'd helped create the songs. My expectation was that I'd get royalties when the album sold, perhaps not insignificant sums. I'd also be getting paid by clubs around the country to perform these songs, perhaps for many years to come. So giving them the publishing fees just gave them their own skin in the game. I was happy to share the wealth, if it came. I was even happier to set up what certainly had to be one of the first—if not *the* first— all-black music-publishing companies.

This *business* thing—I liked it! I liked being responsible for rising or falling by my own decisions. I also liked working with black professionals who understood where I came from and what I was trying to do. When I'd started out, there were no black agents or managers, no major black club owners. There were still hardly any, and certainly none in the movie business. No black movie executives, no black entertainment lawyers, no black screenwriters. The whole entertainment hierarchy was predominantly Jewish. I'd been represented by a lot of smart people— I had more Jews in my life than some Jews—but none truly understood the black experience. So now I created Belafonte Enterprises, Inc., and rented office space at 157 West Fifty-seventh Street, right across from Carnegie Hall. The music-publishing company became one subsidiary of BEI. For film projects, I formed HarBel Productions, both to scout for good scripts and to pitch them to the studios, not just as some supplicant on bended knee, but as a business—a black business—coming at them on their own level. Another arm of the company handled my concert tours. Yet another backed Broadway plays, among them, thanks to producer Phil Rose, Lorraine Hansberry's great *A Raisin in the Sun*.

All this black corporatizing stirred mixed reactions in the entertainment world. I was described as arrogant; often when I left a meeting, some friend who remained would tell me that as soon as the door closed, a white executive would mutter, "Who does that nigger think he is?" Even among whites in the industry who never used the N-word, the whole concept of BEI rankled. Black people weren't supposed to make contract demands. They were supposed to be grateful for what they got. But even among the naysayers, BEI commanded respect—and for me, respect was what it was all about. It *was* the moral mission.

RCA Victor planned to release *Calypso* toward the end of 1956, after *Belafonte* had had its run. But old conventions were falling away; Elvis Presley's debut was doing so well that RCA had decided to bring out his second album sooner rather than later. So why not do the same with me?

I left the timing to RCA. But not the cover. The first mock-ups I saw had me with a big bunch of bananas superimposed on my head. I looked like Carmen Miranda in drag, only in bare feet, with a big toothy grin, as if I were saying, "Come to dee islands!" I nixed that one, and two or three others that similarly engaged in racial stereotyping. The one I approved had no props at all: just me in a green shirt on a red backdrop. RCA's marketers were chagrined. But not for long.

By July 14, 1956, *Calypso* had risen to number three on the *Billboard* album chart, just behind Elvis. On September 8, it hit the number one spot—and kept hitting it, off and on, for thirty-one weeks. No album had done that before.

But there was more: *Calypso* stayed on the *Billboard* chart, usually in one of the upper slots and then fading ever so slowly, for ninety-nine weeks. Not until Michael Jackson's *Thriller* would an album stay longer on the charts. I could hardly begrudge him. Not only was Michael supremely talented, he had a good and generous heart. When I asked him, not long after *Thriller,* to help in an effort I had in mind for African famine victims, he did a lot more than lend his name and write a check. He co-authored "We Are the World."

All through the last half of 1956, Elvis and I traded top places with each other on that *Billboard* chart. I'd been around a bit longer, but Elvis was now huge, after his scandalous, hip-gyrating television appearances, and so not surprisingly, his follow-up album, *Elvis,* knocked *Calypso* out of the top spot by early December.

Here, though, is the historical fact: At the end of that landmark year, generally conceded to be the birth year of rock 'n' roll, the best-selling album wasn't *Elvis Presley* or *Elvis.* It was *Calypso.* Critics took bets on which kind of music would prevail, rock 'n' roll or calypso. Even well into 1957, many critics predicted calypso would win. John S. Wilson, reviewing my next album in mid-1957 in *The New York Times*, would declare, "Reports from the epidemic areas of popular music suggest that Elvis Presley and rock 'n' roll are giving way before the onslaughts of Harry Belafonte and Calypso."

By the end of that next year, of course, the raw power of Presley's rhythm-and-blues rock 'n' roll would dominate the charts, and calypso as a trend would peter out. Fortunately, I'd kept my repertoire varied, and so managed not to peter out with it. In my act, I never performed more than a handful of calypso songs, even when the trend was at its peak, and my follow-up album, *An Evening with Belafonte*, had folk songs from around the world—from "Hava Nageela" to "Danny Boy." I was deeply aware of the consequences of being pigeonholed.

Calypso's success startled the industry and set a trend. A very talented folk trio, the Tarriers, had a hit with their own version of the "Banana Boat Song." One of the Tarriers would soon be better known as an actor: Alan Arkin.

Much as I loved having *Calypso* make history and sell a million copies, I was also thrilled that by the summer of 1956 it had pulled up the earlier *Belafonte*, because with two such different albums at the top of the charts, I couldn't be seen as *just* a calypso singer. A couple of times, with *Calypso* at the top of the charts, I put on classic calypso clothes for *The Ed Sullivan Show* or *The Colgate Comedy Hour* and sang "Day-O" against an elaborate banana-boat backdrop. But then I put an end to that, and for the longest time afterward, I never sang the "Banana Boat Song" publicly. I didn't want to be put in a box and categorized. Somehow I'd known, from that first audition in the Royal Roost, that I would command respect or not perform at all. Not just as an entertainer, but as a black entertainer. Race was the cutting edge in everything I did. To let myself be turned into an object of ridicule would undermine not just my stage persona, but my purpose as well.

All through this time, I kept going to Janet Kennedy for psychotherapy. Of course I said nothing to her of my new misgivings about her husband as my manager, so the therapeutic process, if it had had any value before, had a lot less now. What was the point of having a therapist if you couldn't share your greatest concern with her? But one day I realized I was dealing with a far larger issue.

Janet, I'd noticed, always encouraged me in our sessions to share the details of my political life with her. She was fascinated by Paul Robeson; she wanted to know what I talked about with him. Instinctively, I avoided sharing details of his private thoughts about his personal life. And about Stalin and communism—he'd begun to have his doubts, especially as Russian artists that he'd met began to disappear, but the last thing he wanted was to give J. Edgar Hoover and the rest of his U.S. persecutors any reason to crow. Whatever insignificant news I did pass along, though, Janet seized on. What was that about? I wondered.

Then, with Jay, I mentioned that some black friends had come to me with a real estate investment scheme in Harlem, and it looked pretty good. I asked Jay for a check, and he balked. "It sounds like a bad idea," he said. It might be, I said, stiffening, but these were friends and I wanted to take that chance with them. Once again, Jay's face turned red, and his voice rose to that high-pitched squeak. My timing was bad, he said. He'd invested most of my portfolio into soybean commodities, and to undo that package right now would be costly.

Who *were* these Kennedys? And what was their real agenda with me? Had they come at me from any different angle, I would have asked myself that question long before. In my personal life, I was a tough judge of character; as a performer, I'd learned to be a tough negotiator. But they'd sensed the soft core that lay within. At first I'd fought to keep them from it. But the whole point of analysis was to open up. With Janet's gentle prodding, I'd come to believe that I *had* to let them in, or spend the rest of my life haunted by my demons. And it had worked! As soon as I'd put down the armor and let them in, I'd felt so much better. For the first time I could express my real feelings. Even with the women in my life I hadn't done that. Especially with the women. But what if the same two people who'd made it their mission to win my trust had an ulterior motive? I didn't know what to believe. All I knew was that I needed help.

Through a friend, I contacted a lawyer named Charlie Katz, a very shrewd, tough, left-wing guy who worked for the longshoremen's union. Katz had contacts in some of the same political groups that Jay Richard Kennedy had professed to be part of in the 1940s. Katz said he'd start investigating. Meanwhile, I should just avoid rousing any suspicions.

For the next few months, I kept up my regular schedule of sessions with Janet. Her curiosity in Robeson was unmistakable now, but rather than take note of it, I would just nudge the conversation down another track. And with Jay, I stopped pushing the Harlem investment idea.

Then, at last, I heard back from Charlie Katz. "I have to see you," he said.

"Let me take a look at my calendar," I said.

"No calendar," Katz said. "I'm flying in today. You meet me at the airport. We'll talk in the car."

Charlie's story was, quite simply, mind-boggling. The name Jay Richard Kennedy, he explained, was fake. I was dealing with one Samuel Richard Solomonick, former treasurer for the American Communist party's Chicago operation. At some point, Katz relayed, Solomonick had absconded with a lot of the party's money, gone south of the border, invested it, and gotten entangled in some financial fraud. When the FBI had caught up with him on the fraud charge and learned of his past with the Communist party, they'd given him a choice: go to jail or become a spy for the agency.

He'd chosen the latter.

The FBI had then given Solomonick a complete makeover, according to Katz's sources. Plastic surgery, a new identity, and a new past. He was now Jay Richard Kennedy, an Irish-born laborer who'd come to the Midwest, survived the Dust Bowl, and worked a string of different jobs. What about his Hollywood novel, *Prince Bart*? I asked Katz. Was that a fake, too?

No, Katz said. The man we now knew as Kennedy really had written that book. He wasn't without talent, and like all good con men, his lies were wrapped around a kernel of truth. But at the same time, he was working for the FBI to establish contacts with various high-profile, left-leaning artists, actors, writers, directors, and entertainers, win their confidence as a sympathetic friend, and try to substantiate ties with any hard-core communists they knew.

I was all for exposing the little creep—calling the press that day. Katz shook his head. Kennedy, he pointed out, had all my money under his control, with power of attorney. If I went public, he could make life difficult for me. He might also sue, claiming I'd libeled him. Even if I won in the long run, I'd be in for a messy fight. "Let's do this my way," Katz said.

Katz called Kennedy's office to make an appointment. He was now representing me, he said, and he had matters to discuss. Kennedy kept him waiting an hour in his outer office, then greeted him with a curt "So you're here to talk about that bum?"

"Yes, Mr. Solomonick," Katz said most pointedly, "that's exactly what I'm here to talk about."

The instant that Katz uttered the name Solomonick, Kennedy fell back in his chair, his face red, gagging in what almost appeared to be an epileptic fit. In raced his secretary. "What have you done to him?" she demanded of Katz. Kennedy waved her back out and had her close the door behind her.

Grimly, Katz ticked off his terms. He wanted Solomonick to surrender his power of attorney, hand over all my money, and sign papers promising never to bring any legal claim against me. In return, we would sign a nondisclosure agreement, which he would sign as well, stipulating that neither side would divulge any details of the situation or go after each other in any way.

And that's what we did. To my surprise and relief, Solomonick hadn't stolen my money or invested it badly. It really was in soybeans, and soybeans, as it turned out, were a good investment that year, so I got all my money back and then some. I did lose all the new Hollywood friends I'd made through Jay Richard Kennedy. Richard and Ruth Conte were furious when they heard that I'd abruptly dropped Kennedy as my manager. They saw it as a betrayal on my part, as did Gene Kelly, Anthony Mann, Robert Ryan, and the rest of Kennedy's circle. By the terms of our agreement, I could say nothing to disabuse them of that notion, nor warn them that Kennedy was their enemy, not their friend.

What lay behind this strange skulduggery? Without question the FBI was using Solomonick to dig for incriminating information about me, Paul Robeson, and other outspoken progressives. In retrospect, the whole exercise seems nutty and ridiculous, but in those early, crazy Cold War years, it was pursued in deadly earnest. I could have told those faceless FBI agents behind the scheme, if they'd asked me directly, that I was loyal to America and our Constitution, certainly more than any of them were. I no more advocated the downfall of the United States government than they did. When I spoke out on political issues, it was with the full understanding and appreciation that I lived in a democracy where I *could* express those views. But they had chosen to waste a lot of time and taxpayer money trying to prove otherwise.

· · ·

Unburdened of a manager and a therapist, not to mention two surrogate parents, I managed to land my next big Hollywood role on my own, just by answering the phone.

Darryl Zanuck, the imperious head of Twentieth Century–Fox, didn't ask me if I wanted to star in his next film, *Island in the Sun*. In typical Zanuck fashion, he just told me I was doing it. "You're more than perfect for it," he told me. "Quite frankly, there's no one else I can even think of casting for the role. If you don't sign on, I won't make the film. God knows I've got enough people telling me not to do it." Assuming I did sign on, I would be matched up for the third time with Dorothy Dandridge, but she wouldn't be my love interest. That would be the very beautiful Joan Fontaine.

Alec Waugh, the older brother of novelist Evelyn Waugh, had reached the best-seller list the year before with his steamy tale of passion and politics set in the West Indies. With the success of my album *Calypso* coming right after it, the Caribbean was suddenly hot. And Zanuck was right: who better to play the movie role of a people's leader on the fictional island of Santa Marta, giving fiery political speeches in one scene and singing calypso songs in the next?

Everything about *Island in the Sun* made it seem a story Waugh had written with me in mind—though he hadn't. For me, Santa Marta was just Jamaica with the name changed. David Boyeur, the black political activist I was to play, seemed a mirror image of myself. Maxwell Fleury, the well-bred Englishman running against me for political office under the island's new constitution, was like all the English transplants I'd seen at the Pigous' dinner table in Kingston. (And so was James Mason, who played him flawlessly.) I liked the prospect of breaking another color barrier, a very important one at that. I would be the first American Negro to play a romantic lead in a feature film opposite a white leading actress.

Everything seemed perfect, until Zanuck, having rounded out his cast, declared he was hiring Robert Rossen to direct. To me, and to almost everyone I knew, Rossen was the worst choice. He'd grown up as Robert Rosen on the Lower East Side, absorbing his Russian-Jewish parents' left-wing politics, then joined the American Communist party in 1937 and remained a member for ten years. That wasn't what I had against him—not at all. What infuriated me was that after taking the Fifth before the House Un-American Activities Committee in 1951 and being blacklisted for two years, Rossen had reversed himself, gone back to HUAC, and offered up fifty-seven names of "communist" colleagues. Many of those he named spent the next few years in jail or scraping for work, while Rossen resumed his career with *Mambo* in 1954 and *Alexander the Great* in 1956. I didn't want to contribute to his ongoing rehabilitation, but I had no choice; I'd signed my contract. If I backed out, the studio would have every right to sue, and would. I had misgivings about that, but I had to pick my battles. I hadn't become an actor to speak for the souls of other men. I was in the real world, fighting for work as a black actor when there was almost no work to be had. Let Rossen fight his own demons. I had a movie to make.

The filming—most of it, at any rate—was to take place in Grenada. Shrewdly, Zanuck decided to make a press junket of it, sending a plane full of European and American journalists along with the cast and crew to soak up the Caribbean sun and presumably write long datelined reports. When we landed first at Port of Spain in Trinidad, we held a press conference, both for our junketeers and for Caribbean journalists. The questions were all softballs, until a Trinidadian journalist raised her hand.

"I have a question for Mr. Belafonte," she said. "I'd like to ask you, sir—have you any conscience? That you would take the songs of the people of this region, cheapening them, changing them, and singing them in a way no one ever heard of, and then have the audacity to steal the title 'King of Calypso' with no regard for the culture of the Caribbean?"

The room got very quiet, all eyes on me.

"First of all," I said, "let me say that I have never personally laid claim to be 'King of Calypso.' That was the decision of those I work for." That was true; to my great embarrassment, and over my objections, RCA Victor had promoted me that way. I knew just how presumptuous that would make me look in the islands, especially in Trinidad, where the annual calypso festival produced a new "King of Calypso" by popular acclaim.

"But even if I could be the true King of Calypso, I wouldn't want to be," I went on. "Because although I admire how clever and how interesting calypsonians can be in the songs they write and sing, I also find that most of those lyrics are not in the best interests of black people, because their songs are always filled with the need to make Europeans laugh at us. They glorify and dig deep into promiscuity, they go into genitalia. . . . I'd rather sing to the honor and glory of the region, and the beauty and dignity of our women."

There was another silence as the Trinidadian journalist, and the rest of the room, took that in. And then the caravan moved on. For some time afterward, I knew, that journalist's perception dogged me, and calypsonians here and there disparaged me. But already, my versions, popular as they were, were wending their way back into the Caribbean culture. Eventually, all those very same calypsonians would be singing their songs my way! And the different versions they'd sung before would be forgotten.

Grenada was beautiful, the cast top-rate, but by the second day of shooting, we realized our director was a full-fledged alcoholic. Rossen wasn't just a run-of-the-mill drunk who got juiced at night. He was drunk all day, so much so that he rarely made it to his director's chair for shooting. Instead, he'd dictate notes in his hotel room each night to his script adviser, Elise Gaige. The next day, she'd direct us herself, relaying his comments and changes while Rossen slept through the morning. On the rare occasions when he showed up, we literally couldn't understand what he was telling us, so much was he slurring his words. Clearly the guilt he'd felt at handing up those fifty-seven names would haunt him for the rest of his life.

As detrimental as Rossen was to the production, though, *Island in the Sun* was its own worst enemy. Its story line had not one but two interracial romances; in addition to mine with the elegant Englishwoman played by Joan Fontaine, Dorothy Dandridge played a pharmacy clerk who gets romanced by a white governor's aide. Dorothy ends up flying off to a new life with her own British lover (played by John Justin, a Peter Lawford type), while my romance with Joan Fontaine ends in a smoldering stalemate. Yet in neither romance do the characters kiss or even embrace! To his credit, Zanuck had pushed the film through knowing its interracial romances would anger or at least discomfit a large number of moviegoers. But he'd made clear in the columns that there would be no interracial kissing. Not even a peck on the cheek. Asked about this by one columnist, Zanuck airily declared, "There is no scene that calls for kissing. There was no conscious effort to avoid it."

That edict left us acting scenes that had no credibility. Out by the old sugar mill overlooking the valley, Joan and I have our first moments alone, and exchange passionate looks. "Do you still feel that anyone whose skin is different from yours is an enemy?" Joan asks me.

"Do you think I do?" I ask in return.

But there the scene ends. No kiss, no embrace, just—cut! It was absurd. How could two characters in the islands feel this strong mutual attraction and not do anything about it? Not only would our relationship look foolish onscreen, but the whole picture would seem false.

Over dinner one night early in the filming, Joan and I hatched our own subversive attempt to remedy this. We had another romantic scene the next day. In this one, I was to slice open a coconut with a machete and offer it to Joan so she could sample the milk inside. What I did the next day was hand it to her and watch, intensely, as she drank. Then I took it back, my eyes on the place where she'd put her lips. Slowly and deliberately, I put my lips where hers had been. Then I took the sip that consummated the moment. For anyone who followed it carefully enough, the scene would have, in its own way, a passionate climax.

Even I knew we couldn't consummate our onscreen romance by going to bed together. Audiences weren't ready for that. It would have killed Joan's career—if Twentieth Century–Fox didn't kill the movie first. But at our nightly dinners—all of us at a long outside table, drinking rum in the torchlight—we railed at our complicity, as actors, in suppressing hard truths. To be honest, I did more of the railing than anyone else. "The Irish don't have this problem—their ethnicity is all over the place," I'd say. "The Italians—same thing. But not with black people. There's always someone external to our culture and ethnicity telling the story of who we are." After several nights of listening to me go on about ethnic origins, Joan smiled sweetly and pointed. "Harry," she said, "could you please pass the ethnic butter?"

Perhaps in part because we couldn't express any passion onscreen, and also because we were, after all, in the islands, lulled by those sultry breezes, there was a lot of serious flirting off-set. My own possibilities were limited; Julie had come to Grenada to watch the filming, and I was certainly happy about that. But a very beautiful, raven-haired twenty-three-year-old Joan Collins, playing the sister to James Mason's expat Brit, caught my eye, and I would be less than honest if I didn't say there was some heat there. One night back in Los Angeles, I would invite the whole cast of *Island in the Sun* to my show at the Cocoanut Grove. Away from the prying press on Grenada, our mutual attraction would not be denied. I guess I felt a little escapism was justified, and who better to escape with than Joan?

One of the few who didn't at least fantasize about a romance in

Grenada was Dorothy Dandridge. Mindful of the lurking press, Dorothy made sure not to be seen alone with any of the actors; she knew how quickly a drink at the bar might be telegraphed to the tabloids as a Hollywood romance. Our own relations were totally circumspect, since her affair with Otto Preminger was now public knowledge, and I had Julie at my side. Sadly, Dorothy was unhappier than ever. She'd realized Otto would never leave his wife, and she swelled with anger whenever she spoke of him. She felt the frustration that all mistresses feel, of being, for one reason or another, second best, and that had a special sting because second best was how she was still treated by Hollywood, even after her Oscar nomination. She was offered either starring roles in second-rate films or supporting roles in major productions. *Island in the Sun* was a perfect example of the latter. The story simply didn't have a black female lead, so Dorothy had settled for a supporting role with very little meat to it. Though Julie and I did our best to shore up her spirits, we knew the truth: There just wasn't a place for a black leading lady in Hollywood. Not yet, at least.

All fall, Marguerite and I talked sadly but calmly, mostly by phone from opposite coasts, about how to divide our lives. She was quite sad about the outcome of our marriage, but she wasn't fighting the divorce. She just wanted to understand what had gone wrong. The easy answer was that my career had pulled us apart, but even she knew there was more to it than that. Politically, I had embraced left-wing causes that discomfited or even appalled her. For her part, Marguerite had immersed herself in Catholicism, which I just couldn't abide. I said I was willing to grant her full custody of Shari and Adrienne, but I wanted the absolute right to be able to spend as much time as I wanted with them, and the right to choose their schools.

As Marguerite boarded a plane in New York for Las Vegas in mid-January 1957, a reporter asked her if she had any hopes of salvaging her marriage. By now, our divorce plans had become public. "Miracles happen," she said, and perhaps she hoped for one. Marguerite had decided to establish residency in Vegas, as I had for legal reasons. She was viewing it as an extended vacation with Adrienne and Shari, whose hands she held as she boarded the plane. Perhaps in some corner of her mind she thought that when I joined them, I might see the light.

When Marguerite and the girls arrived in Vegas, I felt a lot of conflicting emotions, above all guilt at the prospect of not being a full-time dad for the girls. But the die was cast. On February 28, her six weeks duly spent, Marguerite filed her divorce suit. It was granted right there at the county courthouse.

For the last two weeks of my Riviera engagement, I immersed myself in the show. I felt grateful for the distraction it provided. One night Elvis caught the show with Ann-Margret as his date, and came backstage to say hello. Elvis couldn't have been more decorous; he insisted on calling me "Mr. Belafonte." Maybe it was just everything I was feeling at the time, or maybe our year of chasing each other on the charts had made me competitive, but his manner seemed country-boy slick, and his music seemed derivative. Only later would I learn that Elvis had hung out for years with a lot of black musicians and come by his style legitimately. But he did perform with such put-on flash that over the next years, I noticed, he inspired a whole generation of rhythm-and-blues players who thought they could put that flash on and be Elvis, too. Oddly, almost no American performers ever tried to pick up on the rich Caribbean music culture I'd borrowed from, aside from the Tarriers. What I'd done was mine, and consciously or not, no one ever tried to imitate me. Maybe I should have been insulted, but I took it as a compliment.

When I wasn't onstage, my emotions kept churning. I felt relief to have my marriage to Marguerite behind me, but heartsick to have waved good-bye to Adrienne and Shari at the airport. Sometime early in the Christmas season, Julie became pregnant. She was now in Los Angeles, where her parents lived, waiting for my next move. I made it on March 7, proposing to her that night on the phone. I had a day off the next day, I told her: Let's do it.

In the early morning hours of March 8, right after my last show, I flew to San Diego, where Julie met me. Together with her father and Phil Stein, the manager of my newly formed film production company, HarBel, we drove across the border to Tecate, Mexico, for an appointment at the mayor's office. When we arrived, the mayor was nowhere to be found, nor was anyone else at his office. We'd chosen Tecate because it was a small outpost where no one would be likely to recognize me. We needn't have worried; the streets were empty, aside from a few vagrant dogs and a hungover mariachi band. We tracked the mayor down in a bar across the street; he was more than half in the bag. He spoke no English, and we spoke no Spanish, but we all laughed a lot. Over at his office, he solemnly married us—in Spanish—and, after taking our money, signed our wedding license and presented it to us. "Wait a minute," I said. "These aren't our names!" The mayor snatched up the license and examined it blearily. Sure enough, he'd just married, or perhaps remarried, two local citizens of Tecate. Only after a lot of back-and-forth that involved paying the mayor more American dollars to issue a new license did we drive north as man and wife.

For now, Julie and I agreed, we would keep our marriage secret. Perhaps we wouldn't even announce it until our child was born. I was worried, frankly, about how the press—and the black community— would react to the speed with which I'd remarried, and the marriage's racial implications. I wanted to minimize any backlash. With luck, we would ease the news out so casually that it would be "old" by the time anyone noticed.

We didn't have that kind of luck.

10

Back in New York, Julie and I settled quietly into a new apartment off Central Park West on Eighty-fourth Street, just steps from the basement pad I'd shared with my buddies a decade and seemingly a lifetime ago. Not quietly enough, though; within days, a reporter from the *New York Amsterdam News* started sniffing around. The reporter claimed he came to our apartment disguised as a census taker and asked for Mrs. Belafonte. "I'm Mrs. Belafonte," Julie said, thus cinching the story. But that was sheer fiction, a cover-up for the tip the paper had gotten from some supposedly reliable source.

To the *News,* and the black community it served, my secret marriage to Julie was a hot and controversial topic. "Many Negroes are wondering why a man who has waved the flag of justice for his race should turn from a Negro wife to a white wife," the paper observed, adding, "Will Harry's marriage affect his status as matinee idol?" I didn't have to wait long to see how it played in certain prominent black circles; though no one said a word, I somehow slipped off a number of guest lists for dinners that spring. The fact that Julie was Jewish carried its own nuance in the tribe—both tribes, actually. Behind my back, I suspected, some members of both were muttering their disapproval, and predicting my speedy demise.

To an extent, I understood the outcry. Marguerite and I had been a picture-perfect couple on a pedestal, role models for a lot of American blacks who saw us not only as a great success story but also as embodying the highest family values. Divorce pushed us—or rather, me—right off that pedestal. And marrying a white woman when the ink was barely dry on my divorce papers left me and my image in a questionable place.

Or did it?

The best strategy, I decided, was to go on offense. So I reached out to *Ebony*, the black *Life* magazine, with its vast national readership, and offered its editors a scoop. They could have the story, I told them—our story, Julie's and mine. Better yet, I would write it myself. The editors grabbed at it. This would give me control over the story, and a tacit seal of approval from the biggest force in the black mainstream media. With that, I knew I had a strong hand.

WHY I MARRIED JULIE, ran the cover line, over a photograph of Julie and me in front of a Charlie White painting on our living-room wall in the Eighty-fourth Street apartment. "I believe in integration and work for it with all my heart and soul," I wrote. "But I did not marry Julie to further the cause of integration. I married her because I was in love with her and she married me because she was in love with me." I gave *Ebony*'s readers a bit of a window into my problems with Marguerite—the long absences that had strained our marriage; the moodiness that made me hard to live with—and I explained, in more detail, how I'd met Julie, how much she'd impressed me with her deep sensitivity to black culture, how as a dancer with the otherwise all-black Katherine Dunham Dance Company she'd often stayed in colored-only boardinghouses with the troupe when they were on tour. With her upbeat, life-affirming spirit, I wrote, Julie was far better able to deal with my moods, and we had so much in common—both in the arts and in politics—that I knew we would make a good match. If there was any doubt left in *Ebony* readers' minds that all this was for the best, I ended by reiterating my commitment to black causes—a commitment that would grow only more significant now that I had just signed a $1 million contract with RCA Victor records, and a multiyear contract with the Riviera, earning $200,000 for each monthlong gig.

That certainly got readers scratching their heads. After all, wasn't the budding civil rights movement all about integration? Wasn't I a leading figure in it? Wasn't I then walking the walk by making my own life an example of what integration could be? For those who insisted on seeing interracial marriage as somehow at odds with integration, the sheer scale of my earnings was daunting. What other black figure in America was willing to tap that kind of money for the cause?

That May, I went to Washington with Julie to participate in a

"Prayer Pilgrimage for Freedom" on the steps of the Lincoln Memorial. The goal was to prod the Eisenhower administration to fulfill the promise of the U.S. Supreme Court's *Brown v. Board of Education* decision after three years of virtual inaction. In retrospect, it was a kind of dry run for the 1963 March on Washington. Many of the figures who would lead the movement through its biggest battles to come were there: my childhood hero A. Philip Randolph of the Brotherhood of Sleeping Car Porters, Roy Wilkins of the National Association for the Advancement of Colored People, and members of the newly formed Southern Christian Leadership Conference, among them Bayard Rustin, Fred Shuttlesworth, Ella Baker—and Martin Luther King, Jr., its founding head. King, in that evenhanded way I'd come to appreciate, blamed both political parties for failing to enact the court's historic ruling. "The Democrats have betrayed it by capitulating to the prejudices and undemocratic practices of the southern Democrats," King said to "amens" from the crowd of some forty thousand. "The Republicans have betrayed it by capitulating to the blatant hypocrisy of right wing, reactionary northerners." King ended with a blunt cry: "Give us the ballot!"

Up on the dais with me and Julie, separated from us by a clump of celebrities—Sammy Davis, Jr., Ruby Dee, Sidney Poitier, and the great singer Mahalia Jackson—stood Marguerite, there in her own right as a now-prominent figure. At one point she and Julie exchanged a look and an awkward, silent greeting. It was the first time they'd set eyes on each other. But then, gracefully, they both turned back to the crowd and the cause they'd come to support.

Like a celluloid version of my interracial romance, *Island in the Sun* reached theaters that June, to mostly good reviews above the Mason-Dixon Line and wrathful reactions below it. The Ku Klux Klan staged a propaganda campaign, burning Darryl Zanuck in effigy and threatening to torch any theaters that showed the film. Exhibitors in several southern cities—Atlanta, Charlotte, Memphis, New Orleans—duly banned the film. A bill was even introduced in the South Carolina legislature, declaring that any theater in the state daring to show the film would be fined.

Zanuck hit back hard. He declared he'd pay for any damage to theaters caused by the showing of the film, and he vowed that if damage were done, he'd sue the KKK for violating federal commerce law by interfering with interstate trade. Interestingly, that was the same argument the U.S. Supreme Court would use a few years later when it banned segregation in bus terminals because the buses were crossing state lines and so were subject to federal law. Zanuck had the law on his side, and the clout to have that law enforced. Duly cowed, the KKK only stirred publicity that helped bring in the crowds. In the South, so many blacks came streaming into the larger towns to see the film that the theaters established "colored-only" movie days. I'd thought the film would do poorly, both because of its interracial romances and because of the meek way it treated them. Instead, it would go on to be the year's sixth-highest earner, after blockbusters like *The Bridge on the River Kwai* and *Sayonara*.

Yet if Americans liked *Island in the Sun*, they also made judgments, not all of them favorable, about the actors in its two interracial romances. They seemed to approve of, or at least not condemn, John Justin and Dorothy Dandridge for their white man–black woman romance. They felt very differently—as they always had—about a romance between a black man and a white woman. Many bought into the notion that black islanders went after vacationing white women; that was to be expected. So it wasn't my career that was singed. But white audiences—at least white males—didn't want to be reminded that white women were often attracted to black men, that some even vacationed alone in the islands and sought out local color. Joan Fontaine's character clearly felt that pull, and moviegoers punished her for it.

The epitome of lily-white English elegance, Fontaine had starred in a major film virtually every year for two decades, matched up with Hollywood's finest leading men, from Laurence Olivier to Gary Cooper. Now her onscreen romance with a black man seemed to taint her in the minds of the moviegoing public. She starred in two films right after *Island in the Sun*, but I suspect both were lined up beforehand. Then came a three-year dry spell, followed by *Voyage to the Bottom of the Sea*, hardly the kind of voyage Joan Fontaine could have wanted to take. And after one or two other films, nothing more. Perhaps when she made *Island in the Sun*, she was reaching Hollywood's cutoff age for leading ladies. But this was still a precipitous drop. She hadn't done *Island in the Sun* for the money; none of us had earned much up front for a film expected to do modestly, at best. Nor had she done it to please Zanuck;

she had too much box-office draw to be his pawn. I believe that she'd done the role of Mavis Norman to make her own quiet stand against racial prejudice. And more than any of us, she paid a price for that.

All in all, I thought *Island in the Sun* came out pretty well for a film that pussyfooted around race issues and had a director too drunk to work. Along with controversial story lines, it had a charming cast, and intrigue, in a Technicolor island setting. It wasn't art, but I'd go so far as to say that half a century later, it's still worth watching. Unquestionably, though, its theme song, which I wrote with Lord Burgess and performed in character, fared better than the film it graced. "Island in the Sun" wasn't adapted from some island classic. We wrote that one from the ground up, with social realities tucked into its island images. "*I see woman on bended knee / Cutting cane for her family / I see man at the water side / Casting nets at the surfing tide. . . .*" Not only did the song outlast the movie, it went on to become a greater favorite than "Day-O" in my repertoire, especially in Europe, where for decades it was my most requested number.

I cut another album of Caribbean songs that year, and "Island in the Sun" was on it (*Belafonte Sings of the Caribbean*), but I also brought out that album of international folk songs (*An Evening with Harry Belafonte*). If I had any doubts I'd survive the passing calypso trend, they were put to rest that July and August of 1957 at the Greek Theatre in L.A., where I played the longest run for any individual artist in its nearly thirty-year history. From what I could tell, no one in those audiences had any problem with my marital status, either. Instead, the combination of *Island in the Sun* with those albums and sold-out concert dates created a kind of conflagration of fame, leading to major magazine profiles, a six-part series in the *New York Post*—then a liberal, highbrow newspaper—and more. It was all quite exhilarating, and more than a little unnerving. Added to all this, I was immersed in the civil rights movement, and fully engaged with the most prominent black man in the world—Dr. Martin Luther King, Jr. So much for expected backlash from my detractors, not to mention the loss of faith among my fans.

For the doubts that still lurked behind my stage persona, and the rage that all too often surfaced, psychoanalysis might seem the last thing I'd have tried after my nightmarish experience with Jay Richard and Janet Kennedy. Thanks to the Kennedys, I was far more of an emotional wreck—and now far more paranoid—than I'd been before. Yet what else could I do *but* go back for more, hoping this time I'd find the right analyst? If you have a bad tooth and your dentist makes it worse, you don't go to a shoemaker to get it fixed!

Fortunately, I found Peter Neubauer, a Freudian so respected in his field, with so many distinguished affiliations, that I could rest assured he was, at least, not some fraud or FBI informant. Peter was old-school, an Austrian Jew who, like Freud, had received his medical training at the University of Vienna. He'd fled the Nazis (like Freud), eventually coming to New York to join the staff at Bellevue Hospital while building a private practice. More important than these impeccable credentials, Peter was wise and warm, perhaps the most empathetic person I've ever met. I walked into his office as a patient deeply wounded by poverty, as a thirty-year-old black man riding a wave of enormous and confounding popularity, fame, and wealth, as a political activist struggling to integrate my activism with my professional and personal lives, and haunted, as a father, by the fear that I would fail my children as my father had failed me. I was one very intense patient—an angry and suspicious one at that—and after my painful experience with the Kennedys, it took me a long time to trust Peter deeply enough to let the transference process begin again. But that time passed, and I did come to trust him, and for the next fifty years, I remained his patient, sometimes coming to three or four sessions a week, other times, while on tour, perhaps, letting weeks or months go by between visits. I came not only to trust Peter, but to regard him as in a sense my best friend— a man I loved dearly, whose passing, when it came in 2008, left me truly devastated.

It was Peter who asked to meet my mother, and told me afterward how much he admired her indomitable spirit. But it was also Peter who gently asked how old I had been when my mother had left Dennis in my care. I came to think Peter knew my mother better than I did, and so when I got the idea to move her to L.A., around the time *Island in the Sun* was released, I felt pleased that Peter approved.

Until then, my mother had refused to let me move her to a better apartment, with her husband, Bill Wright, and their two children. She did accept regular checks, but all the while bemoaned her lot. New York was too cold or too hot, her husband was a no-account, and now my brother, Dennis, was in California, stationed at Camp Pendleton as a U.S. Marine, so she never got to see him. Why not move to the West Coast, then? I suggested. I could see she was intrigued, despite her best effort to hide it, so on my next trip to L.A. I bought her a nice four-bedroom house on Victoria Avenue, close to the Ambassador Hotel and its Cocoanut Grove nightclub, now a fixture on my circuit. I had the place furnished and put TV sets in every room and a new car in the driveway. I didn't tell her the house and car were hers; I just flew the family out to L.A., installed them in the house, and told them to enjoy a month's vacation and see how they liked it. When my mother admitted grudgingly that it was rather nice, I had her New York furniture boxed and shipped out there, and arranged to be at the house myself when it arrived. "Welcome home!" I told her. "This is your house."

My mother was bewildered, but not Bill Wright. He loved it. Bill found handyman work in the neighborhood, and Millie seemed to settle into the paradise that was L.A. in the late 1950s.

I thought I'd made my mother happy at last.

I should have known better.

While I was in L.A., I talked to producers about possible films—not just as Harry Belafonte, but as the principal of my newly formed independent film company, HarBel Productions. To my delight, United Artists pledged some serious money for me to commission scripts and work with writers—on subjects and themes of *my* choosing. Of course UA might decide not to produce what I came up with, but I liked the way this new approach felt. We were partners in business, with mutual respect and lawyers on both sides of the table. That fall, *The New York Times* wrote that HarBel "could turn out to be one of the most important developments in the American Negro's long and drawn-out struggle for representation on the nation's movie screens."

In late September, I made my first deal: I would work with independent producer Sol C. Siegel on a film we were calling *End of the World*, based on a post-apocalyptic sci-fi novel called *The Purple Cloud*, published in 1901 by British writer M. P. Shiel. When MGM sent me the script, I was stunned. Clearly it was written for three white characters: two men and the woman they fight over as the three survivors of a nuclear blast. To offer the role to me seemed a radical move for a Hollywood studio. For me it was a romantic lead, and if the female role went to a white actress, as MGM assured us it would, I would have another chance to contribute to the national conversation on race.

Hopefully, this time with a kissing scene, too.

. . .

By now, heading up from L.A. to Vegas felt almost like coming home. The Riviera treated me like royalty. I'd settle into the hotel's largest suite, overlooking the Strip and the desert beyond, do my two shows, then stroll into the casino, still wearing my red satin toreador's shirt, tight black pants, and mohair jacket. I had a formal, even chilly demeanor that daunted most of the fans who approached me. "Hi, Harry," they'd begin, but when they felt that distance I projected, they'd start to stammer and call me "Mr. Belafonte" instead. I wasn't being arrogant; I was protecting myself. As a black star performer in white America, I never knew what was coming at me next. Earlier in my career, I'd heard some doozies. A drunk white southern woman approached me on the casino floor, wrapped her arms around me, and said, "I have to tell you, Mr. Belafonte, having met you and heard you sing tonight, you've made me look at coons in a whole new way." These things happened! I was always polite—I'd shake any stranger's outstretched hand and say hello—but nearly everyone got the message: Don't patronize me. Everyone, that is, except Bruce the pit boss.

Bruce was a bulldog of a guy who radiated raw physical power, with slicked-back hair, a flat, sullen face, massive shoulders, and big, restless hands, through whose heavy fingers poker chips flew in an oddly menacing manner, as if he were readying for a fistfight. "Hello, big man," he'd say as I went by. "When you gonna give us a play?" I knew attitude when I heard it. But what could I do? Complain to the management that the pit boss was calling me "big man"?

Every night, I'd hear the same subtle taunt from Bruce as I walked by. "Hello, big man . . ." Finally, after the last show of my last night, I stopped at his table. My first month at the Riviera had just earned me about $200,000. "Okay," I told Bruce. "I'm in for a thousand."

The game was blackjack, which in those days was played with one deck; not until later would the Vegas casinos start using shoes to prevent brainy players from calculating the odds, as cards got played, of hitting a 20 or 21. I wasn't a card-counter, but I'd played my share of blackjack in the navy. I'd also played tonk, a fast game similar to gin rummy, and poker. I'd played for money, sometimes for hundreds of dollars a pot. But in those games, I'd kept to my limit—the memory of losing Aunt Liz's ten dollars to that three-card-monte dealer in Harlem was still all too vivid—so when I lost what I had, I called it a night. More often than not, I won.

That night, my first night ever gambling in Vegas, I started winning, to Bruce's obvious displeasure. And then I kept winning. As my chips accumulated, I started playing multiple squares—three or four with each hand. A crowd began to gather as Bruce grimly watched the cards being dealt into the night. By 4 a.m. I had $40,000 in chips. That was when Julie and a couple of friends came over to tell me I had to go. "Come on, Harry, we've got a plane to catch." So I had my gate—my excuse to leave. Another dealer came over to take my chips to the cashier's window as Bruce stood in sullen silence. Back came stacks of bills, more cold cash, by far, than I'd ever held in my hands. Holding that cash felt good. Really good. Too good.

Coolly, I peeled off $1,000 and handed it to the dealer. Then I turned to Bruce, and with my free hand, flipped him a $100 chip. Bruce acted reflexively, catching the chip in one of his meaty hands before he could think. I flashed him a big grin. "That's for you, big man."

As we headed out to the airport with cash-stuffed cases, the exhilaration of that score—and my parting line to Bruce—went through me like an electric charge. I had won. I had *won*. But in winning, I had reawakened an addiction. Like caffeine, like cocaine, the high from that night had seeped into my veins. I couldn't wait to get back for more.

Vegas was at the start of its golden era—two decades or more of high rollers and top entertainers. Loyalty was part of what made the place work. I stayed loyal to the Riviera, as did a weirdly eclectic group: Noël Coward for one, Tallulah Bankhead for another . . . and Marlene Dietrich! Other stars were loyal to other resorts: Jack Benny, for example, always played the Sahara. As for the Sands, it was Dean Martin's place, and even more so, Frank Sinatra's.

My friendship with Frank had begun in the formal way that friendships did among Vegas entertainers: by attending each other's shows. I went up to his suite afterward; he came to mine. He was always courteous, even deferential, but we both knew I wasn't Rat Pack material. When I walked into his suite, there might be half a dozen guys drinking and joshing around: Dean Martin, Joey Bishop, a few high rollers who might or might not be gangsters, also a few musicians and, more often than not, Sammy Davis, Jr. As soon as I came through that door, I felt the mood change. Everyone toned down and straightened up. I felt like the high school principal making a surprise visit to a popular teacher's class. The students and that teacher had a camaraderie that I'd just interrupted. Suddenly everyone was on their best behavior. Both the teacher and the class were pleased to see me, but maybe happier to see me go.

The elephant in the room was race. With his black musicians, Frank had an easy, bantering manner. He was always the boss, but he kidded around, and his band members kidded back—just so much, of course, and not any further. Frank wasn't a racist—far from it—but some of those jokes did touch on race. Add Sammy to the mix, and suddenly the banter took on a new edge. It was Sammy who did that, making fun of himself, playing the clown in Frank's court—the clown in blackface. He was the one who'd say he was not only short and ugly but black— and Jewish. Now you might hear a joke, from someone in the room, about how were they going to find Sammy in the parking lot after the show unless he flashed a grin? And maybe someone would be headed down to the casino and on his way out rub Sammy's head for luck.

Only then I'd walk in. And so the mood would settle.

We had a lot in common, Sammy and I. We were about the same age. We'd both made it on raw talent and no training; neither of us knew how to read music. Both of us had broken through in 1951, I at the Village Vanguard in New York, Sammy at Ciro's in L.A. We'd started performing in Vegas at about the same time, too, both of us playing to white audiences, because that was who came to Vegas. For that matter, neither of us ever sang to black audiences anywhere we played; as high-end entertainers, we played to the people who could afford the tickets, and they were, with rare exceptions, white. How could we do otherwise, when the choice was taking maybe $5,000 a week to play the Apollo or taking $25,000 to $50,000 for a week in Vegas? Only through the mass medium of television did we reach black audiences, and with television, of course, the connection was impossible to measure.

But there the similarities ended. Sammy, with his vaudeville roots, had learned to shuck and jive from an early age, and he just couldn't seem to drop the act, even as a star in Vegas. Everything about him onstage oozed deference and accommodation. Like Mr. Bojangles, he was, at heart, the poor black entertainer, desperate to please his white overseers. Offstage he had his babes and his booze, but always kept this out of the white venues he played. When he played the Frontier in Vegas, he went along with staying in the colored-only rooming house at the edge of town, and, on order of the management, stayed out of the Frontier's restaurants and casino. He let himself be governed by the same Jim Crow treatment I'd been met with on my first gig at the Thunderbird and vowed never to accept again.

Sammy had broken color barriers in Vegas, no doubt about it. Each next resort that took a black headline act meant another barrier down. But here, too, there was a difference. I'd broken barriers on my own. Sammy had Frank. It was Frank who'd made Sammy legit to a larger audience, then brought him into the Rat Pack, pushing his star that much higher. Sammy needed Frank not just for his career, but for his entire sense of self-worth. To have Frank include him as one of the Pack was the single greatest honor of his life. And so Sammy, lifelong song-and-dance man that he was, lived to keep the master entertained. He constantly demeaned himself, breaking into his little-black-boy routine. His distress at his blackness, his looks, was forever at play.

By the only yardstick that mattered in Vegas, Sammy was doing better than me; he got paid a bit more by the week. And he had an enormous gift. I couldn't begin to dance like Sammy; I never tried. But he felt threatened by me, no doubt about it. No other black performer had challenged his turf the way I did, playing the Copa and the Waldorf and the Cocoanut Grove as a solo act, then doing the same in Vegas. All this was an attack on his uniqueness. No other black performer had had access to Sinatra and the Rat Pack before, either. Not Nat King Cole or Billy Eckstine or Louis Armstrong. The fact that I could mix in his circle and still keep my dignity as a black man—that ate away at him.

At the same time, Sammy and I were friends. The brotherhood in Vegas was pretty small, after all. Instinctively, its members supported one another. When he was with Frank, I suspect that Sammy made fun at my expense—how pompous or grand I was. In public he embraced me: *"My greatest friend, in whose presence I am humbled."* So I can't say I was entirely surprised when he asked me to serve as best man at the wedding he'd scheduled in a hurry, to get out from the contract on his life put out by Harry Cohn and the mob.

Was it really Harry Cohn, the volatile Columbia studio chief, who ordered that hit? I can't prove it, but Sammy sure thought he had. Cohn was furious that Sammy had embarked on a torrid romance with Kim Novak, one of Columbia's top contract stars. Cohn felt that Novak's box-office appeal would be severely tarnished if her secret romance with Sammy became known. When the lovebirds insisted on staging more trysts in some of the world's most expensive hotels,

Cohn supposedly called one of his many mob connections and sent out the word that Sammy was to be severely punished. Or so Sammy believed. Sammy had a lot of gambling debts, too, and that might have had something to do with it. All I know is that when he sought me out at the Warwick Hotel in Philadelphia, he was truly terrified.

We drove to the Jersey shore together—I don't remember why, exactly, but I remember being in the backseat with him as we rolled along the waterfront, just like in the movie—and Sammy told me how much in debt he was to the mob, and how vulnerable to Cohn. Okay, I told him, here's what we'll do. Sammy's record contract was nearly up; I'd just started a record label under Belafonte Enterprises. I would advance him a couple of hundred thousand dollars to pay off some of his markers and give him some breathing room. He would record on my label, and we would use the proceeds to pay back those loans over time. In the car, he told me how touched he was by my offer, that I was going to the plate for him. I remember him saying, "I only have one eye left. They're not going to get the other one." But nothing ever came of the idea. Later, I got word back that Sammy had thought it rather presumptuous of me to think I could step into his life and play that much of a role, have that much power over him.

What Sammy feared, more than anything else, was that the mob would go after his good eye. Three years before, he'd lost one of his eyes in a horrific—and bizarre—car accident en route from Vegas to L.A. At the wheel of a brand-new Cadillac, Sammy had driven into a multicar collision that threw him forward. Unfortunately, that particular make of Cadillac had a large bullet-shaped cone protruding from the middle of the steering wheel—a jazzy new design touch. The cone went directly into Sammy's left eye, destroying it and leaving it dangling on his cheek. He was lucky to be alive; when he recovered, he acquired a glass eye. That day in the car, he told me he'd been threatened directly: Cohn's thugs would take out his other eye—and break his knees—if he didn't offer convincing proof that his romance with Novak was over. Convincing proof meant more than telling Cohn the two were through. Sammy was going to have to get married, right away, to someone else, and make the press buy it as legit. "You gotta do this for me," Sammy pleaded. "If you're there, that'll validate it."

Inwardly, I felt put off by the request. Staging a fake marriage, with a real minister and real vows, violated some ethic I hadn't known I had. "Wouldn't it make more sense to have Frank do it?" I asked.

"No, man, it's got to be you."

Sammy kept at me, pointing out, among other reasons, that I knew how terrifying it was to lose an eye, let alone two. That was true; not long before, I'd undergone two operations to fix a retinal detachment in my right eye, the one I'd injured as a child in Jamaica with my grandma Jane's scissors. I had hardly any vision in that eye as it was, but a little was better than none, which was what I was facing before those two operations. For nearly a month after, I'd had to wear bandages on both eyes when I was at home, then wear special corrective eyeglasses to train my right eye to track with the left one again. "Okay, man," I said with a sigh, "I'll play the part." Only later did I learn Sammy had asked Frank first, but Frank had begged off, saying his efforts would be better spent trying to get the contract hit canceled.

One day in January 1958, an awkward group convened in the Emerald Room of the Sands Hotel in Vegas. The bride was one Loray White, a gorgeous black singer who performed at the Silver Slipper, a small place on the Strip. Sammy had gone out with her once or twice, and guessed, correctly, that she'd be game for this charade. What he didn't anticipate was that Loray, who had a serious crush on him, would take the offer seriously, even after being advised of the terms: $10,000 and a house in return for marrying him and appearing in public as his wife for a year. Art Silber, Jr., Sammy's longtime manager, later related in his vivid memoir of life with Sammy, *Me and My Shadow*, that Loray broke into tears when she heard the proposition. "Sammy, don't you know I've loved you for years?" Loray said. "You don't have to make a business deal with me. I know we could make this work." When Sammy told her he was in love with someone else, and there would be no intimacy in this "marriage," Loray gave him a radiant smile through her tears. "If that's the only way I can get you, I'll take it."

Just before the ceremony, a friend of Kim Novak's slipped Sammy a box with a white bow on top. Inside was a blue plaid blanket with a little silver dove pin. Sammy's hands shook as he took it out of the box. This was the blanket that he and Kim had somehow made a symbol of their relationship. They'd made love on it, wrapped themselves up in it, and carried it with them on all of their furtive trysts. It was all Sammy could do to keep from weeping on the spot.

At the reception afterward at the Moulin Rouge, away from the press, Sammy started drinking. And then he kept drinking—Jack Daniel's, straight—and started wailing. As he grew drunker and more belligerent, his bride grew increasingly distraught. It was a dreadful party, more a wake than a wedding, and Julie and I slipped away as soon as we could.

Whatever my presence contributed to the ruse, the press bought the story, which played all over the world. Cohn died of a heart attack the next month, whether from agitation at reading more about Novak's love life or not, no one could say for sure. As for Loray White, she stayed on in Sammy's life longer than the contracted year, extracting, in bitterness, a lot more from him than $10,000 and a house before walking away.

In that world capital of quickie weddings, I helped launch another truly terrible marriage that season, only this one was worse, because it involved my old friend and unrequited love Dorothy Dandridge.

Julie and our newborn, David, were with me when Dorothy came to visit us in Vegas. Dorothy was alone again, having broken off her romance with Otto after realizing he had no intention of divorcing his wife, estranged as they might be.

The first night we took her to dinner at the Riviera's nicest restaurant, Dorothy made a major impression on the maître d', a Greek named Jack Dennison. That was understating it; the very sight of her sent him right into orbit. This wasn't as improbable as it might seem. At a top Vegas resort like the Riviera, the maître d' had a lot of juice. He decided which high rollers got comped for suites and shows; of more interest to Dorothy, he helped book the talent. Dennison sent Dorothy lavish flower arrangements every day of her stay at the resort, and more when she got home. Soon he arranged for her to come perform at the Riviera for far more money than she would have commanded from a more objective booker. Having her there several weeks at a time, he was able to lay on so much devotion that she let him talk her into marrying him.

It was a disastrous choice. Dennison turned out to be pathologically abusive, the very kind of man Dorothy had sought so long to avoid after her first abusive marriage. All the flowers and flattery were just the flip side of a terrible, unquenchable jealousy. Soon he'd cut her off from all her friends, including Julie and me. Julie and I couldn't forget that it was through us she'd met this creep. Why couldn't she have traded on her fame to marry well, as Lena Horne had done in marrying Lennie Hayton, the most prominent conductor and arranger at MGM?

All the while, Dorothy's career was spiraling downward. Aside from *Island in the Sun*, the only two movies she'd made since her Oscar-nominated role in *Carmen Jones* were two low-budget flops. When Samuel Goldwyn offered her the chance to play Bess in his movie adaptation of *Porgy and Bess,* the choice filled her with anxiety. To me, the whole Gershwin production was racially demeaning; when Goldwyn offered me Porgy, I turned him down, and advised Dorothy to do the same. Instead, she signed on, and Sidney Poitier stepped in as Porgy. (Sammy Davis, Jr., took Sporting Life, one of the supporting roles, Pearl Bailey and Diahann Carroll two of the others; that was about it for Hollywood's roster of black marquee names at the time.) Just as shooting was about to start, Goldwyn changed directors, from Rouben Mamoulian to . . . Otto Preminger. Their romance dead and buried, Otto treated Dorothy cruelly on set, often sending her off in tears. Though she was nominated for a Golden Globe for her performance, the film failed when it came out in 1959, and Dorothy slipped into a serious depression, only made worse by her abusive husband.

Jack Dennison was just one of dozens of rough characters I came to know at the Riviera in that period. Most were mobbed up to some degree, but I treated them all with courtesy—unless, like Dennison, they proved undeserving of it—and nearly all, in return, treated me the same way. Of all of them, the one I liked and knew best was Gus Greenbaum, the Riviera's manager, a very senior member of the Chicago syndicate.

Greenbaum was a killer; he'd ordered the deaths of at least two associates found to have robbed one of the syndicate's other Vegas hotels. But to me, and to Julie, he seemed avuncular. He liked me, not only because I brought in more high rollers but because I could engage him in long conversations about Israel. Greenbaum was fascinated by me, but all the more so by Julie, who could talk politics for hours. He took to coming up to our suite every day around 6:00 p.m. just to chat. "How are things going with you two?" he'd ask.

One evening, Greenbaum came in looking rattled. He walked over to the huge bay window. "Hey, Hesh, come over here," he said. "Hesh" is Yiddish for "Harry." When I joined him by the window, he said, "Hey, Hesh, you see that?" At that time, the Riviera was the only high-rise building on the Strip. All I could see beyond it was desert: dancing tumbleweeds, and scrub brush, and little sandstorms in the distance. Nothing could have looked more desolate.

"The desert?" I asked. "Yeah, sure, I see it."

"Buy it," Greenbaum said quietly.

"Buy it," I echoed.

"Yeah, buy it. That's where it's all going."

"Only if I can partner with you," I said, only half joking.

Greenbaum shook his head. "You don't want to partner with me, Hesh," he said. "Just buy it."

Days later, the Riviera's attorney, Harvey Silbert, came up to my room looking very depressed. "Gus has been murdered," he said. "In Arizona. They tied him up and cut his throat, so we know it was a hit."

It was common knowledge, Harvey told me, that Greenbaum had gotten sloppy in recent months. Drinking, drugs, womanizing, and gambling had led him to start skimming from the Riviera's casino operations. When his bosses in Chicago had caught on, Greenbaum knew his days were numbered. He'd gone down to Phoenix with his wife on a leave of absence, hoping just to fade away. But you didn't do that with the mob. The grim twist was that Greenbaum's wife had had her throat slashed, too. That was unheard of in mob hits; you didn't kill your target's family. Harvey guessed that Greenbaum's killers had been torturing him for information when his wife unexpectedly walked in. They'd had no choice, he theorized, but to murder her, too.

The news shook me to my boots. What I kept thinking about, over the next days, were those fateful words by the bay window: *You don't want to partner with me.*

I would keep playing Vegas at least one month a year through the 1960s, eventually moving over to the new Caesars Palace, as would Sinatra and the rest of the Rat Pack. But I was cutting down on the club circuit now. I felt profoundly grateful to the rooms that had helped make my name, the shining lights of that great nightclub era: the Waldorf's Empire Room and the Copacabana in Manhattan; the Palmer House in Chicago; the Venetian Room in San Francisco; and the Cocoanut Grove in Los Angeles. But I'd spent the better part of a decade on that circuit without much relief. I wanted to think out my next move. I knew I wanted to dig a lot deeper with folk music. I wanted to do more, too, for social causes—not just write checks and appear at the occasional rally, but find some more profound way to make use of my fame, as Paul Robeson had done before me.

Instead of doing the usual clubs again, I launched my first tour of Europe. The one stop I hesitated to make was Berlin. Frank Sinatra had canceled plans to sing in Germany and said he wouldn't care if the country turned into a parking lot. I understood how he felt. Any American who'd lived through World War II—and certainly any American who'd seen wartime service in Europe—had a deeply ingrained resistance to seeing Germans as anything but Nazis. My conductor and arranger, Bob DeCormier, felt even more strongly than I did. Bob had had part of his right arm shot away in the Battle of the Bulge. He'd lost his mobility with that arm; it had healed in a fixed position, though fortunately one that allowed him to hold a baton, which he could then lift and lower. Bob was appalled at the thought of playing in Berlin. But George Marek, the head of RCA, urged us to get over our qualms. Sales were good in Germany, and could, he felt, get a whole lot better if we appeared.

In late June 1958, I went over on the *Île de France* with Julie and David, along with Bob DeCormier and his wife, Louise. First we spent four weeks sightseeing together. Then, in early August, I did a week of concerts at London's Gaumont State Theatre, performing for four thousand fans so enthusiastic that they nearly destroyed the place. (They did manage to tear the doors off a foreign sports car I'd arrived in.)

Paul Robeson, as it happened, was making a triumphant return to London, too. For eight years he'd been denied the right to travel outside the United States, his passport held by the FBI under the McCarran Act, because of his public statements of solidarity with the Russian people and other political views deemed subversive by J. Edgar Hoover. In the interim, I'd arranged and paid for Robeson to broadcast across the United States–Canadian border at a peace rally, where he spoke to throngs of Europeans who were trying without luck to get U.S. visas because they came from Iron Curtain countries. On another occasion, I'd financed and organized a broadcast from Robeson's brother's AME Zion Church in New York, in which Robeson sang to an audience of Welsh coal miners, one of his most loyal constituencies. He conducted that whole concert by long-distance shortwave telephone. Now, his passport returned at last as a result of a U.S. Supreme Court ruling that found the judgment unconstitutional, Robeson had arrived in England to the hero's welcome he deserved. By chance, his big return concert, at Royal Albert Hall, was on the same night as the first of mine at the Gaumont State.

To the press, the presence of two black American singer-activists in

London concerts the same night offered an irresistible chance to conjure up a bogus controversy. BELAFONTE LAUDED; ROBESON DECRIED, read one headline the next day. In the tabloids' version, Robeson was the old man, over the hill, his voice diminished; I was the new Robeson. Part of the spin was that Robeson was more confrontational in his politics; I was gentle and warm. Angered, I called a press conference to denounce the stories. It was clear to me, I said, that this smear was the work of anti-communists convinced Robeson was red. Nevertheless, one English reporter persisted, wouldn't it be fair to call my singing more . . . lighthearted than Robeson's? I took umbrage at that. "It's because Robeson made his protest that we can be more lighthearted now," I said. "In fact, if there had been no Robeson, there would have been no me."

Robeson came to hear me on my second night at the Gaumont State. After the show, he came backstage to greet me, his massive figure filling the doorway of my dressing room just as the U.S. ambassador attempted to get through. There was an awkward moment: Who would go first? Robeson deferred to the ambassador. "Please, go ahead, I can wait," he said to this factotum of the government that had caused him such grief. "Anyway," he added, utterly deadpan, "our conversation will take much longer. We have much more to talk about."

Even from the air, Germany seemed a different world: gray and lifeless. When our prop plane landed at the Berlin airport, a small gathering of reporters awaited us, but otherwise the place seemed almost deserted. Bob DeCormier and I slid into the back of a big open-air touring car, followed by several others. The wartime rubble was gone, but every block had gaping, open lots, like missing teeth, where bombs had fallen. We were in West Berlin, of course, but even here, martial law applied, forbidding more than a handful of citizens to congregate in any public place. That, we were told, was why only a few fans awaited us outside our hotel, waving but silent as we disembarked.

When Bob and I had checked in to our respective suites, he came over to check out mine, and we sat for a while talking over the upcoming show. From the street below, we could hear a faint hum, like a swarm of mosquitoes. The hum grew louder, until we realized it was a chant. It sounded like *Sieg Heil! Sieg Heil!* My windows had wooden shutters, which were closed, so I walked over and opened them. Below, on the street, were thousands of college-aged students, massed in flagrant violation of martial law. And what they were shouting was . . . *Har-ry! Har-ry! Har-ry!*

Still, we had second thoughts when we got to the theater. The orchestra awaiting us for rehearsal was a sea of German faces, all about our age. All Bob could think, as he stood in front of them with his baton in the air, was *Which one of you motherfuckers shot me?* He brought down his baton, with his injured right arm, and the music began, but his discomfort was all too clear. Finally, during a break, a trombonist came over to him. "You and I have worked together before," he told Bob.

Bob was startled. "Really?" he said.

The trombonist nodded. "I was part of the Free German forces in Belgium after the Battle of the Bulge. I played with you in the house band at that joint in Brussels where they gave out free booze and food."

Bob brightened, and so did I when he introduced me to the trombonist. Now he saw the orchestra a bit differently.

That night, the acclaim we got was like no other I'd ever received. When I got to the Hebrew folk song "Hava Nageela," the crowd roared and started singing—shouting, really—with me, clapping and stamping their feet. It was, I realized, the closest song in my repertoire to a German beer-hall song, with its chantlike syncopation. But how strange was that, a German audience giddily singing a Jewish anthem only thirteen years after the war?

That giddy response, I knew, was about more than music. My presence symbolized my solidarity, as an American, with West Berliners, but with East Berliners, too—with all those oppressed by the Cold War. It showed that a top American entertainer cared enough about them to seek them out and embrace them, at a time when America seemed both formidable and remote. And the gratitude I felt in return from those German audiences—the warmth and love—would be among my greatest rewards as an entertainer.

Another highlight of that European swing came in Brussels, where my performance inaugurated the American pavilion of the World's Fair—the first World's Fair since before the war. To my delight, America's greatest ambassador came to hear me sing. Eleanor Roosevelt and I had corresponded since meeting one night the year before, during one of my Waldorf engagements, when she told me she'd seen me as a fledgling actor at the American Negro Theatre in that spring 1948 production of *Sojourner Truth*. After the Brussels concert, she wrote about me in her "My Day" column. "He was received with tremendous applause and came back and did one encore. I think the audience would have brought him back indefinitely, though the hour was already very late, but the management finally turned the lights on, so the crowd had to leave." The next day, Mrs. Roosevelt came to visit Julie and me at our hotel, and dandled little David on her knee as she discussed world affairs. David responded by urinating on her. Julie and I were appalled, but not Mrs. Roosevelt; she just laughed and made a joke of it. "Well, little man! Thanks for your opinion!"

On my return that fall, I agreed to join another march on Washington—another harbinger of the great march to come. Like the one that would change the world in 1963, this march was organized by A. Philip Randolph, the legendary head of the Brotherhood of Sleeping Car Porters, whose Harlem parades I'd watched with such awe as a child. Randolph envisioned a mass rally of students, once again demanding peacefully but pointedly of President Eisenhower that he follow through on the Supreme Court's decision in *Brown v. Board of Education* and integrate the public schools and colleges of the South. I traveled from New York to Washington with a thousand students, to join a gathering of ten thousand in all at the Washington Monument. The scheduled headliner was Dr. King, but he was recovering from being stabbed in New York, so at Randolph's urging, I stepped into the breach and delivered an impromptu speech. I felt my stomach tighten as I stepped to the microphone, but as I heard my voice carry over the crowd, I let the flow of my phrases rise and fall with their own momentum, as I'd heard Martin do so often; I was no King, but I trusted my passion to get me through, and it did.

We had no permit to march to the White House that day, but we did anyway. We'd asked President Eisenhower to meet with us, and he had declined; that day he'd arranged to be in Georgia playing golf. With the television cameras rolling, I went up to one of the White House guards and said that on behalf of the thousands of Americans with me, I'd come to see the president. The president, I was told, was not available. Well, then, I said, here's a petition, with thousands of signatures, asking him to assure that the Supreme Court's ruling on public school integration be heeded at last. Would he see that this petition reached the president? The guard, studiously ignoring the television cameras, said he would. "Are you sure the president will get it?" The television cameras bore witness to the guard's reply. "Yes," he said, "I'll make sure he sees it."

I didn't expect Eisenhower to act with any alacrity on the pleas of ten thousand students, and in that, I wasn't disappointed. But leading the march that day, I felt something new—the power of that crowd. For the first time I felt: We are omnipotent. We will not be stopped. Later, Martin would say that one of his greatest strategic decisions was recruiting me to the movement. I was on board, all right.

Whatever he asked of me, I would do it.

11

I was moving closer to a new life, one in which the fight for civil rights would take precedence over almost everything. But how to strike the right balance was the trick. I hadn't forgotten the Robeson lesson; I wanted to be sure I always had enough money to support my family, and not let my causes overwhelm their needs. Yet by now I was having almost daily talks with Martin. The more he and I spoke, the more I realized that the movement was more important than anything else. I was feeling my way with all this, in the fall of 1958, when I ran into a color barrier so blatant and infuriating—in Manhattan, of all places—that I put my existential balancing act aside. This one was going to take all the money and celebrity I could throw at it, in equal measures, right away.

Now that we were a family, Julie and I had started searching for a larger apartment than the one we'd found off Central Park West. Our first thought was to rent on the Upper East Side, but every broker we contacted seemed to blanch when we walked in. The message, conveyed either implicitly or overtly, was that we'd be happier in some other neighborhood. I heard the message loud and clear, and I sent back one of my own, by calling a press conference to announce I'd filed a formal complaint with the city. One of those who heard the news was Eleanor Roosevelt.

"I am sure that every New Yorker was shocked the other day to read that Harry Belafonte and his charming wife and baby were finding it practically impossible to get an apartment in New York City except in what might be considered segregated areas or in a hotel," Mrs. Roosevelt wrote in her nationally syndicated column on October 20, 1958. After condemning, in her gentle way, the discrimination still rampant in many New York neighborhoods, she added, "I can think of nothing I would enjoy more than having Mr. and Mrs. Belafonte as my neighbors. I hope they will find a home shortly where they and their enchanting little boy can grow up without feeling the evils of the segregation pattern."

On the phone, Mrs. Roosevelt went further; she invited Julie and me and David to move in with her! She had a lot of space, she told us, and didn't need it all, and she'd love to have us as tenants. I thanked her profusely but told her if I were to accept her offer, I'd be walking away from a battle I needed to fight.

Not long after, Julie and I fell in love with a four-bedroom rental at 300 West End Avenue, one of those great old drafty Upper West Side apartments with not only a living room but a library and pantry. Except that when we tried to rent it, the apartment was somehow suddenly unavailable. Furious, I sent a white friend—Mike Merrick, my publicist—in as my stalking horse. Now the lease was readily conferred. Mike passed it on to me, I signed it with my own name, and the lease was countersigned. Apparently the building manager didn't know who I was. Julie and I moved our furniture in first, then showed up to take occupancy. Within hours, the building manager became aware he had a Negro as a tenant. He passed on the word to the building's owner, who didn't like this at all.

The owner, as it turned out, was Ramfis Trujillo, an international playboy who'd romanced Kim Novak after her breakup with Sammy Davis, Jr., and illegitimate son of the dictator of the Dominican Republic. His own skin color was high-yellow Spanish, but he clearly saw himself as white, and in his building he'd maintained the neighborhood's unwritten covenant against blacks. A billionaire thanks to his father's years of tyranny, Ramfis was used to having his own way. He relayed word that I must pack up and leave. I declined.

We had a one-year lease, which gave me exactly that much time to pull off my plan, because Trujillo, after failing to bully me into leaving right away, was surely not going to offer me the chance to renew. First, I set up a dummy real estate company. Then I set up two others, one for each of the sympathetic tenants who'd agreed to be my cohorts. With that, our three dummy companies began bidding against one another to buy the whole thirteen-story building.

If the building's managing agent found this sudden interest in 300 West End Avenue baffling, he never said so. In fact, our offers were coming at a time of real change in the New York apartment market. Rental properties were growing less profitable for their owners. The whole concept of co-ops was just starting to take hold. What we were proposing would soon become a trend. We would buy the building outright from its owner, then try to sell as many of the apartments as possible to the tenants who lived in them. Any tenant who preferred to keep renting could do that. We had to hope most of the tenants would buy, though, or the money I was putting up to finance the scheme—more than $2 million—would be tied up in bricks and mortar for years.

It all worked like a charm. Just as my one-year lease was about to lapse, our absentee billionaire owner accepted the high bid. Actually, it wasn't very high; part of what made our timing good was that the Trujillos were under increasing political pressure, and both father and son were looking to build up their liquid assets in the event that they had to flee. I now owned my apartment . . . and the building. As most of the other tenants stepped up to buy their apartments, too, the money I'd invested came flowing back.

One holdout was my fifth-floor neighbor, a widow who preferred to keep renting. I started thinking about how large a place Julie and I would have if we took over that one other apartment on the floor and combined the two. With our neighbor's blessing, I not only bought her out, paying market value for an apartment she didn't actually own, but found a rental apartment for her in another building, into which she happily moved. Now we had a twenty-one-room apartment, with nearly seven thousand square feet!

As other tenants left, my partners and I meted out the apartments to friends, some of whom were black, some of whom had experienced the same discrimination I had in my own New York housing search. Lena Horne got the penthouse. Later, Ron Carter, my favorite bass player, got a nice apartment, too. We didn't just invite black friends, though; our goal was integration, not reverse segregation. Eventually, 300 West End Avenue became known as "Harry's building." Strictly speaking, that was no longer true; when the building went completely co-op, I no longer owned any part of it besides our fifth-floor combined apartment. But I was glad to have a home that was mine.

Julie and I would live in that cavernous apartment for nearly half a century, raising our children and entertaining a glittering array of guests. Among our first were Martin and Coretta King, just back from a trip to Europe; they came by one evening in March 1959 and put their feet up with us for a home screening of the about-to-be-released *The Diary of Anne Frank*. Martin would come to think of it as his home away from home, staying with us on many of his New York trips; on occasion, he brought with him two or three of his closest advisers, and by the mid-sixties, the apartment was one of the movement's New York headquarters. Soon, Senator John F. Kennedy would come to visit, seeking my endorsement in his race for president. Eleanor Roosevelt would come to visit, too, though more often we went to see her, driving north to the family compound in Hyde Park, New York, for some of the most rewarding evenings of my life.

At seventy-five in 1959, Mrs. Roosevelt was still active in various humanitarian causes, one of which was the Wiltwyck School in upstate New York, for mostly black children who had committed serious crimes but were too young to be incarcerated. We had been introduced to Wiltwyck by both Mrs. Roosevelt and Dr. Viola Bernard, Julie's distinguished psychoanalyst, who had helped establish the school. Mrs. Roosevelt cared deeply about the welfare of these children, and our relationship, which had been fond but formal, deepened when I agreed to give back-to-back benefit concerts for Wiltwyck at Carnegie Hall, on April 19 and 20, 1959. Along with Millard Thomas, Bob DeCormier, and the rest of my standard backup combo, I used a forty-seven-piece orchestra.

The result, I have to say, was historic. I loved being up there on the Carnegie Hall stage for such a worthy cause, and I had a wonderful time, bantering with the audience between songs—every bit of which remains ingrained on the live double album that RCA Victor released later that year. Until that time, almost the only performances recorded live were Norman Granz's jazz events. *Belafonte at Carnegie Hall* was a milestone, not just in RCA's decision to record a live musical performance, but in its use of brand-new stereo recording equipment that captured the music crisply and complexly, better than if we'd recorded it in a studio. The album stayed on the charts for three years, and is generally regarded as one of the best live albums ever done. Mrs. Roosevelt liked the performance, too. "Here was one man, young and slim and gifted, a superb showman and actor, who sang his way into the hearts of a great audience for the benefit of a group of little colored and white boys who have found themselves entangled with the law," she wrote in her column. "These boys appealed to the kind hearts of Mr. and Mrs. Belafonte when they met [them] last summer, and the program on Monday night was the result of that visit."

Both before and after those concerts, Julie and I drove up to Hyde Park as overnight guests on the family estate at Mrs. Roosevelt's beloved Val-Kill Cottage. We would spend our afternoons engaged in archery—one of Mrs. Roosevelt's passions, for some reason, though she'd gotten too old to use the bow herself. Or we'd drive into town for groceries in Mrs. Roosevelt's Fiat sports car, a gift from her son Franklin junior, who owned the northeastern U.S. Fiat franchise. Mrs. Roosevelt was, of course, a very tall woman, nearly as tall as I was, and to fit comfortably in the driver's seat, she had to have the convertible top down. Even then, it was quite a scrunch. To my shock, she was a fast driver. Quite fast, in fact. I found myself gripping the passenger door, and pushing an imaginary brake with my foot, often fearing the worst. I didn't know how the news of our tragic deaths would be played, but I did know I'd get second billing.

At dinners in the cottage's cozy dining room, Mrs. Roosevelt would have a lively group of five or six, never more than eight. A number of them were African leaders, for Mrs. Roosevelt had worked hard to get their newly independent countries admitted to the United Nations. I met the son of Habib Bourguiba, first president of Tunisia, and Achkar Marof, the U.N. ambassador from Guinea. It was through Mrs. Roosevelt's introductions that my own intense interaction with Africa began.

Another rising African leader I met was Tom Mboya, a young Oxford-educated Kenyan labor organizer who foresaw that Kenyan independence from Britain, whenever it came, would fail if the country had no educated public servants. He had the vision of getting scholarships from American universities for talented Kenyan students, and then flying planeloads of them from Kenya to the United States. I pulled together a benefit for him in Harlem, then made appearances along with Jackie Robinson to raise funds for the airlift. A catalyst was Cora Weiss, a spirited activist who helped arrange a meeting between Mboya and then-Senator Jack Kennedy that led the Kennedy family foundation to help underwrite the effort. The first airlift brought eighty-one students and was a great success in everyone's eyes—except those of the British government, which accused us of meddling in their affairs. We responded by staging a second airlift, and planning more to come.

Julie and I went to dinners at Mrs. Roosevelt's Manhattan apartment, too, and there another eclectic group would gather. One guest I remember meeting there was U.S. Supreme Court Justice William O. Douglas. I felt shy around him at first, but he quickly put me at ease. I'd never met anyone as self-confident as he. I'd have thought a man who makes decisions that affect the heart and soul of the nation would be more guarded. Bill wasn't like that at all. He was very open and very direct, and when he spoke of social inequity, race, war, or politics, it was with real passion. He had a great disdain for war, keen doubts about the military-industrial complex and where it was going, and a deep commitment to civil rights. I adored the man, and when he took me seriously, I felt greatly rewarded. For Bill to regard me as his friend was to me far greater validation of my social and political views than a gold record or a starring role in a Hollywood film. Not long after we met, I found I needed a trustworthy lawyer. It was Bill who recommended a man who had been his law clerk, Sidney Davis, and who, for the rest of his life, became my adviser and legal counsel.

At Val-Kill or in Manhattan, Mrs. Roosevelt's guests would often just be family. Relaxed and happy, Mrs. Roosevelt would tell stories I remember half a century later. I suppose in response to some frustration I was probably airing one night about not being able to nudge President Eisenhower into doing more for civil rights, she told me about the time that A. Philip Randolph had gone to dinner at the White House. President Roosevelt had asked him for a candid view of what the administration needed to do for civil rights. "Don't hold back," the President had said. So Randolph talked and talked, taking the President to task for not using his bully pulpit. Over cigars and brandy, the President finally held up his hand. "I've heard everything you have to say, Mr. Randolph, and I don't disagree. I do have the bully pulpit. I could do a lot more to change what's wrong with this country, and it's my intention to do that. But I have to ask you for one big favor that will ensure I get on with this job expeditiously."

"What?" said Randolph.

"Go out and make me do it."

Mrs. Roosevelt told me that story to make a point. All of us pushing for integration would have to do more than hold a rally now and then. Without an active mass movement to make the government truly uncomfortable, our elected leaders would not do anything—not because they didn't want to do something, but because they needed political pressure to make decisions that many of their constituencies would resent.

On another night, Mrs. Roosevelt told us the Brussels sprouts story. At the height of World War II, correspondence between President Roosevelt and Winston Churchill fell into enemy hands and was eagerly pored over by the Nazi hierarchy. The Nazis' best code breakers focused immediately on the mention of Brussels sprouts. Churchill had told Roosevelt how much he'd hated the Brussels sprouts served at the last dinner the two men had shared. They were one of the foods he most disliked, and he hoped never to have them again! Roosevelt responded, Churchill came back with more on Brussels sprouts, and the Nazis became convinced that the two were writing in code about the major Allied invasion of Europe that would surely come somewhere sometime soon. But no, Mrs. Roosevelt told us, they were actually just talking about . . . Brussels sprouts.

Not all the talk at Mrs. Roosevelt's dinners was so light. She had a prophetic view about school integration. She saw its political necessity, but she warned against it. She felt that using the school as the vanguard for integration put an unfair burden on both students and teachers. Better, she argued, to integrate all public housing. If neighborhoods were integrated, schools would fall in line. To dump the issue onto the schools and give them no choice was, she felt, the cowardly way for society to get past segregation. But she was, of course, fierce in her opposition to segregation and injustice in any form. She never abandoned the Democratic party, but fundamentally, I think, she was a socialist. She felt government should do more—even more than her husband had done in his four terms in office—to level the playing field so that the underclass had a fair share of social benefits and job opportunities. She well understood that race was the greatest barrier to that more equitable vision, how even the smallest nuances of race— all the small, quotidian human encounters a black man had in white America—shaped expectations on both sides of the racial divide. I came to feel that more than almost any white person I'd met, Mrs. Roosevelt had expunged any prejudice she might have grown up with and was, in the truest sense, a humanitarian.

Sadly, in April 1960, Mrs. Roosevelt was badly injured by a car in New York City, and her health rapidly declined. Two years later, Julie and I would read of her death with profound sadness, knowing, at the same time, how fortunate we'd been to have had her in our lives at all.

I don't know that Mrs. Roosevelt was a mother figure for me, though she did possess a lot of the traits I wished my own mother had: curiosity, open-mindedness, a happy spirit. Millie was trapped within her shell of sorrow and self-pity, unhappy as she could be. But at least, I would have said, she still seemed her feisty self. Until, one day in the late 1950s, I got a call from the Idlewild Airport police.

"Sorry to bother you, but we have a situation," reported a policeman from the old New York airport (now John F. Kennedy). "We have a woman who's been here two days, says she's your mother."

I'd had a number of so-called relatives from the islands try to contact me, bearing some surname variation on "Belafonte" and hoping for a little family handout. "Yeah, great," I said. "What's her name?"

"Goes by Millie. Says she flew in from L.A. Lives on Victoria Avenue."

I got a limo right away, and went as directed to the airport's little police office. Millie was sitting on a bench beside it, her hair askew, with bundles at her feet. A homeless person. My mother.

"What happened?" I said. I was in shock.

My mother started to cry, though behind her tears, I could feel her rage. "The worst thing you ever did was put me in that house with that man. I can't tell you what a living hell it has been." In the limo, she went on and on about poor Bill Wright—in her book just another faithless, feckless man who'd betrayed her. I knew Bill. He was a sweet, rather passive fellow, always willing to work, if happier with his feet up. While my mother was in L.A., I'd sent my checks to a post office box that only she knew about; I didn't want Bill to get too complacent. But in no way did he merit this steady stream of vitriol from my mother.

I had to face facts: My mother was no longer possessed of a rational mind. In the weeks that followed, I tried to find her an apartment in Harlem that she'd like. Something was wrong with every place we saw. Finally she settled, unhappily, for a brownstone walk-up apartment on 143rd Street and Convent Avenue, a one-room apartment with a sink but no toilet; the bathroom was down the hall. Like some Dickensian character, she was trapped by her past, forced back to these meager circumstances because they'd shaped her, and they were what she knew. Soon enough I got her belongings boxed and shipped back from L.A.— Bill Wright, not surprisingly, chose to stay in the Victoria Street house, so this marriage, too, was over—but there those boxes stayed in her little apartment, unopened, for years to come. "I'll be moving soon," she'd tell me when I visited. "Why open them now?" But every time a broker showed us nicer apartments, she'd grimace and shake her head.

I was in New York most of the time now, and I was predisposed to movie projects that planned New York shoots. *End of the World*, the post-apocalyptic tale I'd agreed to star in for MGM, had a chilling, empty New York backdrop. Sol Siegel, the MGM producer, arranged for various Manhattan streets and landmarks to be cleared of all cars and people. No flashing traffic lights, either—the Department of Transportation saw to that. And what was always a mystery to me was the deal he cut with the pigeons. Not one bird ever flew past our lens.

We did have a lot of very authentic-seeming post-nuclear debris, an eerily apt setting and story for a time of peak Cold War paranoia, with fallout-shelter signs posted on every building and schoolchildren routinely ordered to hide under their desks in preparation for the coming blast. Long before the coming of technical special effects, the movie did a great job of evoking a post-nuclear New York in an almost poetic fashion, not by what it put into the picture but what it left out: all signs of life.

I felt excited about the script I'd signed off on, even if I wasn't entirely sold on the film's new title: *The World, the Flesh and the Devil*, a phrase from the Book of Common Prayer. For the first twenty pages, I am onscreen alone, wandering the streets in search of other people, my survival the lucky consequence of having been an engineer trapped in a coal mine three thousand feet below sea level when the blast occurred. Finally, I meet another human being: a beautiful woman, to be played by Inger Stevens. We fall in love and make our peace with the apocalypse, only to have a third survivor—to be played by Mel Ferrer—alight from a small boat. Now the story becomes a romantic tangle and, inevitably, a racial one, too. There was a lot of opportunity in those scenes.

Those first scenes of me alone—my shouts echoing against Wall Street's empty caverns—seemed to go just fine when shooting began. Then Inger Stevens appeared, and our mutual attraction began to spark. A day or two later, shooting was suspended. The studio wanted a few minor script changes, we were told by director Ranald MacDougall. Back came the script, changed beyond all recognition. Apparently the powers at MGM—either Sol Siegel or his overlords—had broken out in a cold sweat over the daily rushes: too much interracial intimacy. Now the romantic scenes were completely gone. Instead, my relationship with Inger Stevens was neutered, the last half of the movie rendered all but meaningless.

I was *furious.* Barely able to speak, I threw the script against a wall and stormed off the set. I was through. Once again, I was confronted by the country's schizophrenia on race. On the one hand, I'd just appeared on the cover of *Time* magazine, accompanied by a long, reverent profile inside. Yet the same sort of white decision makers couldn't abide the thought of me touching or kissing a white woman. Wasn't that the whole point of having my own production company involved, to protect me from just this sort of racism?

Jay Kantor, my agent at MCA, called first, pleading with me to finish the film. I told him no. The next call was from Marlon Brando, another of Kantor's clients. "I've been there, man," he said. "I know what you feel. But I know what will happen if you walk off. They'll crucify you. You'll be blacklisted—for keeps. This is very, very serious, what you're doing."

I ranted on for a while, but I finally saw Marlon was right. I had no exit clause to fall back on, and no say over the script. On this one, MGM ruled.

So I went back and finished the film, with all its obvious, irreparable flaws, and when it came out, in May 1959, it flopped, as I knew it would. "The evidence," wrote Bosley Crowther in *The New York Times,* "is that a good idea, good direction and good performances—at least by Mr. Belafonte and Miss Stevens, to a lesser degree—have been sacrificed here to the Hollywood caution of treating the question of race with continuing evasion of more delicate issues and in polite, beaming generalities." It did go on to become a cult favorite.

For my beautiful Swedish-born co-star, Hollywood's squeamishness on the question of race was to have far greater consequences. Despite a number of film successes over the next decade—*Hang 'Em High, 5 Card Stud,* and *Madigan*—Inger often struggled to find work, and began to be passed over for leading roles as the next generation of ingenues came up. Inger was especially vulnerable. She'd secretly married a black actor, Ike Jones, and knew that if word got out, she'd be all but unemployable. Harry Cohn had acted brutally when he forced Kim Novak to stop seeing Sammy Davis, Jr., but he knew his market. One April day in 1970, Inger was found dead in her kitchen from an overdose of prescription drugs washed down with alcohol. She was thirty-five.

I spent the summer on my now-established concert circuit, from the Carter Barron Amphitheatre in Washington, D.C., to the Greek Theatre in L.A., and up to the Riviera in Vegas. Summer was the season for large, outdoor amphitheaters where I could play to bigger audiences. Now, as part of that circuit, I flew to London for the first of several European concerts. And it was in London that I had a most unexpected—and life-changing—encounter.

I'd come back to the Dorchester Hotel at about 1:00 a.m., after a giddy opening night and after-show party, where I'd had my share of Champagne. As I passed through the lobby, the concierge discreetly flagged me down. "Excuse me, Mr. Belafonte," he said. "A priest and some gentlemen have been waiting for you. Shall I tell them to go?"

I looked over to see a white priest, in clerical collar, flanked by three black students with skin so dark they were almost surely African. Great, I thought: a Catholic missionary with his converts, hoping to convert me. But as the priest stood and timidly waved, he looked so pitiable that I went over to greet him. "Mr. Belafonte, I so apologize for encroaching on your privacy," the priest began, "but we are in a truly desperate situation, and you're the only person I can think to ask for help."

I sat and listened.

Father Trevor Huddleston was, in fact, an Anglican, not a Catholic. As I quickly realized, he was the kind of priest I liked: a social activist. English-born and educated, he'd been sent to South Africa by his church and come to abhor the apartheid regime. He'd essentially founded the anti-apartheid movement in Britain. In his latest effort, he was promoting a searing documentary called *Come Back, Africa*, made by an American filmmaker, Lionel Rogosin, that laid bare apartheid's ruthless cruelties. *Come Back, Africa* had just caused a sensation at the Venice Film Festival and won the prestigious Italian Film Critics' Award, but the news had traveled, and down in South Africa, the government was furious. Its leaders had declared that everyone involved in the making of the film would be punished severely—and if existing laws didn't cover this outrage, new laws would be written. The students who were with Father Huddleston had all appeared in the film and come to Venice to help promote it. Now they were in a terrifying limbo. If they returned home, they'd be thrown in jail—or worse. But their visitors' visas would soon expire, and the British government had shown no inclination to grant them political sanctuary. Perhaps if I saw the film and was moved by it, I might be able to help.

I did watch the film the next day, and was riveted, not only by the atrocities it depicted but by an amazing young singer who appeared in a scene set in a *shebeen*—an illegal speakeasy. The singer, a young woman, was both gorgeous and gifted; her extraordinary voice seemed to capture all the hope and despair of black South Africa. When the film ended and the lights came on, a door opened and in walked the singer, along with the students and Father Huddleston. The singer's name was Miriam Makeba.

Makeba, I learned, was already South Africa's best-known female black singer, revered as the "Nightingale." She'd recorded scores of gospel and jazz tunes, as well as traditional African songs, with an all-girl group called the Skylarks. Yet when we met, what struck me was her humility. She wasn't just humble, but meek. She took my hand in both of hers and bowed, which embarrassed me, but I thought if I told her to straighten up, she'd be *more* embarrassed. Later, she told me that the gesture was tribal, indicating respect by a youth for her elders. Some elder! I was thirty-two, to Miriam's twenty-seven. I told her how much I'd adored hearing her sing, and how wonderfully melodic her songs were. Not just melodic but, to an American ear, startlingly fresh and original. I said I'd be happy to introduce her to American record producers and agents—after I did whatever I could to help her obtain British or American visas, if that's what she wanted. I would, of course, try to help the students, too.

From my civil rights work, I had a network of activists throughout Europe, figures of political influence working for world peace. Though the peace movement focused primarily on building channels of communication between the Soviet Union and America, with the goal of uniting both peoples in peace to stop their governments from waging war, it would soon embrace the anti-apartheid cause as well. With a few phone calls, I found Miriam and the students a lawyer to take on their cases pro bono. Their visas were extended, and the students immediately began establishing a cultural base for South Africans in London. It was a propitious time; another new transplant from South Africa to London was Oliver Tambo. A founding member with Nelson Mandela of the African National Congress Youth League, Tambo had been served with a banning order by the apartheid government, and at

Mandela's urging, left South Africa to promote the ANC from abroad. For thirty years he would be based in London, raising funds and promoting the anti-apartheid cause, while Mandela remained jailed and incommunicado.

For the moment, Miriam didn't need my help to get to the United States; Lionel Rogosin had arranged to fly her to New York for a debut at the Village Vanguard. I went to hear her perform, though even before she came out on that tiny stage, I had a bad feeling about it. The Vanguard was billing her as South Africa's most famous jazz singer. Miriam wasn't really a jazz singer; she was a Xhosa tribeswoman from Johannesburg who sang traditional songs like "The Click Song," with the Xhosas' distinctive tongue-clicking sounds, and "Pata Pata." Instead of singing what she knew that night, she launched into American standards—better done by Ella Fitzgerald, Sarah Vaughan, and others—with a strong South African accent that only got in the way. I could see people at the nearby tables looking wonderingly at each other. I had a pretty good sense of what would happen if she kept this up: She'd find herself on a plane back to South Africa, her American singing career over. That night, I took aside the critics I saw in the audience—*The New Yorker*'s Pop Whitaker was one—and asked them, point-blank, to hold their reviews. Give me a few weeks to work with her, I pleaded. She's just gotten bad advice, I told them—she's so much better than this.

I told Miriam the same thing. America didn't need a South African Ella Fitzgerald. It needed Miriam Makeba doing her own music. We walked the streets and talked for hours. Miriam told me about growing up as the youngest of six children in conditions so desperate my own childhood seemed comfortable by comparison. As an infant, she'd been imprisoned with her mother when her mother was charged with brewing and selling beer—a crime for blacks in South Africa. When she was six, her father had died, and the family had struggled even more. At least both her parents had introduced her to traditional music. After winning a missionary school talent contest at thirteen, she'd begun making a name for herself as a singer. But she'd then made the mistake of marrying, at seventeen, an unfaithful and abusive man. All too soon she was back in her mother's home, the marriage over, with a daughter known as Bongi. Her career had begun to take off in her early twenties. But then she'd signed a long-term contract with a record company, a contract that apparently made no mention of royalties. What, she said pitifully, should she do?

I told Miriam to let me put some musicians together. They'd start rehearsing with her. She'd become an official arm of my company, Belafonte Enterprises, and when she was ready, she'd perform with me on my next concert tour. She would need a lawyer to hammer out the financial arrangements—a lawyer of her choosing, not mine—and she would need a bank account. To give that account a little heft, I would deposit into it $25,000 of my own money. That was my gift to her; it wasn't against her future earnings. It would just be her cushion, so she could live in New York on her own. I told her in no uncertain terms that she would have to learn to be responsible with money, to pay her taxes, to keep from overspending. And I warned her to avoid talking publicly about apartheid. Unfortunately, the U.S. government was closely allied with South Africa's regime, and hardly any of its citizens had a clue as to how bad apartheid really was. Speaking out as a foreigner—a black foreigner—would jeopardize her visa. This wasn't hypocrisy on my part; I just knew the lay of the land. I could get away with speaking out because I was an American citizen; paranoid as our government was, it couldn't deport me. It could send Miriam back in a flash. Just work on your music, I told her: *your* music. Politics could come later.

When I laid out the details of the bank account, Miriam's eyes grew wide. "You're like my big brother," she said, and for the rest of her life, that's what she called me: Big Brother. As soon as I started spending time with her, I sensed the emotional scars she'd incurred from growing up in a world of violence, inflicted by both the authorities and her own people. Her docility was both a defense and a way to hide the damage beneath. Like many young victims of extreme abuse, she'd put her pain in different drawers—drawers she could close when she needed to, so she never had to deal with the accumulation of all those hurts.

When I felt she was ready, I helped Miriam land a spot on Steve Allen's TV show. Aside from *The Ed Sullivan Show*, there was no better way to debut on national television; the show had an audience of sixty million. Miriam appeared on November 30, 1959, and received exuberant reviews the next day. Twenty-four hours later, she walked out once more onto the tiny stage of the Village Vanguard. This time I'd packed the house with high-powered friends—Marlon, Sidney, Nina Simone, Anthony Quinn, Robert Ryan, and more. Miriam's very appearance wowed them: She wore a resplendent outfit made for her by John Pratt, one of the great theatrical designers of his day and, as it happened, husband of dance troupe leader Katherine Dunham. Later,

Miriam would say she nearly forgot her lyrics as she looked out at that star-filled crowd. But she didn't, and the crowd adored her.

Afterward, I went up to Max Gordon to ask how long an engagement he could give her, and on what terms. Gordon said he was happy to give her four weeks, but I could forget about negotiating on her behalf. He would pay her what he wanted to, because he was her manager! He pulled out a document, dated from that first unfortunate debut, showing that he and Lionel Rogosin had signed her as their client. Now that I'd made her a hot property, Gordon and Rogosin intended to cash in. Worse, Miriam's percentages were minuscule. This was hardly better than chattel slavery. Steaming mad, I pulled Rogosin over—he was there that night, too—and told them both that if they dared enforce this contract, I would do everything in my power to see that they were disgraced. After some grumbling, they gave in and tore it up. Then I went to work on Miriam's other contract—the one she'd signed in South Africa for terms just as unjust, with a company called Gallotone Records. Not only was the contract shamefully ungenerous; it prohibited her from recording outside South Africa. First I wrote a friendly letter to Mr. Eric Gallo, saying what I thought I could do to help build Miriam's career in the United States. When I got what amounted to a "Drop dead" reply, I went to George Marek, who oversaw my albums as head of RCA Records. RCA, as it turned out, was Gallotone's distributor in South Africa. Within forty-eight hours, Miriam was free of that contract, too, and signed, instead, to a proper contract with RCA.

A little more than a decade earlier, four gods of jazz had glided out onto the stage of the Royal Roost to give a trembling rookie his break. Now with Miriam, I felt I was paying back a little chunk of that karmic debt.

That October, along with Marlon, I tried my hand at being a theater producer, with a French comedy called *Moonbirds*, by Marcel Aymé, starring Wally Cox, our onetime fellow student at the New School. It told a quirky story of a French teacher who discovers he has the power to turn people into birds. There were a few future notables in the cast—actor William Hickey for one—but the critics were merciless, and after opening on October 9, 1959, at the Cort Theatre, *Moonbirds* fell to earth exactly one day later, after three performances.

Hollywood was confounding me, too. What could I do to keep my next film—assuming that as a black leading man I could find one—

from being rewritten halfway through shooting by some timid studio boss? Only, I realized, by putting the whole package together myself—story, director, co-stars—and going to the one studio I felt I could trust: United Artists, run by the staunchly liberal Arthur Krim and a man I truly loved, Max Youngstein. Along with Arnold Picker, they were collectively making films in a way that overnight changed how Hollywood would be doing business.

I'd loved a noirish crime thriller called *Odds Against Tomorrow*, by William McGivern, a southerner whose hard-boiled novels had led already to two great film noirs, *The Big Heat* and *Rogue Cop*. On behalf of HarBel Productions, I sent the novel to screenwriter Abe Polonsky, best known for his Oscar-nominated original screenplay of *Body and Soul*, the dark, brilliant boxing classic of 1947 starring John Garfield and Canada Lee. "You know you're taking a risk if I write the script," Abe told me. I knew: Polonsky had refused to name names before the House Un-American Activities Committee in 1951 and seen his career screech to a halt—ironically, thanks to Robert Rossen, my drunken director on *Island in the Sun*. I told him not to worry; I had talked to the powers at United Artists, Max Youngstein and Arthur Krim, who were already doing their part to hire blacklisted writers, and they were my backers. Hollywood was still cowed, so blacklisted writers had to use pseudonyms. Not just dreamed-up fake names—that was too easy for some anti-communist zealot to uncover—but the names of real writers who hadn't been blacklisted and were willing to help those who were. I went to John Oliver Killens, the highly respected black novelist I'd first met in Harlem through the Committee for the Negro in the Arts. Killens agreed that we could use his name instead of Abe's, though Abe, of course, would get the money for the script he'd written. If anyone questioned us, Killens would claim the script as his own. The co-writer we hired, Nelson Gidding, had worked on several of director Robert Wise's films. He was an untarnished writer we could take to meetings and screenings; he could also be on set to make changes as shooting got under way.

Odds Against Tomorrow is a bank-heist story, but one in which race plays a determining part. The planner of the heist is a white ex-policeman, played by Ed Begley, who's worked out every last detail of the heist he wants to pull off at a small Pennsylvania bank. He hires me because he needs a black deliveryman for his scheme, to be admitted through the bank's back door with a delivery of coffee. To round out his trio, he hires a white ex-con and seasoned bank robber, played by Robert Ryan. The twist is that Ryan's character is a hard-core racist. How the three of us struggle to work together and pull off the heist, amid sharp racial divisions, is what gives the film its power.

As co-producer of the film, along with United Artists, I had final say not only on the cast but on the director as well. When I felt Abe's script was ready, I sent it to Bobby Wise, who'd cut his teeth as the film editor on *The Hunchback of Notre Dame* with Charles Laughton and *Citizen Kane* and had gone on to direct movies in all genres, from horror to sci-fi to war stories to film noir. Robert loved the script as much as I did and had no qualms about working with a blacklisted writer using a pseudonym.

Once again, as with *The World, the Flesh and the Devil*, the filming was done in Manhattan. The difference was that this time, everything went better than I'd dared hope. Wise shot in gritty black and white, focusing almost entirely on the three bank robbers as they prepare for the heist. Visually, the scenes have an almost surreal quality: the streets desolate, the city bleached out and eerily silent. Wise actually used infrared film in some of the sequences, making the Manhattan skyline look black, with white clouds. The film, in all of its aspects, is top-rate, the tension among the three robbers almost suffocating.

Upon its release in October 1959, *Odds Against Tomorrow* brought me the best reviews I'd gotten as a movie actor. Everyone, both in front of and behind the camera, was highly praised. Even the music was terrific; composed and performed by John Lewis and the Modern Jazz Quartet, it went on to be one of the year's top-selling screen-score albums. Taut and bleak, *Odds Against Tomorrow* could stand with the best of the fifties film-noir genre. It still can. It had only one problem: It made no money. Half a century later, it remains a favorite of film buffs, the first film noir made with a black lead character and, as far as I know, the last. *The New York Times*'s Stephen Holden has called it "sadly overlooked." But as I knew in my new capacity as film producer, the bottom line is . . . the bottom line.

I made no more movies that year or the next. I made none for the next decade. The critics all agreed I'd been good in *Odds Against Tomorrow*, and as an entertainer, I remained at my peak. Why, then, no more movies? The truth is I was tired of fighting Hollywood. Tired of trying to push the studios into making films with black male leads who fell in love with their leading ladies the way white stars did. Scripts kept coming to me, some for films that went on to become box-office hits. But in every one of them, the black male lead was neutered. Judging by those roles, you'd wonder if black men even knew what it meant to fall in love, much less to have sex. Two of the more memorable ones that were offered to me were *Lilies of the Field* and *To Sir, with Love*. In one, a handyman on a cross-country jaunt stops to help a bunch of German nuns trying to build a fence. No romance *there*. In the other, a teacher tries to inspire his unruly students. Clearly teaching is a full-time job; no romance there either. Sidney Poitier took both of those parts, and they rocketed him up to new, stratospheric heights of stardom. Everyone loved Sidney in those roles. Ironically, his dark skin, which he felt worked against him in those early days at the ANT, now proved a decided advantage. Yet Sidney, for all his blackness, never looked like an angry black man, and even in *In the Heat of the Night*, where he did break his mold and went so far as to slap a white man (I sure sat up when I saw that), Sidney radiated a truly saintly calm and dignity. Not me. I was a lighter-skinned Negro . . . and an angry one. I didn't want to tone down my sexuality, either. Sidney did that in every role he took. I don't want to put the full rap on race. Sidney is a wonderful actor, and he mesmerized audiences with all his performances. But he knows as well as I do that these nuances were fundamental to his success.

Television, for me, seemed far more open than Hollywood's film community. In the fall of 1959, CBS and Revlon called me in for a top-secret meeting. Revlon had just spent a ton of money on a new show called *The Big Party*. The idea was to throw a lot of celebrities together in a black-tie cocktail-party setting and invite the television audience in. Each week a different superstar hosted: Rock Hudson the first week, Jane Wyman the second week, and on and on. Most of them had never been on television before. On any given show you might see the likes of Sammy Davis, Jr., and the Will Mastin Trio tap-dancing their way down the wide flight of stairs, passing José Greco and his flamenco dancers clicking their heels on their way up. You might pass a big-name comic in the kitchen tossing salads and flipping pans while doing his monologue. In the next room you might find Nat King Cole at the piano, while Judy Garland was in the adjoining room singing to a small group. It was chaos made up of a parade of stars. Every well-known comic in show business, every singer, every dancer had been solicited to take part. Each segment was ninety minutes long. Despite the celebrity wattage, the show was tanking badly. When they invited me to join, I declined the offer. But they were most persistent. I told them I did have some thoughts about a different kind of variety show, if CBS and Revlon would like to hear them.

I knew that CBS and Revlon were fairly desperate, and not just for a way to solve the *Big Party* problem. CBS had produced, and Revlon had sponsored, *The $64,000 Question,* which had mesmerized the nation until the truth came out the year before: Revlon, almost certainly in the person of its CEO and founder Charlie Revson, had manipulated the questions to favor some contestants and push aside others. Single-sponsor quiz shows had been a huge moneymaker for the last several years; now, in the wake of the scandal, they were gone, and both CBS and Revlon needed something to replace them. I knew one other thing: Black women were a big audience for Revlon. The complexions of white women were fairly similar, so they bought similar beauty products. Women of color had a whole panoply of skin tones. Thus, more varied beauty products. I might have a largely white audience in Vegas, but on television I could bring them *all* in. And I was happy to do it . . . if Revlon wanted to meet my terms.

First there was the money: $200,000. That's what Revlon would pay for the show—period. However much I wanted to spend producing the show, the rest would be mine. I could spend $200,000 ordering up the most splendid sets in the history of television and not earn a dime, or stand myself in front of a bare backdrop, sing the whole hour, and keep the $200,000. My choice. But also, I told them, I wanted free rein to choose the talent I did employ, both in front of the camera and behind it. Revson said fine.

Where did I want to go with this opportunity? I started envisioning a portrait of Negro life in America told through music. What better way to promote understanding than with music that reached millions of Americans in sixty minutes? *Tonight with Belafonte* was to be virtually commercial free: There would be some time to introduce the show and wrap it up, but in between there would be no commercial breaks. That was one of my terms, and a television first.

I started by hiring a young director whose work I'd admired on *The Andy Williams Show,* a Revlon summer-replacement variety hour. The show had caught my attention because of its spare sets, straight camera shots, and lack of the usual producing frills. When I met with the director, Norman Jewison, I told him I had something similar in mind for my show. Forget it, he said. Revlon, because of creative differences, had just fired him from *The Andy Williams Show.* I told Jewison not to worry; I was making the hiring decisions. At the first production meeting, I told the assembled CBS and Revlon executives that Jewison was my choice. They blanched, but what could they do? Then I told them the name of the singer I wanted to feature, along with myself: Odetta. There was a long silence.

"What's an Odetta?" one of the executives asked dryly.

"She's a singer, looks like Paul Robeson," I said.

The executives turned green. But what could they do? They'd agreed to my terms.

The show aired on December 10, 1959, to excellent ratings. Odetta, the Alabama-born singer, reached a far larger audience that night than in any appearance she could have made in the clubs of New York and San Francisco. She made a name for herself in the heartland; soon she would be known as the "Voice of the Civil Rights Movement." Norman Jewison's direction gave him back a career: He would go on to direct *The Judy Garland Show* for CBS, which led to films like *The Cincinnati Kid* with Steve McQueen, *The Russians Are Coming, the Russians Are Coming*, with Alan Arkin, and *In the Heat of the Night*, probably Sidney's best picture, along with a lot of other memorable films. As for me, I won an Emmy that year for *Tonight with Belafonte*, the first Emmy ever awarded to a black television producer.

CBS and Revlon were happy, too. They wanted more. We negotiated five more shows, and on my terms. Each show would be an hour; I would have complete control; and it was pay or play, which meant if for any reason Revlon or CBS didn't shoot or air the shows, they still had to pay me.

A local phone directory gave me the idea for the first of these five hour-long specials. In those days before ZIP codes, the city was divided into larger postal zones. One of them, Zone 19, went from Forty-second to Fifty-ninth streets, and from Riverside Drive over to Fifth Avenue. Within that broad swath, I realized, one could hear, on any given day and night, most of the world's musical styles and cultures, from classical in Carnegie Hall to show tunes on Broadway to bebop on Fifty-second Street, but also salsa in Latin bars, jigs in Irish joints, the music of Israel in synagogues and the Yiddish recitals in theaters—the list went on and on. Why not a variety show with a song from each culture and genre within that small, dense district? The show was called *New York 19*.

Everyone thought it was a great idea. But as I would learn when the show aired the next year, television had its own racial stigmas, as hard to deal with as those in the film world.

That Christmas season, fresh off the triumph of my first television special, I opened a one-man show at the Palace Theatre in Times Square. For all my lingering doubts and demons, even I could feel I was breathing the rarefied air at the top of the mountain. The Palace, in 1959, was sacred ground, high above the club circuit, higher even than the Greek Theatre and other outdoor amphitheaters. And unlike any of the Vegas clubs, it was steeped in theater history. From its opening in 1913 as the ultimate vaudeville venue, the Palace had gone on to host all the entertainment greats, from Will Rogers to Ethel Barrymore and Harry Houdini. Having an engagement on that stage was far greater than getting your star on Hollywood Boulevard. Mine lasted fourteen weeks, shattering the Palace's record for one-man shows. The lines went around the block, the critics raved, and the Palace rocked. Did I care if I never made another Hollywood movie? Sure, but not that much. Besides, there were more important things in the world to worry about.

One morning in early February 1960, recovering from another night at the Palace with a cup of strong coffee in the kitchen of my West End Avenue apartment, I opened *The New York Times* to a story that electrified me. Down in Greensboro, North Carolina, four black college students had staged a sit-in at the local, segregated Woolworth's lunch counter. Refused service, they'd continued to sit at the counter for hours. Over the next days, as they kept returning, hundreds of fellow students joined them, and similar sit-ins spread throughout the South. So poignant were the news pictures of those sit-ins—the black students sitting at the counter, surrounded by jeering whites who often doused them with mustard and ketchup—that President Eisenhower, not known for his bold defense of civil rights, actually spoke out in support of the students. All they wanted, he pointed out, was to enjoy the rights of equality they were guaranteed by the Constitution. In July, the owner of the Greensboro Woolworth's would capitulate, desegregating his lunch counter; others would follow.

There was a radical, mind-blowing lesson in this. The country's preeminent civil rights group, the National Association for the Advancement of Colored People (NAACP), hadn't desegregated the lunch counters. Nor had Martin Luther King's SCLC, or the Congress of Racial Equality (CORE). The four original students had staged that sit-in on their own, and hundreds of students across the South, unaffiliated with any group, had followed their example. Students had power—the power of their independence. They didn't have jobs they stood to lose if they protested. And when they did protest, they stirred widespread sympathy if angry policemen tried to intervene. Black or white, these were America's *children*, after all, still more innocent than not, and as youths, their protests had a special, universally appreciated moral gravitas.

I had a number of phone conversations with Martin as the sit-ins spread. He saw the potential for students to play a central role in the civil rights movement now. They could be the solution to a problem that had vexed him ever since the Montgomery bus boycott. The established groups, including his own, were dominated by what he called the elders. By that he meant traditionalists like Roy Wilkins of the NAACP and James Farmer of CORE and A. Philip Randolph of the Brotherhood of Sleeping Car Porters, but also, even more so, by the ministers who occupied positions of influence in all those groups. The ministers might talk the talk, but many balked at confrontation. They didn't want to upset the white powers in their communities. Nor did they want to alienate the bourgeois blacks who made up most of their congregations. Students sensed that. They knew they needed a group of their own. Soon, they would form one—with Martin's blessing but without any help from the SCLC—and call it the Student Nonviolent Coordinating Committee, or SNCC. I didn't know it yet, but those students would have a profound impact on my life—as I would on theirs.

News of the sit-ins spread far and wide—as far as South Africa, where, on March 21, thousands of black protesters gathered in the township of Sharpeville, outside Johannesburg, for a nonviolent action of their own. The apartheid government required them to carry identification papers called pass books, seizure of which by the authorities was in itself cause for arrest: a perfect system of oppression. The protesters massed without their pass books, daring the authorities to try to jail them all. Mahatma Gandhi had preached this very form of civil disobedience; overwhelm the government's jails, he reasoned, and the government would have to compromise or collapse. "Jail, no bail" would become a rallying cry of the American civil rights movement, often to great effect, but on that day in Sharpeville, as the crowd grew to five thousand, police opened fire point-blank. At least sixty-nine people were killed, many of them shot in the back as they fled in panic. The Sharpeville Massacre, as it came to be called, stirred angry strikes and riots and led the government to jail more than eighteen thousand people. It also made the world recognize, for the first time, the brutality of apartheid, and led the United Nations to condemn the government. Furious and defiant, the ruling National party outlawed the African National Congress, among other groups; soon Nelson Mandela would be jailed, and the long bitter standoff between South Africa and the rest of the world would begin.

I spent long hours talking about all this with Miriam, whose friends and family were in immediate danger. Miriam was especially worried about Hugh Masekela, a brilliant young horn player still living in South Africa, whom Miriam would eventually marry. Soon Hugh would be banished from the country, and I would help him resettle in the United States, paying for him to go to the Manhattan School of Music and helping him get his musicians' union card. For Miriam, the best thing I could do was put her front and center at my concerts, and let her be the stirring symbol of black South African talent, beauty, and grace. I didn't have her open my shows, for fear the crowd would dismiss her as an opening act. Instead, I always came out at the start, grabbed the crowd, sang half a dozen or more songs, and only then introduced her. Miriam would sing songs of her own while I went offstage, I'd come back for a duet or two, and, after thunderous applause, Miriam would take her bows and I'd finish the show. To me, that seemed the best way to promote her.

On May 2, I did that with Miriam at Carnegie Hall, and also brought on Odetta. I loved sharing a stage with her. That night, I had the Chad Mitchell Trio on as well, and the whole package became a best-selling live double album, *Belafonte Returns to Carnegie Hall*. It earned a Grammy nomination for Best Album of the Year; I earned a Grammy nomination of my own for Best Male Vocal Performance; and then I won an actual Grammy, for Best Folk Performance, for "Swing Dat Hammer," a single from an album of chain-gang songs that same year.

Not long after the Carnegie Hall concert, a black political operative named Frank Montero reached out to me on behalf of presidential candidate John F. Kennedy. That surprised me. By now, I was clearly tied to the civil rights movement in general, and to Martin Luther King, Jr., in particular. Nothing I'd read about Kennedy so far suggested that either was an interest of his, and I didn't know why I was being approached. But I figured out why soon enough: Jackie Robinson.

Kennedy had routed Hubert Humphrey in the early Democratic primaries, and Humphrey had dropped out, leaving Kennedy the clear leader in the field. Unfortunately, as he edged closer to the nomination, Kennedy, and more so Montero, his black adviser, began getting signals that the Democratic nominee might not be able to count on the black vote. Kennedy was an unknown quantity to the black community, and his Catholicism put off many in the black Baptist Church. Baseball legend Jackie Robinson had a special beef with the candidate because of Kennedy's role in defeating the 1957 civil rights bill in the Senate. Also, Kennedy hadn't held his gaze when they met. Robinson felt that Kennedy was acutely uncomfortable with Negroes. So Robinson, formerly a Humphrey man, had transferred his support to Richard Nixon. That was huge. Robinson felt that Nixon, as vice president under Eisenhower, had shown sympathy toward blacks when the administration sent troops into Little Rock, Arkansas, in defense of the black students and the *Brown v. Board of Education* ruling. Robinson's feelings about Nixon were misguided, but he had made his move, and a lot of bourgeois black voters were inclined to agree with him. The Kennedy camp saw me as a potential counterweight to Robinson.

"Don't look to me," I told Montero. "You Massachusetts guys may think Kennedy's great, but down here in New York, we're for Stevenson." Adlai Stevenson was just a write-in candidate, after his two crushing presidential-election defeats in 1952 and 1956. But we Stevenson fans were a loyal bunch. I said thanks but no thanks to the counterweight offer.

Montero was persistent, though. He kept calling, until one day he asked how I would feel if Kennedy paid me a social visit. "Visited me?" I echoed. Montero explained that the candidate was campaigning that week in New Jersey. If I didn't mind, he'd like to come by the apartment late in the day. Sure, I said. I'd be happy to have the senator come visit.

The Secret Service arrived first, then the senator. "I understand that you and others have reservations about me," Kennedy began. By "others," I gathered he meant Negroes. Kennedy fixed me with a cool, clear gaze. "Let me tell you a bit more about where I stand."

In his winning Boston accent, Kennedy rattled off a number of campaign positions, and then a lot of polling results. Not once, in his disquisition, did I hear the phrase "civil rights." He concluded by saying he understood I had to stand by Stevenson through the convention, but would I endorse him in the general election?

"I'm fascinated that you and the Democratic machine find me so important," I said. "Fascinated and flattered. But you're making a big mistake if you think I can deliver the Negro vote for you. If you want the Negro vote, pay attention to what Martin Luther King is saying and doing. You get him, you don't need me—or Jackie Robinson."

Kennedy seemed puzzled by that. Why, he asked in so many words, was King so important?

I looked into those eyes for a hint of irony, but saw none. Kennedy was young, but his politics were old-school. To him, I could tell, the black vote was just a constituency you bought each election, if not with dollar bills and vague promises, then with star endorsements and public lip service, as well as contributions to the black churches and community organizations. Later, I would learn the Kennedy campaign had an Office of Minority Affairs, occupied by one old machine politician from Chicago whose primary function was to present a black face whenever needed. Among the white preppy Kennedy staffers, the office was known as Uncle Tom's Cabin.

"There's something bigger going on here that you need to learn about," I told the presidential candidate. "Six years after *Brown v. Board of Education*, schools in the South are still segregated, Negroes are being lynched for trying to vote, and a lot of us aren't going to take it anymore. Civil rights is a freight train and it's headed your way."

Kennedy said he was all for civil rights, but I had to realize that the whole southern wing of the Democratic party was segregationist. There was only so much any Democratic president could do.

"Get Negroes the vote, and they'll more than make up for all those segregationists," I told him. "Who do you think constitutes the majority in all those southern states?"

When the candidate left, after more than an hour, I felt I'd reached him, but just barely. I called Martin to report on my meeting, and shared my misgivings with him. Kennedy, I told him, was cold, calculating, and unschooled in the now-sacred cause of civil rights. At the same time, I acknowledged, he was whip-smart and knew how to listen. I said if the candidate called him for a meeting, Martin should find the time. Kennedy did, and the two men met on June 23, 1960, in the Central Park South apartment of Kennedy's powerful father. It was a short talk, Martin told me later, with no sparks on either side. In fact, the two were fairly nonplussed by each other. Kennedy, of course, wanted

King's public endorsement; King declined to give it. King wanted a passionate commitment to civil rights; Kennedy's assurances were lukewarm at best. But both sensed, as smart politicians, that they might be able to help each other.

Though none of the three of us knew it as yet, the stage had been set for a curious, long-running drama, in which Kennedy and King would test each other warily, again and again, wondering how much each could trust the other, seeking common ground in private even as they staked out their differences in public. As they did, I would find that I, too, had a role in this drama, as the mediator, the go-between, the one uniquely placed to explain one to the other. First, the coolly patrician Democratic candidate would have to become president. And then he would have to decide how much he could trust a black entertainer, one whose every move was chronicled in public, to be a reliable emissary.

After Kennedy won the nomination, I had some serious talks with Arthur Krim and a few other Hollywood Democrats—Paul Newman and Frank Sinatra among them—and did come out for Kennedy. I made a television commercial for him in Harlem, in which we sat in upholstered chairs with a little table between us, and the candidate told me earnestly how committed he was to civil rights, and then I looked into the camera and said I'd be voting for Kennedy; how about you? On the wall between us, a cockroach was crawling: a perfect symbol of the poverty that lurked beyond this little set, I thought, though of course the producers wiped it from the film. I remember Jackie Kennedy being at the shoot, very pregnant with John-John. The Kennedy camp ran the commercial throughout the South, hoping to galvanize black voters in Atlanta and other large cities where some were actually registered. The backlash from southern white Democrats was swift and extreme; I think the commercial ran just once across the region before being yanked.

Then, two weeks before the election, I had a chance to see if I'd made the right choice in supporting Kennedy. All summer and fall, the lunch-counter sit-ins had kept spreading throughout the South. On October 19, Martin Luther King was among those arrested in an orchestrated series of sit-ins in Atlanta. King's group, one of eight, requested service at the Magnolia Room, a fashionable place in the

Rich's retail complex. The owner had King and his cohorts arrested and charged with trespassing.

King was jailed, along with thirty-five student protesters from the various sit-ins, after refusing to post bond of $500 each. "Jail, no bail!" Over the next days, as hoped, the protesters' refusal to leave jail unless charges were dropped created headaches for Atlanta's elected officials. The city's mayor had the sly idea of declaring that Senator Kennedy wanted the protesters released. He asked one of Kennedy's closest advisers, Harris Wofford, what he thought of that plan. Wofford was appalled. With the race neck and neck, the last thing Kennedy wanted to do was show public support for King and the protesters. If he did that, whatever tenuous support he had among the South's yellow-dog Democrats—white, mostly racist members of the party—would evaporate.

That much I understood. But then, overnight, the game changed dramatically. A judge in another county issued a bench warrant to the Atlanta judge, ordering him to keep King in jail for possible violation of a suspended sentence on another charge. The previous May, King had been charged with driving with an Alabama license after moving his residence to Georgia. For this misdemeanor, the judge in that case had issued him a twelve-month suspended sentence. The sit-in charge seemed to violate the terms of that sentence. The next morning, King was conveyed, in handcuffs and shackles, to that other judge's jurisdiction, and sentenced to four months' hard labor on a chain gang.

I was on the phone to Coretta King as soon as I heard the news. She was overwhelmed. Every hour that Martin spent on that chain gang, we knew, his life was in danger. What was there to keep some white supremacist on the gang from killing him with a blow of his pickax? Not the police guards, that was for sure. Six months pregnant, Coretta wept at the prospect of bearing her next child—her third—alone or, worse, as a widow.

I started calling everyone I knew who might be of help, starting with Harris Wofford. "If Kennedy really wants the black vote, the best thing he can do is get Martin out of jail," I told him. Wofford drew up a letter of protest for Senator Kennedy to sign, but the campaign rebuffed it. A private deal had been struck with Georgia governor Ernest Vandiver, Jr., Wofford was told. Vandiver would get King released if the candidate stayed quiet. Wofford was sworn to secrecy on this, so to Coretta, and to me, the Kennedy camp seemed utterly unresponsive.

When news came that Martin had been transported to a maximum-security prison and put in solitary confinement, I started calling every Hollywood celebrity I knew, starting with Frank and Sammy, to get them to call Kennedy. I called labor leaders, too. I even called Jackie Robinson, to see if Nixon might be able to help. But I got no response from Nixon's camp. Nor from Martin's father, universally known as Daddy King, who, like many other black Baptist preachers, had come out in support of Nixon, allying themselves with the Republicans not only as the establishment party but the party of Lincoln.

Then, as suddenly as the nightmare had begun, it ended. The county judge who'd ordered King remanded to the state road gang without bail now reversed himself. King could leave the maximum-security prison after posting a $2,000 bond.

Over the next days, the truth came trickling out. Robert Kennedy, so cold to Harris Wofford's behind-the-scenes pleas that his brother get involved in the King case, had had a change of heart. In the beginning, I did get through to Bobby. But he had promised me nothing, and seemed to wish the whole problem would just go away. Apparently, what moved him to action wasn't anyone's pleading. Instead, as a lawyer, he felt affronted by the county judge's flouting of fundamental law. No one charged with a misdemeanor was supposed to be denied bail—period. Bristling, Bobby had called the judge to remind him of that.

Initially, the Kennedy camp tried to deny the story, and for good reason; Bobby's call to a sitting judge on a case was as much a violation of legal ethics as the judge's denial of bail on a misdemeanor. To the candidate's relief, the story petered out quickly in the mainstream press. In the black community, though, word spread like wildfire: The Kennedys had gotten Martin released.

Daddy King was both relieved and grateful, and as an old-time political fixer, he wanted to do the honorable thing: make a public declaration that he'd changed allegiance from Nixon to Kennedy. Nixon hadn't even returned his calls while Martin was in jail; Bobby Kennedy had made the call that got his son released. Daddy King started pushing Martin to endorse John Kennedy, too. But Martin didn't endorse Kennedy, and more than anyone else, I was the reason why.

"You can't afford to endorse him," I argued in one long-distance call after another. "You don't know this man, you don't know what he'll do in the course of his administration. If you anoint him and become his black mouthpiece, you'll pay a huge political price if he lets us down. You won't be able to retreat from that endorsement. You have to stay above this fray." My endorsing him was one thing. Someone of King's stature and moral responsibility, I knew, was quite another.

A summit meeting to hash out the issue was held at the Fifty-seventh Street offices of Belafonte Enterprises. Daddy King was there, along with several fledgling movement leaders, including Clarence Jones and Cleve Robinson. At the meeting, King's lawyers and chief political fixer, Stan Levison, agreed with me completely. But how, we wondered, could King fail to do something for the Kennedy camp? It was Levison who came up with the answer. King wrote an open letter, saying he was "deeply indebted to Senator Kennedy, who served as a great force in making my release possible." But he stopped short of an endorsement because, as he put it in a formal statement, his role as a civil rights activist demanded that he stay nonpartisan. Word came back that the Kennedys were furious with us for derailing King's endorsement. After the election, in a meeting with Bobby Kennedy at his home in McLean, Virginia, we rehashed the story and he gave me a wry smile. "It's true we were angry," he acknowledged. "But we could see it was politically shrewd, a clever move."

Any number of factors might be said to account for Kennedy's razor-thin victory that November, from his father's political sway in Cook County, Illinois, to Nixon's flop sweat in the televised debates. But one of those factors, clearly, was the gratitude felt by blacks for Kennedy's role in securing King's release from that Georgia road gang. The Sunday before the election, Wofford organized the secret printing and dissemination of a pamphlet to black congregations around the country. The pamphlets reached their audience, and from pulpits in black churches around the country that morning, ministers came right out and told their congregations how to vote. And those that could, did.

I had little time to savor the afterglow of Kennedy's victory. I was working day and night on New York 19, my next Revlon-sponsored variety show, and the first in the newly contracted series of five. I'd lined up John Lewis and the Modern Jazz Quartet along with jazz singer Gloria Lynne; among the dancers was one Julie Robinson, along with Arthur Mitchell and members of the New York City Ballet. It aired on CBS on November 20, 1960, and once again, the critics doled out a lot of praise. "Mr. Belafonte wandered in Sunday night in an easy little epic entitled New York 19, that had more charm, spirit and movement than you could find in a barrel of Ed Sullivans," declared the *Los Angeles Times*. "The air of casual informality with which the singer examined a slice of New York was fitted together with the precision of a Swiss watch."

Some months later, as I began planning the hour that would run in the fall of 1961—the second in the series of five—I got a call from Charlie Revson. On the phone he was warm and inviting; he asked me to come in for a meeting at his office—just the two of us.

Over lunch in his private dining room, Revson started harrumphing about how, as a Jew from Montreal, he'd endured his own share of discrimination, and understood the evils of oppression. Then he brought up the show. "Good ratings," he told me. "Good reviews. Very nice. But we're getting some response that says you should do it all black."

"What do you mean, exactly?" I asked. But I knew what he meant: The singers and dancers on the show were of different races.

"Some of our stations in the South are having a problem," Revson explained. "They're okay with an all-black cast. They just don't want to see white singers and dancers on the stage together with them."

"Mr. Revson, let me tell you something," I said. "If you'd asked me to put on a flowery shirt and sing more calypso tunes, and dance more, because that's what white people would like, I would consider it. Because I'm fully aware of the opportunity you've given me. No other black artist in America has the platform you've given me. But when you tell me no whites, you've crossed a line: morally, socially, and politically. There's no way to square it. I cannot become resegregated."

"Okay," Revson said, "if that's how you feel." By four o'clock that afternoon, I had a check from Revlon, a very big check for the balance due on the four future shows that Charlie Revson had just killed.

I thought seriously of telling my audiences, and the media, exactly what had transpired in Charlie Revson's personal dining room. I wanted the world to know what a coward he was, colluding with, and appeasing, southern racists, but embarrassing corporate America would only underscore my reputation as an angry black man lurking behind the sunny stage persona. *New York 19*, with its black and white dancers, had had some small impact on segregation if the racists were braying about it—better to keep the impact a positive one.

As I played back my meeting with Revson over the next days, I had a little epiphany. Here I'd been fighting for the last few years to change Hollywood, and then television, to push them both into casting black actors in dignified, substantive roles, to have black leading men who did all the things that white leading men did—chase villains and rope horses, make money and make love—with leading ladies black *and* white. Time and again, I'd failed. My epiphany was simple. The movies and television weren't all-powerful arbiters of culture. They just reflected the culture. Doing battle with them was like fighting a mirror.

To change the culture, you had to change the country.

And only one thing would change the country: the movement.

Later, Kennedy would come to be seen as the president who took on segregation, a great champion of civil rights cut down before the law he called for came to pass. That was true, in a sense, though no one in the movement, on the eve of his swearing-in, expected too much of him. At that juncture, I think it would be fair to say, both he and his brother Bobby, about to be confirmed as U.S. Attorney General, hoped civil rights would just simmer on a back burner while they ruled the country with the help of the party's southern segregationist wing. Still, this was a new beginning, and none of us could fail to be dazzled by the dashing new President, his elegant wife, and the entire Kennedy clan. For those of us invited to participate in the inaugural gala the night before Kennedy's swearing-in, it was the party of a lifetime, orchestrated by one of the new President's closest friends, Frank Sinatra.

Kennedy had asked Sinatra and Peter Lawford, husband of Kennedy's sister Pat, to produce the gala with just a few weeks' notice. They called in all the greats, from Ethel Merman and Nat King Cole to Lena Horne, Sir Laurence Olivier, Anthony Quinn, and Leonard Bernstein. Olivier was on Broadway in *Beckett*, and Merman was starring in *Gypsy*, so Sinatra just bought all the seats in both houses for the evening in order to get the stars onboard. Of all the obvious luminaries, only Sammy Davis, Jr., was absent. Former ambassador Joseph Kennedy had decided that Sammy's recent interracial marriage to May Britt, at which Frank had served as best man, made him too controversial for the evening—at least for those southern yellow-dog Democrats who'd helped put John Kennedy over the top. My own marriage to Julie wasn't remotely an issue; we didn't carry the baggage that Sammy did. Sammy was a loose cannon, stirring controversy with everything he did—the girls, the gambling, the booze—and, typically, he'd managed with his marriage to May to make as much tabloid news as possible. Sinatra was appalled to have to relay the news to Sammy, and Sammy was doubly crushed, both by the Kennedys' brush-off and by Frank's willingness to go along with it. As for myself, I didn't find out about it till later. On the night of the gala, I saw a lot of black faces—Nat King Cole, Lena Horne, Ella Fitzgerald, Mahalia Jackson, and Sidney—and felt good about that.

The day of the gala—January 19, 1961—heavy snow began falling early over the capital. By nightfall, Washington was paralyzed. Undeterred, Frank arranged to have school buses transport the stars from their hotels to the National Guard Armory, and to have snowplows clear the way for each bus convoy. Once they arrived at the armory, there were even special little footbridges to get the ladies in their gowns across the snowdrifts.

The gala was well worth the journey. Gene Kelly did a song-and-dance version of "The Hat Me Dear Old Father Wore." Ethel Merman stood right in front of the President-elect and belted out, *"You'll be swell! You'll be great! / Gonna have the whole world on a plate!"* Nat King Cole sang "The Surrey with the Fringe on Top," and then I gave the room my best "John Henry." Frank, not to be outdone, did "You Make Me Feel So Young," and Jimmy Durante sang "September Song." For the finale, Frank had the best songwriters in the business work up a medley of popular songs, with humorous new lyrics for the occasion, each ditty to be sung by a different one of us. I sang "My Bobby, My Bobby, He Loves Me," to the tune of "I Love My Baby—My Baby Loves Me," and got an appreciative grin from the President and the prospective Attorney General.

A new era had begun for the country, the civil rights movement—and me.

PART TWO

12

I wasn't an artist who'd become an activist. I was an activist who'd become an artist. Ever since my mother had drummed it into me, I'd felt the need to fight injustice wherever I saw it, in whatever way I could. Somehow my mother had made me feel it was *my* job, *my* obligation. "And don't ever give in," I can hear her say still. "Don't let them get you. You fight, boy. You *fight*." So I'd spoken up, and done some marching, and then found my power in songs of protest, and sorrow, and hope.

I'd worked for a lot of causes since then, gone to a lot of rallies. But at the same time, I kept my priorities clear. It was hard enough to have scaled the highest peaks of the entertainment world: Broadway, Hollywood, the record business, television, and Vegas. No way was I going to slide back down those peaks any sooner than I had to. Behind the Harry Belafonte audiences saw—smiling and relaxed—was a grim perfectionist. And woe to the musician who missed his cue, or the agent who fouled up a booking—this man had a temper. After all, I had a lot to lose! And so when causes made greater and greater claims on my time, I took care to keep the franchise intact.

Now, as the fight for civil rights in America grew fiery, I found myself getting more involved, not just as a celebrity presence but as an active member of Dr. King's inner circle, and as a mediator behind the scenes. I did my best to maintain my commitments as an entertainer. But sometime at the start of the 1960s, the balance tipped. For all the passion I still showed onstage, as a man, I felt far more immersed in a movement that could not—must not—fail.

Half a century later, I sometimes wonder: Was it worth it? Was I wise to give so much of the money I had to the movement? I assumed I'd be a wealthy man when I grew older, and although I live comfortably, I'm not. There are several reasons for that, but giving millions to the cause is certainly one of them. Speaking out as much as I did in the sixties probably hurt my career as well. I can't measure that. I can't see how many people in the audience slipped away. I just have to assume I might have sold a few more records, maybe hosted a few more television variety shows, and appeared in a few more movies, if I hadn't become Harry Belafonte, political activist, instead of Harry Belafonte, singer and actor who sometimes helped a cause.

The irony is that as much as I did for the movement in public, I did much more in private. For starters, I really was right in the middle between Martin Luther King, on the one hand, and the Kennedys, John and Bobby, on the other, as a new administration took office and hopes rose for change. And whatever hits I took to my wallet and career, I have no regrets about that.

"Ask not what your country can do for you—ask what you can do for your country," the new President declared in his inaugural address. One thing Americans could do, as of March 1, 1961, was join the Peace Corps, created by Kennedy with a stroke of his pen. Soon after, I got a call from Sargent Shriver, the President's brother-in-law and newly named Peace Corps director. Shriver told me he had the perfect post for me.

The Kennedy clan hadn't reached out to me because they liked the way I sang. Wherever they looked in the civil rights movement, I had already made it my business to be there. And not just as a celebrity lending his name. In that tense moment when Martin was imprisoned before the election and a lot of southern votes hinged on what the Kennedys did, I had demonstrated that what I brought to the table occupied a strategic space, not only with Martin but with all the players around him. Also, my instincts were based on genuine experience and legitimate observation, and carried value both in counseling the Kennedys to help Martin and in counseling Martin on how much we could expect from the Kennedys. Neither the President nor his brother Bobby yet appreciated how much of an issue civil rights would be on their watch.

But they did see Martin as the movement's leader, and me as a conduit to him, one they felt more at ease with than a goodly number of the southern Baptist preachers who made up most of Martin's circle.

At the same time, the Kennedys saw I had a larger portfolio. As an entertainer, I was known now around the world. My concerts in Germany in 1958 had created a lot of goodwill for America that was not as easily achieved by a politically appointed ambassador. Through Eleanor Roosevelt, I'd met leading figures in several of the newly— or soon-to-be—independent African nations; when they came to the United States, I was on their itineraries. I'd introduced Miriam Makeba to audiences at home and abroad; even without speaking out, she'd come to embody the plight of Africa and the hope of the peoples of Africa. Plus I'd helped sponsor the Airlift Africa program, which the Kennedy family foundation had funded in part. With Kennedy in the White House, more airlifts were scheduled, not just from Kenya but from other emerging African nations. Hundreds of students would benefit, including Barack Obama, Sr., whose studies in Hawaii would be underwritten by my friend Tom Mboya's and our African-American Students Foundation.

I represented, in short, an opportunity for outreach, both in the States and abroad—but also a risk. I could be helpful. But in the beginning, there would be many concerns. How does such a public celebrity maintain the kind of confidentiality that is necessary? How does a high-profile entertainer balance his self-interest when dealing with the likes of Walter Winchell and Dorothy Kilgallen—influential columnists hungry for information, who could help my career—with the strict discretion necessary for shuttling between the White House and the civil rights movement? It was a difficult challenge, but the Kennedys sensed I could manage it. And so came the offer by Shriver, endorsed by the President, to become the "cultural adviser" to the Peace Corps, focusing on emerging African nations. I was also asked to sit on the Corps's new governing board. Unofficially, I suspected, my greater role was to talk Martin and the other civil rights leaders into doing what the administration hoped they would do.

During this time, perceptions were being shaped. My growing closeness to the Kennedys raised questions by some in the movement who saw this relationship as a threat. Malcolm X, for instance. There was so much about Malcolm that I admired, even agreed with, but since he and I did not see eye to eye on some important issues, I never had the opportunity to talk to him in any reasonable way about the specifics of my involvement with the Kennedys. I was never able to help him, or even let him come to a more enlightened understanding of who I was and what I was doing.

One day that spring, Julie and I brought three-and-a-half-year-old David with us for a celebratory Oval Office meeting with the President. As the grown-ups stood talking, David wandered over to the President's desk and started investigating the desktop objects that were, for him, right at eye level. Noting this, the President went over to hand him a legal pad and pen. David sat in the President's chair, drawing for a minute, then came over to tug the President's jacket. "It doesn't work," he said, holding up the pen. The President tried it. David was right. "David," said the President, "I'm sorry to have to tell you, a lot of things around here don't work."

I was hardly immune to the Kennedy charm, but I viewed the President and his Peace Corps offer with a certain wariness. I knew he viewed me the same way. We had mutual interests, but we sensed they might diverge. All across Africa, nations were in upheaval. In Kenya, the British had savagely quashed the Mau Mau uprising, but soon would surrender their colony, just as Tom Mboya foresaw. Algeria and other French colonies were lurching in chaos and violence toward independence, too. And South Africa's white ruling party had just voted to become an apartheid republic free of the British Crown. All these and others were Cold War pawns, and wherever Kennedy looked, he saw rebels armed by Russia. I knew he would tend to support right-wing leaders who parroted the anti-communist line, no matter how repressive they were. After all, this was the American way. My views would be more nuanced. But for now, we could agree that sending America's top black entertainer to Africa would show a lot of goodwill, and might even bring some political dividends.

I knew I was being used, but I was using the Kennedys, too. Africa had fascinated me ever since I was a boy hearing my mother talk of Marcus Garvey and his pan-African dreams. The continent's role in World War II had only deepened my interest—and my empathy. Black African troops had gone into battle for the Dutch, the French, and the British, fighting for the same cause and dream that American blacks did: to vanquish the armies of white supremacy, and reap the fruits of true democracy. The war's aftermath had left them as disillusioned as it did us. Hitler and Stalin were gone, but the colonies they came home to were just as repressive as before. The difference was that they, like American blacks, resisted oppression, and began demanding the freedom they were due. By the late 1950s, American and African blacks saw themselves as allies in a common struggle. So my interest in Africa was not just about retracing roots or reveling in African music and dance. It was about forging a bond in the fight for human and civil rights. Eleanor Roosevelt had started me on this road by introducing me to Africa's new leaders. Now I could be, for them, an emissary from Washington. It was all pretty irresistible. And I knew exactly what I wanted to do first: go to the newly independent Guinea as a guest of its highly charismatic president, Ahmed Sékou Touré.

I'd met Sékou Touré through his ambassador to the U.N., Achkar Marof, one of Eleanor Roosevelt's introductions. In many ways, Sékou Touré was the most beguiling of the new young African leaders. Just five years older than I was, stunningly handsome, with coal-black skin, high cheekbones, and a dazzling smile, he swept into a room like a prince, wearing a white fez cocked at a rakish angle and brilliant white ceremonial robes. That man knew how to make an entrance. You had no choice but to stare at him, and when he chose to return your gaze, you felt rooted to the spot. He had strong, poetic hands that he'd gesture with as he started to talk, and in a sense they expressed his power. You didn't see force in the shape of a fist; you saw the poetic use of it. But if he disagreed with what he heard, the smile could vanish, and Sékou Touré would strike another pose. His eyes would start to flash as he launched into a rebuttal during which no one dared to interrupt him.

To all of Africa, Sékou Touré was a hero who'd stood up to France and paid the price. Three years before, Charles de Gaulle had assumed emergency power as France's "premier" and, as part of his plan to revamp both France and its restive colonies, grandly offered the colonies a choice. They could become members of the French Commonwealth and enjoy its patronage and protection. Or they could have their independence and cut all ties with the mother country. In fact, de Gaulle had played the only card he had. France's foreign influence had already taken a heavy hit with its defeat in Vietnam. Now Algeria was pulling away from French control in its bloody war of independence, and the rest of France's African colonies might well follow if not given this sop. Most colonies took the deal; of all the French colonial leaders, only Sékou Touré, who was the first to respond, dared go it alone. De Gaulle was enraged. Before pulling his military out of Guinea, he'd directed it to ransack the capital of Conakry, blowing up schools and government buildings, destroying the electric grid and the harbor, to show what came of spurning la France. The damage was devastating.

Guinea was still a ruin when I arrived, but Sékou Touré was doing his best to turn it into a utopian socialist state. As he explained over our first dinner, at the former French embassy, he'd made the farmer the most important figure in the country. He'd done all he could to encourage farmers to remain deep in the rural interior, from building schools in remote areas to establishing distribution lines to bring their goods to the capital. He knew all too well the chaos that ensued when a country's rural poor flocked to the city. All this he explained in French, while Achar sat between us, translating.

Sékou Touré talked of Guinea's natural resources—bauxite, diamonds, gold, and more—but with me he stressed the country's cultural riches. Guinea's drummers were Africa's finest. Its dancers were world-renowned, performing in magnificent masks and costumes. I was the new Peace Corps representative from America; I must see for myself! And so, the next morning, we boarded Sékou Touré's helicopter for a tour of the country that was both exhilarating and a little zany.

We flew first to Nzérékoré, in the southernmost tip of the country, where a military contingent in splendid uniforms stood at attention on the tarmac. Sékou Touré inspected the troops, so I walked behind him, inspecting them, too, as official photographers snapped away. *Damn*, I thought, *wait till Sidney sees this*. A cortege of long black cars awaited us. Sékou Touré and I got into the second car, and we headed off, led by a convoy of motorcycles. The presidential car was a convertible, and Sékou Touré rode with the top down so he could wave at and be seen by his loyal subjects. Unfortunately, the dirt road was dry, and the lead car kicked up clouds of dust, so Sékou Touré had his driver pull into the lead, and ordered the motorcycles to drive well ahead.

Sékou Touré, I soon saw, was an inveterate catnapper. He'd slide back in his seat, close his eyes, and be asleep almost instantly. It dawned on me that perhaps he was giving himself little rests from my company; talking through an interpreter was tiring, and we had a long way to go. Invariably, when he woke up, Sékou Touré would hawk up a huge gob of spit and aim it out his open window, then fish from his pocket a long white silk handkerchief not unlike my uncle Lenny's, and wipe his mouth. Every so often, while he was sleeping, a short tropical cloudburst would force the driver to pull over and put up the electrically operated windows and convertible top. Soon the rain would end, back down would come the windows and ragtop, and we'd be on to the next village.

The United States was providing no aid to Guinea, for the bone-headed reason that France was our ally and France was still mad at Sékou Touré. What a waste, I thought. Just by making the humanitarian gesture of fixing the infrastructure France had destroyed, we could earn Sékou Touré's goodwill and start pulling the rest of West Africa our way. As a first step, I suggested, why not a cultural exchange? The dancers and drummers and singers I heard on my tour were so remarkable, their tribal differences so dramatic; why not get them over to Carnegie Hall and the Carter Barron? Back in Conakry, I suggested that Guinea work up to this by building a national arts center where all its brilliant performing and fine arts could be showcased and studied, and also preserved as change came in the post-colonial era. There was, in fact, no theater at all in the city. "Who will pay for that?" Sékou Touré asked dryly. "Your President?"

"Your dancers," I said. "The richness of the Guinean culture. People will come to see them, and the money will follow."

By the time I left, I'd sketched out a plan to bring a whole contingent of American theater talents to Guinea, from performing-arts-center architects to stage and set and costume designers. They'd build a center that expressed the country's artistic spirit. I hoped that, as it progressed, the Kennedy administration would chip in. But until it did, I would underwrite the project myself. On that, I gave Sékou Touré my word.

In Washington after my trip, I reported first to Sarge Shriver, then to the President himself. I gave them both my best pitch for embracing Guinea. The idea that I put before them was that, through the Peace Corps, we would recruit all the theatrical talent we would need. During the volunteers' two-year stay in the Corps, that talent would work on this major cultural development and get the process started. Sékou Touré's commitment to culture was unique. Although, like everyone else, Guinea's citizens delighted in the arts, they viewed working in them as a lesser profession, something only the poor would do. Sékou Touré thought the opposite, and I saw an opportunity for the Peace Corps to play a role.

As we moved along with our discussions, I sensed futility. Like most countries in the developing world, Guinea had accepted aid from the

Soviet Union; the fact that Sékou Touré had had nowhere else to turn, iced out as he was by France and all of France's allies, had no sway at all. Cultural exchanges, maybe. Political ties? Not likely. The Kennedy administration did seem pleased that it had taken the risk of signing me up. But if they thought I'd be their loyal subject on civil rights, they learned otherwise when the first Freedom Riders ran into violent opposition in May 1961.

Activists from the Congress of Racial Equality (CORE) had decided to test a recent U.S. Supreme Court decision declaring that state segregation laws could not be enforced in interstate bus and train stations. Despite the ruling, Greyhound and Trailways stations, as well as train stations, still had white-only bathrooms, water fountains, and waiting areas.

Inspired in part by the Greensboro sit-ins, CORE planned a non-violent action of its own. Thirteen CORE volunteers would take Greyhound and Trailways buses from Washington, D.C., through the South and ignore the COLORED ONLY signs in the depots' waiting areas, restaurants, and bathrooms. Highly trained in nonviolence, they understood the violent rage they would be confronting, how likely it was that they would be beaten, maybe even killed. No matter what happened, they pledged not to strike back.

At the Greyhound terminal in Anniston, Alabama, one of the buses was met by a club-wielding mob. When its tires were slashed, the bus careened away with fifty cars in pursuit, only to grind to a halt and be set afire, its riders nearly burned to death inside. When a second bus reached the Anniston Trailways station, thugs rushed aboard to beat some of the riders with bats and iron pipes. Somehow that bus was able to pull away, bound for Birmingham, where yet another mob lay waiting. The Freedom Riders were set upon, many dealt head injuries so severe they needed stitching up at nearby hospitals. At that point, CORE's leader, Jim Farmer, decided enough was enough, and he directed the Birmingham Freedom Riders to fly to New Orleans.

Up in Nashville, Tennessee, SNCC leader Diane Nash viewed things very differently. She felt the Freedom Rides would appear to have failed unless at least one of the buses completed its route. Her fellow SNCC-ers agreed—and so the Freedom Rides became a SNCC production. I had huge admiration for Diane, and started conferring with her by phone about how I might help. I weighed in on what the route should be, where the Freedom Riders could safely stay each night, and what to do if they were again attacked. I wasn't the only one who underwrote the Freedom Rides, but I certainly was a principal backer. If the Kennedys had asked me whether I was funding the Freedom Rides, I would have told them. But they didn't.

The Kennedy administration, caught by surprise when a photograph of the burning bus in Anniston circulated around the world, was now doing all it could to discourage any further confrontation. To them, the Freedom Riders were as much to blame as the angry mobs. Our hope was that the Freedom Riders would stir enough anger to draw more national press, while avoiding real harm under the watchful eye of federal agents. When I called Bobby Kennedy to get some reassurance of that, he was very discouraging. He told me that, barring a national disaster or threat to national security, he couldn't just call out federal troops. The governors of those states were in charge. He had no authority. Bobby urged me to get SNCC to call off the whole thing. "This is hardly the time to stage a confrontation that just embarrasses everyone," he told me. By "everyone," I knew he meant the President. He didn't need to add that the President was about to go to Vienna for a top-level summit with Soviet chairman Nikita Khrushchev. The last thing the White House needed was news footage of American Negroes being beaten by white policemen—perfect propaganda for the Soviet Union to make its case that the land of the free was anything *but* free. I told him the SNCCers had made their decision, and there was nothing I could do to stop them. "You say you have no authority," I said. "Well, I have no authority, either."

In those phone calls, Bobby was anything but sympathetic. I was reminded of what Martin had said when the President-elect named his brother U.S. Attorney General. We hadn't forgotten Bobby's role as a twenty-seven-year-old legal counsel to Senator Joe McCarthy in his rabid persecution of suspected communist spies and sympathizers. "Somewhere in this man sits good," Martin said. "Our task is to find his moral center and win him to our cause." He was asking us to engage in a new aspect of nonviolence: to look the enemy in the eye and establish a mutual humanity. To us, the chances of doing that with the cold and tightly wound Bobby Kennedy seemed very dim indeed.

Now a bus from Nashville, with Freedom Riders from SNCC aboard, again arrived at the Birmingham Greyhound terminal to be met by an angry mob. This time the police held back the mob until Birmingham's police commissioner, Eugene "Bull" Connor, arrived to order the students arrested. Eerily, at 11:30 the next night, he personally transported them from the jail to the Alabama-Tennessee state line, where he let them out to find their way home. Instead of retreating to Nashville, the Freedom Riders drove back to Birmingham in a car sent from Nashville by Diane Nash.

The next day, I was on the phone to Bobby's assistant attorney general for civil rights, Burke Marshall, as the Freedom Riders made their way to Birmingham's bus terminals and tried to board buses for Montgomery. Bobby had sent his personal assistant, John Seigenthaler, down to Alabama to negotiate with Governor John Patterson; the buses eventually left, bound for Montgomery, with a huge state police escort. At the city line, however, the police fell away. When the Freedom Riders reached the Montgomery Greyhound terminal, the largest and most violent mob yet materialized. John Lewis, at the start of his historic career in civil rights, was knocked unconscious. So was John Seigenthaler.

At last, Bobby's moral center seemed to stir. A night later, Dr. King arrived in Montgomery to address a packed church, only to have an angry mob block the doors from outside. As a result of long, tense talks between Bobby and Governor Patterson, National Guards arrived to let the congregants out at 4:30 a.m. Bobby also secured the Freedom Riders' safety for the next leg of their trip, from Montgomery to Jackson, Mississippi. As part of the understanding, though, the Kennedys let the governors of both states uphold their Jim Crow laws in the bus stations. That was one hell of a concession, and it showed us that Bobby was perfectly capable of selling us short to keep the peace. His heart was in making his brother look good, not battling for civil rights. But Freedom Riders kept pouring into Jackson, and their arrests proved Gandhi right again. The state grew tired of tending them, especially with the continuing federal scrutiny. Eventually, Bobby would push the Interstate Commerce Commission into abiding by the Supreme Court's ruling. With that, COLORED ONLY signs would come down in bus and train stations across the South.

"What *else* do they want?" Bobby asked me with some irritation one day that June over lunch at Hickory Hill, his sprawling family estate in Virginia, after the Freedom Riders had won their initial victories. By "they" he meant the whole alphabet soup of civil rights groups causing all that trouble in the South: SNCC, the SCLC, CORE, and the NAACP. I'd come down to give a series of concerts at the outdoor Carter Barron amphitheater in Washington, D.C., and Bobby and his wife, Ethel, had come to hear me. Knowing I was playing to an influential crowd, I'd snuck a little politics in, with new lines for old songs like "Michael Row the Boat Ashore": *"Mississippi on your knees, hallelujah / Another bus is on the way, hallelujah . . ."*

Over lunch, I tried to explain why desegregating bus and train stations, even lunch counters, was not enough, and why waiting any longer to pull down the rest of Jim Crow was not an option. The SNCCers stood ready to stage more "direct actions," as they called their acts of civil disobedience: illegal gatherings meant to provoke mass arrests. No one could make them back off—not Bobby, not me, not even, and perhaps especially, Dr. King. "If you want to know what they're going to do next, just read Gandhi," I said. "The whole blueprint for what the movement is doing is right there. In fact, if you hand out copies to everyone in your Justice Department, you'll all be ahead of the game."

"Staging protests isn't nearly as powerful as registering voters," Bobby argued. "If you want real power, get out the vote."

Ethel was at that luncheon, too; it was to celebrate their wedding anniversary. Of all the Kennedy women, she was the one I would end up admiring most. She wasn't playacting. She looked at you and immediately got what you were about. Often in the coming years, when Bobby was balking at something we wanted him to do for the movement, I'd take my case to Ethel. "We have to talk to him," she'd say, and she would. How often she'd bring him around, I couldn't say for sure, but on the issues she chose to help us on, I knew she would prevail.

Bobby was right, of course, that registering black voters was crucial. But was it more important than staging protests that shocked the system? That was the question I found myself debating the next day in my suite at the Hotel Woodruff, with a dozen young SNCCers. Ella Baker, SNCC's matriarch, had called me to ask if I'd meet with them, and there was nothing I wouldn't do for Ella. She'd started with Martin in the Montgomery Improvement Association, yet she was also the one who'd urged young, disaffected members of Martin's Southern Christian Leadership Conference to go off and form SNCC. I had not only agreed to meet with the SNCCers but offered to pay their way to Washington from Nashville or wherever they were, and put them up for the night.

John Lewis wasn't one of the SNCCers who came to my suite that day. For one thing, he was in jail in Mississippi with a busload of Freedom Riders. Even had he been free, though, he would have wanted no part of a meeting with Harry Belafonte, the singer who'd gotten so close to the Kennedys. He feared I would try to talk the SNCCers into focusing on voter registration, and out of staging more direct actions, just as the Kennedys wanted. Voter registration would put more Kennedy Democrats on the rolls while sparing the administration any further embarrassment. How, John would ask angrily when he got out of jail, was registering voters an act of Gandhian nonviolence?

Even more off-putting to many of the SNCCers, I was a "King man." In the year since SNCC's founding, Martin had gone to great pains to praise it and say he well understood the need for young activists to have their own group. But Martin had lost a lot of respect when he'd declined the SNCCers' plea to join them on a Freedom Ride. "I think I should choose the time and place of my Golgotha," he'd declared, managing in one unfortunate statement not only to sound timid, but to compare himself to Jesus. From that point on, SNCCers would call him "De Lawd," and roll their eyes at what they saw as his highfalutin airs. I was Martin's confidant, the SNCCers well knew. Why have anything to do with me? As the dozen or so SNCCers filed into my suite, I realized I had doubts of my own. For one, I didn't want to be their sole source of funds. For another, I worried that aligning myself with any one group would pigeonhole me. I wanted to be able to speak out on issues as a citizen, not as a member of the board of SNCC.

The first thing that struck me was how young the SNCCers were; many were eighteen years old, none more than twenty-one. Most had already been tested by the first Freedom Rides. They'd literally stared down death and kept on, undeterred. They had the quiet confidence of battle-tested militants, and they knew their power; they, not the SCLC, had lately drawn the world's attention to the savagery of segregation. They had little interest in heeding Dr. King *or* the Kennedys. But as we kept talking, I sensed them beginning to trust me as my own man, not Martin's or the Kennedys'.

On the tricky issue of voter registration, I was surprised to hear that these particular SNCCers saw it as the single most important initiative the movement could undertake. They also knew it was the most dangerous. There was nothing more threatening to southern whites than blacks getting the vote in states where blacks were the clear majority. A lot of other SNCCers sided with John Lewis in feeling that direct actions were more effective, but that, I would learn, was typical of SNCC. Every issue got hotly debated. The group was fiercely democratic; everything it did had to be approved by a majority vote, and all votes were equal. Other groups—the SCLC, the NAACP, CORE—had their boards of elders who made decisions. Not SNCC. That was what they'd left the SCLC to get away from. Tempers flared, but somehow, with everyone so committed to the movement, decisions got made and progress followed. Among all the causes and groups I've known in my decades of activism, SNCC was unique.

Even before the students spelled out the details of their plan—mobilizing northern volunteers, opening field offices, canvassing the southern black communities—I knew I would have to help. That day, I wrote SNCC a check for $40,000. That was serious money in 1961. I sort of suspected I was signing on to be SNCC's major angel for years to come. There weren't a lot of other black angels with deep-pocketed robes flying around in the wings! But I would never regret that commitment.

Nearly half a century later, in April 2010, I would listen to our nation's first black U.S. Attorney General speak at SNCC's fiftieth reunion. How much difference had SNCC made? Eric Holder would ask rhetorically. Enough, he would say, "that you can draw a straight line between the forming of SNCC and my fifth-floor office at the U.S. Department of Justice. Enough that you can draw a line from SNCC to the White House, and our first black president."

Those were pretty good returns on investment.

I was plunging deeper into the movement, but I hadn't let my day job slide. Miriam Makeba was with me on tour that whole summer and fall, from an outdoor concert at the Forest Hills Music Festival (in that all-white enclave with housing covenants against blacks), where we sang in pouring rain while the band took cover, to a sold-out three-week stand at L.A.'s Greek Theatre, to Harrah's in Lake Tahoe, where the waiting list for our opening-night concert had 1,700 names. I had a new album out, *Jump Up Calypso*, that became one of my best sellers and my sixth gold album. But I was still taking care not to let calypso dominate my repertoire, which was why for my next album, *Midnight Special*, I mixed up folk and blues, and in so doing made a little music history with a very young Bob Dylan.

For the title track, I'd planned to have Sonny Terry play harmonica. That was an easy choice; Sonny was the world's greatest blues harp player, best known for his amazing collaborations with blues guitarist Brownie McGhee. Sonny and Brownie had shared stages with me that summer, and I adored them both. But with an orchestra due to assemble the next day, I got news that Sonny was sick in bed in Mississippi. Millard Thomas, my steady guitarist—the one who'd nearly burned down a hotel in St. Louis with both of us in it in the early days—said he had a young guy who could take Sonny's place. The next day, a skinny, scraggly-haired kid no more than twenty years old sauntered into the studio with a brown paper bag. He emptied it onto a table, and four or five harmonicas fell out. "Mind if I hear you all run through it one time?" he asked. "Midnight Special" was a standard blues song, but sure, I said, why not?

When we'd done our run-through, Bob nodded, chose one of the harmonicas, and asked for a glass of water. We started in again. Just as we reached his part, Bob dipped his harmonica into the glass of water, then shook off the water and began to blow a very funky harp. When he was finished, we listened to the playback and nodded. It was right on the money.

We told him as much, but the kid didn't linger. I'm not sure he even shook hands good-bye. On his way out, he tossed the harmonica he'd just played into the trash. I thought, Well, he certainly didn't think much of *that* song. I had the sense he viewed me as an elder, and maybe not a worthy one at that. Two years later, he played a few songs at the March on Washington. He sang with Joan Baez, whom I associated with a nasty put-down of me in a *Time* cover story on emerging folk-singers. Whoever called me "Belaphony" in the story was too cowardly to be quoted by name, and maybe it wasn't Baez, but she was the folkie on the cover, so I blamed her! And I assumed her buddy Dylan probably felt the same way.

All wrong—dead wrong. Baez harbored no such feelings, nor did Dylan, as I discovered in 2004, when I picked up Dylan's memoir, *Chronicles, Volume One*. Here I'd nursed a wounded ego all these years, stung by a slight that even then I had to admit had no real basis in truth. (Was it the *way* he'd thrown that harmonica in the trash?) It turned out that Bob bought the cheapest harmonicas he could find, because they yielded a crude sound, and once you dipped the harmonica in water and blew as hard as you could, the harmonica was no good; you had to throw it out. Bob's harp-playing on *Midnight Special* marked his first time in a recording studio. He'd been too shy to say what he felt about me. He sure made up for it in *Chronicles*. He wrote:

Harry was the best balladeer in the land and everybody knew it. He was a fantastic artist, sang about lovers and slaves—chain gang workers, saints and sinners and children. . . . Harry was like Valentino. As a performer, he broke all attendance records.

He could play to a packed house at Carnegie Hall and then the next day he might appear at a garment center union rally. To Harry, it didn't make any difference. People were people. He had ideals and made you feel you're part of the human race. There never was a performer who crossed so many lines as Harry. He appealed to everybody, whether they were steelworkers or symphony patrons or bobby-soxers, even children—everybody. He had that rare ability. Somewhere he had said that he didn't like to go on television, because he didn't think his music could be represented well on a small screen, and he was probably right. Everything about him was gigantic. The folk purists had a problem with him, but Harry—who could have kicked the shit out of all of them—couldn't be bothered, said that all folksingers were interpreters, said it in a public way as if someone had summoned him to set the record straight. He even said he hated pop songs, thought they were junk. I could identify with Harry in all kinds of ways. Sometime in the past, he had been barred from the door of the world famous nightclub the Copacabana because of his color, and then later he'd be headlining the joint. You've got to wonder how that would make someone feel emotionally. Astoundingly and as unbelievable as it might have seemed, I'd be making my professional recording debut with Harry, playing harmonica on one of his albums called *Midnight Special*. Strangely enough, this was the only one memorable recording date that would stand out in my mind for years to come. Even my own sessions would become lost in abstractions. With Belafonte I felt like I'd become anointed in some kind of way. . . . Harry was that rare type of character that radiates greatness, and you hope that some of it rubs off on you. The man commands respect. You know he never took the easy path, though he could have.

Not everyone I knew was inclined to heap such generous praise upon me. If I felt my head swelling a bit, if my feet were starting to rise off the ground, I knew there was one person I could always count on to cut me down: my ex–mother-in-law, the all-too-present Mrs. Byrd.

Somehow, despite my *extremely* generous divorce settlement with her daughter, not to mention that little Adrienne and Shari, when they stayed with me, had rooms of their own, Mrs. Byrd was not appeased;

she made this clear by trying to turn my daughters against me. Her influence on Adrienne was somewhat limited; I'd nurtured my first-born for her first eight years. But I'd had no closeness with Shari—by the time she was born, Marguerite and I were estranged, and I'd left the family when Shari was barely two years old—so Mrs. Byrd had a pliable subject on which to work. When the girls came to the apartment, seven-year-old Shari would hang back warily while her older sister settled right in. Soon enough, Shari would start having fun, too. But then that phone would ring, and Shari would get on the line, and start nodding as her grandmother filled her head with warnings. By the time she hung up, she'd be whining and crying that she wanted to go home. "Tell your mother to stop programming the kid," I'd tell Marguerite. But nothing worked.

Finally I exercised the right I'd retained in our divorce to say where the girls would go to school, and sent both Shari and Adrienne to a boarding school in Lenox, Massachusetts, called Windsor Mountain. It got them away from their meddlesome grandmother, yet was close enough that I could drive up to see them on weekends. As I did, I fell in love with the region and bought a 180-acre hilltop farm in Chatham, New York, in between Manhattan and the school, so we could spend cozy country weekends as a family. The very idea filled me with joy; I'd never had a country place. For months I spent every free moment directing its renovation, making decisions about furniture and curtains. In the course of that, Julie's parents, quite elderly and frail now, came to realize they needed special attention. So I bought a little farm adjacent to my property, and they moved to a house at the bottom of my hill, one that met all their needs. Up in the main house, my daughters loved their bedrooms, and four-year-old David loved his.

Julie wasn't so excited about ours.

I guess I hadn't asked Julie what she thought about spending quiet weekends in the country. It never occurred to me that anyone wouldn't want to, much less my wife. A major and somewhat arrogant oversight on my part. Country life bored her and country winters appalled her. She was a city girl. She had a circle of very close girlfriends in New York, all black dancers from the Katherine Dunham company. They made for quite a cultural mix. One, Jackie Wolcott, was married to Michael Goldman, the son of a powerful Jewish banker and a Rothschild descendant. Another, Dolores Harper, had settled down with an Italian guy, Joe Autori, who managed a fleet of garages. Frances Taylor, the third, was married to Miles Davis, no less. And then there was Julie, married to me! They called themselves the Sadies, after *Miss Sadie Thompson*, the 1953 movie musical starring Rita Hayworth as a strutting hussy. The Sadies were free spirits, with their own flirty style, not diminished in the least by marriage and motherhood. The one nonfemale addition, who had absolute access to their most private moments, was Vanoye Aikens; he happened to be Katherine Dunham's leading man and the only one who could lift her. The Sadies got together on their own, spoke French and Spanish, smoked cigarettes, drank quite a bit, and stayed up late. They had no real interest in the countryside, and Julie had very little interest in being there without them—especially because, like many city girls, she'd never learned to drive and didn't want to learn. She did appreciate having her parents nearby, but an occasional weekend was more than enough for her. Only then did I realize how dependent we were, Julie and I, on the distractions of our New York lives to make our marriage work. It wasn't a sign filled with promise.

I was giving a concert in Connecticut the night that Gina, my fourth and last child, was born in New York's Mount Sinai Hospital: September 8, 1961. For all the decades of analysis I've had, I cannot say exactly why it is that I chose the name Gina only four months after Sidney Poitier chose to name *his* latest newborn Gina. Nor can I say why Sidney chose to name his third daughter Sherri, in July 1956, some two years after I named my second child Shari. But I think it's safe to say that these were not coincidences.

Even when months passed without our seeing each other, my life and Sidney's remained intimately intertwined. Mostly we cheered each other on, had great fun, and knew that no one else could understand exactly what we'd been through, where we'd started, and what it felt like to be in the space we shared. And when one of us felt overwhelmed by the strange, lonely business of stardom as a black man in white America, we knew there was only one other person to turn to. Which was why Sidney made a point of flying to Miami one day in December 1961, while I was playing the Cafe Pompeii at the Eden Roc Hotel.

Sidney was a wreck. His father, Reginald, had just died after a life of poverty and backbreaking work. Sidney had been one of the pallbearers, solemn and stoic like the others, but later his grief came flooding out. For all his success, he remained unhappy—uncertain about his career, stifled in his marriage. His Juanita, like Marguerite, was a light-skinned beauty from a black bourgeois family. She even had straight hair like Marguerite. And like Marguerite, she was Catholic, her values conservative. Sidney's Hollywood success had put the same sort of distance between him and Juanita that my own success had between Marguerite and me.

In my hotel suite, Sidney shared his doubts with me, and with Julie, who'd come to Miami with me and was tending our newborn with a full retinue of hotel staffers on call. Despite our friendship, despite all the adoring people who surrounded him, despite even his four daughters, Sidney felt profoundly alone. He knew this sense of apartness could be traced not only to the poverty of his childhood and his parents' problems and now his father's death, but also to the darkness of his skin—a barrier between the man within it and nearly everyone he encountered. The irony of his situation was not lost on him. In both of his latest triumphs, *A Raisin in the Sun* and *Paris Blues*, his skin color heightened his character's dramatic impact. But none of his Hollywood successes had made him any happier. He was posing a question that he wouldn't have asked anyone else. Where do you go with this money and power and adulation from white folks, as a man of race? And if none of it keeps you happy for long, what do you do about *that*?

Sidney had an answer, but it wasn't an easy one. During the filming of *Paris Blues*, he'd fallen in love with Diahann Carroll, whom I knew not only from *Carmen Jones*, but because she was married to Monte Kay, the onetime boy manager of the Royal Roost who'd given me my big break! Diahann had looked a little scrawny in *Carmen Jones*, but she sure had blossomed since then. Now she was one of Hollywood's three leading black actresses, along with Lena Horne and Dorothy Dandridge. Sidney was madly in love with her, but both he and Diahann felt deeply conflicted about ending their respective marriages. Sidney felt not only guilty but anxious: How could he hurt Juanita this way? How would his children cope? And selfishly, how would a divorce affect his career? He felt he wasn't emotionally stable enough to go through all this.

I'd faced all those questions, as Sidney well knew. The parallels were all there. I had been married to Marguerite when I met Julie. On occasion, I told him, I'd been all but paralyzed by the guilt and rage and fear I felt in contemplating divorce, especially given that my father had left my mother, and even more so as a black star whose marriage to a beautiful black woman was an inspiration to the black community. "You can't do this alone," I told him, "and you can't just unburden your heart to us and hope that solves the problem. It helps, but what you need is a very good analyst—and a lot of time."

I told Sidney about Peter Neubauer, and how I'd finally come to trust him after my nightmarish experience with Jay Richard and Janet Kennedy. "All right, so I'll go to him," Sidney said.

Julie shook her head. "I don't think so," she said. "Too close a connection." She was right. Peter was far too professional to take on a patient's best friend, knowing that I'd be part of Sidney's story. "But try mine," Julie added. "She's amazing."

"'She'?" Sidney echoed.

Julie explained that Dr. Viola Bernard was not only a distinguished psychoanalyst but a tireless civil rights advocate. As a white liberal, she'd pushed for more black psychiatrists in her profession, and worked with Eleanor Roosevelt in helping the troubled youths of Wiltwyck. She'd also signed on to the study with Dr. Kenneth Clark that persuaded the U.S. Supreme Court that segregation adversely affected the mental health of children, which led to the court's ruling in *Brown v. Board of Education*. Sidney still seemed dubious about going to a woman analyst; how could he be honest with her? But he went, and then kept going, four or five times a week, just like me. Almost immediately, his sessions led him to tell Juanita he wanted a divorce.

That week, Sammy Davis, Jr., was in Miami with a gig at the Fontainebleau, and Floyd Patterson was training somewhere nearby for a fight. One evening all five of us gathered in my hotel suite—Sammy, Floyd, Sidney, me, and Julie—and a hotel photographer, at our invitation, came up to record the moment. Four stars at the top of their game: famous, charismatic, with money in the bank, and all of us, behind our smiles, wrestling with the puzzle of what it meant to be black stars in white America.

Sidney and I were still talking in Miami when just north of the Florida state line, Martin Luther King was arrested for leading a prayer march in Albany, Georgia. The official charges were obstructing the sidewalk and parading without a permit. The truth was that Albany's police chief, Laurie Pritchett, was clamping down on a mass uprising of daily marches and demonstrations that was growing way too successful.

The Albany Movement had started with a sit-in on the very day the Kennedy administration officially desegregated interstate bus and train stations after months of Freedom Rides. The Kennedys were furious. How ungrateful could these black folk be? Charles Sherrod, a twenty-four-year-old SNCC volunteer and Freedom Ride veteran, had rallied Albany's rural black population by saying exactly what the Kennedys didn't want to hear: It was time to strike down Jim Crow in all its forms, not just at the bus and train stations. As the protests spread, Martin arrived with reinforcements from the SCLC, and Chief Pritchett decided enough was enough. On December 16, Martin was jailed along with hundreds of others. He declared he'd stay in jail indefinitely—"jail, no bail"—but in the cell he found himself sharing with two others, a private drama began to unfold. One of his two cell mates, a local black doctor who'd been voted head of the Albany Movement, was overwhelmed by his imprisonment and appeared to be suffering a mental breakdown. Martin feared the doctor might not last much longer behind bars.

Within forty-eight hours, Martin and his cell mates agreed to be released. Martin was put in the awkward position of trying to explain why he'd agreed to leave jail after all, without embarrassing the local doctor by disclosing details of his mental distress. To all watching, he seemed to have lost his nerve. Certainly he'd accomplished nothing; Police Chief Pritchett was able to say that aside from desegregating its bus and train stations on federal order, Albany had made not one concession in its Jim Crow laws. Nor would it—with Martin's release, the Albany Movement deflated like a pricked balloon. So smoothly had Pritchett defused it that Bobby Kennedy called to congratulate him on keeping the peace. Soon it would be said that Pritchett had "killed the Movement with kindness," and Martin, for a long time, would look like a loser.

I heard a lot of anger when I talked to the SNCCers about Albany. They'd done all the hard work. They'd gotten the Albany Movement started, done the door-to-door organizing, made the marches happen, and for what? So Martin could do what he always did: come in at just the right moment, get all the media attention, then fly off to his next high-profile appearance. With his about-face on "jail, no bail," Martin had really outdone himself this time. The movement had lost its momentum, and he was to blame.

I saw both sides of that bitter divide, and sensed I might be able to help. One day in February 1962, I hosted a delegation of SNCCers in the red-walled living room of my New York apartment. I listened as they reeled off their many grievances against Martin and the SCLC: how aloof and self-important Martin was, how overly cautious, how out of touch he was with the students who at this point led the movement. In their scorn, the students ridiculed the whole King family: Martin and Coretta for their too-fancy clothes and social affectations, and Martin's father, "Daddy King," with his bragging and swaggering, as if the whole movement were his congregation. All these charges were grossly exaggerated. I came in for some hits, too, not just for defending Martin but for thinking that the movement had to have a star, as if it were a Broadway play or Hollywood movie. The whole point of SNCC was to cause social change as a group of equals, no one more important than the others, no one even telling the others what to do. Which was true: If you were down in Mississippi as a SNCC volunteer, registering voters, and you said you had a better way, no one stopped you. You just went and did it.

I told the SNCCers I had nothing but admiration for what they'd done. They had the DNA for courage and struggle, going places where no black preacher, including Martin, dared go. I admired their militancy, and I understood their chief grievance: They were doing the hard work, and Martin was getting the glory. But they needed to know that Dr. King's commitment was profound, and that SNCC wouldn't exist without the foundation he'd laid down. They needed to give the man his due.

Then the doorbell rang and in came another guest: Martin. He had no airs that night. Humbled by his failure in Albany, he took great pains to make the SNCCers aware of how much he valued their efforts. Martin knew that a lot of the SNCCers there had lost patience with him. As the evening wore on, though, a grudging respect filled the room. The SNCCers left no doubt that they were going to do exactly what they thought it right to do. No one, including Martin, was going to dictate to them. But they did agree to let the SCLC work with them. And so for the moment, the divide was bridged, and the question became not whether the two sides would work together, but what their next target should be. They had to pick it with enormous care. If they chose a city where the police had learned, like Chief Pritchett, to hide their hatred under a veneer of politeness, they wouldn't succeed in showing the world the true face of segregation. If, on the other hand, they chose a place where the authorities were too unrestrained, the next campaign might descend into widespread violence.

For nearly a year, where to strike next would remain an open question. And then, with a sudden clarity, both sides would agree on the answer.

13

To hear stories of the movement all these years later, you might think no one ever stopped marching long enough to crack a smile, much less tell a joke. Not true. Just inside the front door of the Manhattan apartment where I now live, I keep a large framed photograph of Martin and me taken in the early sixties. It's a picture of us cracking up at something one of us has just said. It's a good reminder that even in the movement's darkest days, we still had room for humor.

That was especially true at the end of the day, when Martin was staying over, which happened so often that the apartment became his home away from home. Julie would bring out his bottle of Harveys Bristol Cream, and Martin would make a big deal of checking to see if anyone had drunk any since his last visit; he marked the level just to be sure. At the oak bar in the corner of the living room, I'd mix drinks for Julie and myself, and bring them over. It wouldn't be long before we were laughing at something—like the way Ralph Abernathy, Martin's heavyset aide-de-camp, snored in that jail cell in Albany, Georgia, so loudly he kept Martin awake all night, so loudly that Martin was convinced it was Ralph's snoring that had driven their third cell mate, that poor local doctor, out of his wits. "Never again," Martin would say with Baptist fervor about sharing a room with Abernathy. "Never again, sweet Jesus!"

Time was filled with laughter with everyone in my life, even in that grim, going-nowhere year for the movement between Albany and Birmingham. I never let a conversation go more than a minute without finding something funny to say. That was just my way. I laughed with my wife and children. I teased the people around me. With good friends like Sidney and Bill Attaway, there was *always* a lot of laughter. In my shows, after that trademark intense opening, I always threw in some humorous songs and tried to get the audience going. And then there was Vegas, a whole other kind of fun, not only because I packed them in at the Riviera, but because, thanks to Bruce the sneering pit boss, I'd rediscovered my love of gambling.

I played the Riviera every year now, for at least three or four weeks, and when I did, I did a *lot* of gambling. I would come into the casino after my last show and nod politely but coolly at the gamblers who looked up as I passed. Usually I'd stop at the craps table, or see who was in for chemin de fer, and let the heat steer me to one or the other. I brought heat of my own; when I had the dice at craps, or took over the bank at chemin de fer, the bets really went up. Sometimes I hit it big. More often, if I stayed in, I started to lose. The worst luck always came when I let the game get personal. I'd find myself sitting next to some arrogant oilman in a ten-gallon hat—the kind of guy who called me "Mr. Belafonte" to my face and probably "nigger" to my back—and stay in, trying to win at his expense. Or a beautiful woman would sit down to play, and we'd start trading looks, and my game would go to hell. I knew that those beautiful women were often shills, sent by the house for just that purpose when a bettor was doing too well. But you couldn't prove it, and it was bad form to ask.

When I lost, I kept losing; I once ended up down as much as $200,000. This was serious gambling. But I loved it—in a nerve-rattling, adrenaline-pumping way. I'd sign a marker; my debt would be charged against my contract. The pit boss would be instructed to call upstairs if I lost $100,000, just to confirm that I wasn't drunk or angry. They were happy to take my money, but I was too important to upset, so they'd much rather have me stop for the night, and stay cool, than keep on losing. While Gus Greenbaum was alive, he'd try to talk me out of getting in so deep. "We don't need your money," he'd say. After he died, there were others who played that role. But as my salary rose, I could take the losses and still be standing, so they went only so far in their gentle expressions of concern. Some weeks, I lost half of my salary.

When I did lose, I stayed pretty cool. I didn't like showing the crowd how I felt, and I could sip a single drink all night, so I didn't get sloppy the way so many gamblers did when those free drinks kept appearing, as if by magic, beside them. I had a lot of show-biz friends, though, who really detonated when they hit a cold streak. And for all of them, alcohol was a key component.

One was Alan King, the comedian. I'd met Alan years before on the Borscht Belt, when we were both playing Grossinger's and the Concord. Alan was the smartest dresser I'd ever seen: the bow tie tied just right, the perfectly pressed white shirt with diamond studs and cuff links, the pinkie ring, the big cigar. Despite his caustic stage image, he was one of the kindest and most generous-spirited comics in the business. Whenever I called him for a civil rights benefit, Alan was right there. And funny. Once, at an early benefit for Martin and the SCLC at the Harlem Armory on West 143rd Street, he took the stage, impeccably dressed, and shot his cuffs as he surveyed the all-black audience. "Before I go any further," he said, "you should understand you've been backing the wrong King. He wants to get you into Woolworth's. You stick with me, I'll get you into '21.' " The crowd went crazy.

Alan's game in Vegas was craps. He'd have his big cigar in one hand, the dice in the other, and just before he rolled, he'd declare to the croupier, "Double on the hard eight!" It was hard enough rolling an eight with a three and a five, or a six and a two. But getting two fours—that was tough. And doubling his bet on the hard eight—that was taking a wild chance. In craps, you never have the table to yourself. Anyone else can join in and bet on your roll—or against it.

One night, a little old lady in a funny hat kept betting a hundred dollars against Alan's rolls, on which his bets were often up in the thousands. I could see Alan getting tense, but what really unhinged him was the croupier, who kept speaking in rhyme: "Don't leave the gate before you play the hard eight." Alan gave him a murderous look. "I don't mind losing my money," he said, "but I don't need to lose it in rhyme." With that, Alan gave the old lady a get-lost glance, as if trying to break his hex. Then, with a show of defiance, he doubled his bet, and the croupier, out of instinct, said, "Out of the door, come on a hard four . . ." Once again, Alan lost. He kept rolling, the old lady kept betting against him, and then the croupier let loose with another rhyme. Giving a drunken Tarzan shout, Alan leaped across the table and started strangling him. The guy was turning blue before the pit boss and a pack of security agents pulled Alan off.

Billy Eckstine, the great bandleader and crooner, was another hot-headed craps player, and the more he drank, the hotter he got. One night I went over to the Thunderbird to catch his act, and ended up at the craps table with him and Dinah Washington, the great blues and jazz singer. Dinah was married—she managed to accumulate eight husbands before her tragic death at thirty-nine in 1963—but she was with Billy that night. She had a little pet name for him, "Beezy." On this night, she was over at the blackjack table, losing small stakes, while Billy was losing big-time at craps. Onstage, Billy was a great romantic; offstage, he was a womanizer, and a fairly hard, crude one at that. I watched as Dinah sashayed up behind him while he was in the middle of a roll. "Beezy," she said, "I need another hundred." Then she touched him. Big mistake! Billy put down the dice, turned to her, and said, "Give you a hundred? Bitch, if your brains were on fire I wouldn't piss in your ears, unless I could piss gasoline." I was pretty shaken by that. It was like seeing the devil emerge from Billy Eckstine's smooth and handsome features. But even Billy was tame compared to Frank.

Sinatra was, of course, the king of Vegas. When he blew into town, off a private plane, whisked to the Sands in a long black limo, it was "Yes, Mr. Sinatra" this, and "Yes, Mr. Sinatra" that. He got his high-roller suite of choice, and drinks and meals for his whole entourage. All on the house. Frank never had a tab, but he did have debts. All of us had debts. What he did with his, we never knew, though we certainly wondered, when he flew off to New Jersey to sing at some mobster's birthday party, if that wasn't payback.

With Frank it was always baccarat with a big ring of people. Frank would be at one end and, on occasion, I'd be at the other. Frank would start out cool, though even then, you sensed his lethal edge. You knew the house was watching with a big smile; our presence juiced up the whole casino. Everyone from the high rollers to the old ladies playing one-armed bandits bet more and drank more and then bet again. Frank's drink was Jack Daniel's, and as the evening wore on, his eyes would turn hard and glossy. When he was winning, he had that glow. He'd crack jokes with whoever had come in with him—Dean Martin or Joey Bishop, or sometimes Peter Lawford—and handle his liquor well. But when he started losing, look out. Many a night he'd punch another player in the face, and then his bodyguards would intervene. If he felt the croupier was to blame for his luck, he'd call out in a loud voice to have him replaced, and if the croupier hesitated, Frank would swing at him, too. I melted away at the first sign of real trouble, and when I next saw him, I'd just pretend that the incident had never taken place. In truth it didn't bother me—it was just what happened when you put gambling, booze, and women together and the party went on all night. I liked Frank's swagger, and I appreciated that he never, ever disrespected me. But that was the year—1962—that the Kennedys cut their ties with Frank, wary of his mob connections. Furious at them for the rest of his life, Frank bristled at my continuing closeness with the Kennedy clan. So our friendship was never quite the same.

For all the racism I'd faced when I first came to Vegas, now I found the Strip, oddly enough, almost free of that taint. My ironclad contracts helped: no discrimination allowed! But I'd come to realize that on the casino floor, no one much cared what color you were. The only color that mattered was green.

That wasn't true when I left the Riviera's cozy cocoon. The next racial slight might come on a New York street corner: the cabdriver with his light on who sped right by me as I hailed him, and then, just half a block down, picked up a waiting white passenger. That happened a lot. It might even come while I was on tour, from someone who knew exactly who I was, and dealt the race card anyway.

That was how it happened in Atlanta, in June 1962, when I came down to give a fundraiser concert for the SCLC. Since Atlanta had a great concentration of middle-class blacks, and since my visit began with a press conference at which I was awarded the keys to the city, my guard was down a bit. After the conference, I checked into the Atlanta Cabana Motel without incident. Then Martin and Coretta and I, along with Miriam Makeba, who now sang at most of my concerts, made our way down for lunch to the motel's fancy restaurant, the King's Inn. The name seemed pretty ironic that day. Despite the hotel's policy of accepting blacks, the restaurant's management had a different view; we were denied service.

Martin felt the incident was somehow his fault because he and Coretta had recommended this particular hotel. He gave the manager a penetrating stare, until the man finally said, "I'm sorry, those are the rules." When I got over my surprise, I was almost amused. Only a week or two before, I'd dined with the President, after attending his birthday party at Madison Square Garden, the one where Marilyn Monroe sang her famous rendition of "Happy Birthday." And now I was hearing I couldn't enter a run-of-the-mill coffee shop.

Word got around fast. The newly elected mayor of Atlanta, a white liberal reformer and civil rights advocate named Carl Sanders, called us to apologize, and forced the restaurant to serve us after all. I knew his heart was in the right place; at my request, he'd already started removing the WHITE and COLORED signs from the bathrooms and water fountains and seating areas of the civic center where I was to sing that evening. But this was still the South. When I walked into the center to rehearse, I saw pale silhouettes on the walls where the signs had been, a perfect metaphor for the attitudes that lingered on.

That was the fall that James Meredith announced his plan to enroll at the University of Mississippi, and the state's Jim Crow governor, Ross Barnett, cried, "Never!" The Kennedys, more fed up now with segregationists than with civil rights activists—though it was always a close call—sent the U.S. Army to plow through a state police blockade in the college town of Oxford, with its pretty courthouse square, and keep Meredith from being mauled by a bloodthirsty mob. Meredith stayed on, enduring countless affronts, to graduate from Ole Miss. But as brave and triumphant as his one-man crusade was, it only showed how far the movement had to go. Eight years after *Brown v. Board of Education*, the fight for civil rights was seriously stalled.

I could feel that frustration with the marchers was growing. The Kennedys were a perfect example of that. We needed a big win to counteract the apathy and exhaustion and to get the nation—the world—charged up again. We were all suffering from fatigue and, worse, redundancy. There was a killing sameness to each rally or march, from the staging and organizing, to asking our same donors to fund it, to making the same case—when they asked us how this time would be different—that we'd made countless times before. We needed a victory—a big, game-changing, history-making victory.

I can't say for sure who first suggested Birmingham, but history would tilt toward the Reverend Fred Shuttlesworth, whose Birmingham parsonage had been bombed. By that fall, SNCC was pushing Birmingham, too. By any measure, Birmingham was the true nerve center of the Jim Crow South. The most nonnegotiable place. It had segregated lunch counters, restrooms, and water fountains. It had black city workers in menial jobs with no hope of advancement. It had a nickname, "Bombingham," for all the homemade bombs detonated by Klansmen in the city's black community. It also had, in Eugene "Bull" Connor, a racist police chief with a hair-trigger temper. If we could break the back of segregation here, we'd regain our momentum. If we failed, the movement would be looking for an appropriate epitaph. I don't think anything we did sent as much fear to the White House as the prospect of Birmingham. I don't think in the civil rights movement there was anything else that carried that kind of potential outcome. It really could break the back of segregation.

We knew what the stakes were—what we might win and what we might lose. Which was why we called the Birmingham project "Go for Broke."

Soon after New Year's, Martin let himself be persuaded by several in his camp, myself among them, that the SNCCers were right: Birmingham, Alabama, was the ultimate target. When it was concluded that he had no choice but to get involved, the question was how. We avoided making plans on the phone; we suspected all our phones were tapped, at one time or another, and that turned out be true. So we used code words, and met at my apartment, one of the few places that felt truly safe. Later, we would learn that FBI agents had gone so far as to set up surveillance microphones in motels where Martin was staying, listening to his conversations through the motel room walls. Our paranoia was hardly misplaced.

I brought the two camps together at our strategy meetings: the young SNCCers and the SCLC. The SNCCers wanted Martin's participation, but in a plan of their devising. That was unrealistic. When you brought Martin in, you got his whole circle. These were some of the very elders from whom SNCC had split. The SNCCers rolled their eyes at the SCLC; they saw them as a lot of timid preachers and hangers-on, more focused on puffing themselves up than taking bold action. The elders, for their part, had trouble masking their condescension toward the SNCCers. Even Martin, in private, would express some exasperation. He felt that for all their courage, they really didn't appreciate the dangers inherent in what they were proposing, especially in Birmingham. They were noble, but also naïve, he thought, and Martin was worried—very worried—about what might happen to them. In this mediator role I'd neither sought nor expected, I did my best to keep egos stroked and tempers in check.

Martin was right to be worried, but the SNCCers weren't as naïve as they seemed. They'd seen some hard times down in Mississippi, during the voter registration drive I'd helped launch eighteen months before. Perhaps our most unsung hero was Bob Moses, SNCC's lead organizer in Mississippi. He was a Harvard-educated philosopher who'd left academia behind for arduous movement work, a man of almost no words with most of us, but a charismatic leader who inspired by putting his body on the line, right up front, again and again. He and his brave recruits had run up against a state legislature that seemed to take rich amusement in raising one barrier after another to their campaign. One new rule required that all voter applicants have their names published in local newspapers. Registered voters—which was to say whites—were also allowed to question the "moral character" of new applicants. Along with the deep, pervasive fear that all rural blacks had of being beaten or lynched, the new rules had all but doomed the drive.

And then, in Greenwood, SNCC's center of operations in the state, fire and violence erupted. The wood-frame house that served as SNCC's office was torched, a SNCC volunteer named Jimmy Travis nearly died in a drive-by shooting, and a local black resident was hit by shotgun fire as he entered his home. That led to an angry confrontation between SNCC and police. Moses and another man were attacked by a police dog, and eight protesters, including Moses, were jailed. By the time the eight were given the maximum four-month sentences each for disorderly conduct, civil rights leaders, the national press, and activists such as comedian Dick Gregory had descended on Greenwood. Under all that pressure, the Greenwood authorities blinked. The eight jail sentences were suspended; Moses and the others walked out free. For a day, or two, they were euphoric. Then it began to sink in that this drama had no more acts. The press and civil rights leaders had left; the Greenwood office of SNCC was still a smoldering ruin; and the voter registration drive had failed.

It was all up to Birmingham now.

Very soon, in looking at Birmingham, we considered the issue of arrests. Martin decided if it came to that, and it almost certainly would, he would have to be among the first arrested. Stan Levison, Clarence Jones (Martin's attorney), and I agreed, but some of his circle protested: Wouldn't he be more needed outside? But Martin, still feeling the sting of Albany, was adamant. The only question was how long he should stay in, and then, when the point had been made, what we would do about bail. We knew the bail for Martin would be high; at the same time, we'd have to bail out others so that Martin didn't appear to get special treatment—the grave mistake of Albany, Georgia. We would need a big war chest for bail. That, I knew, was where I would be needed most.

To help raise bail money for Birmingham, we staged a "secret" fundraiser at my West End apartment on March 31, 1963. The secrecy was because we didn't want to reveal to the public our geographic target or our strategy. Along with a few famous actors—Sidney,

Anthony Quinn, Fredric March—and other notables with deep pockets, we invited all the powerful journalists we knew. At least the ones we trusted. We wanted them in on the story before it happened, so they could write not just with authority but with understanding. Tom Wicker and Anthony Lewis of *The New York Times* were mainstays for us, but so, too, were James Wechsler of the *New York Post*, Murray Kempton of *The New Republic*, and Governor Nelson Rockefeller's influential press adviser, Hugh Morrow. The whole liberal establishment was there that night, in on the "secret" related by Martin, Ralph Abernathy, and, among others, Fred Shuttlesworth, who by now had been the target of not one but two assassination attempts in Birmingham sanctioned directly by Bull Connor.

When the press and paying guests had left, Julie and I sat up with Martin and his advisers. Only then did Martin allow himself his ceremonial glass of Harveys Bristol Cream. But even that did nothing to break the tension he clearly felt. That evening I noticed, for the first time, that Martin had developed a little facial tic. With no particular regularity, his head would yank a bit to the side. Later, when I asked him about it, he said it was nerves—a little reaction to some upsetting thought or new anxiety. It was easy enough, that night, to see what had set the tic off. The prospects for violence in the weeks to come could hardly be greater. Martin truly agonized over putting marchers in danger. But as he well knew, the power of nonviolence was greatest when confronted by violence, and he was pragmatic enough to know, like a general on the eve of battle, that not all his troops would escape unscathed. Always, we came back to the question of the local youth: whether we could strategically afford to encourage them to participate, and if so, how we'd protect them. Martin was deeply aware of the moral implications of urging young people to become involved. The serious injury or death of even one young protester would be devastating not only for his or her family but for all of us—for the whole movement. Yet there was also a moral power in putting youth on the streets: the most innocent among us marching to say that segregation will not stand. The news images of those young people in the streets standing up to uniformed policemen would be powerful, too powerful to ignore.

The question was just how violent Bull Connor's troops would be.

Strangely enough, one of Martin's concerns on April 3, when sit-ins kicked off the Birmingham campaign, was that Connor might no longer be a factor. Some months before, a number of influential Birmingham businessmen had agreed that Connor was too powerful and provocative—bad for the city's image and bad for business. Rather than mount a divisive campaign to replace him as police commissioner, they slyly contrived to eliminate the job and create a new mayor–city council structure. Not surprisingly, Connor had decided to run for mayor himself. But the city fathers had persuaded a more moderate candidate, Albert Boutwell, to run against him. So close were the results of the March 5 election that a runoff had been scheduled for April 2. Martin had wrestled with whether to postpone those first sit-ins; if Boutwell won and Connor were broomed aside, the city might put a peaceful end to its segregation laws. Then again, it might not. A new administration might just as well dillydally into the Easter holidays, which would rob the movement of all momentum. And if somehow Martin reenergized the campaign after that, he might be met by the "kill-'em-with-kindness" approach that Police Chief Laurie Pritchett had used so well in Albany, Georgia. Bull Connor, as it turned out, lost the April 2 runoff. But he had decided to challenge the results in court. While the outcome remained in limbo, both Connor and Boutwell acted like winners, forming separate administrations. Which meant that as the first sit-ins occurred, Connor was still in control of the Birmingham police force. We were deeply concerned about Connor. But in a strange way, we needed him, too. His fiery temper and brutal tactics were the true face of segregation we needed the world to see.

While Connor's fate hung in the balance, the first sit-ins and protests sputtered like wet kindling. Dozens, not hundreds, of protesters showed up. After eight days, only 150 had been carted off to jail, fewer than on the first day of the Albany Movement. When a judge issued a stern injunction banning all protests of any kind, and promised serious jail time for any who dared violate it, the campaign looked doomed. Not even Martin's close aides seemed eager to test the judge's resolve, especially not after Alabama's recently sworn-in governor, George Wallace ("Segregation now, segregation tomorrow, segregation forever"), and Bull Connor drafted a new bail policy that would apply only to Birmingham. The maximum bail bond for a misdemeanor had been $300. Now, if their bill passed, it would be $2,500. The movement could handle a few of those, but not too many.

After retiring to a bedroom to pray for guidance while his advisers waited outside, Martin emerged to declare that he would march in defiance of the judge's injunction. And so he did, on Good Friday, April 12, 1963, with Ralph Abernathy somewhat reluctantly beside him. At first only a few dozen protesters followed. But as he made his way up the streets of Birmingham, hundreds of black bystanders came out to cheer him on. They knew the sacrifice he was making. This was the real thing. The two leaders were duly arrested, along with fifty or so others. Martin, at Bull Connor's express orders, was put in solitary confinement, without even a mattress to sleep on, just a bed frame with metal slats. By the time Martin's cell door shut, Clarence Jones, his lawyer, was on the phone to me in New York. He was terribly worried. Martin had vowed "jail, no bail," but what if solitary confinement proved too much for him? Clarence wouldn't even be able to talk to him all weekend, he'd been told. He had enough money to bail out Martin and Ralph if needed, but the city had just declared no further bonds would be granted to the jailed marchers because the SCLC had inadequate assets. I said I'd do what I could.

As always when Martin was jailed, my first call was to Coretta, to sympathize with her and to see what I could do for her. This time, as soon as I said hello, another phone started ringing in her house, and then another. Meanwhile, I could hear her three older children running around in the background. Coretta had just given birth days before to her fourth child, Bernice Albertine. "Who's taking care of Bernice?" I asked her.

Coretta said she was taking care of Bernice herself.

"What about the other children?"

"Just me," Coretta said with a sigh.

"No one's in that house with you?"

"No," Coretta said. "It's just me."

"What about a secretary or a housekeeper?" I asked.

"No," Coretta said. "Martin won't permit it. He feels he can't afford the help, and if he did, people would think he was living too high."

I knew what Martin earned as a preacher: about $6,000 to $7,000 a year. Even in 1963, that wasn't a lot of scratch. Maybe he couldn't afford help, but how could Coretta cope with four children alone?

"From this moment on," I told her, "you're going to have a housekeeper and a secretary, and I want you to identify a driver who can take you wherever you need to go. And if anyone wants to know how you can afford that, you just say Harry's paying."

I carried through on my promise that very day. I felt pretty good about it until my accountant, Abe Briloff, saw the entry in my accounting books. "You can't have these people on the company payroll," he told me. "They don't work for your entertainment company; you can't deduct their wages from your taxes. If you want these people to work for the Kings, you have to pay for them out of your pocket, after taxes, one hundred percent. Otherwise you'll get your head handed to you."

I did as Abe said. Not long after, Martin was audited. As soon as those IRS agents got to the notation about "staff," they pounced. Where, they wanted to know, was Martin getting the money to pay for this staff?

"Harry Belafonte," Martin said.

In a matter of hours, there were two IRS guys in my New York office, putting a lock on my files, examining how I handled all my corporate money. When they got to "staff—Dr. King," Abe produced the records—taxes paid on the money I paid them, staff withholding taxes paid, too. It was all 100 percent clean.

Those IRS agents looked so disappointed.

Later, when the journalist Taylor Branch was combing through FBI transcripts, researching his Pulitzer Prize–winning trilogy on Martin and the civil rights movement, he came upon an amusing chat between Martin and a friend. Martin related that he and his father had had a conversation about housekeepers. Martin's father complained that his cost him twenty-five dollars a week. Highway robbery, Daddy King exclaimed. "I told him I paid my housekeeper a hundred dollars a week," Martin told the friend. "That really shamed him." Martin laughed. "But I didn't tell him Harry was paying for it."

Within an hour of getting Clarence's call, I'd wired $50,000—most of it raised, some of it my own—down to Birmingham for bail bonds. I hoped I'd get that money back, but you never knew for sure with southern bail bondsmen. Often weeks or months after a case had been settled one way or another, the money would somehow be stuck in the entrails of a southern city's court system.

All that Easter weekend, Martin remained in solitary confinement. Once again, I called Bobby Kennedy, among many others. How could Bobby sit by while Martin was suffering in these barbaric conditions? "Tell Reverend King we're doing all we can," Bobby said wryly. "But I'm not sure we can get into prison reform at this moment." Bobby had made clear that he and the President opposed the whole Birmingham campaign; so far, nothing Bull Connor had done inclined them to interfere with the state's authority. Bobby was especially irked that Martin had "chosen" to remain in jail when he could easily afford the bail to walk free. I tried to explain that choosing "jail, no bail" was not some bid for martyrdom. It was one of the tenets of nonviolence. "This ain't no game," I told Bobby. "It's the real thing. Maybe it's time you open your copy of Gandhi."

Finally, on Monday, Martin was allowed a visit from Clarence, who told him I'd sent the $50,000. Clarence told me later that Martin beamed at that. He was thrilled, not only that he and Ralph could be sprung at a time of their choosing, but that others could be, too. I'd told Clarence I was good for whatever else he needed, and Clarence passed that on to Martin as well.

Cheered as he was by that news, Martin scanned the newspaper that Clarence brought him with growing indignation. A group of Birmingham clergymen had written a letter urging the black community to end its protest, and criticizing Martin for staging the campaign. The moderate Boutwell administration would surely take power, with promises of healing, and the last thing the city needed at this delicate juncture was civil strife. Agitated, Martin began drafting a reply, writing on the only paper he had: the margins of those same newspapers. Eventually, his scribbled notes, linked by numbers and arrows, would be typed up clean and published as a "Letter from Birmingham Jail." One day the letter would be seen as one of Martin's most eloquent testaments, beautifully explaining the need for nonviolent actions to make a community confront unjust laws. It was, at the same time, such a rebuke to the American clergy, putting Christianity—or at least their version of it—to severe test. I would read that letter often in the years to come; for me, it was all about sacrifice: how much the clergy was willing to sacrifice for the greater good of mankind.

For the moment, though, the letter was obscured by the rush of oncoming events.

Martin and Ralph were released on bond that following Saturday, April 20, along with the marchers who'd joined them. Yet even with its leader back in charge, the campaign seemed to drift. So did Birmingham's political stalemate; both administrations were still awaiting word from a judge as to which would take office. They could agree on one thing: When Fred Shuttlesworth applied to both for a parade permit for May 2, both administrations turned him down. That was when the true miracle of Birmingham occurred. The city's children, hundreds and then thousands of black Birmingham schoolchildren, marched, without a permit, into the teeth of Bull Connor's police. James Bevel, formerly of SNCC, now of SCLC, had pushed Martin into using the children at this juncture. But no one could have anticipated how many would respond to the call, why thousands would rush forth right into the phalanx of uniformed police. Even Taylor Branch, in his definitive trilogy, cannot say for sure. And why thousands more followed them, many as young as six or eight years old, is one of the mysteries of the movement—for me, as powerful a show of faith and Christian spirit as I've ever seen.

Those next days remain, for me, a montage of grainy black-and-white news photos. The high-pressure water jets turned on ten-year-old children, slamming them down on the pavement. Groups of schoolchildren singing, terrified, as police with guns and billy clubs bear down upon them. Children emerging in flocks from the Sixteenth Street Baptist Church. Children everywhere, confounding the police by coming from all directions. And, of course, the picture that shocked the world: high school student Walter Gadsden bitten in the abdomen by a snarling police dog.

Hundreds of children were jailed each day, seventy-five to each cell built for eight. The next waves of children weren't coached or encouraged by the SCLC or SNCC; they just came out on their own. When Birmingham ran out of room, hundreds more were put outside in barbed-wire encampments. Finally Birmingham's "big mules"—its leading businessmen—threw up their hands and agreed, with prodding from the Kennedys, to negotiate with Martin. The talks went late into the night, producing what seemed a compromise agreement. Before he could sign off on it, Martin was hauled back in front of a judge, along with Ralph Abernathy, for a hearing in regard to their unlawful parade on Good Friday. After refusing to post their respective $2,500 bail bonds, both men were put in jail again. Not until the children were all set free, they said, would they seek their own release.

The Kennedys were furious. In such a volatile climate, the compromise might fall apart while King and Abernathy whiled away these precious hours in prison, making a moral point that seemed, to the pragmatic Kennedys, an exercise in self-indulgence. Obviously the children would be let out of prison soon enough, one way or another; why did Martin have to make a martyr of himself by tying their release to his? It seemed to Bobby that both Martin and Bull Connor, for their own different reasons, might privately want the violence to escalate at this point. That was when Bobby called me in New York. This was a maddening situation, he said. Martin wouldn't let the SCLC bail him and Abernathy out of jail, but, clearly, he needed to get out as soon as possible so the Birmingham deal could be drawn up and signed, and the children then let out of jail. Could I send down $5,000 myself to bail the two of them out?

I'm sure that at other times in American history, a U.S. Attorney General has called on a private citizen to ask him to resolve a national conflict by wiring $5,000 of his own money. I just can't think of any. I was happy to do it. "It's on its way," I told Bobby. "The only problem is, I'm not sure the SCLC will use it." In my latest talks with Clarence Jones—the one person with whom Martin was able to communicate— I'd learned that Martin was adamant. He would not be bailed out until the children were bailed out, too.

Bobby said he'd get back to me. He then called a prominent black businessman in Birmingham, A. G. Gaston, who'd held himself aloof from the protests until the day he'd looked out his window to see a black schoolchild being hurled up the street by a high-pressure water jet. Gaston was no great admirer of Dr. King, but he was horrified by Bull Connor's troops and wanted an end to the mayhem. At Bobby's request, he took $5,000 from his own bank and sent it right over to the court. To their surprise, and somewhat to their dismay, Martin and Ralph were duly released.

By then, Bobby was back on the phone with me. He understood that if the children weren't bailed out soon, Martin would get himself jailed again. That in itself would spark action on the streets. And Bull Connor would then do all he could to provoke a full-scale riot. Any more violence, from either side, would kill the compromise and fan extreme reactions. What Bobby needed was the money to bail out two thousand incarcerated children.

"Bobby," I said, "I'm not sure I can do that."

"You don't have to," Bobby said. ""What I'm about to tell you will not be repeated. You're going to get a call from Mike Quill. He'll be a resource for you. You may get calls from other resources, too. I'm working on that." Bobby paused. "I'm in an extremely vulnerable position," he added, "as the Attorney General, getting personally involved in a case that has huge federal ramifications—a case I may have to try if this gets out of hand. For me to be showing any favoritism to victims in the case could become highly problematic."

I said I understood, and I certainly did. But I also knew—and I told him this—that if he didn't deal with the situation today, it would be twice as bad tomorrow. There would be twice as many children, and the potential for violence and tragedy would be far, far greater. Helping to get these children out of jail, as part of the larger solution to this whole quagmire, was something he simply had to do.

I'd had some tense innings with Bobby. Too often he'd seemed a cold pragmatist, more intent on protecting his brother than promoting civil rights, which, as Attorney General, was his job. But I felt that at last I'd found his moral center, just as Martin had predicted we would. I knew, too, that he'd come, at last, to trust me, and that I mustn't betray that trust. I did check with Martin to be sure he was onboard. He was. He, too, now sensed that Bobby was doing all he could to resolve the crisis by bailing out the children. Together, Martin and Bobby had estimated that they'd need at least $160,000 for the task. The only people with access to that kind of money on a weekend—at least for a Democratic administration—were U.S. labor leaders, of whom Mike Quill was one.

When the phone rang a short while later, I recognized the thick Irish brogue right away. Mike Quill was the legendary head of the Transit Workers Union—founded by New York City subway workers and bus drivers. He was one scrappy guy. "It's a sad day in America when the cops put kids in jail for nothin'," Quill growled. "We gotta get those kids out." I told him I was grateful for his help. "Lord, yes, we'll do what we can," he said. "I'm sending a courier over with a check for fifty thousand dollars."

By then Bobby had also called Walter Reuther of the United Automobile Workers. Reuther had told Bobby he could come up with a good chunk of that $160,000. George Meany, president of the AFL-CIO, said he was good for $80,000. David McDonald of the United Steelworkers kicked in $40,000, and my friend Cleveland Robinson, a black New York labor leader representing store workers, helped with another sizable chunk.

In the midst of all these calls back and forth, Bobby called to ask if Mike Quill's courier had arrived yet. The intercom rang as we were talking. "That might be him now," I said.

"I'll wait on the line," Bobby said.

I put the phone down and went to check; it was indeed the courier.

Bobby waited until the courier rang the doorbell and handed over his check. "Okay," I told him, "it's in my hands." Only then did he ring off.

While we were waiting for the other checks, I put in a call to Hugh Morrow, Governor Rockefeller's press man. I knew Hugh and knew that in his own buttoned-down way, he supported our cause; he had come to that "secret" fundraiser for Birmingham in late March.

"Hugh," I said, "I know you wrote a check at that party. But now I need another favor."

Hugh heard me out, and came back with good news: Governor Rockefeller wanted to help. I told Hugh that Clarence Jones was flying up to New York to gather all the checks and bring them down to Birmingham. Hugh told me to have Clarence call him at home on Sutton Place as soon as he arrived. "He's not getting in until after midnight," I warned. Hugh said that wasn't a problem.

Clarence called Hugh at about 1:00 a.m. from LaGuardia Airport.

"Mr. Rockefeller would like to help," Hugh told him. "Can you meet us at nine o'clock tomorrow morning at the Chase Manhattan Bank on Forty-seventh Street and Sixth Avenue?"

"But tomorrow's Saturday," Clarence said. "The bank will be closed."

"Please, Mr. Jones, just meet us at the bank."

At precisely 9:00 a.m., Clarence was ushered into the closed bank by security guards, and then downstairs to its central vault. There, beside the vault, were Hugh Morrow and Governor Rockefeller. As the three shook hands, the guards spun the vault's combination locks and turned its immense wheels. In a moment or two, the gleaming vault door, two or three feet thick, swung silently open on well-oiled hinges. Clarence was dumbstruck, he told me later. "I mean I'm an educated Negro," he said, "but I sure never stood in front of an open bank vault door before." Inside were stacks of bills wrapped in cellophane. Governor Rockefeller strolled into the vault like he was walking into his private study, came back with a stack in either hand, and put them on a table in front of Clarence. "I hope this is enough," the governor said with a little grin.

"It's a hundred thousand dollars," Hugh explained.

Hugh went on to say that the governor wanted this done in absolute secrecy. If word got out, Rockefeller might be seen as trying to buy black votes for next year's presidential race against fellow Republican Barry Goldwater. Clarence said he understood. In fact, as I'd warned Clarence on the phone the night before, we needed to keep this a secret from the Kennedys, too, just as we needed to keep the Kennedys' involvement a secret from the Rockefellers. Both sides wanted to help the children of Birmingham, but politics dictated that we keep the sides well apart.

"So is that it?" Clarence asked. "I just take the money?"

"Not quite," Hugh said. He gestured to a clerk sitting at a typewriter, who asked for Clarence's full name and address. He then put before Clarence a demand promissory note with Clarence's name on it. Clarence knew what that was. It meant that he was getting a loan, payable on demand by the lender. What if the Chase Manhattan Bank demanded the money back next week, while it was still in the hands of Birmingham's bail bondsmen? Clarence would be liable for it. But what choice did he have? *I'm not even going to tell my wife I've signed this*, Clarence thought as he signed the paper with a shaking hand.

At the Birmingham motel where Martin was staying, local and national reporters gathered at noon for what the King camp had said would be important news. Martin and the "big mules" had signed off on the terms of their agreement, but Martin wouldn't sanction it until he knew he could get the children released at exactly the same time. Too many parents, over the last days, had harshly criticized him for letting the children be part of the campaign at all, and for the terrible conditions to which so many of those children had been exposed. They called his decision immoral. He might have noted that SNCC had called on the children to march—which was true—but that was inside baseball to the parents.

An hour passed, then another, as Martin waited to hear if Clarence had collected enough money to free the children. Only when he learned that more than $160,000 was actually being transferred to the city's bond clerks did he let the press conference begin. Graciously, he let Fred Shuttlesworth address the press first. In ringing words that would long be remembered, Fred Shuttlesworth proclaimed, "The City of Birmingham has reached an accord with its conscience."

The money we'd raised in those twenty-four hours freed thousands of children. I worried for days afterward that we wouldn't get the bail money back. But that didn't happen in Birmingham—perhaps because the sums were so huge that no bail clerk could claim to have lost track of them, perhaps because Bull Connor and his fellow commissioners were gone, banished by a judge's ruling at last, and the more moderate Boutwell crew was in, doing what it could to heal the city.

That next Tuesday, Clarence Jones was back in his office in lower Manhattan when his secretary announced that a messenger from Chase Manhattan Bank was in the reception area, insisting on handing an envelope to Clarence in person. Annoyed and apprehensive, Clarence came out, signed for the envelope, and then opened it as the messenger disappeared into an elevator. Inside was the promissory note he'd signed on Saturday morning. On it now was written, "Paid in full." Not only was Clarence off the hook; Governor Rockefeller had made the $100,000 a gift to the movement.

For the civil rights effort in America, Birmingham was the turning point. Bull Connor and the segregationists he stood for had nearly stopped the movement cold, and if they had, I don't think Martin could have come back from that defeat. I think he would have lost the last of his power and credibility. The children had saved him. They'd saved us all, putting their lives on the line with an innocence and passion that finally proved more powerful than the fire hoses, and the attack dogs, and the police with their guns. Their purity came shining through, and the white citizens of Birmingham were simply shamed into surrender. It was the most astonishing victory of nonviolent action that any of us had yet seen.

Without Bobby, the children might have stayed in jail a crucial few days more. Violence might have erupted as angry parents filled the streets. Bull Connor might have declared martial law, and Birmingham might have gone up in flames, taking the delicate truce with it. Bobby deserved enormous credit, and I sensed, when I told him so, that he took quiet pride in having done not just what needed to be done, but what was the right thing, too.

That didn't mean the Attorney General was now a convert to the cause. His cause was still protecting the President, in whose interest it still was to pay as low a price as possible. We could push for desegregation one city at a time, but even after Birmingham, President Kennedy saw no political gain in pushing for a federal civil rights bill. The yellow-dog Democrats and Republicans would just kill it in committee. The President and Bobby both felt that all of us in the movement should recognize this reality, and appreciate all they were doing behind the scenes to inch the ball forward. Those secret calls to the union leaders for Birmingham bail money? They were just the latest example. The Kennedys would do more, if we would just work with them in this quiet, back-channel way.

But Birmingham had lit a match. If one southern city could be forced to integrate, why not every other? In Jackson, Mississippi, Medgar Evers of the NAACP demanded the mayor grant the same concessions. Sit-ins and bloody arrests followed. How to contain this spreading conflagration? Bobby took a suggestion from Dick Gregory that he get in touch with James Baldwin, the black writer and activist who'd just published *The Fire Next Time*, his searing essays on race relations in America. Perhaps Jimmy Baldwin would have some intelligent and helpful ideas. Bobby duly invited Baldwin to lunch at Hickory Hill. On the spur of the moment, he suggested that Baldwin gather some representative black voices for an evening of private, off-the-record conversation in New York. Bobby meant the very next night, when, as it happened, he would be in New York, staying at his father's Central Park South apartment.

"So I'm down here having lunch with Bobby," Baldwin said when he reached me by phone from Hickory Hill. "He'd like to meet with a group of us. . . ."

Baldwin and I were very close. We'd met in the 1950s through the Committee for the Negro in the Arts and other left-wing groups that had drawn the FBI's attention. Baldwin was a true intellectual, with a Noël Coward–like flair that intrigued me, and when he moved to France, I visited him with some regularity, drinking wine and sharing stories at the modest villa and vineyard he kept at Saint-Paul-de-Vence. When he came back to America to reengage himself in the struggle, our friendship hit a new level. With the publication of *The Fire Next Time*, he was traveling and lecturing throughout the South, articulating his own racial ideology.

I was glad to be called, but also a bit wary. "What's the agenda?" I asked.

"There's so much anger out there in the black community," Baldwin said. "Even Martin can't get his hands around it. Bobby wants to understand that anger better, to know how to respond."

To me this was puzzling. With all the history that had passed between Bobby and me, what did he not yet know about anger in the black community?

"And who's going?" I asked.

Baldwin said he was reaching out to Lena Horne and Lorraine Hansberry, the author of *A Raisin in the Sun*, and a handful of others. Someone from SNCC, for sure, someone from CORE.

I said I'd go, though on thinking about it, I wondered if we weren't just being set up. I loved Lena and Lorraine, but what could they tell Bobby that the movement leaders couldn't convey with more thought and authority? The more I heard, the more I thought this whole enterprise, from Baldwin's perspective, was froth combined with naïveté.

And I wondered what Kennedy's agenda was. Perhaps the Kennedys were trying to ease us into taking a more moderate line than SNCC or even the SCLC. They might then use that as leverage in the upcoming reelection campaign.

I walked over the next evening, May 24, 1963, to find a real hodge-podge of guests at the Kennedy apartment on Central Park South. It was a perfect coterie for a cocktail party, but a slightly odd group to brief Bobby on the latest in U.S. race relations. A number of the guests were Baldwin's functionaries: his literary agent, his lawyer, and his secretary, among them. Lena Horne and Lorraine Hansberry were there, as promised. So was Clarence Jones. The distinguished black psychologist Kenneth B. Clark was there; the studies he had done in the 1940s to gauge the impact of segregation on children, with the help of Dr. Viola Bernard, had helped influence the Supreme Court in its landmark *Brown v. Board of Education* ruling. There, too, were a couple of young activists from CORE and SNCC. Bobby emerged from the apartment's recesses, accompanied by Burke Marshall and a press aide, and after hors d'oeuvres and a light buffet, Bobby addressed the room.

He started by thanking everyone for coming. Then he got to his message. He ticked off all the things the administration was doing to help our cause. He also pointed out the political realities. "We have a party in revolt," he said, "and we have to be somewhat considerate about how to keep them onboard if the Democratic party is going to prevail in the next elections." Instead of recognizing that, he said, more and more blacks in America appeared to be heeding the radical messages of extremists like Malcolm X. If that continued, Bobby said, it would only bring trouble.

At first the conversation was civil. But as it unfolded, it took in the incipient Vietnam War, and the assumption that young black and white men would fight together if the country needed them. Wasn't that the spirit in which whites and blacks should be working—a patriotic spirit for the greater good of America?

A young black man grew more and more agitated as Bobby went on in this way. Finally the young man said, "I don't know what I'm doing here, listening to all this cocktail-party patter. What you're asking us young black people to do is pick up guns against people in Asia while you have continued to deny us our rights here."

Jerome Smith was a young volunteer for CORE who'd joined in the first Freedom Rides and, like John Lewis, been subjected to savage beatings. Unlike Lewis, he was about fed up with nonviolence, and he knew a lot of others who felt the same way. The next time police responded with guns and dogs and hoses, Jerome said, he would be ready—with a gun of his own. "When I pull the trigger," he told us, "kiss it good-bye."

Bobby was stunned. The one thing he took for granted was that all Americans would be patriotic if confronted by a common enemy.

Trying to ease past the awkward moment, James Baldwin asked Jerome how he felt about picking up a gun to fight for America if it actually declared war. "Never!" Jerome cried. "These are poor people who did nothing to us. They're more my brothers than you are." Not for another year would America send combat troops to Vietnam, but the Kennedy administration was heavily involved, and getting more so every day.

"You will not fight for your country?" Bobby retorted. "How can you say that?"

Back and forth went the tense exchange, until Jerome said that being in this living room with Kennedy made him want to vomit.

At that moment, Lorraine stood up to say she felt sickened, too. "You've got a great many very, very accomplished people in this room, Mr. Attorney General," she said, and then pointed to Jerome. "But the only man who should be listened to is that man over there."

Bobby turned red at that. I had never seen him so shaken. And now, with the floodgates opened, others spoke, too. In that room, it was almost as if all these people had suddenly realized they had this one chance to say what they really thought to one of the most powerful figures in the U.S. government, and no one, not even Bobby, was going to stop them.

Bobby listened to another few minutes of this and then indicated the evening was over. Clarence took that opportunity to go over to him and say quietly that he and Martin appreciated all the administration had done to help resolve the Birmingham crisis. Bobby replied icily that he wished that Jones had said something publicly in defense of the administration at the Birmingham press conference—not about the union bail money, just to give the administration some credit.

I wasn't exempt from Bobby's anger that night. "You know us better than that," he said to me when I came over. "Why don't you tell these people who we are?"

"Why do you assume I don't?" I said. "Maybe if we were not there telling them who you are, things would not be as calm as they are."

"Calm?" Bobby echoed. "With what's going on in the streets?"

"Yes," I said, and then I criticized him in return. "You may think you're doing enough," I said, "but you don't live with us, you don't even visit our pain. Obviously, progress in America is in the eyes of the beholder. What you observe, Bobby, and what you want to see of us, is based upon the needs of the political machine. What we need is well beyond that. The problem is the failure of the power players to see us for who we really are and what we are really experiencing. Those children in Birmingham are our children, not yours . . ."

Before I had finished, Bobby turned to Burke Marshall. "Enough," he said, and turned on his heel, out of the living room and down a hall. His aides spent a few minutes trying to bring the temperature down, but it was a futile effort. With grimaces and glares, we muttered our good-byes and left.

At about 12:30 a.m., I got a call at home from Jimmy Baldwin. "It broke in the *Times*," he said.

"What?"

"Our evening. With Bobby. It's in tomorrow's *New York Times*."

"How the fuck did that happen?"

Jimmy denied he'd done it, though he admitted he'd talked to the *Times* reporter.

"Did it ever occur to you that you didn't have to do that?"

Baldwin was quoted in the morning's story, and most of us believed he was responsible for it. In truth, though, almost everyone in that room had a relationship with the media. Any of us could have been the leaker.

Reading the story the next morning, I had a sick feeling. I felt we'd done a great disservice to Bobby—not by saying what we felt, but by embarrassing him in print. We'd also hurt our cause. Whether Bobby would even talk to me again, I had no idea. I felt sure that the trust we'd built up was seriously eroded, if not altogether swept away.

In a sense I was right. Bobby was angrier at me than he was at Clarence; he felt I'd personally betrayed him. Still, we would have no choice but to talk again, sooner than I could have imagined, about how to deal with a march on Washington.

14

I'd barely finished the *New York Times* story the next morning when Martin called. He wanted every detail of the evening with Bobby. "Disaster," I said with a sigh. But when I relayed Jerome Smith's fighting words, Martin had a different view. "Maybe it's just what Bobby needed to hear," he said. "He's going to hear a lot more of it if the President keeps dawdling on that civil rights bill."

Martin sensed what history would confirm: Birmingham had changed everything. Jim Crow *would* go. The only question was by which means: violence or nonviolence. Martin worried every day now that young, angry activists would stop heeding his pleas for nonviolence and, as Jerome had warned, pick up the gun. If the Kennedys understood that, they might be pushed at last into taking on Congress. "Philip keeps talking about a march on Washington," Martin said, meaning A. Philip Randolph. "It sure would bring the movement right to the President's door. Maybe it's time."

It was a huge gamble. If we called for a march and the turnout was meager, Martin would lose a lot of the clout and credibility he'd just gained. But from now on that would always be his challenge. Each choice would be defined in absolute terms. If we missed our target, we were out. If we succeeded, we were welcome to take on another adventure. But this much we knew: If he failed to act on the idea of a march on Washington, this fateful moment would pass, and with it, perhaps, his last chance to stage a massive exercise in nonviolence before the streets of American cities north and south filled with rage and resentment, guns and blood.

I urged Martin to take the chance, and told him I'd start making calls to actors and entertainers who might lend their names and presence. That very day, I happened to speak with Paul Newman, whom I'd known since my days at the New School, when he was at the Actors Studio and I would sit in on classes; he and Joanne Woodward agreed on the spot to participate in the march. So did Marlon, whom I reached on the West Coast. When I called Martin back to say all three had signed on, I could hear the excitement in his voice. "I wonder," he mused, "what the Kennedys will think of that. . . ." Martin appreciated the nuance: Newman, Woodward, and Brando were all strong Kennedy backers. For them to sign on so readily to a march undertaken, in a sense, as a challenge to the Kennedys—that would send quite a signal.

To everyone's surprise, the President heeded another, very different signal just days later, when Governor George Wallace made a dramatic show of blocking two black students from enrolling at the University of Alabama. The President startled his aides by declaring that on that very night, June 11, 1963, he would deliver a speech announcing he was, after all, submitting a comprehensive civil rights bill to Congress. "The events in Birmingham and elsewhere have so increased the cries for equality," the President told the nation, "that no city or state or legislative body can prudently choose to ignore them. . . . We face, therefore, a moral crisis as a country and a people. . . . A great change is at hand, and our task, our obligation, is to make that revolution, that change, peaceful and constructive for all."

We couldn't have asked for a more strongly worded declaration. Martin was in tears. So were a lot of other people I talked to that night. So was I. Our jubilation was shattered, though, when word came that Medgar Evers had been shot dead late that night in his driveway. The KKK and their brethren wouldn't go down without a fight.

With the Kennedys, as we had learned, progress came as one step forward and two steps back. Or maybe two steps forward and one back. The President had just called for a civil rights bill. So as far as Bobby could see, there was no longer any reason to stage a march on Washington. Why, he asked me in our next phone talk, were we bothering with that? Our target now, I said, was Congress, not the Kennedys. We had to show all those yellow-dog Democrats and Republicans that a broad cross section of the country wanted this civil rights bill.

Bobby had one reason after another for why we should cancel the march. By marching, we'd only jeopardize the bill, not enhance its chances. Congress didn't like being told what to do by a crowd outside its door. If the march did reach the scale we predicted, it would overwhelm Washington's local police force. And that was alarming, because a crowd that large would have "crazies" of all kinds, including, Bobby suggested, violent ones. It was true that in SNCC's ranks, I was hearing more and more talk of militancy. In Michigan, the Students for a Democratic Society (SDS) had sprung up to fight racism by any means necessary. Malcolm X and his Nation of Islam had publicly rejected nonviolence as a strategy and mocked Martin as a "chump." But so far, all that was talk. At the other extreme, Bobby warned, the Ku Klux Klan might disrupt the march, perhaps with gunfire; the FBI had been picking up a lot of alarming threats on monitored calls.

"Every time the FBI weighs in with 'intelligence,' it's always to fan fears of violence," I countered. "The FBI has no reason to fear us on that score. If they really think white extremists may be a threat, then you need to do whatever you can to contain them. And if that means federal troops, then so be it."

Did I realize, asked Bobby, how much all that federal protection would *cost*?

"Are you telling us that we should abandon our constitutional right to freedom of assembly as a cost-saving measure?"

The point was, said Bobby, that it would be money—taxpayer money—needlessly spent. Civil rights would come with or without a march on Washington.

"Bobby," I said, "I appreciate the position you're in. But you're not going to stop us. So you better start getting used to the fact that it's going to happen, and start trying to help us make it work."

That message seemed to reach the President. Shortly after, Martin and other civil rights leaders were invited to the White House to discuss the march, among other matters. The President asked Martin to come to the Oval Office first for a private chat. After pleasantries, as Taylor Branch reported in *Parting the Waters,* the first book of his remarkable trilogy on King and the civil rights movement, the President had Martin step out into the Rose Garden. It was a bit bewildering, but the President soon made himself clear. The FBI had come up with credible evidence that two of Martin's closest advisers, Stan Levison and Jack O'Dell, were active, high-ranking communists, manipulating the SCLC on behalf of the American Communist party. By having this chat in the Rose Garden, the President seemed to be implying that he himself was under surveillance—presumably by J. Edgar Hoover—and had to step outside the Oval Office to give Martin this secret counsel, for fear that Hoover would regard it as tipping off the target of an FBI investigation.

This was not the first time Hoover had struck. From the earliest days of the bus boycott in Montgomery, Martin had relied on a New York organizer and intellectual named Bayard Rustin. It was Rustin who, when boycotters began to be hauled off to jail in the wake of Rosa Parks's arrest, told Martin this was the best thing that could happen. The black community, Martin included, was appalled by the very idea of jail and the social stigma it carried. Bayard was the one who told Martin about Mahatma Gandhi and the tenets of nonviolence. "You should be as willing to go to jail," he declared, "as a bride to go to bed on her wedding night. Going to jail is precisely what we should be doing." For the past several years, Bayard had been an integral member of Martin's kitchen cabinet, counseling him almost every day. But Bayard was vulnerable, for the reason Martin and all of us knew: He had been sentenced to sixty days in jail after pleading guilty to a morals charge for homosexual acts. Not long before Martin's Rose Garden stroll with the President, Hoover had threatened to expose Bayard's criminal record and, in so doing, smear the whole SCLC as a den of iniquity. Only later would the staggering hypocrisy of this charge become clear: The FBI director was himself gay and, according to biographer Anthony Summers, an enthusiastic cross-dresser in his private time. Tragically, Martin had felt compelled to cut Bayard loose. And now this.

Martin was shocked. He asked the President what proof there was of either man's communist activities. Kennedy wasn't at liberty to provide more specific evidence, he said, but the FBI had it, Martin could be sure of that. Keeping Levison and O'Dell on staff, the President warned, could ruin Martin's credibility and kill the movement. Clearly, it would keep the Kennedys from being able to work with Martin on passing the civil rights bill.

In a New York hotel room not long after, Martin related his meeting to half a dozen of his inner circle, including O'Dell, but not Levison, who was away on vacation. O'Dell was appalled. Everyone knew of his youthful support of communist-related causes, he said. He had no regrets about any of that. But the rest of it was just Hoover's fantasy; O'Dell had no involvement with the American Communist party.

Nor, he felt sure, did Stan. Martin listened. And then, after the meeting, he came over to my apartment to ask what I thought he should do.

I didn't know O'Dell that well, but I'd come to admire Stan Levison enormously. A nonpracticing lawyer and fundraiser for various left-wing causes, Stan had made money in real estate and car dealerships, then spent a lot of it fighting for the victims of the McCarthy era, specifically Americans targeted by the McCarran and Smith acts. He did that, I felt sure, not as a communist but as an American outraged at how those acts denied fellow Americans their constitutional freedoms. With the lynching of Emmett Till in 1955, Stan had turned his attention to targets of Jim Crow in Mississippi. That had led him, in turn, to Martin and the Montgomery Improvement Association. Soon Stan was Martin's most trusted aide. In person, he was completely nondescript: short, a little on the chubby side, bespectacled, and very quiet. But he was a brilliant tactician and tireless fundraiser. Again and again, he came in with wise advice that steered Martin away from some pitfall, or toward some opportunity. He was also a brilliant speechwriter who contributed significantly to nearly every speech Martin gave. The President had Theodore Sorensen, who'd come to know Kennedy so well that he could tailor phrases perfectly to the President's sensibility and speaking style. Stan did that for Martin. "I know Stan's not a communist," Martin said. "At least, I certainly think he's not. But to have the President and the Attorney General and the director of the FBI all telling me otherwise—that's somewhat overwhelming."

I told Martin that from a personal point of view, I felt the worst thing he could do was kowtow to the administration and banish his trusted advisers based on not a shred of evidence. We should stand and be tested. Because if they pulled that thread once, they would pull it again; most of us had marched in some communist-backed rally against racism, or signed some letter of social protest sponsored by a group that had some communist ties. "But here's the thing," I said. "Stan is a man of tremendous intellectual capability and moral integrity. So put it to him. And let's see what he has to say, since he's usually right about things."

With Stan still away, Martin could push off that decision. O'Dell required immediate attention. Unlike Stan, he was a full-time paid staffer on the SCLC. If the price of continuing Kennedy support on the civil rights bill was letting O'Dell go, regardless of how unfair that might be, Martin could do that. The stakes were simply too big to stand on principle here. Reluctantly, Martin told O'Dell he had to leave. So guilty did he feel about this, however, that he urged O'Dell to stay until he found another job. This quickly reached the Attorney General. Back came word that soon was not soon enough. O'Dell had to be gone right away. Heartsick, Martin complied. By then, Stan was back from vacation. As I'd suggested, Martin asked him what *he* thought it best to do. Stan was unequivocal. "I'll resign," he said.

Perhaps Martin should have taken Stan at his word. Instead, still acting out of guilt, he had Clarence Jones tell Bobby Kennedy that the matter had been resolved. Martin would no longer have direct contact with Stan. Since Stan was an independent businessman based in New York, Martin could simply stop being his client. That, Clarence cheerfully noted to Bobby, would keep the FBI from taping any conversations between the two men. Clarence asked Bobby if there was anyone else at the SCLC that he would suggest Stan not contact directly. Kennedy grew apoplectic. Here was Martin's lawyer—the same lawyer who'd patronized Bobby at the disastrous Central Park South get-together a month or so before—asking Bobby to collude with him in protecting Stan Levison from FBI scrutiny, implying that all of this was a game and that Stan would maintain some back channel to Martin. So angry was Bobby, especially after the fiasco of the Baldwin evening, and the ensuing story in *The New York Times*, that he proceeded to sign off on Hoover's request to wiretap Clarence. Bobby also brooded hard about whether to approve a wiretap on Martin himself. In the end, he backed off from that, but as Taylor Branch noted, the wiretaps on Clarence made the FBI privy to conversations between Clarence and Martin—essentially opening Martin's private life to FBI scrutiny.

Stan did stop talking directly to Martin—for a while. The truth was, though, we needed Stan too much to let him go, especially with the March on Washington looming. He was just too powerful a chess player. So risking the Kennedys' rage, and perhaps with the civil rights bill hanging in the balance, Clarence and I became Stan's secret conduits to Martin. I didn't call Stan at his office; he didn't call Clarence or me directly, either. Instead, I'd go to a friend's house and call a third party, who would relay the message that Stan should call their mutual friend. Stan would then go out to a pay phone and call me at that friend's house. Both parties were then on "safe phones," as we called them, and the FBI was, we hoped, left out of the loop.

Through these covert conversations, Stan kept in touch, closely enough to guide us as we organized the March on Washington. Closely enough, too, to help Martin write one of the most famous speeches of the twentieth century.

A. Philip Randolph had cautioned Martin not to schedule the march too soon. Endless logistics were involved. It was like planning the Normandy invasion. Randolph knew what he was talking about; he'd planned a march on Washington as far back as 1941, until a last-minute political compromise with President Roosevelt led him to call it off. So Martin set the date for late August, and Randolph, along with the rest of us, began reaching out to organized labor. We all hoped that a hundred thousand people would show up. But only if you had labor working with you could you feel pretty sure you'd get that kind of crowd.

The first calls went out to the leaders who'd pulled together the Birmingham bail money, among others. Walter Reuther of the UAW, Mike Quill of the New York Transit Workers Union, John Lewis of the United Mine Workers, and Moe Foner of 1199, the New York hospital and health-care workers' union—we needed all these leaders to commit troops. All did, though not without getting something in return. If the unions were going to lend their muscle, they wanted a march not just for civil rights, but for workers' rights, too. So now we were planning "The March on Washington for Jobs and Freedom." Some worried that the march might lose its focus on civil rights. Martin didn't. If one hundred thousand people massed in front of the Lincoln Memorial, he said with a laugh, no one would care about the march's name. Just its motive!

I started making calls of my own, to corral more stars.

There was nothing new about putting a star onstage to draw a crowd. Woody Guthrie and Pete Seeger had headlined all those union benefit concerts I went to in the forties, and if they weren't there, Paul Robeson was. A lot of us had grown up with that—seeing the power of celebrity to help social causes—and as our own stars had grown, a whole generation of us had kept faith with that sense of mission. My thought was: Why stop at two or three? Why not get them *all* onstage?

I called Tony Bennett. Without missing a beat, he said, "You got me." I called Shelley Winters, Diahann Carroll, Lena Horne, Billy Eckstine, Burt Lancaster, James Garner, James Baldwin, Sidney Poitier, Tony Curtis, Ossie Davis and Ruby Dee, Jackie Robinson, Josephine Baker, Robert Ryan, Leonard Bernstein, Sammy Davis, Jr., Joseph

Mankiewicz, and more. Every one of them said yes. Partly they agreed to come because they were friends of mine. But this cause was so just, so undeniable, everyone wanted in. And the larger our group got, the more power it had. Everybody felt that—even the Kennedys. With all of us aboard, there was simply no doubt the march would happen. And it would be huge.

When I went back to Martin to tell him who'd signed on, he was, of course, highly pleased, but to my surprise, he paused and then said, "That's a lot of friends."

Yes, I said, I was very proud of that.

"All quite liberal."

"Well, sure."

"Have you reached out to anyone across the divide?"

I told him I didn't see how I could reach out to Ronald Reagan, or George Murphy, two of Hollywood's best-known Republican actors. I really didn't know them at all. I did know Charlton Heston; he was on the other side of the divide.

"What did he say when you spoke to him?"

"I didn't speak to him."

"I think it would be in our interest," Martin said, "to have such a presence."

I pondered how to do this. Then I called Marlon. I told him I hoped he'd chair the march's Hollywood delegation. "Someone needs to lead the posse," I said. "But I'd like to exploit you a bit."

"A bit?"

I chuckled. "Yeah, I'd like to ask Charlton Heston to join us, and I'd like to propose that he co-chair the delegation with you."

Marlon groaned. If I had such a galaxy of stars, he said, why did we need Heston? I pitched Martin's point, and Marlon gave a grudging sigh. But then I added one of my own. The fact was, I said, that Heston knew he wasn't a great actor. Behind those iconic good looks and macho swagger was an insecure guy who yearned for the approval of his peers. Co-chairing a Hollywood delegation with Marlon was exactly the blessing he needed. And he would help our cause. Charlton Heston marching with us would be a powerful image for mainstream America. "Okay," Marlon said with a laugh. "Enough! You got me."

So I flew out to Heston's home and proposed that he and Marlon co-chair the Hollywood delegation. Heston gave me a look—that craggy, deep Charlton Heston look. "Co-chair with Marlon?" he echoed. "I'd be delighted."

And could we bring the Hollywood delegation to Heston's home for a press conference when we announced that?

No problem.

I called Martin as soon as I got back to my hotel. "We got Heston!" With that, Martin's spirits went way high. Now he, too, knew the march would succeed, and lead us where we needed to go. How could it not? We had Moses!

The Kennedys were cautiously onboard now, reassured and impressed by the star power. Instead of some gathering of scruffy activists, this march was starting to sound almost glamorous. Not, though, to J. Edgar Hoover. Behind the scenes, he was our biggest adversary. On an almost daily basis, he preached fire and brimstone in his interoffice memos. The nation would be destroyed! Communists everywhere! He had his agents call each of the actors and entertainers I'd lined up, warning them the march might be violent, and urging them not to attend. When the march turned out to be peaceful and joyous, the stars would seem to have done a modest thing by showing up. But ignoring those dire FBI warnings, in the days before the march, took some courage.

When he awoke on August 28, 1963, Martin felt deeply anxious. What if no one came? What if violence broke out? What if people died? But by 9:00 a.m., one hundred charter buses an hour were rolling into Washington. Twenty-one long trains drew up to Union Station. At the Washington Monument, where a morning concert was to kick off the rally, tens of thousands gathered. Almost more astounding than the numbers was the complexion of the crowd: black and white in almost equal proportions, all happy and excited together. Martin could stop wondering whether anyone would come, and so could we.

Joan Baez started by singing "Oh, Freedom," and an amazing array of performers followed: Peter, Paul and Mary, Odetta, Josh White, and Bob Dylan. I could take no credit for getting any of them there, and in fact missed the concert. I'd had my hands full recruiting the celebrities who would join me at the Lincoln Memorial for the afternoon speeches. Just getting the Hollywood contingent onto a plane in L.A. the day before, and getting them from the Washington airport to a hotel, was a full-time job; keeping track of all the other celebrities arriving from New York was a second job. Or maybe a third—I lost count.

Not long after noon, I got my whole gang down from their hotel rooms and onto a bus that took us to the far end of the reflecting pool.

Tens of thousands of people had already made the walk here from the Washington Monument; many were cooling their feet in the reflecting pool. Less than half a mile away, discreetly hidden, were tanks and other combat vehicles, and troops armed to the teeth. But with not a hint of violence emanating from that crowd, the military might would remain where it was. Most in the crowd would have no idea it was there.

We could have been let out right behind the Lincoln Memorial, but I'd decided we should take the risk of walking the length of the reflecting pool and interacting with the crowd. The power of that moment was something I've never forgotten; I can feel it still. To see Burt Lancaster walking by—that was good for a double take right there. But then to see Marlon and Charlton Heston, and Sidney Poitier, Paul Newman, Mahalia Jackson, James Garner, Tony Bennett, Lena Horne, Diahann Carroll, Sammy Davis, Jr., one after another after another, in a posse, shaking hands as we all went by, talking, offering uplifting words: The effect was electrifying. I've thought a lot since then about the power of celebrity harnessed to social causes, whether it does any more than give a crowd a thrill and stroke a few stars' egos. Maybe, sometimes. But not that day. Not with the whole country at a tipping point on civil rights. As a group, we played more of a role in most Americans' daily lives than their priests or pastors, their politicians, or even their teachers. We were the ones singing America's songs, starring in its movies and television shows, presiding at all the communing places of American mass culture. To see us all together, moving as one, saying by our presence here that *segregation would not stand*—that was powerful. And for all the power we were sending through that crowd, so much more was being beamed by television cameras into living rooms across the land.

Behind the Lincoln Memorial, we had our own little holding pen, with tables of drinks and sandwiches. For a while we just mingled. The union leaders were there, too, and writers—everyone whose presence I'd thought would help elevate the occasion. Burt Lancaster chatted with Walter Reuther, Jimmy Baldwin hung with Charlton Heston, Sammy and Marlon talked as Marlon displayed an electric cattle prod that the Birmingham police had used to shock fleeing children. Finally we all took our seats on different levels behind the podium, and Camilla Williams sang the national anthem. I looked out and realized I would never again, in my life, see so many Americans gathered in one place. Not just 100,000, but more than 250,000—more people than we imagined in our wildest dreams. And not out of anger, or demagoguery, but hope. What, I wondered, must J. Edgar Hoover be thinking at that moment, holed up in his dark little den at the FBI?

Julie and I were seated to the right of the podium just a row or so back. So we were perhaps ten feet from Martin, looking at him from behind, when he launched into his historic speech. As usual, he had a little envelope with scribbled notes—just the highlights he wanted to hit. He never had more notes than that. I heard his voice echo back from the speakers, over the crowd, and for a while just let myself ride the cadences. Occasionally he spoke a little too fast, but not on this day. He took his time, and let his phrases settle. I'd heard him speak many times and so I recognized phrases and themes I'd heard before. Today they were spun in a slightly new order. At some point, I sensed that that new order was improvisation; by either accident or intent, he'd departed from his prepared points. Yet miraculously, and magnificently, this speech became the synthesis of every speech he'd ever made, and the best of all of them. From behind him, Mahalia Jackson called out gently, "Tell 'em about the dream, Martin." And as he did, I heard something new: a tone of confidence that this enormous crowd had brought him. Change *would* come. Jim Crow *would* go.

Back in my hotel suite afterward, good friends gathered: Marlon, Paul Newman and Joanne Woodward, Shelley Winters, Sidney Poitier, Ossie Davis, and Ruby Dee. The march was so overwhelmingly successful that we couldn't get our minds around it. Not one incidence of violence! Every television report was glowingly positive, not just about the mood of the crowd but about the prospects for the civil rights bill. The president had even received Martin back at the White House after his speech, along with Roy Wilkins of the NAACP, Walter Reuther, and A. Philip Randolph. "Maybe we should stay a few days," I suggested to my friends. "We could meet in groups with Republican congressmen about the bill." There I was again, pushing my friends too hard. This time, after gauging the mood, I let the suggestion drop.

A television was on, and at some point we gathered in front of it to see a live roundtable interview with all the top civil rights leaders, including Martin. "Wait a minute," I said. I looked more closely at the moderator and nearly fell off my chair. "My God!" I said. "It's Jay Richard Kennedy!" My old financial adviser! The con man–turned–FBI informer!

I hadn't seen him since I'd ended our fraught relationship—not in person or on television. He wasn't a television moderator. So how could he be there now, on this public television program, sitting with the country's leading civil rights figures? It blew my mind.

When I had an opportunity to speak with Martin a day or two later, I asked him what he knew of the program's moderator. He said he'd gotten the impression that Jay Richard Kennedy was an adviser to James Farmer of CORE, one of the panel's other guests. This turned out to be true: Kennedy had weaseled his way into Farmer's good graces and become a confidant. In his conversations with the FBI, as transcripts later showed, Kennedy would pitch Farmer as the smart and accommodating civil rights leader the government should work with, while characterizing Martin as "dumb" and, at the same time, an active agent of Peking, whom the FBI should sideline at any cost. Soon Kennedy would also worm his way into Frank Sinatra's inner circle, becoming the singer's financial adviser, at least for a while. He would go on to infiltrate the Black Panthers, even becoming the paramour of one of the Panthers' female leaders. Was he a mole for the FBI in these chapters of his strange life, too?

All this I learned years later. At the time, I just wondered aloud, with Martin, what Jay Richard Kennedy's true role might be. I told Martin my story, probably violating my legal agreement with Kennedy by sharing it. As far as I could see, though, Kennedy had changed the playing field by putting himself in close proximity to Martin and the other civil rights leaders. I had a higher obligation now, to make Martin aware of what a dangerous character Kennedy was. My story astonished him. Not surprisingly, Martin shared it with Clarence Jones, who passed it on to Stan Levison. And then I was in for a far greater surprise.

The next time I saw Stan in New York, he told me there was something I needed to know. Usually Stan seemed so unflappable. Not now.

"Okay," I said. "Hit me."

"My ex-wife was your analyst."

I tried, without success, to get my mind around that.

"I was married to Janet," Stan said. "Back in the forties. We got divorced. She then married Jay Richard Kennedy." He held up his hands. "I don't know what it means but . . . it happened."

Now my mind was totally blown. Could this really be a coincidence? Stan filled in what he could. Janet really was a psychotherapist; with Stan, she'd also participated in various leftist causes of the forties. Somehow, Stan had met Jay Richard and got into business with him—a chain of car washes or laundries in Latin America, as I recall. Stan hadn't known much about Kennedy; only that when his marriage broke up, Janet went off with him. Whether she'd known of Jay Richard's communist background, Stan had no idea. Had the FBI forced her to be an informant, too? Who knew? It was possible, we agreed, that Janet might have remained unaware of Jay Richard's past as Jacob Solomonick, and known him only as Jay Richard Kennedy, novelist, screenwriter, and financial adviser. But then why had Janet, in my sessions with her, kept trying to worm out information about Paul Robeson, if not to pass it on to her husband?

Whatever Janet's role was, Jay Richard had been a very malevolent force in my life—and in Stan's. I knew *I* was a target; after our legal separation, more than one of Kennedy's clients had relayed nasty stories he'd spread about me. I'd supposedly cheated him, betrayed him, and, of course, failed to appreciate the great boost he'd given to my career. It seemed only logical that if Kennedy were still an FBI informant, he'd have done all he could to throw dirt on me. But what about Stan? Was it too much to imagine that Jay Richard Kennedy, out of spite toward his wife's first husband, had provided the FBI with disinformation about Stan that had led J. Edgar Hoover to zero in on him? Kennedy had motive enough, and the FBI would surely chase any whisper. This was, after all, the height of the Cold War, a climate of spies and double agents, plots and counterplots. The Cuban missile crisis was still reverberating; *The Manchurian Candidate*, with Frank Sinatra as a former U.S. prisoner of war brainwashed by the communists to kill on remote command, had perfectly captured the country's ongoing paranoia. I felt twinges of paranoia myself. In the days after Stan told me about Janet, I wondered, occasionally: Was Hoover right? Maybe Stan *was* an active communist, taking his orders from Moscow. Maybe he was in league with Janet *and* Jay Richard Kennedy, manipulating Martin and his whole circle. But then I would talk to Stan again, and think, Nah, impossible. The guy was a mensch. And he was.

Years later, when I filed Freedom of Information Act requests with the FBI for any and all transcripts related to me, I got a lot of jumbled, very redundant, highly redacted pages. They did confirm that the agency had combed my past for every rally and cause I'd had anything to do with, searching for the remotest communist ties. It had done that back in the early 1950s, when my name showed up in *Counterattack* magazine, and concluded I wasn't a member of the Communist party or a threat of any kind. But in 1957—after Jay Richard Kennedy and I broke apart—there was Kennedy in the FBI files, identified as formerly Samuel R. Solomonick, telling the agency that while Harry Belafonte enjoyed great popularity, he was "generally disliked by the Negro people." Eight years later, there he was again, telling the FBI that I, like Martin, was "an agent of the Peking government."

Censored though they were, the files confirmed that Jay Richard Kennedy had been an FBI informant over a period of years, at least from the mid-1950s to the mid-1960s. But not, perhaps, a very respected one. In a 1965 interoffice memo relaying Kennedy's charge that I was an agent of the Peking government, the agent sending the report noted that Kennedy "would not give any facts to substantiate this allegation." The agent also noted that Kennedy had been my manager some years before, and was still bitter over the loss of his client. Another agent wrote that Kennedy furnished "nebulous information." He added that Kennedy "attempted to impress interviewing agents with his influence, social standing, power, and wealth." That same year, another FBI interoffice memo would note that "Jay Richard Kennedy, a self-styled racial expert who claims considerable influence over James Farmer, head of CORE, feels he should have a talk with the director about racial matters and that he may communicate with him to arrange for an appointment." The director, of course, being J. Edgar Hoover. Back came this reply: "We have, in the past, explored results of some of [Kennedy's] speculation and determined it unfounded in fact. Accordingly, it is felt that it would be a waste of time for the director to give this man an audience."

So was Jay Richard Kennedy an FBI informant at the time he represented me in the mid-1950s or not? Did he seek me out, through Janet, either at the agency's direction or at his own initiative to spy on me and so leverage his standing with the agency? Or was he a spy without portfolio at that point, exacting revenge only after our unhappy split by going to the agency and smearing me as best he could? On this, the FBI files would offer flatly contradictory versions. One document would confirm that Jay Richard Kennedy was a "confidential informant of the Office of Security circa 1958 through 1969 and reported to this office primarily on matters pertaining to the activities of various civil rights leaders." But another internal FBI memo would note that Kennedy was interviewed by bureau agents as early as 1954. My own suspicion was that Kennedy had conducted a personal vendetta against Stan Levison, as his wife's ex; got the FBI interested; and then started ratting on me. I could have sought out Kennedy and demanded that at last he tell me the truth. But how would I have known if he was telling it?

When I sift through the history of the civil rights movement, I'm struck by how almost every triumph was followed, in days or weeks, sometimes hours, by some grievous crime of hate, as if Jim Crow were a living, breathing, snarling being, and the hatred of every last racist in the South were concentrated in him as he pulled another trigger or lit another fuse. Medgar Evers's murder on the night of President Kennedy's historic civil rights speech was one such instance. The four black Sunday-school girls murdered by a bomb in Birmingham's Sixteenth Street Baptist Church, less than three weeks after the March on Washington, was another. The heinousness of this act, carried out by Klansmen who planned their bomb to explode in the middle of a Sunday morning, was truly beyond human understanding. The girls—three of them fourteen years old, the other one eleven—had gone down to the women's lounge in the basement to primp for the morning's youth service. They were the ones closest to the bomb when it went off.

Martin, when he preached at the funeral for three of the girls, declared, "They did not die in vain." He was right, for the shocking murders shamed and silenced many of those in Congress planning to vote against the civil rights bill. How could America be said to have done enough for civil rights when Sunday-school girls could be killed with impunity?

President Kennedy's assassination, two months later, left a larger, darker stain on the country, one that extended far beyond the fight for civil rights. But its effect on civil rights was profound; the president who'd finally listened to his conscience and called for a sweeping civil rights bill would leave that bill as a legacy the entire country felt bound to see through.

I was in Paris when I heard the news, visiting the set of the jewelry-heist film *Topkapi*. I'd gotten to know Jules Dassin, the blacklisted American director who'd started a new career in France, and Melina Mercouri, the Greek actress whom he'd soon marry, when they came to a concert I gave in Greece. Since then, we'd often seen each other in New York, and established a custom of sending little tchotchkes to each other. Dassin was directing *Topkapi,* and Mercouri was starring in it, along with Peter Ustinov, and I spent a delightful few hours at the Boulogne-Billancourt studio, watching this dazzling ensemble work together. Afterward, we drove into Paris for dinner. News of the assassination came over the radio, but of course in French. None of us quite understood what was being said. We rolled onto the Île Saint-Louis, and climbed up to the large, rambling apartment of our host and hostess, the American novelist James Jones and his wife, Gloria. We heard the news from Gloria as she opened the door. Everyone was sitting in tears in front of a television set as those terrible, grainy clips of footage played again and again. I felt the bottomless grief that all of us who lived through that time did. But I also thought: What if some black radical did this? I needed to get back into the circle with Martin and prepare for the onslaught if that were the case.

I didn't go to the funeral. I didn't want to invade the Kennedy family's personal space. For all the conversations I'd had with Bobby, and the handful of talks with the President, I never regarded myself as an insider. I never made that presumption. I was a contact, a conduit, a useful character. That was enough for me.

As images of the funeral reverberated in all our minds, and a new president inherited the challenge of passing the civil rights bill, I flew to Africa for a celebration full of joy and promise: Independence Day for Kenya. With me I brought Miriam Makeba and several musicians, though not Millard Thomas, who sadly had died of cancer. Miriam and I were received like visiting royalty. We sat in the reviewing stand as tribe after tribe paraded by. On one side of us was Jomo Kenyatta, the country's first prime minister, who vowed that tribal rivalries would be buried and forgotten in the new republic. On the other was Prince Philip, representing the British Crown. At some point, the British flag was lowered, and the Kenyan flag hoisted up to take its place. Carefully, the British flag was folded and handed over to Prince Philip, who put it on his lap. I was within earshot as he turned to an aide. "You know," he said with that casual tone of entitlement that royal breeding brings, "I never really appreciated the vastness of the British Empire until I started receiving all these bloody flags."

After the ceremony came the concert, in a vast amphitheater, to which we walked with all the tribes. There among them were a number of very proud, and very tall, Masai warriors, who were simply transfixed by Miriam. After greeting us with much flattery, one of the

Masai started talking and gesturing toward Miriam, and then to me. Finally a translator stepped in. "He would like to know," the translator relayed, "if you would be good enough to sell Miriam to him for ten head of cattle."

I declined their kind offer as gently as I could, and managed to refrain from teasing Miriam until we'd moved on. But that moment, in its own way, showed just how deeply rooted tribal customs were in the new democracy. Independence in Africa, as Sékou Touré and other new leaders were finding, was hard to achieve, but even harder to manage.

Miriam and I were working beautifully together, united in our desire to bring African music to America, and just as eager to take American folk songs abroad. Our concerts together were always sellouts, and soon we would record an album, *An Evening with Belafonte/Makeba*, consisting only of African songs, that would win a Grammy Award. I'd loved bringing Miriam to American audiences, and since then, I'd also helped the young African horn player Hugh Masekela immigrate to the States. Hugh was Miriam's boyfriend, and briefly her husband, but he was also a great talent who, like Miriam, quickly made his own career. For me, it was all part of paying off that karmic debt to the legendary jazz players who'd given me my break at the Royal Roost. I was happy to do it. But for Miriam and me, the ride was about to get a little rougher.

Miriam was an international figure now, a top entertainer, and with that profile came the power to speak her mind. In 1963 she'd testified before the United Nations on apartheid, and while the U.S. government hadn't deported her, South Africa had deprived her of citizenship. Briefly, she was a woman without a country, though Guinea, Belgium, and Ghana issued her passports in solidarity; she ended up with nine altogether. Fortunately, Miriam had brought her daughter, Bongi, to the United States from South Africa, so she was protected that way, too. She earned enough to have a full-time African nanny for Bongi, and a nice New York apartment, which she opened to visiting African students.

Most belonged to activist Stephen Biko's Pan-Africanist Congress (PAC), a group more militantly anti-apartheid than Nelson Mandela's African National Congress (ANC). I was staunchly pro-ANC, so that caused some tension between Miriam and me. So did the fact that some of the more radical members of SNCC—the ones rejecting nonviolence as a strategy—were hooking up with PAC, often directly through Miriam.

I began to feel Miriam was getting into deep waters, not just politically but personally; there were a lot of drugs in this scene, and not just soft ones. I found myself warning Miriam to clean up her act, which only made her resentful. I could hardly have predicted where Miriam would end up. But the vibes were disturbing.

I can't remember if, in worrying about Miriam's career, I worried about my own. Perhaps not. I still sold out amphitheaters; I still commanded top concert fees in Vegas. The truth was, though, that tastes were changing. I had my core audience, both large and global. But the British invasion had begun. In February 1964, the Beatles made their first appearance on *The Ed Sullivan Show*. In about six minutes, they played two songs and changed the world. I was still very hot; the very next month, Ed Sullivan gave me twenty-two minutes on a single show to sing five numbers with backup singers and a band. No one had ever had twenty-two minutes before on *Sullivan*. But that giddy sense of being the hottest thing in show biz—that would start to fade. My albums would win acclaim, but *Belafonte at the Greek Theatre*, which came out in 1964—and won a Grammy nomination for Best Folk Recording—would be my last to break the Top 40. No one stays the champ forever.

The very way music was changing—going electric, getting louder—had a profound effect on my voice. I was, at heart, a cabaret singer. I had the chops to play hotel rooms and dinner clubs with a microphone and a single spotlight—I could have done that forever and never lost my voice. Pushing to be heard over Broadway orchestras without a microphone had marred my clarity and tone. As my backup band went electric to keep up with the times, I began to do serious injury to my vocal cords. I didn't want to go back to Dr. Max Jacobson, who was now treating patients so indiscriminately that he would prescribe amphetamines without even seeing them. Instead, I went to a Dr. Max Salm. He'd treated a lot of stars, which made him arrogant. And the more popular you were, the more arrogant he became. You needed him, he didn't need you. He really played God. He looked down my throat, saying nothing for what seemed the longest time. "You can rest your voice, and eventually you'll be fine," he said when he'd finished his exam.

"How long is 'eventually'?" I asked.

"Three or four months."

I gasped. "That would be a catastrophe," I said. "I can't cancel that many concerts."

The doctor shrugged. "Or . . . ," he said, "you can have me remove the node I see on your vocal cords. Your choice."

It wasn't much of a choice. Dr. Salm made his preference clear, and gave me every assurance that all would go well. Who was I to question him? So he gave me a little local anesthetic right there in his office, and "popped out" the node in a matter of minutes. "Now just rest your voice for ten days, and you'll be fine," he said with a dismissive wave of his hands.

My voice was never the same. My vocal folds, instead of being parallel, were bowed. And Dr. Salm had left a lot of scar tissue, so the folds could never close correctly after that. I took vocal lessons to try to change the way I sang, to no purposeful end. From critics, I'd never received anything but raves. By the early 1970s, though, I noticed that the critics seemed to be getting younger—the old guys were retiring— and that they had less interest in the songs I sang. I reacted by turning up the volume. The more I did, the more I strained my voice.

Each day, whether or not I had a concert that night, I talked with Martin, or Stan, or Clarence. Often, too, I talked with Bobby, who would remain as U.S. Attorney General for some nine months after his brother's death.

One day, I got a call from Jim Forman of SNCC, still down in Mississippi. Vietnam was just a smudge on the horizon; President Kennedy had sent advisers, but the Gulf of Tonkin and the military escalation that followed were still months away. Yet a suspicious number of young black men in Mississippi were being drafted. More suspiciously, a lot of them were SNCC volunteers. Coincidence? Jim thought not, as did I. So I called Bobby and told him where I thought this would go. SNCCers who got drafted would either go to Vietnam and become military agitators, or be draft resisters and conscientious objectors. Either way, it wouldn't help the U.S. military. At the same time, it would kill SNCC's voter registration drive, which in turn would hurt the Democrats.

There was a long pause on the line.

"Well," Bobby said at last, "this is not so simple."

He understood, he said, that southern draft boards were probably going out of their way to draft local SNCCers. But if Bobby was seen as intervening in the recruitment process, that would be toxic for him.

Not only would he look unpatriotic; he'd seem to be engaged in a self-serving maneuver to boost the ranks of Democratic voters. Still, he appreciated the problem.

"Who are the most important ones?" he asked.

I rattled off the names of some I thought were in jeopardy, and then Bobby ended our exchange with no commitments. He never called me to say what he'd done, and I never asked. But almost overnight, the all-out campaign to draft SNCCers came to an end.

We spent a lot of time strategizing, in the spring of 1964, about how to help get the civil rights bill passed, and speculating on whether President Johnson was secretly trying to kill it. At that moment, its outcome was uncertain at best. The House had passed it, but in the Senate, West Virginia's Robert Byrd was leading a filibuster that would last fifty-seven days. Even if it did pass, we'd come to realize, it was only half a loaf. It outlawed discrimination in public places based on race, color, or national origin, and it called for desegregating public schools. But while it also declared that voters be treated equally, it failed to rule out literacy tests and other Jim Crow tactics meant to keep poor blacks from the voting booth. Integrating lunch counters, bathrooms, and schools was important, but without a free and fair vote, southern blacks would still be second-class citizens in a racist society, with absolutely no political power.

That spring, Bob Moses, the quiet but fierce leader of SNCC's voter-registration drive in Mississippi, declared that a new approach was needed. In addition to small, localized drives, he wanted an army of college students to blanket the state. Mississippi Freedom Summer, as he called it, would register all the literate black voters it could find, and educate the rest to be literate; part of the plan was to set up makeshift schools. Somehow, SNCC would have to recruit hundreds of college students, train them, get them down to Mississippi, manage them while they were there, and keep them fed and housed. The organizational challenge was formidable. The cost would be staggering. Long before I got that desperate call to bring $50,000 in cash to Greenwood, I knew that SNCC would be counting on me for more money.

The big debate that spring was about who we should enlist. Black college students would be at far greater risk in rural Mississippi than white students. A lot more white students were lining up, too. In the Northeast's top colleges, heading south for the summer to register black voters suddenly seemed the thing to do: a noble mission and, as much, a real adventure. But a lot of SNCCers balked at the prospect of

Harvard men and Yalies swarming into Greenwood and brandishing their Ivy League educations. Since I was supplying a lot of the bankroll, I got to weigh in on that, and what I thought was: Hell, yes, bring on the white students. I knew that to a growing number of SNCCers, the movement had taken on new meaning: not integration but a separate and equal black society. That wasn't my view. I shared Martin's dream, of a world in which no one's skin color made him better, or different. It was the reason I pushed so hard to have white students come to Mississippi.

SNCC wasn't the only group that launched Mississippi Freedom Summer. CORE was another. In fact, two of the three young activists who vanished on June 21, Michael Schwerner and James Chaney, were affiliated with CORE; the third, Andrew Goodman, was from SNCC. By then, the Democrats had broken the filibuster on the civil rights bill, and the Civil Rights Act was signed into law by President Johnson on July 2. As we feared, it did nothing to protect the voting rights of poor southern blacks; we would have to bring mass registration drives into every southern state. Our only other choice was to push for a new federal voting rights bill, which seemed a near-impossible feat. Whatever course we chose, Schwerner, Chaney, and Goodman would not be with us. On August 4, FBI agents, acting on a tip, found their bodies buried on a farm near Philadelphia, Mississippi. (Not by chance would Ronald Reagan choose to declare his first presidential candidacy in that bloodstained town. Whites and blacks would know all too well that he was signaling his support of Jim Crow.) That was when Jim Forman called me, desperate to keep Mississippi Freedom Summer alive, and Sidney and I found ourselves flying to Jackson with that doctor's satchel.

Walking with Sidney into that Elks Hall in Greenwood to jubilant cheers would be one of the most gratifying moments of my life. But Greenwood was scary—it really was. Standing before that audience, I wondered if some Klansman wasn't fixing us in his crosshairs, about to squeeze off a shot. I felt ashamed of that thought as I scanned the crowd and noticed how many had bandaged heads and arms. Among the thousand brave souls who fanned out each day that summer with clipboards in hand, some inevitably came back beaten and bloodied. But my fear returned in the morning, when Sidney and I spent some time at Greenwood's latest SNCC headquarters—another wood-frame house, not burned down yet—and strolled down Main Street. Nearly everyone—white and black—was armed. We saw black farmers brandishing shotguns, unheard of in the South, staring down whites who rolled by in pickups with full rifle racks. This was war.

When we gave the SNCCers that money, I set aside $10,000 of it as a reserve. With any luck, they could get their army of volunteers through August on the other $60,000. Seeing how frayed everyone's nerves were in Greenwood, I had a thought as to how that $10,000 should then be spent: on a recuperative getaway for ten or twelve of the SNCCers who'd carried the heaviest burdens these last three years. I saw signs of serious fatigue among them, and I felt very concerned for their emotional welfare. I feared that without some sort of physical and spiritual rest, grave mistakes would be made and our cause derailed. I wanted to take them somewhere far away from Mississippi, somewhere they'd never imagined visiting but would excite them as soon as they heard the name: Guinea, in West Africa.

I first bounced the idea off Achkar Marof, Guinea's ambassador to the United Nations, whom I'd first met through Eleanor Roosevelt, and through whom I'd first gone to Guinea as Sékou Touré's guest. Africa was a subject of growing fascination throughout the movement. Many SNCCers were talking about reconnecting with their African roots. Some, most notably a young, ambitious northerner named Stokely Carmichael, were donning African tribal clothes. (I would notice, over the next years, that it was always SNCCers from north of the Mason-Dixon Line who wore African dress; southern blacks had no interest.) Yet none had actually gone to Africa. Seeing Guinea would be a life-changing experience for these battle-weary veterans, and I knew President Sékou Touré would enjoy meeting them. Achar's eyes lit up at the idea. In just days word came: The young Americans were invited, and would be given all the attentions accorded to foreign dignitaries.

Rest was needed all the more after the Democratic Convention in Atlantic City in late August and its heartbreaking floor fight. To break the lock that white segregationists had on Mississippi's state delegation, Bob Moses had founded a new Mississippi Freedom Democratic party. If he could just get enough Democratic delegates from other states to give the MFDP their blessing, its own, mostly black delegates would be seated and given the power to vote. A lot of Democratic delegates around the country strongly sympathized with the MFDP—they'd seen those pictures of Birmingham and other brutal confrontations, and wanted to help. But to President Johnson, this was an appalling prospect; the whole yellow-dog Democratic South might well walk out of the convention if the MFDP was seated, dooming his election hopes.

No one was a shrewder strategist than LBJ. All too soon, despite widespread support, the MFDP was iced out of the proceedings.

For that and a hundred other reasons, Bob Moses was the first name on my list for the Guinea trip. He tried to back out, claiming he didn't want special treatment, but the others brought him around. Another clear choice was John Lewis, who'd nearly lost his life at that Montgomery bus station, and risked it many times since. And then there was baby-faced Julian Bond, who ran SNCC's office in Atlanta. James Forman joined the list. Along with a handful of others, we added Fannie Lou Hamer, who'd worked so hard to launch the Mississippi Freedom Democratic party. Fannie Lou's speech on the floor of the Democratic Convention had been so riveting—and so powerful, broadcast as it was on national television—that President Johnson had sent word to the press corps that he had an urgent announcement to make, just to pre-empt the live coverage of Fannie Lou, then nattered away about nothing as the cameras rolled. Fannie was one of the great leaders of our movement, a Mississippi sharecropper's daughter who'd faced armed southern troopers without fear and had a limp, the result of a brutal beating, to show for it. If anyone deserved a vacation, it was Fannie.

We left for Senegal on September 11, 1964, and flew from there to Conakry on Air Guinée, which in itself was a shock for some in the group: The pilot and the flight attendants were black! Presidential emissaries were there to whisk us through security in seconds, then drive us in long black cars to the former French embassy, a sprawling estate with beachfront bungalows. Dinner, we were told, would be at the presidential palace in an hour or two. We were settling in, and unpacking, when President Sékou Touré drove up, unannounced, to welcome us personally. Most of us gathered ourselves pretty quickly, but when I knocked on Fannie Lou Hamer's bungalow door, I heard her singing in the bathroom.

"Fannie, the president is here. Can you come?"

Fannie whooped with laughter. "Yeah, right," she said. "Well, just tell His Excellency that I'll see him in a couple of hours. I'm having my bath, darling."

"Fannie, I'm telling you—the president is here."

There was a silence.

"Are you telling the truth?"

"Yes."

"Good Lord, you're serious!" Then a lot of splashing.

Five or six minutes later, Fannie Lou emerged, her hair still wringing wet. She stopped dead when she saw Sékou Touré, in his white fez and white robes, flashing a grin of welcome at her. He came over, kissed her on each cheek, and said how pleased he was to meet her. With that, Fannie threw her arms around him, buried her face in his chest, and wept.

I understood completely. Neither Fannie nor any of the others had ever seen a black head of state. The very idea, after enduring beatings and police dogs and constant oppression by the only authority figures they knew—white ones—was overwhelming. To these bone-tired activists, Sékou Touré was a symbol of true freedom and self-rule. To have him sweep in, with his title and authority, and say, "Welcome home"—well, it was no wonder Fannie dissolved in tears. The rest of the eyes there weren't so dry, either.

True to his word, Sékou Touré treated our group like dignitaries, hosting feasts and spectacular displays of Guinean drumming and dancing. I went along for some of that, but I also had work to do; my plans for a cultural center in Conakry were well under way. Initially, I had hoped to have the program staffed by Peace Corps volunteers, but when I'd sent that suggestion up the chain of command, it had been quashed. I knew that wasn't Sarge Shriver's fault. No U.S. administration was going to help Guinea as long as France was boycotting it. Instead, we'd recruited some twenty American theater hands to live in the capital and travel around the country, researching and recording tribal artists and rituals. I'd paid those salaries myself—and was still paying them, except during the occasional stretches when we landed private funding.

Ralph Alswang, one of Broadway's greatest set designers, had worked up detailed sketches of the center, which would arise from a central plot of land donated by Sékou Touré. In its design it would resemble a chief's hut, only one as big as an auditorium, cast in concrete and steel. From the roof's concrete surface, water would run down the walls in a constant stream to cool the interior. The water would also run inside, along the lip of the stage, to keep the performers especially cool. Tethered to the complex would be small satellite buildings, one for drama, one for music, one for ballet, and so forth. On an offshore island we dubbed the "Isle of Dance," we built barracks for dancers from all over Guinea, where they could live and practice while they prepared to tour the United States. We even planned their diets, incorporating Western food little by little so they'd acclimate to it and not get sick when they traveled. Sékou Touré himself came up with a name one day for the traveling troupe. We were looking at a map of the country. "Djoliba," he said, and pointed to the Djoliba River that flowed through Guinea to become a source of the Niger. "You can safely say that all of the dances done in Guinea come from the Niger. So why not call it Ballet Djoliba?"

By now, Sékou Touré had found some money to help underwrite the project. The Johnson administration, unfortunately, had no more interest in contributing to our cultural exchange than the previous one had. U.S. policy was preposterous. We gave Guinea nothing, our allies did the same, and so Sékou Touré had no choice but to accept aid for his desperate country from the Soviet Union and China, the only available sources of it. For that, Guinea was viewed as a communist satellite.

Evidence of Soviet aid to Guinea appeared modest—as far as I could see—and in some regards amusing. One afternoon we drove by a field with hundreds of large, identical vehicles of some kind. "Snowplows," Sékou Touré explained. "The best in the world."

"Does it snow in Guinea?" I asked.

Sékou Touré shook his head. "But they will be very useful. Our roads get so muddy in the rainy season that trucks and cars get stuck. Even the paved roads are impassable because of mudslides from the hills. So we'll use the snowplows to move all the mud. We haven't used them yet, though."

"Have you not had much rain?"

"Oh, yes, lots of rain. But we need to redesign the snowplows before we can use them. The exhaust pipe runs through the plow's cabin, you see."

I wondered if Achar had mistranslated. "The exhaust pipe runs through the cabin? Why?"

"To heat the cabin," Sékou Touré explained. "Very useful in the Russian winter. Here it makes the cabin so hot that the drivers can't bear it. We're waiting for some Russian engineers to come change the design."

The spell, for the SNCCers, was broken all too soon by worrying news from back home. SNCC's fault lines were suddenly much wider. The moderates still advocated nonviolence. But for many in SNCC, the short, tragic story of the Mississippi Freedom Democratic party had been the last straw. As John Lewis would note in his autobiography, *Walking with the Wind*, the SNCC, in taking on Mississippi's all-white delegation, had played by all the rules, only to see their effort crushed by raw, racist politics. Their patience with nonviolence was spent. From now on, SNCC would go an increasingly radical route, and I would find myself mediating not just between SNCC, on the one hand, and Martin on the other, but among these new SNCC factions, the most radical of which would soon become the Black Panthers.

For all the angry rhetoric, the final break lay some months off. Before it, there would be one more campaign that all of us could fight together: to cross a bridge in Selma.

15

Almost a decade had passed since my fateful meeting with Martin in the basement of Harlem's Abyssinian Baptist Church. Since then, I'd done all I could to uphold my vow. I had no doubt that in helping the movement, I was serving a sacred cause. But I was also helping my friend. By the fall of 1964, I would go so far as to say we were the best of friends. Not that Martin didn't have other close friends. But the trust and love we shared was, for me at least, unique.

Like all close friends, we loved to talk. When Martin stayed in the apartment overnight, Julie would cook a simple kitchen dinner, and then we'd adjourn to the red living room, our shoes off and our feet up. (The first time he did that, I noticed that for a man of modest height, Martin had *big feet.*) Eventually Julie would pad off to bed, but we'd stay up late into the night talking. We talked about everything, but to me, the most interesting discussions we had were about the existence of God.

Martin truly believed. I admired his faith; I envied it. I just couldn't make that leap myself. To me, faith as practiced all around me was blindly tied to religion, and religion was preachers in Harlem and Jamaica passing the hat for Jesus and driving off in fancy cars. It was my mother's last resort, only it never made her happy. It was nuns invoking the Christian spirit and rapping my knuckles with sticks. It was priests blessing Italian troops on the newsreels, sending them off to slaughter defenseless Ethiopians. I failed to see any good in the hypocrisy of all that.

None of this Martin denied. But none of it troubled his faith.

All right, then, I would say, let's just talk concepts of faith: theological constructs. I was willing to accept that our life on earth was more than an accident of evolution, but who could say what force was behind it? Unlike other preachers I'd known, Martin made no effort to convert me to his religious views. In those late-night talks, he answered my questions and shared his faith, but never proselytized. I admired Martin's faith, but even more, I admired the values he lived by. Unlike those preachers of my youth, Martin had virtually no possessions. His commitment to the poor was profound. I had never met anyone as true to the teachings of Christ. His kindness, his sense of justice, above all his humility—these were astounding to me. He was the first pure spiritual force I'd met. And while I kept my doubts, his spirituality changed my life. Even now I hear his voice with great regularity, and continue to be guided by it. Paul Robeson had been my first great formative influence; you might say he gave me my backbone. Martin King was the second; he nourished my soul.

I don't mean to imply that those talks were all abstract and philosophical. Not at all. We spent a lot of time—most of the time—strategizing. What city should we take on next? What new act of nonviolence would really shake things up? As an entertainer, I'd always rehearsed with deep intensity, going eight or ten hours at a stretch, often forgetting to eat. I was that same way in planning a next campaign—and so was Martin.

That fall, for all his triumphs, Martin felt more beleaguered than ever. There were fault lines and factions at his own SCLC, deep tensions with SNCC and the other movement groups. The strategy of nonviolence was under increasing challenge. At the same time, the Johnson administration was telling Martin that even one more nonviolent campaign would be too much. The country had had enough trouble absorbing the Civil Rights Act; a voting rights bill was out of the question. The pressures Martin felt weren't just political. Death threats came with unnerving frequency. Often he heard about them from the FBI. Yet this was the same FBI that under J. Edgar Hoover was wiretapping his conversations in motel rooms. If he didn't know for sure that Hoover's agents had tapped conversations in which he talked of extramarital trysts, he had to suspect as much. He never knew when Hoover might try to ruin him. But he would soon find out.

As close as we were, Martin never touched on those trysts in our late-night talks. I think he would have been embarrassed to tell me about them; they were for bull sessions with his constant traveling companion and aide-de-camp, Bernard Lee, or perhaps with Andy Young, who in Martin's circle had the keenest appreciation for sexual adventures. Nor did Martin meet available women through me, as Coretta may have thought. But he did lay bare some feelings about his marriage and the trade-offs he'd made. Back in college, Martin had fallen in love with a white girl—the daughter of a cook at the college cafeteria—and told friends they intended to marry. Black classmates questioned that: What black church would hire a pastor who had a white wife? And what would his parents say? Martin felt he could withstand the fury of Daddy King, but not his mother's broken heart. After much soul-searching, he ended the romance and started looking for a more socially acceptable mate. Coretta Scott was a proper bourgeois prospect, with light skin, straight hair, and social ambitions. With her as his perfect partner, he'd landed his first ministry, at the Dexter Avenue Baptist Church in Montgomery. The bus boycott had come barely a year later. Suddenly Martin was a hero, a role model, a husband and father, but also a young man who'd left his preferred love behind to make the bargains of a throne.

He had a lot of conflicted feelings, but his sense of mission forced him to endure.

I saw Martin and Coretta together a lot, and I did sense a mutual affection. Martin was very sensitive toward her, and very caring. But I felt nothing transcendent between them. They seemed to me a couple who'd made a pact that worked to the advantage of both. I found Coretta very obliging, always ready to make public appearances as the dutiful wife. In return, she expected her audiences to treat her accordingly. She was perfectly suited for all the privileges that came with being Martin's wife—the seats of honor, her picture in the paper, invitations from high black society—and she dressed the part, with pearls and flattering dresses. Her manner was stately and stern. You could never tell an off-color joke around Coretta, or even make a teasing remark if it had some salacious spin. I know Martin chafed at that, and so did I. And I had no idea how he endured her singing. Coretta had studied music at Antioch College, and in her role as preacher's wife, she liked to perform solos for the congregation. I took to stealing a look at the program outside the church before the service, and waiting until she'd finished her song before slipping into the pew. She wasn't tone-deaf, but she wasn't far from it. Soon enough, you knew she'd go flat or sharp. The suspense was almost worse than the note itself.

Given the trade-off he'd made, Martin was fascinated by my own choices. Coretta was my Marguerite; the parallels were all there. And yet I'd divorced Marguerite . . . for another woman. A woman who happened to be white—and Jewish! Another taboo shattered. Martin couldn't get over that. He was so intrigued that I'd done this and my reputation was untarnished. He more than envied me. He would say that, in fact, he admired the strength he thought it took to endure the animus that was a constant in our lives. He turned wistful when he compared his story to mine. I remember exactly where we were sitting when Martin bared his heart about this. He was on the stool in front of the big wooden bar in my living room; I was on the stool behind it. I was like the bartender, hearing out the lonely guy across the bar when everyone else has left. Out of discretion, he never brought up the subject again.

We talked a lot about society's expectations of us, which rules we were bound by and which we could break, as black role models in our respective worlds. Martin's pedestal was a lot higher and more fragile than mine. He wasn't just a role model. He was a moral leader. He knew how little it would take for him to be perceived as a hypocrite. Even his friendship with me was fraught with risk. I was his staunch supporter, but also a force that could give him access to the devil's desires. Broadway showgirls, Hollywood starlets—the smallest exposure to these lures might be used against him. Often these days I brought SNCCers or members of Martin's own circle to Vegas for a few days of R&R, paying their way out, giving them tickets to my show, fronting them a little cash to blow at the casino. I knew better than to invite Martin to Vegas, and he knew not to come. But I think he would have welcomed the experience.

Coretta might have worried that I'd lead Martin astray, except that by the fall of 1964, I'd become as useful to her as I was to him. Along with the household help I now employed for her, I sent a limousine to pick her up at the airport whenever she came to New York. On occasion, she stayed at the apartment, came and went as she liked. Julie and I took her to dinners, to Broadway shows, and more. I'd also taken out a $50,000 life insurance policy on Martin, with Coretta as the beneficiary. We all knew Martin's life was in danger on a daily basis, and yet Martin had no life insurance; he felt he couldn't afford it. These were not acts on my part to endear me to her; I did these things because I could. But they did have the effect of inoculating me against any fears Coretta might have that I was leading Martin into temptation.

That fall came the news that Martin had been awarded the Nobel Peace Prize. He was the youngest ever to win it, and the grandeur of that tribute carried its own risks. Amid the movement groups, envy and resentment swirled. Some SNCCers felt Martin had won for work they'd done. Some in King's entourage felt the same way. I told the grumblers to get real. No one thought Martin had done all the work himself. So many people were committing daily acts of courage in the South for civil rights. But Martin was the *embodiment* of our movement. He was the force. And winning the Nobel might give him the clout to keep young, angry skeptics in line with nonviolence a short while longer.

That hope was put to the test early in the new year, and so, too, was Martin's public image.

Selma, Alabama, was, like Birmingham, a city steeped in segregation, with a top lawman, Sheriff Jim Clark, every bit as brutal as Birmingham's Bull Connor. When students in Selma, with help from SNCC, tested the new Civil Rights Act by trying to enter the city's segregated movie theater, Sheriff Clark's troops dispersed them with tear gas. When the students persisted, a judge issued an injunction forbidding gatherings of more than three people in the city. In a state ruled by Governor George Wallace, voting rights weren't even an issue; for Selma's blacks, they didn't exist. On his way home from receiving the Nobel in Norway, Martin met in Washington with President Johnson, who reiterated that the country needed a rest from civil rights. Martin wavered. But when a delegation of citizens from Selma came to plead for his help in desegregating the city, he felt the calling.

Martin led a first rally in Selma on January 2, 1965, demanding a free and fair vote for all. Weeks of marches and mass arrests followed. After a night of brutal beatings by Sheriff Clark's troops on February 18, a marcher named Jimmy Lee Jackson died of his wounds, and James Bevel of the SCLC first suggested carrying the victim's coffin the fifty-four miles from Selma to the state capital, Montgomery. The plan to take the body was eventually put aside, but not the march to Montgomery.

Martin was out of town, on March 7, 1965, for the march over Selma's Edmund Pettus Bridge that would come to be known as "Bloody Sunday." In juggling his many obligations, he'd found himself pulled between leading the march, which other organizers had set for that day, and fulfilling a commitment to preach in Atlanta. He chose Atlanta—a mistake, as he later admitted to me.

Instead, John Lewis ended up leading some six hundred mostly local citizens over the bridge, into the teeth of Sheriff Clark's armed and mounted troops. John had already shown extraordinary courage on the Freedom Rides. He showed it again in staring down Sheriff Clark and ignoring his order to retreat. The melee that resulted was one of the movement's bloodiest, with mounted policemen mercilessly clubbing and bullwhipping defenseless churchgoers who'd joined the march in their Sunday best. Once again, John was clubbed on the head. This time his skull was badly cracked, his survival a miracle.

Martin told me later that had he led that first march, it might have turned out very differently. It might have looked, in fact, a lot like the second march over the bridge, two days later, which Martin did lead. This time, Martin and his followers reached the foot of the Pettus Bridge, where Sheriff Clark and his troops waited—and then, at Martin's signal, retreated. In private talks with the U.S. Justice Department and the White House, Martin had learned that this second march was scheduled too soon for the federal government to provide adequate protection. A judge hadn't even sanctioned it yet. Unless Martin wanted a reprise of Bloody Sunday, a compromise would have to be struck. Many of the marchers on that second crossing were horrified when they saw Martin waving them back. They felt he'd surrendered before a shot was fired. Bloody Sunday had shocked the world—a costly success, but a success all the same. The second march, they felt, was a disgrace; many felt Martin had betrayed them. And yet as Martin reminded me on the phone that night, compromise was a crucial tenet of nonviolence. If compromise got you closer to your goal, then it was worth any loss of face.

An Alabama judge did, at last, grant permission for a march not only across Pettus Bridge but from Selma to Montgomery. To me, that showed Martin had been right, at least in regard to that second confrontation on the bridge. This time, the marchers would be protected, along their whole route, by the Alabama National Guard. By the end of the third day, Martin expected, the exhausted marchers would need pumping up for the last few miles into Montgomery the next morning. That, Martin told me, was where I could help. Could I get some of my friends to come entertain the marchers at their third-night campsite?

I said I thought I could.

. . .

I was calling on short notice, and yet the cause was so compelling, the news photos of violence on the Pettus Bridge so fresh, that almost everyone I reached out to agreed to come. Nina Simone, Joan Baez, Johnny Mathis, Billy Eckstine, Tony Bennett, Odetta, Peter, Paul and Mary, the Chad Mitchell Trio, and more all said yes.

Sammy Davis, Jr., was especially enthusiastic. "Absolutely, man, I'm in." After I'd used his name in helping promote the concert, Sammy called to say he had to back out. He'd thought he could cancel a performance of *Golden Boy* on Broadway, but his producers, and the play's backers, had raised holy hell about it. "They just won't let me do it, brother. What can I do?"

"Sure, I understand," I said.

Then I put in a call to Hilly Elkins, the top producer of *Golden Boy*. "Hilly," I said, "I need to ask you something. How much is a night's gross for your show?" He gave me a figure. "Okay," I said. "Sammy's told me that you won't let him go because of your obligations to your backers. So I'll take that burden off and buy the night. It makes that much difference to the integrity of the march that he come." We were asking theaters to close down, something only a national crisis would justify. Having Sammy, and showing that his theater was shutting down, had become part of the validation that convinced others to come. If he backed out now, in the twilight moment, a lot of others would have had an excuse for backing out, too. A lot was riding on him.

Stunned, Hilly said he'd see what he could do. A day or so later he called back. "Under pain of death, you can't repeat this," he said, "but Sammy wanted it this way. He didn't want to cancel the show. He wanted us to take the rap for him.

"I've talked to the backers," Hilly added, "and we've decided we'll take the hit—cancel the night and take the loss. Only we can't tell Sammy that, or he'll lose face. So you tell him you bought out the night, and we'll tell him that, too."

When I went back to Sammy and told him I'd bought out the night, he was flabbergasted. "But that's a lot of pokey, man."

"It's that important you be there," I told him. "I can't have anyone think I was pulling a fast one by saying you'd be there when you wouldn't."

On their third and final night, the marchers camped out at the City of St. Jude, a Catholic compound a few miles outside Montgomery's city limits, with a church, hospital, and school that served the local black community. Along with the three thousand marchers sanctioned by the Alabama judge, some twenty-five thousand others gathered at the site, both to show solidarity and to hear all the stars rumored to be coming. I'd spent almost every waking hour for days making arrangements: flying in the entertainers from either coast, lining up transportation from the airport and hotel rooms for them. I'd told them their costs would be covered, and they were. In all, that evening would cost me $10,000. I could handle that. What I couldn't control was the rain.

By early evening, the campsite was saturated, the crowd soaked, and with all that rain, the electrical connections kept shorting out as we tried to set up the sound system. It hadn't occurred to me that we might also need a stage. I'd thought the crowd would be much smaller, that we'd set up on some nearby hillside. Only the ground was so muddy that the mikes and klieg lights kept sinking and tipping. A teenager who worked in the local mortuary had the brainstorm that saved the night.

The young man drove off in his pickup with a couple of his friends and soon returned with a full load of coffins—empty ones, that is. Soon we had our makeshift stage, a first row of coffins embedded in the mud, two or three rows above, and sheets of plywood secured on top of them. The lights kept sputtering out, leaving the crowd in darkness, and dozens of people pressed against the coffins had to be moved out lest they be crushed. But the concert started at last, and the lineup of stars, one after another, sent spirits soaring. Tony Bennett and Peter, Paul and Mary sang; so did Joan Baez and Johnny Mathis. In between musical performances, comics and other well-known figures addressed the crowd. Alan King, James Baldwin, Leonard Bernstein, Nipsey Russell, Anthony Perkins, Mike Nichols and Elaine May, George Kirby, Dick Gregory, Shelley Winters, Ossie Davis, Floyd Patterson—all got up on that stage of coffins and thanked the marchers. Even Ralph Bunche, the distinguished professor and political scientist who had helped form the United Nations with Eleanor Roosevelt after World War II, and had won a Nobel Peace Prize as its chief mediator in settling the Arab-Israeli war of 1947–49, an elder from the black establishment, stood with us on that stage, giving his blessing. I served as MC, and sang "Jamaica Farewell," and brought out Martin and Coretta to rousing cheers. The feeling that night was truly powerful. We would *not* be denied.

The marchers slept that night—if they slept—in the muddy field of St. Jude's. The entertainers were driven into Montgomery to stay in a hotel. I still have my room key from that night. The number of entertainers and writers and others in that group had grown in the last twenty-four hours, and there weren't enough rooms for all, so we put three or four to a room, grouped by gender. At one point in the night, a couple of the men, including my buddy Bill Attaway and Billy Eckstine, donned sheets and went into one of the women's rooms, making ghostlike moans. I was right there with them. For some reason the women didn't appreciate our humor. Not at all.

The next morning, most of us drove back to St. Jude's to help Martin lead the more than three thousand marchers their last three miles into Montgomery. Our presence in force was a message in itself. Alabama state troopers lined the route, their faces like masks. Behind them, white bystanders glared. Many of them shouted, "Nigger, nigger, nigger," or, at the white marchers, "Nigger lover." I looked right at them, one after another, silently. Many just looked away, or met my gaze with hate, but some seemed startled and shamed. A few even waved and smiled.

We were a conquering army, with not a gun among us, as we marched into Montgomery. When we reached the capitol building, Joan Baez climbed aboard a flatbed truck and led us all in singing "The Star-Spangled Banner," "This Land Is Your Land," and "Blowin' in the Wind." I took the mike to address the crowd. "Great day!" I shouted. "Great day!" But I also looked directly at the television cameras and said, "There are millions of us on the way. And every time you think you've given us some severe blow, we come back bigger and better." Later, we would learn that Governor Wallace was in his office, peering out his window at us from behind his draperies.

Without doubt, the horror of Bloody Sunday, combined with the triumph of our final march to Montgomery, helped push through the Voting Rights Act that President Johnson would sign into law on August 6, 1965. That day in Montgomery I was once again struck by how powerful nonviolence could be—if its practitioners were passionate and persistent enough, and if their cause was just. Beaten down, we came back stronger, in larger numbers, again and again, until the marchers became the majority. And when they did, change followed.

Yet once again, the fury of the vanquished led to an act of revenge. This time the victim was a young white woman, Viola Liuzzo, mother of five. Drawn by the images of violence on the Pettus Bridge, she'd told her husband, a Teamsters business agent, that Selma was "everybody's fight," and had come down on her own to help. After the march to Montgomery, she volunteered to take carloads of stars to the airports in Montgomery or Jackson for their various flights home. I remember she was supposed to give Tony Bennett a ride next, but he deferred because he was having too good a time, so she took someone else. It was on the way back from that trip that Viola, accompanied by a young black activist, drew the attention of a car of Klansmen. They chased her 1963 Oldsmobile on Route 80 and killed her with two bullets to the head.

Not long after that, I gave a benefit concert in Detroit for members of the United Auto Workers and civil rights activists. The Liuzzo family was there that night. Afterward they came backstage: Viola's husband and all five children. We exchanged warm greetings and embraces. Suddenly, the next-to-youngest boy came up to me and punched me hard in the groin. Doubled me up! He was crying, his father was horrified, and I was dumbfounded. But I came to appreciate that the boy blamed me for his mother's death. He wasn't right, but maybe he wasn't all wrong. Viola's son, with his inconsolable loss and pain, haunted me for a long time after that.

I guess he haunts me still.

Around the time of Selma, I got an alarming call from Achkar Marof, Guinea's ambassador to the U.N. "The project is in jeopardy," Achar told me. "I can't say anything more. The president wants you to fly over right away."

I was stunned. Everything had been going so well. My team of twenty was over there working away; any week now they would break ground on Ralph Alswang's amazing theater design. What could have gone wrong?

At Achar's direction, I boarded an empty Pan Am plane in New York: a deadhead run, as they called it, just the pilots, crew, and me. When we stopped in Boston, I looked out the window to see a coffin being brought aboard. Some African diplomat had died, I was told; his body was going back home. It felt like an eerie omen.

A car was waiting at the Conakry airport to take me directly to Sékou Touré's palace. With the president was his number one aide, Alassane Diop, who served as translator. Sékou Touré told me, sternly, that the United States could no longer deny its meddling in the Republic of Congo. Like other African leaders, Sékou Touré had had no doubt of the CIA's hand in the 1961 murder of Patrice Lumumba, Congo's first prime minister after the country's independence from Belgium.

Like many leaders who had turned first to the United States for support, only to be spurned, Lumumba had established Soviet ties; his killers took a U.S.-pleasing anti-communist line. Sékou Touré's sympathies lay with the Soviet-backed rebels who'd tried, ever since, to overthrow the government. Through all this the United States had claimed a neutral role, but their complicity, Sékou Touré seethed, was now all too clear. A number of Cuban-American pilots, trained and sent by the CIA to fly B-26 bombers against the rebels, had just been shot down. These were, in fact, Bay of Pigs veterans, recruited because they were neither U.S. citizens nor permanent U.S. residents; if they were captured, the CIA could say they were mercenaries. But no one was buying that, least of all Sékou Touré. As a show of sympathy with the Congolese rebels, Sékou Touré was breaking diplomatic relations with the United States. "I worry that when we do that, the members of your project will be endangered," he told me stiffly. "Therefore, they must leave as soon as possible."

I got very teary when I heard this, but Sékou Touré was firm; there could be no appeal. My team was devastated. Many sobbed as I gave them the news. They'd thrown themselves, body and soul, into this project. They loved the Guinean artists they'd come to know; they saw how vulnerable Guinea's arts were to the vagaries of West African politics. Something very, very precious was being lost.

I went back to Guinea after that, but just once or twice. In my Peace Corps capacity, I needed to focus on other African countries where more progress might be made. When I did visit, I found that the Chinese had put up an arts center on the plot Sékou Touré had pledged to us. It was a crude, square box of a building, utilitarian but graceless.

Sékou Touré was cordial when I saw him on those visits, but the warmth was gone. Our moment had passed. So, it seemed, had the country's moment of hope and idealism. The people were poorer than ever, their handsome president in his palace, cut off, increasingly paranoid. In this darkening climate, Achkar Marof, Sékou Touré's staunch friend and ambassador, was called back from New York. Soon after, he was found hanging from a Conakry bridge.

I was in L.A. the week that Watts began to burn, in August 1965. The outdoor stage of the Greek Theatre, where I performed every night, lay in a natural bowl, so I couldn't see the flames on the horizon. But I did arrange with the mayor to get busloads of kids from Watts brought out to the show each night, and to have them distanced from the violence, and from the stage I made a nightly appeal for peace in the city. It was like asking a forest fire to put itself out. President Johnson had just signed the Voting Rights Act into law, yet even that no longer sufficed. The rioters wanted out of the ghetto, out of grinding poverty and broken public schools and harsh police abuse. They wanted the same freedoms and opportunities that white America enjoyed.

While I was out there, I co-hosted a SNCC fundraiser with Sidney at a Beverly Hills discotheque. Everyone from Richard Burton and Elizabeth Taylor to Burt Lancaster, Marlon Brando, and James Garner showed up, and we raised a lot of money. But the irony of partying at a discotheque while Watts burned was not lost on anyone. I was happy to raise the money, but SNCC's needs were bottomless, and its emerging leader, Stokely Carmichael, made no secret of his scorn for nonviolence. SNCC was happy to take our checks, but I knew that in private, Stokely and his circle were probably as dismissive of me as they were of Martin. We were part of the establishment. Which was to say, in the new phrase of that time, that we were part of the problem, not the solution.

I was back in New York when I got the news that Dorothy Dandridge had died. I wasn't surprised, but I felt profoundly sad, and not a little guilty. Dorothy's marriage to Jack Dennison had all but ruined her. Abusive both physically and emotionally, Dennison had left Dorothy in tatters when their ill-starred marriage ended in 1962, three years after it began. Her marriage had drained her financially, too. She'd taken to singing in smoke-filled nightclubs to pay off her debts, only to learn that her managers had bilked her of $150,000. Worse, she owed nearly that much to the IRS. She'd had to sell her Hollywood home; far more devastating, she'd had to put her daughter in a state mental institution. Relegated to a small apartment on Fountain Avenue in West Hollywood, alone and in despair, she'd suffered a nervous breakdown. The gorgeous, brilliantly talented woman I knew was gone, snuffed out by bad luck, a bad man, but also, I felt, by Hollywood's blatant racism, the reflection, as always, of the country it entertained. I don't think Dorothy meant to kill herself when she died of an overdose of antidepressants on September 8, 1965. But she did not have any reason to keep living. Her story was over.

That fall, SNCC made one last effort to work through the system. In Alabama, Stokely formed the Lowndes County Freedom Organization to register black voters, using the clout of the Voting Rights Act.

State law called for every political party to have a visual symbol, so illiterate voters could identify it. Since the state's Democratic party had a white rooster (along with the words "White Supremacy for the Right"), the new Lowndes County party chose a black panther. That was the genesis of the Black Panther party, which would soon arise, with guns and raised fists, in cities all over the country. The Lowndes County Black Panthers set the tone by carrying guns themselves, and not allowing white SNCCers to join.

I didn't support the new Lowndes County party and its anti-white stance. To me, Stokely was tearing apart SNCC for his own aggrandizement. And while I understood the deep well of anger from which his militancy came, I was firmly committed to nonviolence; carrying guns, I felt, was both dumb and dangerous. Mostly dumb. Our backgrounds heightened the tension between us. Stokely was Trinidadian, and there was always this competitive thing between Trinidadians and other West Indians. You could take us out of the islands, but you couldn't quite take the islands out of us.

The Lowndes County Black Panthers lost that November—possibly as a result of vote-tampering, given that they'd registered more black voters in the county than there were white voters—and SNCC was left $50,000 in debt. I did what I could to help, less by sending money to the group itself than by sending it to individual SNCCers I admired who were doing projects on their own. I couldn't turn my back on Bob Moses; I couldn't walk away from Julian Bond. This, from now on, was how I'd deal with SNCC.

My broader sympathies lay with Martin and the SCLC. Money was tight there, too, in part because of SNCC; news images of the gun-toting Lowndes County Black Panthers were scaring a lot of white supporters away from the movement altogether. Even the most stalwart of our backers, though, were feeling tapped out and tired. We had the Civil Rights Act, we had the Voting Rights Act. Wasn't that enough? When was this movement going to end? More to the point, when were we going to stop hounding them for money? What we needed to do, I told Martin, was broaden our base. I knew there was a lot of goodwill toward the movement in Europe. Why not do a few fundraisers there?

The very idea irked Daddy King. "You can't be going hat in hand to strangers and asking them to solve race problems in America," he harrumphed at a strategy meeting I attended. "That makes our country look bad. You're going to make a lot of white people really mad at us."

"Make them mad," I echoed. "What are they going to do? Lynch us? Drop us in the river and have us disappear? They're already doing that, so what does *mad* mean?"

I knew what Daddy King was really saying. The flip side of Jerome Smith's angry speech to Bobby Kennedy about not wanting to fight America's wars while America was depriving him of his civil rights was a deep-rooted, almost pathological patriotism. Most blacks, even movement blacks, made a distinction between the government that was keeping them down and a gauzy, idealized image of America, its flag waving proudly for all. When Daddy King said he didn't want to make white people mad, he meant he didn't want to go up against the agencies of white America, starting with the U.S. State Department. After some days and more heated words, we reached a compromise. We would go, but do just one fundraiser, at the American Church in Paris. The very name sounded reassuring to Daddy King: a little island of Americans in that sea of foreigners. I knew just how little that island was; the American Church held only about five hundred parishioners. At least it would get us over there.

Only it wouldn't. Days before our departure, the American Church withdrew its invitation. The minister admitted the State Department had warned him not to host a bunch of left-wing Negroes, for fear of disturbing U.S.-French relations. Cold War tensions were also part of the picture: The State Department didn't want a bunch of black Americans criticizing the U.S. government, and perhaps even claiming solidarity with Russia, as Paul Robeson had done in Paris a generation before. Daddy King was almost exultant. "I told you so!" he said. "I told you it wasn't going to work!"

I said, "Give me twenty-four hours."

I called my French gang: Yves Montand and Simone Signoret, Melina Mercouri and Jules Dassin. "Where can we do this?" I asked. In just a few hours Yves called back to say we had the 4,500-seat Palais des Sports. Not only that, but he'd talked to friends in the French labor movement. They would guarantee a sold-out house, including a whole array of stars. And they did; it was an amazing night: La Nuit des Droits Civiques, or Civil Rights Night. Thousands more listened through loudspeakers on the surrounding streets.

The day of the concert, we'd thought about where to go for a celebratory dinner afterward. We were staying at the George V Hotel, and my idea was to go to a place called Jimmy's, which served soul food in the heart of Paris. By the time we got back from the Palais des Sports, a whole mess of takeout that I'd ordered from Jimmy's was waiting in the kitchen of the George V. We gathered in the suite of actor Peter O'Toole, who'd been filming *How to Steal a Million* in Paris: Martin's circle, my French gang, and all the stars who'd participated or attended, including, on the American side, Mahalia Jackson and Odetta. Food was coming, we assured them, and so it did. Peter O'Toole opened his door to see Martin with a napkin over his forearm, holding a large tray of fried chicken from Jimmy's and plainly imitating a waiter. "Dinner is served," Martin said in that deep baritone of his. As the plates were handed out, he went from star to star, dispensing chicken and pausing ever so briefly to give each a sense of his personal appreciation for their contribution. "You have no idea what it means to our folks back home." O'Toole was shocked, but not me. For Martin, I knew this wasn't a spoof. It was an exercise in humility, an act of abject gratitude to all these stars for coming out for him.

I knew that Sweden would be just as receptive as France—I'd performed there, and Martin was certainly a household name throughout Scandinavia after coming to Norway to accept his Nobel Prize—so before leaving the States I called Olof Palme, leader of the country's Social Democrats. In a short time, he, too, had made arrangements. Right after our Paris stop we would perform at Sweden's Royal Opera House, with every major Scandinavian star onstage, and with the concert beamed to all of Scandinavia. The king of Sweden would be our official patron; the money from ticket sales would go right to an account at the Royal Bank of Sweden. The king himself would guarantee that the benefit raised $100,000 for the SCLC.

And that's exactly what he did.

That European swing was one of the most gratifying tours of my life. When you get the U.S. State Department telling Paris to shut you down, and all the embassies not to work with you, and when what was to be a minor fundraiser turns into a major triumph, there's a vindication in that—a very personal vindication. I couldn't help but think again of J. Edgar Hoover in his dark little den at the FBI, and wonder if he was gnashing his teeth at the news of our great success.

Not long after we returned, in the spring of 1966, SNCC made fundraising for the SCLC even harder, by electing Stokely its new chairman. That meant an end to nonviolence as SNCC's credo. At the same time, a hard ruling was reached on SNCC's white members. While not expelled, they were ordered to work on their own, in white communities. I supported the ruling—as far as it went. Whenever a biracial group of SNCCers went out in the field, they looked like what they were—activists. Instead of aggravating those already-tense situations, why not have white activists infiltrate white communities and try to turn them around? Or even infiltrate the Klan? But anger was rising, and with it, the radical view that blacks could never integrate into white society. They needed their own society, their own America, apart. The ruling pointed SNCC in that direction—and that I didn't agree with at all.

A month later, James Meredith, now graduated from the University of Mississippi, undertook a one-man "March Against Fear" across the state to encourage black voters to register. Alone and vulnerable, Meredith was shot by a sniper as he walked down a two-lane blacktop; by a small miracle, he wasn't killed. In the aftermath, Stokely stood before a furious crowd and shouted the words that sent SNCC, and the movement, firmly in a new direction. No more "Freedom Now," Stokely told the crowd. "What we're going to start saying now is *Black Power.*" Enough going to jail for marching, enough bowing down in nonviolence and getting beaten. *Black Power.*

I thought if I'd been jailed twenty-seven times, as Stokely had, I might shout, "Black Power," too. But Martin was still right. Nonviolence set a moral example that moved us forward. Violence set us back. From now on, "Black Power" would define SNCC and dominate the movement. SNCC would give rise to the national Black Panthers, and in the way of all revolutions, each next leader would be more radical than the previous one—from Stokely to H. Rap Brown to Huey Newton to Bobby Seale—until the movement lost its power and direction amid violence and drugs, police harassment and FBI infiltration.

Through much of the next two years, Martin would seem old news, his history-making campaigns behind him. But my faith in him would never waver. And though helping his cause would grow harder and harder, I had made a vow.

When I look back at this period of such political ferment, no single experience defines it for me. Not even Selma. The swirl of it all is what I see. Speaking at a rally one day in Washington, singing the next night at the Greek Theatre in L.A., heading up to Vegas for a four-week stand, making a new record, discovering a new talent, meeting with Martin, with musicians, with SNCCers, African leaders, Black

Panthers. I wanted to do everything, and I did. But why? Why race around trying to please every constituency, like that guy I remember from *The Ed Sullivan Show*, spinning plates on sticks, trying to keep them all spinning so none would fall?

I took that up a lot with Peter Neubauer, my therapist. With his help, I came to appreciate the impact of the constant praise and approval that was hitting me from all sides all the time. That might seem the story for any celebrity, but this was different. Bigger. More complex. It wasn't just adoration I was getting. People were investing faith and hope and trust in me. I was being anointed every day. Of all the black kids in Jamaica and Harlem, why had I been the one chosen to sit with leaders of state, who solicited my opinion? I felt driven to justify people's respect, and with Peter's help, I saw how that had become a cycle. The more I did, the more they respected me; the more they respected me, the more I felt compelled to do.

At the core of all this was my mother, always pushing herself, and in the echoes of her voice, still pushing me, too. I'd long since realized how obsessive this was—a kind of insanity. A decade after abandoning the house I'd bought her in L.A., she was still in that little brownstone walk-up apartment on 143rd Street and Convent Avenue—the apartment with a bathroom down the hall—refusing to accept any help from me, save the occasional check. In a heartbeat she could have had all the comforts; she could have traveled the world. She preferred to stay there in that apartment, driven, fighting poverty with every breath and step because that was who she was; that was her identity. That same head-down, shoulders-squared drive still motivated me, too.

In one regard, the greater influence had been those great jazz players at the Royal Roost and the life-changing break they'd bestowed upon me. I was still paying that karmic debt and would be paying it joyously for the rest of my life. My newest discovery was Nana Mouskouri, the marvelous Greek jazz and folk singer, whom I'd met on tour in Greece in 1960 and then shared stages with all over the United States and Europe.

Nana was extremely shy, even onstage. Not by chance did she hide behind her trademark eyeglasses—heavy-rimmed and upturned, like a librarian's—and her shoulder-length hair, which often hid part of her face while she sang. But she had a glorious voice, an astounding range, and brilliant rhythm—she could sing those complex Greek folk songs in 9/8 or 11/4 and never miss a beat. By the time I met her, she had a large Greek following and was wildly popular with the U.S. sailors stationed at the large military base on Crete. I just helped her broaden her following. I paid for her to come to New York that year. She brought her husband, George Petsilas, who accompanied her on guitar. Before long, Quincy Jones was producing her first American album.

When I finally took her on tour with me, beginning in 1965, Nana, utterly fluent in French, German, and Spanish, made hit albums in all those markets, too, becoming one of the best-selling recording artists in the world. And still she refused to take off those heavy black-framed glasses! Onstage, they seemed to keep her apart from her audience. She stood stiffly, doing nothing with her body to dramatize her singing. I felt that if I could just get her out from behind those glasses, she could open up as a performer. I said as much on the second night of our tour, and she gave it a try, but she felt so awkward and exposed without her glasses that the very next night, she went back to them.

I knew Nana was a woman of churning emotions—you felt that just hearing her sing, which was a big part of her appeal—but I didn't know *how* emotional she was until the day I sat across from her and her husband on our tour bus and realized she was crying. I caught George's eye; he just gave me a little "she's okay" wave. But she wasn't. Her tears turned into racking sobs. Up and down the bus, conversations died, and the musicians exchanged worried looks. Had Nana and George had a serious spat? Had one of her parents died? The sobs went on for some time, almost until our next stop. After we'd checked in, I saw George alone in the hotel lobby and asked him why Nana had been crying. "Ah," he said, "she was reading a Greek tragedy." I looked at him, waiting to hear more. "Well, that's it," he said. "That was the reason. The story deeply touched her." I didn't know whether to laugh or start working up a Plan B for the tour. I was traveling with two strange people!

By the time we stopped touring together, Nana's star was rising so fast that, unlike Miriam, she could now fill big halls and command large sums on her own. It simply made no sense for her to keep touring with me. But we did record an album together, *An Evening with Belafonte/Mouskouri*, and before we parted ways, we played the hottest new house in Vegas, the resort that would become my new home on the Strip.

Overnight, with its opening on August 5, 1966, Caesars Palace transformed Las Vegas. Everything about it, from its fourteen-story tower with seven hundred rooms to the eighteen fountains sending spray high in front of its vast casino, announced that Caesars was now *the place*. The place where Frank would hang his hat. The place where I would, too.

Andy Williams inaugurated the Caesars Circus Maximus room. Nana and I came two or three weeks later. Leaving the Riviera was hard, but, frankly, not that hard with the salary Caesars was offering. My manager, Mike Merrick, told me with a wolfish grin that I wouldn't believe it, and I didn't. I liked the glamour, I liked the room, I liked the pay. As much as all that, though, I liked what Caesar's did for Joe Louis.

Since that Sunday long ago when my mother had barred me from going to see him practice, Joe had vanquished every foe in sight except the Internal Revenue Service. Shamefully, the IRS had hounded Joe for back taxes his accountant had failed to pay. By the IRS's reckoning, those sums had ballooned with interest and penalties. Never mind that in World War II, Joe had gone on one tour after another to entertain servicemen, and done all he could to encourage blacks to join the segregated army. In the postwar years, Joe had been forced back into the ring again and again to raise money to pay the government, until his aging body had given out and he'd taken punishing hits. Who had taken care of Joe when his country did its best to destroy its greatest living sports hero? The mob—that was who. Frank Lucas, the ruthless black gangster who built a global drug empire, grew so disgusted with the IRS's treatment of Louis that he supposedly paid off one of Louis's tax debts of $50,000. At Caesars, owner Jerry Zarowitz, whose Chicago mob connections were never in dispute, did much more. He hired Joe for very good pay—possibly not all of it declared to the IRS—to meet and greet high rollers, and go to sports events representing Caesars. The casino put Joe's daughter to work, too, as a front-desk manager. That place did Joe right.

Joe wasn't at Caesars that first time I played the room, but he arrived not long after, and from then on, I sought him out every time I played there. He wasn't bitter, though he had every right to be. He just seemed resigned to his fate, which broke my heart. I loved to listen to him talk; he had a thick Alabama accent I could barely understand, and his syntax was mangled, but his words rolled out so beautifully. He used a lot of metaphors, and the thing of it was, they didn't always make sense, at least not to me. But that didn't make them any less charming.

With Bill Cosby and
Sidney Poitier on *The
New Bill Cosby Show*

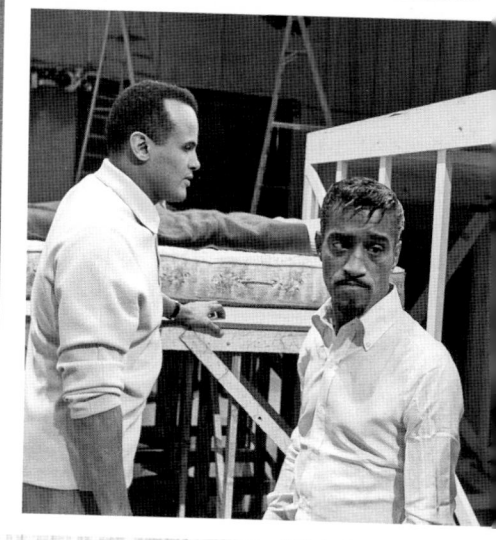

With Tony Curtis

With Sammy
Davis, Jr.,
on the set of
*The Strollin'
Twenties*

With Ed
Sullivan

Guest hosting *The Tonight Show* with guests (right to left) Martin Luther King, Jr., Paul Newman, Leon Bibb, Nipsey Russell, and Ed McMahon, 1968

And Dionne Warwick, 1968

And Paul Newman, 1968

nd the Smothers
others and Bill
osby, 1968

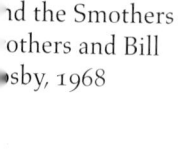

d Robert F. Kennedy,
58

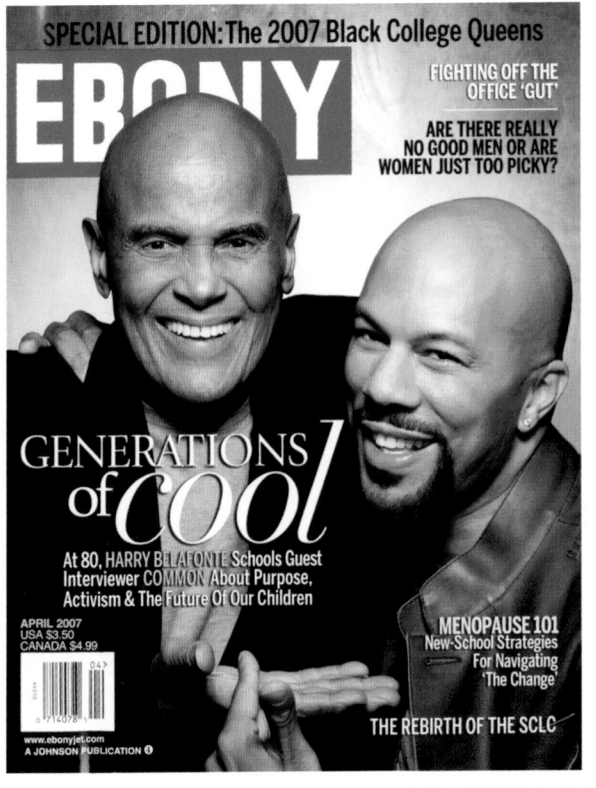

With Common
on the cover
of *Ebony*
magazine

On the cover of *Jet* magazine

In Ethiopia

th my wife, Pam, and
esident Nelson Mandela

With President Bill Clinton

With former governor of
New York Mario Cuomo

Accepting an honorary degree from Columbia University

The first photograph that my wife, Pam, ever took of me, in 1964

With Pam on our wedding day

Our whole family on our wedding day, with officiant former New York City ma
David Dinkins (second row, right)

Another day for "Day-O"

I'd ask him about Muhammad Ali, who'd just changed his name from Cassius Clay. "So what do you make of Muhammad Ali as a Muslim fighting in the ring, when Muslims are supposed to be so peace-loving?"

Joe would nod sagely, and give me a look. "Well, you know, I kind of believe that if a rabbit could throw rocks, there'd be less hunters in the forest."

Joe's patron was a Chicago gangster, no doubt about it. But Jerry Zarowitz, better known as "Z," was also a sweet, erudite fellow in his sixties; you didn't live that long in his world if you were greedy or reckless. Before long, he and I became close friends. Of course I was somewhat predisposed to like anyone who wanted to pay me as much money per week as I was getting and put me up in high-roller suites with all the perks. But that wasn't the only reason. Whenever I needed bail money for friends in the movement, I knew I could count on Jerry to wire it for me, no questions asked.

Jerry didn't just give me the money because he knew I was good for it. He really enjoyed helping the movement. He loved me, loved Martin, loved that we were taking our hits for civil rights.

"Jerry," I said to him one day, "when I ask you for bail money for Dr. King, who's fighting for justice, and campaign contributions for Democrats who want to get tough on crime, that's not actually in your interest, is it?"

Jerry gave me a deadpan look. "Justice," he said, "is always in my best interest. With the Democrats, a guy like me can get his case heard by the Supreme Court. With Republicans, justice starts in the lockup!"

Jerry was right, in a sense, though mob justice was, perhaps, the kind he meant. All these guys had a code; they knew right from wrong in the business they did with one another. As long as they played by those rules, they could, and usually did, lead fairly bourgeois lives. Which was to say that in a city where organized crime ruled, a lot of them had wives and kids, well-kept homes and late-model Buicks. I went to barbecues at mobsters' houses, traded sports talk and drank beers with them. When one pit boss I knew got put in jail, I'd look in on his family every time I came to town, and take his wife and kids to Lake Mead for an afternoon of waterskiing off the big yacht that was mine to use, courtesy of Caesars. I brought them backstage after my shows, arranged for them to see other shows—everything I'd do for any other good friends. The truth was that I felt immensely comfortable with these gangsters and their bosses, and with the casinos that served as their courts. Their world was the one I'd come to know through my uncle Lenny and aunt Liz.

I had just come back home for Christmas and New Year's, and was readying to travel again when I heard from Sidney. Usually I was the one who called Sidney for help on my latest cause, but this time the roles were reversed. As America's uncontested top black movie star now, Sidney brought a lot of power to any cause he took up, and while he didn't take up nearly enough, in my opinion, he did throw himself into the national elections in his native Bahamas in early 1967. A lot was at stake. Lynden Pindling, the island's leading black politician, had rallied his Progressive Liberal party (PLP) to try to win a first-ever black majority in the House of Assembly. Sidney was down there the weekend before the historic election of January 10 when he heard bad news. The PLP had counted on a shipment of walkie-talkies to arrive from America for its get-out-the-vote effort. Somehow, it hadn't arrived. Could Sidney do something? Sidney called me in New York. "Harry," he said, "I need half a dozen sets of walkie-talkies. It is absolutely essential that I have them on this island by tomorrow."

"You been drinking?" I asked.

"Not a drop," Sidney said.

I told him I could probably get the Empire State Building down to the Bahamas more easily on a Saturday night than half a dozen sets of walkie-talkies. This was long before the Internet, or even FedEx. Stores were closed; it was about 8:00 p.m. But I said I'd try. I opened up the Yellow Pages and started matching the names of retailers in those ads to names in the White Pages. Finally I reached a guy who actually was a retailer, and whose store sold walkie-talkies. Only he lived a good distance out of the city. When I'd managed to convince him that I was, in fact, Harry Belafonte, and not Prince Albert in a can, he agreed to drive in on Sunday at 7:00 a.m. and open his store, just for me. He warned me, though, that I'd need permission from the Federal Communications Commission to put them on a plane headed out of the United States. So then I had to call Bobby Kennedy and get him to make a few calls himself. But Sunday morning, I had those walkie-talkies on the first commercial flight to Nassau, and Sidney was at the other end to receive them. In some part because of that better communication through the rural areas, Pindling's PLP won that black majority, and the islands took a giant step toward independence, which they would win six years later. I made Sidney repay the debt before the month was out, dragging him up to a benefit for SNCC at Small's Paradise in Harlem. Those walkie-talkies weren't free!

Sidney was on a remarkable roll, starring in one hit film after another. From his Academy Award for *Lilies of the Field,* he'd gone on to star in *A Patch of Blue,* for which he would win a Golden Globe nomination. And now three of his biggest films were about to appear one after another: *To Sir, with Love, In the Heat of the Night,* and *Guess Who's Coming to Dinner.* Sidney knew how I felt about those roles; in every one of them he was neutered, unless you counted *A Patch of Blue,* in which he romanced a blind white girl who didn't *know* he was black. But to Hollywood, Sidney was the one black actor with whom white America felt comfortable, because of that dignity he radiated, that sexless gallantry. The resentment I felt wasn't directed toward Sidney—I had my stardom; I didn't need his—but at Hollywood and white America. It really burned me that in the midst of the civil rights movement, with Jim Crow laws falling away, the only black who sold movie tickets was one who posed no threat whatsoever to the masculinity of white moviegoers.

Around this time, Sidney joined me in two TV specials that I produced as celebrations of black culture. *The Strollin' Twenties,* which aired on CBS in February 1966, was written by Langston Hughes, whose voice-over prologue began: *"Every Sunday was Easter Sunday in Harlem . . . when people were asked what they were doing, they usually said, 'Goin strollin.' . . . Our show depicts that era. . . ."* Singing and dancing with pride and pizzazz in the numbers that followed were Sammy Davis, Jr., Diahann Carroll, Nipsey Russell, Duke Ellington, and . . . Sidney, who played "the stroller," Hughes's narrator, stopping in on scenes like a rent party to save a family from eviction, a street-corner song-and-dance routine, and a jazz concert at the Savoy Ballroom. *The Strollin' Twenties* was actually the first television show ever written, produced, and performed completely by blacks—a not-insignificant milestone. But for Sidney, it stirred complex and conflicted feelings. After a long period of guilt and confusion, he had obtained a Mexican divorce from Juanita in 1964, only to have her refuse to sign off on it. In New York State, that meant he wasn't yet divorced. During the filming of *The Strollin' Twenties,* Sidney was still struggling to get Juanita's sign-off, even as he and Diahann Carroll tried to set up house in a New York apartment. But when Sidney insisted that Diahann's daughter live with her grandmother awhile so that the grown-ups could adjust to cohabitation, Diahann balked. Her therapist, she told Sidney, had questioned the arrangement. Sidney declared, "To hell with you and your doctor." And that was it for Sidney and Diahann.

The Strollin' Twenties made the cover of *Life* magazine and reached a large national audience. That was enough for ABC to let me produce an even riskier hourlong variety show in 1967: *A Time for Laughter: A Look at Negro Humor in America.* I got Sidney in for that one, too.

A Time for Laughter did more than showcase a lot of great black comic talent. Negro comics on television played to white audiences. If they didn't come out bug-eyed in blackface, they still mocked themselves. They knew white audiences wanted to laugh *at* them, not *with* them, and so they obliged, laughing all the way to the bank. I wanted the jokes and routines Negroes told one another, the humor they shared away from white folk, the humor that came directly from the severity of their lives: poverty, joblessness, prejudice. And I wanted white audiences, as well as black, to hear it.

When I asked Sidney to join in, we kidded each other about those rooftop routines we'd done long ago. "If you'd stuck with stand-up, you'd be on that roof today," I told him.

"Not me," Sidney retorted. "I would have jumped off to escape your jokes."

I gathered the best of the best: from senior statesmen like Redd Foxx, Moms Mabley, George Kirby, and Pigmeat Markham to up-and-comers Dick Gregory, Godfrey Cambridge, Nipsey Russell, and the youngest hot talent of the pack, Richard Pryor. Sidney showed his comic side, and so did Diahann Carroll (the two now on civil terms again, their romance strictly history). My longtime pal Bill Attaway wrote the show—at least, he got the credit. But the comics did most of their own writing and improvising. "Take one of your best jokes," I told them, "and work it up into a sketch." George Kirby played Santa Claus, listening as a black child whispered in his ear. "You're dreaming of a *what* Christmas?" Diahann Carroll sat in a big bubbling pot, about to be eaten by . . . white cannibals. I played a surgeon in the operating theater, performing a complex operation. The nurse kept handing me tools and wiping the sweat from my brow. Finally the camera pulled back to reveal that the patient was . . . a watermelon! To this day, I think the way we opened the show—the billboarding, as it's called—inspired producer George Schlatter to do the same for each episode of

Rowan & Martin's Laugh-In—not quite the cultural impact I'd had in mind, but an impact all the same.

Some white critics grumbled at the final result; they just didn't find one or another of the skits amusing. Perhaps, as the *Pittsburgh Courier*, one of a handful of Negro newspapers of the day, suggested, white audiences would never get it. How could they? The humor that came from a history of being oppressed was like a different language from the humor of those who'd been the oppressors.

In this time of such contrasts, what greater juxtaposition could there be than to have *A Time for Laughter* air on April 6, 1967, just two days after Martin's historic anti-war speech at the Riverside Church in upper Manhattan?

Ever since America had become fully engaged in Vietnam, a fierce debate had raged in Martin's inner circle. Poor blacks were being drafted in disproportionate numbers and sent straight to the front lines, where a lot of them were dying. Didn't our fight for civil rights obligate us to fight this institutional racism? But Martin's dismay with the war went deeper than that. As a pastor and a pacifist, he viewed it as a terrible abomination for all involved: for white soldiers as well as black, for Vietnamese as much as Americans. Yet to speak out against the war carried serious risks for him. He would lose support. How much, no one could predict, but in 1967, a lot of the media were still pro-war, *Time* magazine famously so, and so were a lot of church congregations. President Johnson would be furious, and likely become a political foe. Was all this worth it? In my talks with Martin, I said I thought it was, and so did others. But still I was surprised when Martin began drafting his anti-war speech in my apartment, discarding yellow legal-pad pages of scrawled script as he refined his thoughts.

What fascinated me most about the speech, when I heard it, was its depth of detail. Martin had read deeply on the war's historic origins. In his speech, he explained that history from the perspective of the Vietnamese, and how French colonialism and all the worst American instincts had led us to this place. Rather than dwell on the moral implications, he made a cool, clear case for why we had no business there. When Martin had headed back down to Atlanta, I saw that he'd left those legal-pad pages in his guest-room wastebasket. I retrieved them, and framed them, and for years they graced what I called my civil rights wall: a hallway of movement photographs, letters, and other memorabilia.

Martin's Vietnam speech was bold and brave, not just in raising an early, prominent voice against the war but in doing so while he was fully aware of the cost to his own political power. Afterward the Johnson administration was furious, the President an ally no longer. And while Martin had already lost whole battalions of backers to movement fatigue and fear of the new black militants, now he lost more. Many middle-of-the-road Americans who were inclined to support civil rights still supported the President in a time of war; not to do so, they felt, was to be unpatriotic.

That September, I embarked with Martin on a fairly urgent eight-city fundraising tour for the SCLC. We had guest appearances by Aretha Franklin and Sammy Davis, Jr., among others, at one stop or the next. In Oakland, California, Sammy told the modest audience about his trip to Vietnam to entertain the troops, only to have Joan Baez confront him onstage for supporting the war. In Houston, we got a larger crowd, perhaps because Aretha Franklin sang for us that night, but early into the concert, the hall began to fill with a rank odor. The Klan had put tear gas into the air-conditioning system, forcing us to cut the concert short.

And then in Baltimore, I walked into my dressing room and noticed a state trooper standing at attention nearby. He wasn't just white. He was blue-white. He had a bristling, mean look about him, the kind that sets off alarm bells. All evening, as I performed, he stood backstage, glowering at me. I think Martin drove on to Washington that night; I stayed in a campus lodge at the Univeristy of Maryland. When I got to the front desk, the clerk handed me an envelope. That was weird—no one knew where I was staying. Stranger yet, it was rather heavy.

The envelope contained bullets—six of them—and a letter. "Dear Mr. Belafonte," the letter read. "I give you these six bullets because they will never be used. None of them will ever take a human life, because my experience listening to you and Dr. King made me realize I have been serving the wrong forces. I should be in your ranks. Tonight was transforming for me." It was signed by the state trooper who'd guarded me that night. I keep that letter, and the bullets it contained, at my home in a box of precious objects.

In his remarks at all those concerts, Martin articulated a new goal. He'd come to the conclusion that the movement must wage a broader fight. Not just for poor black Americans, but for all poor Americans.

Martin understood that this would anger the government, and much of the population, far more than demanding civil rights for blacks. He would be saying that the very soul of America—capitalism—was flawed and should be changed. How could it not be, when so many Americans were denied capitalism's benefits and simply tossed into the ranks of the truly, hopelessly poor? For decades, the American labor movement had pushed for justice in the capitalist system, but always on behalf of a particular constituency: miners or autoworkers or farm-workers. Martin wanted to fight for them all, to push for nothing less than a redistribution of America's wealth and power.

When he talked of this "poor people's campaign" at those gatherings, I sensed some confusion in the crowd. So did he. Far from discouraging him, that only made him more certain that he was on the right path. The worthiest causes, he often told me, were never popular at first. The injustices they took on were so ingrained in society that the majority took them for granted, and liked them just the way they were. At no time would a prophetic remark he made be more applicable: "Cowardice asks the question, 'Is it safe?' Expediency asks the question, 'Is it politic?' And vanity comes along and asks the question, 'Is it popular?' But conscience asks the question, 'Is it right?'" As Martin knew, there comes a time when one must take a position that is neither politic nor popular, because conscience tells him he must.

Unlike most in his kitchen cabinet, I endorsed Martin's new campaign without reservation. But I also realized that the goal he'd set was so lofty, it might just be unattainable.

16

When I got the call from NBC in early 1968 inviting me to host *The Tonight Show* for an entire week, it blindsided me. Johnny Carson, late-night talk-show host without peer, seemed to think I'd be an interesting . . . change of pace.

Both of us knew that this wasn't some casual fill-in gig. There wasn't any black talk-show host on American television. The very idea was an oxymoron. And Johnny Carson's seat wasn't just any talk-show host's seat. Carson was the king of late night; the whole country tuned in. My hosting the show would be breaking a barrier of significant proportions. But the potential for disaster was huge. I couldn't go on the air like some overeager comic, trying to please the audience with bright one-liners drawn from the news of the day. I had done Johnny's show many times and, like the rest of America, loved his style, but to attempt to do what he did could have serious ramifications. I'd just look like a buffoon and, more important, blow a chance to reach America with a message of tolerance and understanding. Maybe, I thought, this was not the platform. So I took the easy road. I told Johnny thanks, but no thanks.

Johnny wasn't about to give up that easily, it turned out. I picked up the phone to hear a secretary say, "Please hold for Mr. Sarnoff," and onto the line came the chairman of RCA, owner of NBC, home of *The Tonight Show*. I decided to tweak the great Robert Sarnoff a little bit. "So," I said, "are you calling to give me my weekly show at last?"

In a perfect world, it would have made complete sense for Sarnoff to make me that offer, with my Emmy-winning record for television variety specials. Only this wasn't a perfect world. Sammy Davis, Jr., had been given his own television show two years before, and it hadn't worked out. A decade before, Nat King Cole had broken the color line as America's first black variety-show host. Ironically, his show had the highest audience viewership in its slot, but the hammer still came down hard—very simply, corporate America wouldn't buy in. He was just a bit too black. And although this fact had to be challenged, the trick was how to do so. Sarnoff knew I'd turned down the offer.

"I think you're missing an opportunity here," he said.

I knew the RCA chairman to be a staunch liberal, good on race issues. I was surprised and intrigued when he started framing the offer as a chance to influence racial attitudes.

Over the next few days, I met with the NBC hierarchy, and bit by bit, we talked out what this hybrid of a talk show might be. I would do no opening monologue. Instead, I'd sing an opening song. And I would do no commericals. Ed McMahon, Johnny's sidekick, would have to do all the pitches. Most important, I wanted a handpicked list of guests with whom I had a lot in common, so we could speak with intelligence and passion. The NBC executives countered that they had to approve the list. The miracle was that the names I submitted for the week were approved without a murmur. Now all I needed to do was convince the stars on that list to come aboard.

One Monday night in early February, Johnny's vast audience tuned in to see me chatting with the likes of Senator Robert Kennedy, Lena Horne, Bill Cosby, and the Smothers Brothers. For a lot of black Americans, just seeing me behind Johnny's desk was mind-boggling in itself. In the *New Yorker* profile that he later wrote of me, Henry Louis Gates, Jr., recalled, "For one week in February of 1968, something strange happened to the *Tonight Show* with Johnny Carson: it became the *Tonight Show* with Harry Belafonte. I was a high-school student, growing up in Piedmont, West Virginia, a partly segregated hamlet in the Allegheny Mountains, and television was the only thing that connected any of us there with the larger world. Night after night, my father and I stayed up late to watch a black man host the highest-rated show in its time slot—history in the making."

I started by trying to get Bobby to say what he thought would happen in Vietnam. Bobby dutifully parroted President Johnson's war policy. I told Bobby I knew his opinion didn't coincide with the President's.

Bobby smiled and dodged. I asked him directly if he was running for president, and would he declare it on the show. Bobby flashed another smile and said he was just hoping for a happy ending. Then I asked him what he had seen on his recent travels through Appalachia.

"I've seen despair and hopelessness, and I've seen children who are starving to death in the United States," he told me. "I mean, not 'I read about children who are starving in the United States,' but I've seen children who are starving to death in the United States. And as the reports have said, they will never recover mentally after the age of four."

It was a poignant moment. Bobby wasn't talking like a politician. He was talking like a man with a moral center. Just what I thought America needed to hear.

Lena Horne, elegant and gorgeous, came on to talk about being a grandmother, which astonished Bill Cosby, sitting next to her. "Times have really changed," he marveled. "My grandmother spent most of her time worrying about which tooth would fall out next." Tommy and Dickie Smothers, the bad-boy comics of network television, shared details of skits that CBS had censored—a first, in its own way, for the stars of a rival network. Since I'd asked Bobby Kennedy what he thought of Johnson, I asked Tommy Smothers, too. "I think he's indisputably the best president we have at the moment," he said.

It was an amazing week. Paul Newman came on, not to talk about his next movie, but to play his trombone! I had Wilt Chamberlain, Sidney Poitier . . . as many black guests as white, talking not just about their movies or sports, but about issues of the day. By Wednesday morning, I'd stirred up the entire television-watching South. "Colored on TV," astonished white southerners told one another, while black folks, filled with pride, said, "TV's gone colored."

I wanted Martin as a guest, too, of course, and he agreed to come, though on the day he was scheduled he hadn't shown up by the start of taping. I had faith he would make it, so I greeted the house audience and sang my nightly opening song. Just as I was finishing, I saw Martin backstage, out of breath, gesturing an apology to me. When I brought him on, he told me what had happened. "Everything went wrong today," he said when we'd settled into our chairs. "A meeting ran late, I was late to the airport, the plane got to LaGuardia late. . . . Finally I got in a cab, and the driver recognized me. I said, 'I'm doing *The Tonight Show* with Harry Belafonte and I'm late.' So that driver hit the pedal, and it got very dicey. Finally I said, 'Young man! Young man!' He turned around. 'Yes?' he said. I said, 'I'd rather be known as Dr. King late than the late Dr. King.'"

The crowd laughed, and so did I, but I realized he'd given me an opening for a question that needed asking. "Tell me," I said, "do you fear for your life?"

Martin took a beat. "I'm more concerned about doing a good job, doing something for humanity and what I consider the will of God, than about longevity," he said. "Ultimately, it isn't so important how long you live. The important thing is how well you live."

The audience was dead silent as we spoke; I knew we'd ventured a long way from the territory of one-liners and cute little personal confessions *The Tonight Show* served up as its usual meal. But when the show was over and I thanked the studio audience for coming, their applause was heartfelt. I knew applause; I knew when it was real. This was real.

After days of hearing what nests of right-wing hornets I'd stirred up, I finished on Friday night by thanking NBC and Johnny Carson for a week I'd never forget. Then I added, "I am fully aware of how many of you have been offended by the politics aired on this show this week. None of it was meant to offend. But all of this was consciously arranged by me to give you all a taste of what's being said in rooms that many of you may not know or enter. Thank you for listening."

I thought I was done with TV controversy for a while, but I was wrong. In early March, I flew to Burbank, California, to tape an hour-long special with Petula Clark, the British singer who'd made her name in the United States with the hit song "Downtown." This was Petula's first special. Her sponsor dubbed her the Plymouth Girl after their automobile. I was delighted that Pet, as we called her, had chosen to have me as her solo guest. For one of our duets, we sang an antiwar anthem that Pet had written, "On the Path of Glory." As we were singing, she put a hand on my arm in a spontaneous gesture of solidarity. That, we soon learned, displeased a Chrysler advertising manager who had sat in on the taping to make sure that nothing would mar the sponsor's image. The manager, one Doyle Lott, feared Petula's hand on my arm would offend viewers. He told the show's producer that he found the touch offensive and absolutely unacceptable, and ordered the song reshot without it. The producer, Claude Wolff, who happened to be Petula's husband, refused. Now Mr. Lott went directly to Pet. She and Claude then took me aside and asked what I thought we should do. I felt Pet's dilemma profoundly. The larger ramifications of this incident could have serious consequences for her career. Perhaps, I told her, we should pick another fight, another day, at least while her best interests were at stake.

"Forget my best interests," she said. "What would you do?"

I grinned. "Nail the bastard."

"So we will," she replied, and with Claude's full support, we refused to reshoot.

Word got out well before the show's airing in early April, and when it did, Mr. Lott called me to apologize. He said he'd been tired and had overreacted, and that whoever he spoke with had relayed his words inaccurately. I said nothing until he was done, and then told him, "Mr. Lott, I think you're being disingenuous with me. It was you who said those words. And your apology comes a hundred years too late."

Martin's plan for a gathering of poor people in Washington, D.C., had taken shape by the time he appeared on *The Tonight Show*. Instead of a one-day march, he would bring thousands of poor people, both black and white, along with Mexican-American farm laborers from California, Native Americans, and more, to build a shantytown near the White House. There the protesters would remain until Congress passed an economic rights bill to alleviate poverty in America.

Bobby Kennedy had declared for president at last, and said his first goal was to erase "material poverty." Yet even he was opposed to the plan of a large and sustained public gathering in Washington; Bobby was always worried about the potential for violence. So was *The New York Times*, which editorialized against "emotional demonstrations in this time of civic unrest." Martin called his circle together in my home and, with Stan Levison and the rest of us, pondered long and hard, deep into the night, what our options were, along with the potential consequences. We concluded we would move ahead as planned. Martin spoke to large and excited gatherings around the country about his Poor People's Campaign. On March 27, a week before his assassination, he came up to New York for a big party at my apartment, one of the biggest we had held.

As usual, Martin was late. He always packed too much into his schedule, trying to do it all. This time a stop in Newark, New Jersey, had left him shaken. He'd met with Amiri Baraka, better known as LeRoi Jones, the playwright, essayist, and poet, who had formed a group called New Ark. Baraka identified himself as a black nationalist, and now openly advocated violence. He'd been arrested for carrying a gun during the previous summer's riots in Newark, and with his new group he was threatening to disrupt the city again. Martin had tried to reason with him, with no success. Baraka and his followers had denounced Martin bitterly. They'd scoffed at nonviolence, and vowed to tear Newark down in a matter of days. Martin was concerned that if Newark did blow, it would distract attention from the Poor People's Campaign and much that the movement had already accomplished.

None of this, however, Martin revealed when he walked in, because our gathering included journalists—*The New York Times*'s Tom Wicker and Anthony Lewis, among them. He wanted to stay on point, not muddy the message. As on the eve of Birmingham, we wanted to seed media interest as much as raise money. I sensed Martin's mood, but saw him push it away. Instead, with all the passion he could muster, he talked up the Poor People's Campaign. Only when the journalists and paying guests had left did Martin let his feelings show with the inner circle who remained.

Bernard Lee, Martin's personal secretary and bodyguard, was there that night; he was never far from Martin's side. So was Andrew Young, the future mayor of Atlanta. Stan Levison was long since back in the circle; his exile had ended when Bobby Kennedy stepped down from being Attorney General. Clarence Jones, Martin's lawyer and another of his closest confidants, was there. Julie was there, too, her feet tucked up under her, a glass of vodka in her hand. Her opinions were sought and valued whenever the group met in our apartment.

Martin poured his customary Bristol Cream, but skipped the routine of seeing how much remained. His collar open, his shoes off, he sipped pensively at the oak bar, Andy and Stan and Clarence on either side of him, me as host behind the bar. At first, Martin stayed on the subject of the evening. He spoke so quietly that Bernard, lying on a sofa behind him, soon fell asleep. But as he talked about Washington, and what he hoped to accomplish, he grew increasingly agitated.

"What bothers you, Martin?" I asked. "What's got you in such a surly mood?"

"Newark," Martin said, and proceeded to tell us of his unnerving visit with Amiri Baraka. "Beyond what an eruption in that city would mean, how it would take us off-course, I'm just so disturbed at what I'm hearing more and more. Somehow, frustration over the war has brought forth this idea that the solution resides in violence. What I cannot get across to these young people is that I wholly embrace everything they feel! It's just the tactics we can't agree on. I have more in common with these young people than with anybody else in this movement. I feel their rage. I feel their pain. I feel their frustration. It's the system that's the problem, and it's choking the breath out of our lives."

In the pause that followed, Andy replied, "Well, I don't know, Martin. It's not the entire system. It's only part of it, and I think we can fix that."

Suddenly, Martin lost his temper. "I don't need to hear from you, Andy," he said. "I've heard enough from you. You're a capitalist, and I'm not. And so we don't see eye to eye—on this and a lot of other stuff."

It was an awkward moment. Martin was really angry. But I understood the subtext. Deep down, Andy was ambivalent about the Poor People's Campaign. All the other goals that we had set for ourselves up to this moment were tangible. Almost all of them were focused on justice. But when it came to economics, the goals were more complicated, the lines more blurred. Andy didn't believe that all the victims came from the same level of experience. He felt that there was a critical difference between poor whites and Hispanics, on one hand, and poor blacks on the other. This disparity, he felt, could make the Poor People's Campaign a rocky journey.

The tension peaked. "The trouble," Martin went on, "is that we live in a failed system. Capitalism does not permit an even flow of economic resources. With this system, a small privileged few are rich beyond conscience and almost all others are doomed to be poor at some level." Taking a sip from his glass, he continued, "That's the way the system works. And since we know that the system will not change the rules, we're going to have to change the system."

At heart, Martin was a socialist and a revolutionary thinker. He spoke not just in anger, but in anguish. His voice dropped to a more reflective tone as he continued. "We fought hard and long, and I have never doubted that we would prevail in this struggle. Already our rewards have begun to reveal themselves. Desegregation . . . the Voting Rights Act . . ." He paused. "But what deeply troubles me now is that for all the steps we've taken toward integration, I've come to believe that we are integrating into a burning house."

We had not heard Martin quite this way before. I felt as if our moorings were unhinging. "Damn, Martin! If that's what you think, what would you have us do?" I asked.

He gave me a look. "I guess we're just going to have to become firemen."

Martin flew down to Memphis the next morning, accompanied only by Bernard Lee. The sanitation workers of Memphis were striking, and Martin wanted to show solidarity with them before going to Washington to kick off the Poor People's Campaign. Ralph Abernathy was there to greet him; he was the one member of the inner circle who hadn't been at my home the night before, because he'd been making arrangements for the march that Martin would lead. The crowd was far larger than expected—as many as twenty thousand—but while Martin was greeted with cheers, the mood on the streets was volatile, and the crash of breaking storefront windows, as Martin struggled to find his place at the head of the march, soon made clear that looting had begun. As it spread, Memphis police set off tear gas, and armored personnel carriers rolled in with the National Guard to clear the streets and enforce a state of emergency. The march was a calamity, playing right into the hands of critics who said Martin couldn't keep the movement from falling into violence. When I spoke with Martin on the phone that evening, I'd never heard him sound so upset. He was distraught. He felt strongly that the FBI had fomented the violence to undermine him. "There are forces of evil at work here, Harry," Martin said. "I feel it." Later, FBI files would show that Martin's instincts were sound. Under J. Edgar Hoover's COINTELPRO (for Counter Intelligence Program), the FBI by 1968 had infiltrated political groups it deemed subversive, planted false reports in the media, set movement leaders against one another, and slapped them with phony charges. Before COINTELPRO was dismantled in 1971, it would also be linked to the murders of numerous Black Panthers. Was it paranoid of Martin to think the FBI had tipped the Memphis march into chaos? I don't think so.

Martin was in Washington that Sunday, March 31, to deliver a sermon at the National Cathedral. But then he went back to Memphis. In a phone conversation with him, he said he felt honor-bound to return and lead a more peaceful rally. Martin was calmer now, focused on planning; our conversation was friendly, but perfunctory. I said I'd see him in Washington; I would be there to help him launch the Poor People's Campaign. He thanked me for that; we said good-bye. That was the last time we ever spoke.

In Memphis, Martin checked into Room 306 of the Lorraine Motel under stormy skies, as tornado warnings came over the radio. When he heard that the weather had kept the crowd small at the Masonic Temple where he was to speak, he asked Ralph Abernathy to fill in for him. But when Abernathy got to the temple and saw how disappointed the audience was, he got on the phone and persuaded Martin to come after all.

So many people asked me later if Martin had had some warning that he might be assassinated, if that was why the last speech of his life was so prophetic. I don't know if he had any warning. I don't think so. He'd been a target for so long, and made so many prophetic speeches. Perhaps this was just another one. And yet the final paragraph of it stuns me still.

"Well, I don't know what will happen now," Martin told that crowd.

We've got some difficult days ahead. But it really doesn't matter with me now, because I've been to the mountaintop. I don't mind. . . . Like anybody, I would like to live a long life. Longevity has its place. But I'm not concerned about that now. I just want to do God's will. And He's allowed me to go up to the mountain, and I've looked over, and I've seen the promised land. I may not get there with you. But I want you to know tonight that we as a people will get to the promised land. So I'm happy tonight. I'm not worried about anything. I'm not fearing any man. Mine eyes have seen the glory of the coming of the Lord.

I was in the living room of my apartment the next day, the room where I'd last seen Martin, when our housekeeper, Pearl Gibson, cried out from down the hall in her thick Jamaican accent. "Lawd God, Mr. B., Mr. B., come quick, look at the television." I ran down and looked at the screen, then fell back in a chair. I was immobile, physically and emotionally and psychologically. When I could finally move, my first thought was to call Coretta.

The line was busy. I tried again but couldn't get through. I just sat in that chair, my eyes wet with tears, and dialed again and again.

Finally Coretta answered, crying. I could tell she was making an enormous effort to be strong. I said, "I'm coming down as quickly as I can."

Coretta was at her home in Atlanta; she hadn't been in Memphis with Martin. When I arrived, she greeted me with a hug, too grief-stricken to speak, yet even as she did, the phones behind her were ringing. Everyone wanted her: civil rights leaders, friends, news reporters, the FBI. There, too, were her four children, wide-eyed, silent, needing so much more than any mother could give. "They're sending his body home," Coretta managed at last.

Coretta wanted me to help her pick the clothes that Martin would be buried in. Numbly, she led the way back to the bedroom. Martin's closet held just six or eight suits, all of them dark. With close friends and family, Martin wore jeans and casual shirts. In public, he dressed invariably like the preacher he was: dark suit, white shirt, dark tie, black shoes. I took out one of the suits, and Coretta laid it on the bed like a disconnected shadow.

"Coretta," I said, "I'm going to help you with everything I can. But there's something I want to ask of you, too. This country's going up in smoke, and one of the places it may catch fire first is in Memphis. Some think the march should be canceled. I think the march should go on. I think we need to show that even in death Martin's movement will not be halted."

"You do?" Coretta said.

"Yes, but more important, I think you should lead it."

That snapped Coretta out of her daze. "Me?"

"You're the only force in the universe who can do it as it needs to be done. The whole world will be watching, and your presence, and what you say, will have enormous impact on what this nation will do. The leadership needs your strength and your resolve."

There was a long pause, and then Coretta said, "I'll have to make arrangements for the children."

George Barrie, the head of Fabergé, made his plane available to us. It wasn't the first plane offered that day, but I trusted Barrie not to capitalize somehow on the offer. In the end, Coretta decided to take her three older children; they would bring Martin's spirit and presence with them. The FBI was alerted, and we flew through guarded airspace to Memphis. I stayed with her that whole day—beside her as she led the march, then on the dais as she made a brief, dignified speech that left the crowd in tears. Her presence had a great emotional effect that night on national television, and I think that it helped keep the riots from getting even worse than they did. As it was, Stokely spoke at Howard University in Washington, D.C., the day after Martin's assassination and warned that violence would break out. Violence did break out, and for three days the inner city burned. So did ghettos all over the country. I remembered Martin's talk, little more than a week before, about the futility of violence in our community. Here was Stokely, invoking Martin and violence in the same breath, condoning the chaos that damaged or destroyed hundreds of businesses, with a resulting loss of thousands of jobs. Still, if only in Memphis, I think Coretta's presence helped.

Martin's body was at an Atlanta funeral home, dressed in the clothes Coretta had chosen, when we got back. From there it went to lie in state, in an open casket, at Spelman College. Julie had arrived from New York, and at Coretta's request, we went in first, accompanied by Bernard Lee, to inspect the body before other visitors and the press came in. In that eerie stillness, Julie and I went up to the coffin, and saw where the mortician had puttied the open wound. Somehow there was still a large, discolored gap covering the side of Martin's face, and the tone of his skin on that side was distinctly different from that of his other cheek. It was unsettling, disturbing that the mortician didn't display greater care. Julie reached into her purse, took out her powder puff, and dabbed gently at the discoloration until she got the tone just right.

A day or two before the funeral, I hosted a strategy meeting in my hotel suite. Clarence Jones was there, I remember, along with Berry Gordy, Jr., the founder of Motown Records, and half a dozen others. I felt we needed to be extremely creative at this moment, to think in larger-than-life terms. The whole country was reeling; marches and protests were unfolding north and south. I felt we should do something to provide a focus for all that rage and sorrow, to send a message and set a tone. We could harness the power of all the celebrities who were in town for the funeral and stage a vigil at Atlanta's open-air stadium. The political figures alone included Bobby and Ethel Kennedy, Jackie Kennedy accompanied by her brother-in-law Ted, Nelson Rockefeller, Hubert Humphrey, Eugene McCarthy, and Richard Nixon. There were sports heroes—Jackie Robinson and Wilt Chamberlain—and entertainment figures, including Marlon and Bill Cosby, Aretha Franklin and Stevie Wonder. I felt I could also get other stars to fly in. Just as at the March on Washington, just as at Selma, the celebrities would swell and inspire the crowd, and turn the nation from violence. And it wouldn't be just stars. Ordinary people, too, could speak in the course of the night-long vigil about what Martin had meant to them. Together we would celebrate and honor Martin's fight for civil rights and his commitment to nonviolence, and that gathering would be broadcast all over the world.

We'd talked about the vigil before. Everyone in the room was onboard for it. All but one person—our newest arrival: Sidney. "At this time," he said, "it just seems too daunting a task, on top of the funeral." Too daunting a task for whom? With national television cameras focused on this event, the whole world would be watching. Much could be achieved in helping to calm the nation. All those young people who wanted to hit the streets and burn down America—and eventually tried to do just that—would be directed otherwise. That was my thinking. Sidney's feeling was that if it failed, that would mar the legacy more than any vigil could burnish it.

Sidney started articulating this position without, perhaps, realizing how strongly I felt. I stayed quiet while he went on, but my temper began rising. Julie, who was there with me, responded first. Later, in his autobiography, Sidney would say that "with blazing ferocity she lit into my position with an attack that was obviously directed at me personally. But my view was my view, so I held my ground." That he did, and I held mine. Some in the room began to side with Sidney; others sided with me; but now the idea was tainted by dissension. For those who were looking for that one voice of doubt to get behind, Sidney provided it. Having spread those doubts, he effectively killed the vigil. I was so angry that Sidney and I stopped speaking. Two years would pass before we spoke again.

A lot of people vied for places of influence with Coretta. I saw the beginnings of "Who will possess and be anointed? Who will own this legacy? Who will be steering the ship?" Ralph Abernathy was the number two man at the SCLC. His children were the same age as Martin's and, along with his wife, Juanita, had deep ties to the King family. Abernathy, along with Jesse Jackson and others, had stood on that balcony in Memphis, pointing in the direction of the assassin's gunfire. Already, Jesse was putting out feelers and talking to the press, positioning himself to be the successor. Soon he would go back to Chicago and brandish the "bloody garment" that Martin was wearing when he died. Like Abernathy, he, too, was angling for proximity to Coretta.

I distanced myself from all this, and from the immediate family that enveloped Coretta at the funeral, and during the march from the funeral to the burial ground, as a horse-drawn cortege pulled the wagon with Martin's body, I was well offscreen. At the burial, I did sit next to Coretta, at her express request. Not long afterward, she asked me who I thought should succeed Martin. We both knew she had no desire to take on his mantle, so we didn't even discuss that possibility. But she did not want her influence diminished. Remaining a voice to be reckoned with in the choice of Martin's successor would be one of the best ways to keep herself in the SCLC's innermost circle. She asked if I wanted to be considered. I said no. The vow I'd made that day in Harlem hardly ended with Martin's death. If anything, I was more needed now. But Martin had set up a line of succession by making Ralph Abernathy his vice president. The position was Ralph's to accept or decline, and I knew how much Ralph wanted it. And as much as my heart was in the movement, the more I thought about it, the more I saw troubled waters.

In one of our moments together that week, Coretta gave me the cuff links and tie clip that Martin had worn the day he died. They were among the few personal effects the police had passed on to her. In Martin's breast pocket, the police had found a small leaf-green envelope, along with a handkerchief. One side of the envelope had scribbled notes in Martin's hand for the speech he would have given in Washington inaugurating the Poor People's Campaign. It listed names of dignitaries to mention, and notes on why the Poor People's Campaign was so important. On the other side were typed pointers for the sermon he'd given the previous Sunday at the National Cathedral. Coretta gave the envelope to Stan Levison, who cherished it until his death. At Stan's request, the envelope was then bequeathed to me.

I would have done all I could for Martin's family even if I hadn't been named as one of three executors of his estate. (Harry Wachtel and Stan Levison, both lawyers, were the other two.) That role just formalized the responsibility I felt. The estate itself was meager—$5,000 in joint bank accounts. Martin had earned quite a bit of money from his five books, and $50,000 for the Nobel Peace Prize, but he'd given all that money to the SCLC, Morehouse College, and the Ebenezer Baptist Church. Besides the payout on the insurance policy I had secured on Martin for the family some years earlier, more would be needed. That week, I gave Coretta the first of several checks to help support the family. I knew that once the King Center was set up and endowed, the institute would pay her a salary, and she would be all right. In that transition period, she never had to ask for money; at the slightest mention of financial need, I wrote her a check. I kept in touch with the children, too—Yolanda, Martin Luther King III, Dexter, and Bernice. I didn't call them every day, but whenever I could, I reached out to them.

The center did open soon enough. But not in the way I'd envisioned. I'd thought the center's purpose would be to challenge injustice and nurture grassroots activism in the cause of civil rights, whether for blacks, American Indians, women, or all the dispossessed, whose plight Martin had taken up with the Poor People's Campaign. But no. As Coretta set it up, the center was about polishing Martin's public image. Under its aegis, professors wrote papers, sifting through the minutiae of Martin's life. Meanwhile, Coretta made social appearances at the most elite places. The White House was perfect; the National Guard Armory would do.

I was on the center's board for a while, so I saw all this coming down. Whenever I suggested the center endorse one grassroots effort or another, my fellow board members would throw up their hands. "We have to attract funding," some would say. "We can't offend the funders!"

Still, I was surprised when I got Coretta's invitation to a commemorative dinner for Martin's birthday the next January. It was to be a large, lavish affair in Atlanta. When I looked more closely at the fancy invitation, I did a double take. There among the list of sponsors was Henry Ford II, chairman and CEO of the Ford Motor company. He had just returned from South Africa, where the company had negotiated one of its most crushing labor contracts ever. By this time, the SCLC had established ties with South Africa's government-in-exile, the ANC, and called for sanctions against U.S. companies that did business with the apartheid government. Yet here was "Hank the Deuce," as he was known, heading up the dinner for Martin! When Coretta called to ask why I hadn't RSVP'd, I told her I wouldn't be coming. She was shocked. I told her that even if a Ford weren't coming, I didn't think a fancy dinner should be the way to honor Martin and his legacy. Had she perhaps planned something else for the anniversary, something a little more in keeping with the grassroots theme that I might participate in?

No, Coretta admitted. The effort of organizing the dinner had exhausted her. "How are you honoring his memory?" she asked me.

I told her I was going to Rikers Island, a prison in New York City overcrowded with young black teenagers. "I'm going to speak to the prisoners, the truly poorest among us."

To Coretta's credit, she flew up to New York before the dinner. She spoke to the prisoners, and then she flew back down for her dinner. The King Center continued as it had before, embracing no causes, issuing no calls to action, just playing on what I call the soft side of conscience. None of this obscures Coretta's greatest accomplishment—getting a national holiday proclaimed for Martin. No small feat. But the center, governed by timidity, hasn't even become the beacon of scholarship its founders intended it to be. Noble laureates are welcomed; younger, more cutting-edge scholars are not vigorously pursued. Now, under the leadership of Martin's children, it is basically a crypt with a reflecting pool, selling trinkets and memorabilia and books to tourists and students.

The Poor People's Campaign went on without Martin, but just barely. Rain fell on twenty-eight of its thirty-nine days, turning the Washington Mall into mud and soaking the five thousand or so hardy souls who set up their shanties there. Ralph Abernathy did his best to inspire this ragtag army, but his ego had gotten the better of him. He declared himself the mayor of Resurrection City, and in one speech, he actually said, "Every morning when I get up and look in the mirror I love Ralph Abernathy more and more."

I don't know if even Martin could have made a triumph of the Poor People's Campaign; most Americans, even liberal ones, had no patience with a shantytown of the ever-more-pungent poor on the Washington Mall. But I do know that Martin's absence showed how brilliantly and effectively he'd kept his bickering deputies in line. Was there no one else who could truly lead the SCLC? Stan Levison and I agreed that of all the candidates, only Andrew Young had the necessary temperament and charisma. But in the aftermath of Martin's death, Andrew had grown more reserved. He could be a feisty lieutenant, but not, it seemed, a self-reliant leader. Or perhaps he was recalling that last angry exchange with Martin in my apartment, and doubting whether Martin would have wanted him to take charge. By default, the job was Ralph Abernathy's to take, and he took it.

The tents and shanties were still up on the Mall in early June, when

Bobby Kennedy was assassinated in Los Angeles. I'd spoken with him just days before about campaigning for him. I'd made appearances for him when he ran for the U.S. Senate in New York. Back in February, on *The Tonight Show*, I had encouraged him to seek the presidency. And now that he was running for president, I wanted to help him in any way I could. The days of wondering how we might find and access his moral center were long gone. In his famous trips to see the nation's poor up close, Bobby had been transformed. I had come to admire him profoundly. I had even dared to imagine, for a few giddy weeks after President Johnson shocked the nation by declaring he wouldn't seek reelection, a Robert Kennedy administration that might embrace the goals of the Poor People's Campaign, given all that Bobby had said in the last year about America's poor. Now both Martin and Bobby were gone. On the Washington Mall, the shanties and tents of the Poor People's Campaign lingered until June 24. And then, as if to demonstrate that the whole country had tired of them, bulldozers rolled through the Mall's Seventeenth Street entrance and demolished Resurrection City.

In the wake of Bobby's death, and Martin's, I felt despair but also renewed determination. To abandon their causes now would be a gross betrayal. As always, in moments of moral quandary, I heard an echo of my childhood Catholicism, renounced but never entirely silenced. *How can I be worthy? I must be worthy. How?* Yet I felt tired. Tired of fighting, tired of the movement, tired of Harry Belafonte, political activist. That summer, an interviewer asked me what I was planning to do next for the cause. Maybe nothing, I told him. "I hate marching, and getting called at three a.m. to bail somebody out of jail, sitting on panels and talking to reporters and groups about America's racial problem." All I wanted, I said, was to "watch grass grow, and leaves change color, and see my children grow up."

In that bloodstained political season, I campaigned reluctantly for Eugene McCarthy. In person I found him cold and detached, but he said the right things, and Hubert Humphrey I found to be a craven opportunist. He'd played a central role in destroying the hopes of the Mississippi Freedom Democratic party in 1964 to help assure Johnson's election. As vice president, he'd pushed Johnson's hawkish Vietnam policy, knowing how fraudulent and doomed it was, and a lot of American soldiers, including a disproportionate number of blacks, were dying as a result. Vicious toward critics of the war, Humphrey struck back however he could—in my case by terminating my Peace Corps role with a letter saying the Corps was "reorganizing" and that my services were no longer needed. In a dark time like that, humor was the best response. At the height of the Democratic Convention that August in Chicago, the Smothers Brothers ran an eight-minute skit on their TV program, showing footage of Mayor Richard Daley's truncheon-wielding police battling demonstrators in the streets. I was superimposed in the foreground, singing "Don't Stop the Carnival" in calypso style as if I were there on the streets. CBS went ballistic. They not only pulled the eight minutes, but in its place ran a free commercial for Richard Nixon, then fired the Smothers Brothers—not just censured them but fired them—even as their popularity was soaring with the largest audience share on television. It was that kind of summer.

What I would do next for civil rights was a question I constantly asked myself. I found nothing in what Ralph Abernathy said or did to inspire me to stick with the SCLC. His strategies were insipid, his style off-putting. More than once he said to me, "You don't treat me the way you treated Dr. King." The first time I laughed it off. The second time I told him the truth. "The essential difference between you and Martin is that Martin earned it," I said. "We didn't just blindly throw gifts at his feet. We're willing to serve you, but you have to demonstrate to the entire nation that you can fill that space." The demonstrations were not forthcoming. It wasn't too long after that that Abernathy went Republican and became President Nixon's go-to guy on civil rights. That was about it for me and the SCLC. I kept working with SNCC for a while, but when in 1969 it changed its name to the Student *National* Coordinating Committee to reflect its official rejection of nonviolence, I lost heart. Soon after, SNCC quietly expired, a victim of battle fatigue and anti-white radicalism in more or less equal measures.

Martin's death had seriously crippled the movement he'd begun; that was becoming all too clear. The old groups were sputtering, their leaders competing, the sense of purpose dispelled. The movement for equality among blacks and whites in America was like a peeling poster on a brick wall, papered over with images of Black Panthers raising their fists. All those who had denounced Martin, from either the left or the right, now had a vacuum they could fill with whomever they wanted. Yet in that chaos, no one leader emerged. Everything shut down, all movements ground to a standstill.

What, then, could I do on my own? To me the answer was obvious:

take advantage of the Voting Rights Act and help elect black candidates at every level of the political system. I'd started as soon as the act was passed by joining Julian Bond on the campaign trail as he ran for the Georgia House of Representatives. That same year—1965—I'd helped persuade a young civil rights worker, John Conyers, to run for U.S. Congress in his home state of Michigan; twenty-two terms later, he's still there, the second-longest-serving incumbent in the House. By 1969, enough blacks had won congressional seats to form the Congressional Black Caucus, with Conyers as its dean, but that was just the start. In 1970, I helped persuade Andy Young to run for Congress in Georgia, gave him money, and staged a lot of free concerts. He lost that first time, but he stayed the course and won in 1972. On the city level, I helped Carl Stokes become mayor of Cleveland, Ohio, in 1967; that same year, I helped Richard Hatcher become mayor of Gary, Indiana. These were just the candidates in whose campaigns I played a significant role, with early endorsements and sizable contributions. For an awful lot of others, I made four- and five-figure contributions. If this was the best way to build on Martin's achievements, then that's what I would do, brick by brick, check by check. Most of these figures, not surprisingly, had started as activists and community organizers. They were the few in the black community who had networks of influence up and running; they could best compete with the white establishment politicians. But there was a trade-off. The more of these pioneers we elected to office, the fewer there were on the streets to do the organizing they had done.

At the same time, I was immersing myself in the South Africa sanctions movement. Freeing Nelson Mandela, ending the horrors of apartheid—that was where I saw the greatest need. Close behind were the needs of the newly independent African nations, tipping between hope and despair. I would spend much of the next two decades doing all I could to help.

The sixties had started, for me, with an awakening sense of Africa and its vast potential, not only for its proud tribes and nations, but as the world's black homeland. Now, as the sixties in America came to an end, that homeland seemed only more precious. But also more imperiled. Independent nations were struggling to feed their poor, waging wars as their leaders profiteered. A strange story captured for me a sense of the hope in both America and Africa as the sixties began, and disillusionment in both continents as the decade came to an end. It was a story of three characters I'd known well: Stokely Carmichael, Miriam Makeba, and Ahmed Sékou Touré.

I could see Miriam still as I'd met her in London in 1958, her youth and beauty and talent so radiant. How could I not have helped her? I had no regrets about that, though by the late sixties, Miriam was like a rebellious daughter, flaunting her brand of radical politics in my face, doing more than her share of drugs, and going from one rocky romance to the next. From Hugh Masekela, the South African trumpet player, she'd gone to Black Panther Huey Newton, and now to Stokely. I didn't introduce Miriam to Stokely, and neither told me the news. I had to figure it out by observing Stokely's change of wardrobe. Stokely was accustomed to wearing Levi's and a work shirt, with maybe a denim jacket. One day I went to one of Miriam's concerts, and there, backstage, was Stokely, in one of the finest Nehru suits I'd ever seen. A hand-tailored Nehru suit. On one hand he sported a big jeweled ring; in the other, he held a gold-headed mahogany cane. No doubt about it: Here was Miriam's new man. Miriam had the money now, and she liked to spend it. And both Miriam and Stokely seemed pretty turned on by that.

Stokely had wowed Miriam with his cries of "Black Power" and his national stature as head of SNCC. He'd impressed her that much more by angrily leaving SNCC in 1967 when it refused to boot out whites altogether. (In fact, he was expelled for hogging the limelight and issuing fiery statements without his fellow SNCCers' approval.) Briefly he'd become honorary prime minister of the Black Panthers, but when they also balked at severing all alliances with white activists, he broke with them, too. In the spring of 1969, he and Miriam decided they'd had enough of America's institutional racism, a phrase that Stokely had coined. So they moved to Guinea at the invitation of my old friend Sékou Touré.

For Stokely, who soon changed his name to Kwame Ture after two of Africa's brightest political leaders, Kwame Nkrumah, ex-president of Ghana, and Sékou Touré, this new life seemed, at first, a dream come true. Africa had fascinated him for years; he was one of the northern SNCCers who was now wearing African robes. Sékou Touré made him a special aide, and Stokely came to regard him as a mentor. Miriam got her own plum post, as Guinea's minister of culture. At some point, she also became Sékou Touré's not-so-secret mistress.

Whether that occurred before or after her separation from Stokely in 1973, I don't know. I do know that by then, Sékou Touré had set aside his youthful dreams of creating a utopian socialist state and become a vengeful tyrant who tortured his real or perceived political opponents. The hanging of my friend Ambassador Achkar Marof was just the start. Almost everyone I'd met in the country and come to regard as a friend was being branded an enemy of the state. Thousands of the country's intellectual, military, and political leaders were thrown into Camp Boiro, Guinea's gulag, many to die by torture, starvation, or firing squad. Sékou Touré was said to have syphilis of the brain, but then they say that about all black dictators. Certainly he was paranoid, and with his absolute power, he now kept his people in a state of constant mortal fear, and let them live in abject poverty, despite the country's many natural resources. Stokely and Miriam had to have known Sékou Touré was doing this by the early 1970s, but neither ever said a public word against him.

When Stokely and Miriam separated, Stokely moved back to the United States and grew increasingly paranoid himself. Eventually he came to believe that the FBI had infected him with prostate cancer. Miriam stayed in Guinea and fed Sékou Touré's paranoid fears. As his special adviser, she traveled with diplomatic immunity, and often visited Guinea's embassies abroad, where she came to be feared as much as Sékou Touré himself. Anyone against whom she took the slightest offense, she would write up as a political threat in private reports for Sékou Touré's eyes only. If an embassy official was called back home after a visit from Miriam, that would be it for him.

I had long since stopped visiting Guinea, and fallen out of touch with both Miriam and Sékou Touré, but I did inquire, when I could, about friends I'd made there. One day I asked about Alassane Diop, the Senegalese-born diplomat who'd made Guinea his home. When I'd first met Sékou Touré, Alassane was his best friend; the three of us would stay up laughing late into the night. When I'd been summoned back to hear the bad news about the arts center, it was Alassane who translated at Sékou Touré's side. Now, I heard, he'd been put in Camp Boiro and executed by firing squad. Yet even after this clear indication of Sékou Touré's mental imbalance, Miriam stayed on. That saddened me, but I wasn't surprised. My guess was that as a victim of a paranoid police state in South Africa, she felt, in a strange way, at home in Guinea, and perhaps in helping wield that power she was enacting a kind of revenge.

Years later, after I'd joined UNICEF as a goodwill ambassador and begun visiting Africa in much the same way I'd done for the Peace Corps, I found myself at a conference in Senegal. Way down the hall I thought I discerned a familiar figure. Could it be? "My God!" I cried out. It was Alassane Diop. "You're alive!" Behind him was his wife, Adelaide. I hadn't expected to see her ever again, either.

Over dinner that night, Alassane told me his amazing story. In a sense, he said, Sékou Touré had been right to feel threatened; he had a lot of enemies. But Sékou Touré had grown truly paranoid, and the confidante who did perhaps more than any other to provoke his fears was Miriam. It was Miriam who had given Alassane up.

"I was put in prison," Alassane told me, "and then I was put before the firing squad. Prisoners were shot in the head over an open pit. I closed my eyes, waiting for the bullet . . . but the officer's pistol jammed." The soldiers took that as an omen. Alassane was taken back to his cell and told that his execution would be rescheduled. Just at that time, the president of Senegal, Abdou Diouf, was making a state visit to Guinea. He had heard that a native Senegalese was in prison, about to be killed, and he petitioned Sékou Touré for Alassane's release. As a favor, Sékou Touré released Alassane into Diouf's care. "I came straight from prison," Alassane told me. "I went on the plane in my bare feet."

I told Alassane he must write a book about all this. My old friend shook his head. He wanted to do nothing, he said, that would hurt Guinea's legacy. What about telling the story of Sékou Touré and Miriam? I asked. No, Alassane said. The brotherhood he'd shared with Sékou Touré was too precious for that. As for Miriam, he said, "Remember, Miriam means so much to so many African people. Why destroy the inspiration she still stirs to this day?"

And it was true. Sékou Touré had died in 1984 of heart failure, but Miriam was still a vital figure—Alassane and I were having our dinner in the early 1990s—and after leaving Guinea she had helped push for Nelson Mandela's release. In her last years she became a goodwill ambassador for the United Nations and won international prizes for her charitable work. At the time of her death in 2008, she was giving a benefit concert in Italy to support a writer who'd dared to expose the workings of the Camorra, a Mafia-like cartel. She had a heart attack after singing one of the songs she'd made famous, "Pata Pata," and was eulogized as "Mama Africa." Did all her good works outweigh those dark years with Sékou Touré? Who could say?

The sixties had taken a toll on Miriam as they had on all of us. A lot of us hadn't made it out. When I looked back at all I'd tried to do, my first reaction was despair. So much more needed to be done. But if the energy that had led to two landmark civil rights laws lay fallow—and it did—green shoots would soon be growing from the warming soil. The women's movement, the American Indian movement, gay liberation, and the environmental movement—all these would emerge in the 1970s. A mighty force had been unleashed, and it would not be kept at rest for long. At critical junctures over the last two decades, I had played a role in that unleashing. I felt I'd lived two lives, perhaps three. At the threshold of a new decade I felt almost ancient.

I was forty-two years old.

PART THREE

17

If I'd had a credo for the life I'd lived so far, it might be: Do it all. My days were jammed, my evenings, too, in a constant balancing act between art and activism, tipped toward the latter. All too often, I'm sorry to say, I relegated my family to the cracks and margins: an evening at home between one day's rally and the next day's flight, a stolen weekend at the farm in Chatham to make up for a week away. "My father was serving two families," my son, David, later observed. "Us and the family of Man."

I know that though my intentions were good, I did fill my days with a certain self-importance. But I do believe the deeper drive was for validation, a search for self. Who *was* I? If I just did enough, and then some more, and then some more after that, perhaps I'd know at last. Perhaps, in the process, I'd do well enough, and do enough good, to please the parent whose West Indian voice still echoed in my head. Again and again, my psychoanalyst, Peter Neubauer, led me back to my mother, the source, it seemed, of all my drive and despair.

I called it a balancing act, but *balance* wasn't a word that rightly described my life so far. Now, as I moved toward the half-century mark, I searched for a real balance, between public and private life, work and family, time given and time shared. I'm not sure I ever found it. And then, at an age when most men decide to take their tea by the fire and cherish their long-suffering wives, I wound up throwing my marriage up in the air and starting all over again.

Perhaps balance just wasn't my thing.

I thought a lot, after Martin was gone, about the friendships in my life and how precious they were. Right up at the top was my friendship with Sidney. And yet for two years we hadn't spoken a word to each other. I'd done a lot of stewing about the way he dashed my hopes of a memorial concert for Martin, and I know he felt just as hurt and angry that I'd blown up at him. We were two very proud West Indians, and here's the truth: It takes a *lot* for a West Indian to put his pride aside. Finally, one day in the spring of 1970, I just picked up the phone and called. I had a script I wanted to pitch him, but that was just an excuse. I missed my friend.

The script had come to me from an intern on the set of a small film I'd made the year before, *The Angel Levine*—my first film since *Odds Against Tomorrow* in 1959. Once again, I'd been drawn to a story of race relations. *The Angel Levine* is based on a short story by Bernard Malamud, about a Jewish tailor with a bad back, a sick wife, and no money. He prays for an angel, and gets one, though in an unlikely form; the Angel Levine is a black street hustler who has twenty-four hours to convince the tailor he really is an angel, in order for both to be redeemed. I was reminded of that Jewish tailor who'd let my mother buy those sun-bleached suits in his store window at a generous discount, then taught her how to dye them blue. Along with the mixed cast—Zero Mostel as the tailor, me as the black angel—we had a black screenwriter, Bill Gunn, and an Academy Award–winning Czech director named Ján Kadár, making his first film in English after winning a Best Foreign-Language Film Oscar for *The Shop on Main Street*. Oh— and a Ukrainian actress named Ida Kaminska playing the tailor's wife. But I didn't stop there. I'd decided the making of *The Angel Levine* would be, in itself, an exercise in race relations (and since HarBel Productions was financing it, I could make that decision). I got the unions to agree to let young people of color serve as interns to the various union workers on set. The whole production process was a model for an enlightened, race-sensitized Hollywood. Except that Hollywood had no interest in adopting it, with one exception: Norman Jewison, who would always be a stand-up guy.

At least I got that intern's script out of it.

When he got on the line, I could tell that Sidney wasn't his usual stoic self. He was a bit rattled hearing my voice. With some hesitation, he told me to come on over and tell him the story.

Sidney and I were both based in New York. We both had offices on Fifty-seventh Street, just two blocks apart. Somehow we'd managed never to run into each other on the street in these last two years, but then, New York is like that. The next day, I walked over to say hello again to my friend. Neither of us made any mention of our rift. We just took up as if we'd seen each other the week before.

I reminded Sidney that a decade or so before, we'd talked about doing a black western. Blacks had played a serious role in settling the frontier, but not a single film had ever explored the subject. The script I had in hand, *Buck and the Preacher* by Drake Walker—he was the intern—could be a first step toward remedying that. Its two lead characters were both black frontiersmen, and if Sidney felt as I did about it, we could play those roles ourselves.

I left Sidney with the script, and in less than a day, he called back: He was in. With his string of box-office triumphs, he now had his own production deal. Within reason, he could say what he wanted to do next, and so he informed Columbia Pictures that *Buck and the Preacher* was it.

"You brought the film to me," Sidney said. "So let's make the deal very simple: It's fifty-fifty all the way, and you can take top billing." This was a lot more than generous; Sidney was the world's biggest black movie star now, and I wasn't. I told him I was in for 50/50, but he would take first position on the screen. "This is your kingdom," I said, "and you should reign."

I knew Sidney would make a perfect Buck: a wagon master set on protecting former slaves on their new western homesteads from the labor wranglers who want to press them into work gangs. Sidney was as square-jawed and upright in a cowboy hat as any white hero of a Hollywood western. For my own part, as the rascally preacher who comes along for the ride, I decided this was my chance to stretch. Instead of looking myself, as I'd done in every film I'd made in my matinee idol days, I'd have the kind of fun that my pals from the New School had been having for years, changing into a completely unrecognizable character. I let my hair grow wild and curly. I had the preacher chew tobacco, and stained my teeth, so that my smile looked more like a sneer. And like those fire-and-brimstone preachers I recalled from my early days in Jamaica and Harlem, crying out, "Jesus," and passing the hat, I rattled off evangelical riffs that rolled off my tongue as easily as my own name.

Both of us had money in this game—that is, my production company did and so did Sidney's—so with an eye toward the bottom line, we decided to cut costs by filming in Durango, Mexico. That would have been a smart decision if we'd hired the right director. Unfortunately, we didn't.

Joe Sargent would go on to a successful career (*The Taking of Pelham One Two Three*, *Jaws: The Revenge*), but at the time he took on *Buck and the Preacher*, he'd mostly done episodes of *Lassie* and *The Man from U.N.C.L.E.* The first week of shooting showed a serious drift from the whole tone and sensibility of the script. We were sending film up every day by air courier to be developed in L.A., so the studio was seeing the "dailies" even before we did. No one was happy. So Joe was to be replaced. But now what? We tried calling a few other directors, but no one wanted to parachute into the problem. That was when I started pushing Sidney to take Sargent's place himself. "We have a great crew and cast," I told him. "Everybody's pulling for you. So any problems that come up, we'll solve them together. Don't be afraid to try this."

The studio gave its blessing for Sidney to try a few days in the chair. He was very hesitant, but with a lot of urging from all of us—including Julie, cast as the wife of the Indian chief, and perfect for the part—we helped him take up the gamble. The response to the first viewing of the dailies was encouraging. Finally two young executives flew down to take a closer look. One of them, Peter Guber, would go on to produce many of the most popular films of his generation, from *Rain Man* to *Batman*. After watching Sidney work for a day, he made one of his early executive decisions: Sidney could stay in the director's chair.

For a while, spirits ran high. I wanted my dear friend to succeed, to make his bones as a director and, in the process, break that next race barrier; as far as I knew, there wasn't another black director in Hollywood at this level. I knew Sidney wasn't Martin Scorsese, but then, so did he. I was just grateful the film was getting done—and more, that Sidney was letting me run with my part.

When the film came out in the spring of 1972, Vincent Canby of *The New York Times* gave me some of the highest praise I'd gotten as an actor. "With what I suspect is the complete co-operation of Poitier," he wrote, "the film is stolen almost immediately by Harry Belafonte as a bogus preacher. . . . Belafonte has mellowed considerably as an actor since his matinee idol days . . . and his performance here seems limited only by the simple material. His Preacher is a high-spirited con artist with bad teeth, a patulous eye and some dark memories that give the film its few moments of dramatic distinction." Otherwise, Canby said, *Buck and the Preacher* was a "perfectly ordinary" western. For some reason, the black audiences we'd hoped would come in droves never showed up. Nor did the white ones. *Butch Cassidy and the Sundance Kid* had shown that the western as a genre still had legs, at least when it was leavened with a lot of dry humor. Well, we had dry humor. And weren't Sidney and I the black equivalents of Robert Redford and Paul Newman? Apparently not. But *Buck and the Preacher* would become one of the most viewed movies on TV (or so it appears to me), with endless showings in the wee hours of the morning.

Hollywood is littered with the dead production deals of marquee actors who thought they had the money to make four or five pictures. They did, and they didn't; one bomb usually blows up the deal. *Buck and the Preacher* didn't end Sidney's run, but it did put him on the ropes. He needed a hit, and in the midst of an early-1970s trend of cheap black dramas and comedies—blaxploitation, it was called—he thought he had the answer.

I was in Vegas, working at Caesars, when Sidney called to say he was coming up. He had a script he wanted me to read. I told him to stay for a couple of days as my guest, see my show, and hit Lake Mead. Sidney was a smooth poker player, at times almost lethal. But he skirted the casino like the plague. "No," Sidney told me, "no lake, no poker. I can't do that, and I can't leave the script with you. I need you to read it while I'm there."

With the first few pages of *Uptown Saturday Night,* my heart sank. The story seemed very weak to me, way below Sidney's standards. A guy wins the lottery but loses his ticket; it winds up in the hands of a jewelry thief who doesn't know what he has. So the hapless lottery winner has to seek the help of another gangster to outwit the first one. Sidney would be the lottery winner; I would be Geechie Dan Beauford, one of the gangsters. The whole script was contrived, the comedy trite. I said, "Sidney, if I were you, I wouldn't do this. You just came off *Buck and the Preacher,* it didn't do well, the black audience didn't show up at all. I don't think your career can take another one of those. Wait till you find a script that sings. And wait till you get another great co-star," by which I meant, as we both knew, a white co-star with box-office appeal.

"I don't have that luxury," Sidney said. "I'm committed to make this movie. And I need your help."

So I started thinking about what might make this work. I said, "If this is the script you have to make, you have to figure out how to stay ahead of the audience, because the way this is written, the audience is going to be way ahead of you in no time flat." How? Sidney asked. I was thinking of *A Time for Laughter,* my television tribute to black humor. "Let's get all of those comics," I said. "Put them all in, one after another. Let each one ham it up, do his bit. Just as the audience is starting to get bored with one of them, we'll kill him off and bring on another one. That way, each one can do his bit in a couple of days' work, and you don't need them all there at the same time."

Sidney looked at me hopefully. "It could work," he said.

Everyone wanted to help Sidney, so we had no trouble lining up Flip Wilson, Richard Pryor, and Bill Cosby. I did a comic turn myself, in a send-up of Marlon doing his *Godfather* death scene with slices of orange in his mouth. Pryor, at the height of his powers of improvisation, did hilarious, unscripted bits that had virtually no relation to the story. Who cared? They were funny. Our instincts, as it turned out, were right on the money this time: When it came out in June 1974, *Uptown Saturday Night* made $10 million, a major payday at the time. It was frothy and buffoonish, and audiences—both black and white— loved it. It became the first crossover racial comedy of the decade.

So of course Sidney came back to me and uttered Hollywood's most destructive word: "sequel." "Not this time," I said. "I think we got lucky; we got away with something. But let's not tempt the gods." I was especially nonplussed because the part he wanted me to play this time was so small! It was almost a cameo. Nothing in it stirred my interest. I think Sidney felt I was being ungrateful; after all, I wasn't the most sought-after actor in the world. He felt he was doing me a favor. I didn't. Undeterred, Sidney developed not just one sequel, but two: *Let's Do It Again* and *A Piece of the Action.* Both made money, a lot of money, in fact, and Sidney, who directed and produced the whole trilogy, enjoyed a new ride of economic power in Hollywood. I had no regrets about having turned down the work. But I know Sidney felt slighted, and while that hardly produced another rift, a little coolness crept in.

More than a decade had passed since *Midnight Special,* the album a young Bob Dylan had played on. In that time, I'd come out with more than a dozen albums, from my own studio recordings of folk, calypso, and love songs, to live albums (one at the Greek Theatre in L.A., one in Toronto, Canada), to collaborations with Miriam Makeba, Nana Mouskouri, and Lena Horne. But rock 'n' roll was so powerful and pervasive now! The charts were packed with those titles, and stages I'd once thought were mine were being claimed by James Brown, the Beatles, Aretha Franklin, the Rolling Stones, the Beach Boys, Stevie Wonder, Crosby, Stills, Nash & Young, and a multitude of others. Where was my new field to plow? I thought I might have the answer. I hadn't forgotten the waves of acclaim that met me all over Europe in the summer of 1958. Since then, I'd gone back for the occasional concert—Greece in 1960, those fundraisers for Martin in Paris and Stockholm, a couple of showy galas in Monaco hosted by Princess Grace—but with the constant demands of the civil rights movement, I'd mostly toured the United States. Were they still there, those European audiences? Would they still come out to hear me?

Soon enough, my new Danish promoter, Arnie Warso, put my fears to rest. Barely old enough to drink—or so he seemed—Arnie bore an uncanny resemblance to the little kid on Dutch Boy paint cans, complete with blond bangs. The first time he came to my office in New York to sell me on the tour he felt he could put together, I swept by him through the office's waiting room, sure he was just a messenger. But Arnie was as good as his word; he built up a tour that went from Scandinavia and Belgium through Germany and Austria, Italy and Spain, all in major venues that sold out almost overnight.

For our debut, in Hamburg, Germany, Arnie arranged to have press fly in from all over Europe. This wouldn't just be a concert; it would be a news event! I was eager to face that bank of cameras and microphones—it's amazing, after the reporters go away, how soon you want them back again. And then, once my bags were packed and I was at the airport waiting, I got word that my father had died. When I called Arnie to give him the news, and canceled my flight, a flock of European journalists waiting at the other end concluded that my opening-night concert was off, my whole tour in jeopardy. Arnie put out all the brush fires he could. The concert wasn't canceled, he said, nor was the tour. I would get there as soon as I could.

In our last years, my father and I had reached a real understanding. The terrifying giant of my childhood, beating me bloody, had aged into a passive figure incapable of hitting anyone. Instead of yelling, he talked, and I listened. I didn't entirely forgive him his rages, but I felt I understood the misery he'd lived in with my mother, and the role she'd had in making it worse. With Edith, he was happy, and that impressed me; it impressed me that he made her happy, too. Edith was a U.S. citizen, American-born, and once they were married, my father had qualified for citizenship himself, but for some years he'd hesitated; the old fears of deportation died hard. Finally one day he'd gone to take his oath of allegiance, and I'd vouched for him, swelling with pride as he clutched his little packet of citizenship papers to his chest. Now he was gone.

My mother, still parked in her studio apartment on 143rd Street, wanted no part of the arrangements. As far as she was concerned, my father had died the day he walked out on her. So I sat down with Edith and my brother, Dennis, and we agreed my father would be cremated at a later date. Dennis and I would cast his ashes out to sea off Jamaica. With the details settled, I caught the next flight to Hamburg. Since I'd originally planned to arrive three days ahead of the concert, I still had time. Only now I was arriving just hours ahead. Late, too, was all our equipment—our sets, lights, microphones, amplifiers, and more—which had gone by boat through Holland and been held up for lack of the proper carnet. Our crew was still frantically assembling it all as the concert hour approached. When the black-tied guests streamed in, they were steered to the bar and told to start drinking at our expense. Ninety minutes after the concert's scheduled start, they took their seats, the theater went dark, and I walked out onstage.

As usual, a grand piano was set center stage, with my eight-piece band and four backup singers behind it. In front of the piano, framed by its curve, stood a little table with a glass of water, a black napkin, and, on top of the napkin, my microphone. I liked to walk out unencumbered, bow to the audience, then turn upstage, walk a few steps, and pick up the mike—checking, as I did, to see that my whistles were lined up beside it; I used them when I performed my "Carnival" medley. On this night, when I turned back to face the audience, the whole house was standing. I'd never gotten a standing ovation before I even started to sing. I had to swallow hard to launch into my first song. I started a cappella and the band swung in. What happened after that was pandemonium. Euphoric cheering, thousands singing along, dancing in the aisles, more standing ovations, encore after encore. The next day, headlines like TRIUMPHANT BELAFONTE bannered in newspapers across the continent.

The love that came at me every night of that tour coursed through me in a whole new way. The nightclub applause of my early days was probably just as strong, but I'd never quite believed it was real. On that fateful night at the Royal Roost, I'd walked onto a stage by chance: I felt sure they'd see through me soon enough. Eventually, I'd come to expect the cheers. Not take them for granted—never that—but to assume that as long as I did my best, those waves of tribute would keep rolling in. They did, but I couldn't kid myself. I was in my mid-forties now, with my first gray hairs and a whole generation of talented entertainers coming up behind me. What I felt in Europe was that none of that mattered.

What made all this especially gratifying was that in Europe, I wasn't admired in spite of being an activist. I was admired for my activism as much as for my performing. European audiences saw me as an emissary, expressing liberal American views that were somewhat at odds with official U.S. foreign policy. I never spoke disrespectfully about my country. But I did publicly and repeatedly endorse the nuclear-freeze movement, and I did condemn South Africa's apartheid government.

Occasionally, I challenged the country where I was performing on its own political issues. I had a huge and mostly young audience in East Germany—here, too, my human rights work stirred as much if not more excitement than my singing—and so, rather warily, in 1983, the Communist government of Erich Honecker let me be invited to perform at East Berlin's annual youth festival. I'd never appeared in East Germany before. I said I'd go on one condition: that I be allowed to share the stage with another act of my choosing. I didn't say who. A few days before the concert, my German promoter, Fritz Rau, let slip to the East German press that I'd be sharing the stage with . . . Udo Lindenberg. The press was stunned. Udo Lindenberg was the Bruce Springsteen of West Germany, but with a hard political edge. In his songs he gleefully mocked East Germany's government and its rigid head of state. His latest hit song, played widely underground in East Berlin, declared, *"I have a flask of cognac with me and it tastes very yummy / Which I slurp at ease with Erich Honecker / And I say: 'Hey, honey, I sing for little money in the Palace of the Republic if you let me . . .'"*

The Honecker government could have banned our appearance, but its apparatchiks knew better. Even in a repressive society, youth had power if roused to fury. The morning of the concert, I held a press conference with Udo at my side. The first few questions were all for Udo—dressed scruffily as usual—and he disappointed no one with his teasing, wry replies. Then a journalist stood to address me, and threw me a curve. "Mr. Belafonte, what do you think of the U.S. invasion of Grenada today?"

I couldn't believe I'd heard him right. I thought he meant the United States had invaded Spain. In the Caribbean? The whole idea was preposterous. It sounded like a Marx Brothers movie. I stammered that this was the first I'd heard of it, and I could hardly comment until I knew more. With that, the press conference fell into chaos. Udo and I traded looks of disbelief. We'd thought we'd one-upped the East German regime; instead, President Reagan had one-upped us all with the most unlikely invasion in American history. We did put on a hell of a concert that night, though, and the crowd went wild for us.

I disagreed with almost every tenet of U.S. foreign policy, from the Cold War freeze on any relations with Iron Curtain countries, to Vietnam and its aftermath, to the backing of right-wing tyrants through Africa and Latin America. But I felt a special frustration with America's stance toward an island close to home: not Grenada, but Cuba. To me, Fidel Castro was still the brave revolutionary who'd overthrown a corrupt regime and was trying to create a socialist utopia. Our trade blockade pleased the right-wing Cuban-American community in Miami, but who were those angry partisans? A lot of them were cogs in the corrupt Batista machine who'd lost their plunder and were still mad about it! Long after the Bay of Pigs and the Cuban missile crisis, I still felt the United States should forge an alliance with Cuba that benefited both countries and gave Castro enough space to make his experiment work.

I guess I made that view pretty well known, because one day in early 1974, I got word that Castro would be honored to have Julie and me as his guests at the Havana Film Festival, which turned out to be one of the most impressive film festivals that I have ever seen. We flew to Montreal—the U.S. ban on all direct air travel to Cuba was in effect—and then to Havana. I assumed we'd have a short meet and greet and pose for a picture or two. I had no inkling that this would be the start of a long friendship.

This was my first visit to Castro's Cuba, but not my first to the island. In the mid-fifties, when I'd played the Eden Roc in Miami, I'd taken to flying a prop plane over to Havana for a night of great food and gambling at a casino. Castro was already in the hills with his troops, planning his next moves, and most Americans I met there were cheering him on against the wildly crooked Fulgencio Batista. Soon after Castro marched into the capital in January 1959, I'd seen him in some big rooms in Harlem, raising funds to support the revolution, which needed all the help it could get; Batista had looted the treasury of $300 million as he fled the country.

As part of the blockade, Americans were allowed to spend only a nominal amount of money in Cuba. For us that wasn't a problem; we were guests of the Cuban government. A car whisked us from the airport to the Hotel Habana Riviera, the famous high-rise casino resort on the Malecón waterfront built in the mid-fifties with the secret backing of Meyer Lansky and other Las Vegas mobsters. (Such were the U.S. citizens who'd lost their properties in the revolution, to the lasting indignation of their government.) When, we asked, would we meet our host? Our driver and translator smiled apologetically. As the target of literally hundreds of assassination attempts, they explained, Castro never announced his schedule in advance. We should expect that at some point we'd be interrupted in whatever we were doing and taken to an undisclosed location.

For a day or so we explored Havana and lolled by the pool. Then came word that we should be in the hotel lobby at a certain time. We were warned that we might wait awhile; Castro, as usual, was running late. We didn't care. We were going to meet Fidel! Unfortunately, the hotel lobby seemed to have no air-conditioning. For more than an hour, we sweated in stifling humidity, until I announced to Julie that I could stand no more; I was going up to our room to shower and change.

I was just drying off from a cooling shower when the phone rang. "Señor Belafonte?"

"Yes."

"You are in your room."

"Yes."

"Not in the lobby."

"No."

"Where is your wife?"

"In the lobby."

"Is there anyone else in your room?"

"No."

I'm not sure how I understood this exchange, because I spoke no Spanish.

"Stay where you are, Señor Belafonte."

About three seconds later came a knock on the door. I opened it to see an incredibly handsome young Cuban in military mufti—not rugged jungle but beautifully tailored: revolutionary haute couture. I, on the other hand, was wearing Jockey shorts—and nothing else. I saw, past his shoulder, that the room across the hallway was open and occupied by four or five other military men in mufti, all with sidearms and a couple of AK-47's. My eye went immediately to the one in the full black beard, who strode over to take my hand in his. "Welcome to Cuba, Señor Belafonte," exclaimed Fidel Castro, with a grin at my Jockey shorts. He was as tall as I was—six feet two—which I hadn't expected, with proud, flashing eyes and a broad grin. "You have made the Cuban people so happy!"

I put my pants on at that point, and one of the men went down to bring Julie up. With a beautiful female translator named Juanita at his side, Fidel thanked me for coming and said how much a fan he was of my music. As soon as Julie appeared, I could see he'd just become even more of a fan of hers. We talked in the hotel room for hours, then followed the entourage downstairs to the motorcade waiting outside. Off we sped to the Museum of the Revolution, with its amazing glassed-in atrium of full-grown indigenous trees and plants. The dining room to which we were shown was very grand, the hors d'oeuvres delicious, the dinner superb. As for the cigars—well, that went without saying. Later, when friends asked me if our day with Castro had worn us out, I told them the truth: absolutely not. Castro was so compelling, in both his physical presence and his intellectual passion, that Julie and I were genuinely sorry to say good-bye.

Castro was a film buff—that was clear from his many excited references to American classics. (His all-time favorite was *Gone with the Wind*.) At his urging, Julie and I came back just months later. This time we brought Sidney and his lady friend, Joanna Shimkus, a young Canadian actress whom he'd met when the two were cast together in a heist film called *The Lost Man*. (Like Julie, Joanna was both white and Jewish.) Over the next few days, we saw a lot of films, drank a lot of cocktails with leftist writers like Jorge Amado and Gabriel García Márquez, and listened to some of the world's best jazz musicians play late into the night: Dizzy Gillespie, Stan Getz, and more. Once again, Fidel's men in mufti materialized without advance notice. This time, we were taken first to the Museum of the Revolution, and up to Castro's private office, with a panoramic view of the city.

Castro came from behind his desk to greet us with outstretched hands. He dazzled Sidney with his thorough knowledge of his film career; he seemed to have seen every film Sidney ever made. (I couldn't help noticing that *Island in the Sun* was the one film of mine he knew; he did know most of my songs.) I'd come to realize that he understood English quite well—I could see that from his visceral reactions to what we said—but still he spoke in Spanish and relied on his gorgeous translator. Whether he felt uncomfortable speaking English, or liked his English-speaking guests to feel better informed by having to go through his translator, I can't say for sure.

Castro loved having two of America's top black stars on his turf, not because he was starstruck, but because we *were* black—Castro took pride in presenting Cuba to the world as a truly prejudice-free nation; it was part of his socialist outlook—and also because he knew we admired what he was trying to do. Sidney's doubts about Castro at the time were certainly greater than mine. But we both wanted to believe in the dream, and in the dreamer. Castro was a modern-day Bolívar; there was no other Spanish leader quite like him. Sékou Touré had thrown over his socialist ideals and become a dictator, as had others. I still hoped Fidel would avoid that trap.

We talked a lot in Castro's office that day about the U.S.–Cuba relationship. Despite all the assassination attempts made against him—a British documentary in 2006 would put the total to date at 638—Castro expressed no anger toward the United States. He did bring up President Kennedy's assassination, and sharply rebuffed the conspiracy theories that implicated Cuba. He explained how it made no sense for Cuba's interests to have taken Kennedy out. Why would Castro have wanted that heat, especially if, as the U.S. State Department feared, he was building atomic missiles and hiding them in the hills? We wanted to believe him, and his logic seemed persuasive. So then were Lee Harvey Oswald's efforts to fly to Cuba weeks before the assassination just the meanderings of a crazed lone gunman? The fact that the Cuban embassy in Mexico City held up his demand for a visa to Havana for five days would seem to suggest that. So did Oswald's decision not to go to Cuba when the visa finally came through. But to this day, no one knows for sure—except, perhaps, Fidel.

"Come back and visit us again," Castro said as he shook our hands good-bye. I don't think Sidney ever did, but I made a point of going to the Cuban film festival year after year. When I did, I was put not in the Hotel Habana Riviera but in a "protocol house," government-owned with household staff. I never knew on those visits if Castro would see me, but he almost always did. One day he took Julie and me on a drive to the prison in Oriente Province where he'd been confined before the revolution. Julie's parents were with us that time. When he showed us his cell, he grew very emotional; little by little, the man behind the figure was emerging. At other times we joined him for visits to schools, where the students' rapture at seeing him was unfeigned, as was his pleasure at seeing them. Inevitably on these visits we talked politics, and when we did, I made a point of gently relaying the views and frustrations of Cuban dissidents with whom I'd met—without naming names, of course. Castro would listen, and occasionally take heed, loosening some government edict or other. The most dramatic case came when I introduced him, in 1999, to Cuban rap.

Julie had come with me, as she almost always did, and we were staying in one of the protocol houses, but went for lunch one day at the National Hotel. At a nearby table, I noticed a group of blacks who seemed to be Cuban. I wound up talking to them, and they told me they were rappers. I said I hadn't known that Cuba had rappers. After all, rap is in your face, by definition. How could they be true to rap's spirit in Castro's Cuba? They couldn't perform in Havana's clubs, they acknowledged; to the country's elite, they didn't even exist. But they did perform underground, often for hundreds of people. That night, Julie and I went to hear the ones we'd met. We were amazed. Of course we didn't understand every word and idiom; rap is hard enough to follow in English, much less in a second language. But a translator helped us follow the gist, and I fully appreciated the passion behind what I was hearing.

The very next day, Julie and I had lunch with Fidel, along with his minister of culture, Abel Prieto, a tall, very handsome, very Spanish-looking hippie with long hair and blue eyes. We started talking about blacks in Cuban culture, which gave me an opportunity to bring up the black rappers we'd heard the night before, and what a pity it was that they could only perform underground. I could see that Castro had only the vaguest idea of what rap and hip-hop were, so I gave him a crash course in how they'd swept the planet, how they not only dominated the international music industry but had so much to say about the social and political issues of the day. For Castro to be unaware of how much Cuban rappers were adding to that conversation was truly a pity—not least because I could see how a U.S.-Cuban cultural exchange in rap and hip-hop might start a dialogue between the two countries.

Fidel turned in some bafflement to the minister of culture. "Why are these artists afraid to perform in Havana?"

Prieto had to admit he didn't know much about rap or Cuban rappers, let alone black ones. To Fidel, free speech wasn't so much the issue as racism; if black artists in Cuba were being repressed, that undermined Castro's no-prejudice policy. Lunch was over, so we stood up to take our leave. "Where are you going?" Fidel demanded. I suggested we might head back to our protocol house. "No, no, no. I want you to come with me and tell me more about these rappers."

Whether we liked it or not, we were now part of Fidel's entourage for the day. Out we went to his unmarked presidential car. Fidel slid into the passenger seat, while we got in back. "So," he said, turning back to us, "what is this hip-hop?"

First stop was a graduation ceremony for some four thousand medical students. Despite all the hardships, Cuba had kept up a highly regarded medical system for its citizens, and managed at the same time to send out thousands of newly certified doctors each year to Africa, Asia, and Latin America, reaping an enormous amount of goodwill throughout the developing world. Fidel pulled me onstage to say a few words to the sea of graduates, then launched into one of the marathon speeches for which he was so well known. Finally it was back into the car and off to the next event.

Fidel kept me close, peppering me with more questions on rap. Our final stop was a buffet dinner for Alicia Alonso, Cuba's top ballerina, who had studied with Balanchine, become a great star in the United States, then decided to go back to Cuba and devote her life to building a national ballet company. I was thrilled to meet her, though it wasn't long before I felt a familiar hand on my arm. "And what about white rappers? Are there many?"

"Yes," I said, "but I think what is most interesting about all this is that the largest audience in America for this music is white children. It is an amazing phenomenon."

Fidel considered that thought for a moment and simply said, "Hmm."

When I got back to the protocol house, I looked at my watch: I'd just spent eleven hours with Fidel.

Almost a year later, on my next trip to Cuba, a young woman and two young men approached me and gave me some flowers. I said thank you, but what are these for? The young man said, "For everything you said to Fidel Castro about rap." All three were rappers. Since my last visit, their lives had changed dramatically. Fidel had not only declared his approval of Cuban rappers, he'd dedicated a brownstone in Havana to the nascent Cuban rap movement, and outfitted it with a recording studio, as well as all the equipment of a fully functioning office and communications center. Today those rappers are heard all over Latin America and have carved out a very respectable place in the U.S. rap scene. Some have even decided to live here.

My last visit to Cuba—in the fall of 2009—was, of them all, the most poignant. I was down with a film crew, gathering footage for a documentary about my life in the human rights movement. I asked Fidel for an interview, and for the first time, he invited me to his home. He may have other homes around the island for all I know; this one was a modest house with a swimming pool in the hills outside Havana.

Fidel had had a bad fall in 2004 while stepping down from a stage, breaking a kneecap and fracturing an arm. Two years later, intestinal surgery had left him so frail and despondent that he handed power over to his brother and, as he later put it in an interview, prepared to die. But Fidel is a tough old bird; somehow he'd regained the will to live, and embarked on a program of rehabilitation. The Fidel we saw that day was almost fully recovered—his cane discarded, his handshake firm, his eyes once again flashing with curiosity and passion, though also with some exasperation. "As a musician, you should know rhythm and timing," he grumbled as he greeted me. "Your timing is awful!"

I asked him what he meant by that.

"The playoffs!"

Castro is a rabid baseball fan. He did all he could to encourage promising Cuban players, only to have the best of them defect to the United States to play in the Major Leagues. "In order to see some of Cuba's best players play, I have to watch American baseball," he said. He indicated the TV behind him, and the game in progress.

The revolution hadn't fulfilled its promise, and now was facing its most critical challenge. While he never quite came out and said as much, Fidel clearly knew it. And yet his fascination with world politics was undiminished; he was up on every issue, and despite Cuba's problems, despite the global recession, he was filled with excitement for what might yet be.

Fidel was so charismatic, his energy so powerful, his legacy in some ways so admirable, in other ways so sad. I genuinely liked him, but

I can't say he was my role model. Paul Robeson was my role model. Sadly, by the time I met Fidel, Paul had slipped into his final decline.

I had done my best, ever since our simultaneous concerts in London in 1958, to stay in touch with Paul. It wasn't easy. During a tour of the Soviet Union in 1961, he'd slit his wrists in a Moscow hotel room and nearly died. Admitted for some months to a Soviet sanatorium, he had experienced bouts of paranoia, and come to feel he'd been given hallucinogenic drugs, possibly by the CIA. Back in London's Priory Hospital, he had undergone more than fifty rounds of electroshock therapy, later viewed as grossly excessive. Paul and his son, Paul junior, felt that both the British and U.S. intelligence services were manipulating his treatment to "neutralize" him. Certainly they were monitoring Paul's condition, though perhaps in an effort to keep him alive, not have him die; an FBI memo at the time warned that Paul's death would be used for communist propaganda. Whatever the causes of his physical ill health, I saw enough of Paul to know that he was also suffering deep and enduring depression about what had happened to so many of his friends in the Soviet Union. He had believed strongly in the Soviet promise, and would say nothing publicly against it that would give ammunition to the anti-communist zealots who'd hounded him for so long. But he knew what a genocidal psychopath Stalin had become, and that tormented him.

Paul had moved back to the United States in 1963, living first with his wife, Eslanda, in Harlem, and then, after Eslanda's death, moving into a humble brownstone apartment with his sister in Philadelphia. When I visited him there, we sat on straight-backed chairs in the dining room, in an apartment that held no traces of his life and achievements: no framed photographs, posters, or other memorabilia. This was, after all, his sister's house, but those unadorned walls heightened the sense of a man cut off from his own legacy. Physically, he was reduced from that towering, broad-shouldered force of nature to a stooped and frail figure. Still, he seemed in good spirits, largely, I suspect, because I'd come to discuss the plans for a seventy-fifth-birthday tribute to him at Carnegie Hall.

The idea had come up in conversation with Paul Robeson, Jr., who lived near me on the Upper West Side. When Paul had mentioned in early 1973 that his father's seventy-fifth birthday was coming up, he and I started making things happen. Paul senior planned to attend. But as April 9 loomed, he fell ill, and had to cancel the trip. The event went forward without him: Three thousand people filled Carnegie Hall for a night of music, homage, and love. Everyone from Sidney to Odetta, Dizzy Gillespie to Coretta, James Earl Jones, Ossie Davis, and Ruby Dee was there. Birthday greetings came from President Julius K. Nyerere of Tanzania, President Kenneth Kaunda of Zambia, Prime Minister Indira Gandhi of India, and more. Paul's presence filled the hall, and a prerecorded greeting from him played on a giant screen. "Though I have not been able to be active for several years," Paul told us in halting tones, "I want you to know that I am the same Paul, dedicated as ever to the worldwide cause of humanity for freedom, peace, and brotherhood."

A little less than three years later, Paul died—whether from complications of a stroke, as the doctors said, or just a broken heart, who could say. By a strange coincidence, he died on the very day—January 23, 1976—that I was serving as best man to Sidney for his wedding to Joanna Shimkus at Sidney's mansion in Beverly Hills. Four days later, I joined the throng of five thousand mourners at Mother AME Zion Church in Harlem. Among them were Malcolm X's widow, Betty Shabazz, composer Eubie Blake, and Henry Winston, chairman of the American Communist party. Even in death, Paul was going to show the world he'd stuck to his beliefs. At one point, after many had spoken, we sat in silence, listening to a recording of Paul singing "Deep River" in his inimitable bass baritone. How vividly I remembered that voice, and that towering figure filling the tiny backstage corridor of the Village Vanguard. *"Get them to sing your song, and they'll want to know who you are."* Those words had stayed with me, and so had *his* song, of unwavering courage and character. In all I'd done, he'd guided and inspired me. My whole life was an homage to him.

The death of my brother, Dennis, at about the same time, was a different kind of loss: the sad, quiet demise of a man who'd never dared to dream at all. His whole life had been a ball of tension. He radiated anxiety and rage. His wife had left him when they were young. I doubt he'd ever taken up with anyone again. What Dennis lived for, more than anyone I've ever known, was the movies. He'd go to a first showing and stay in the darkened theater all day. "Your eyes are so red from all that movie-watching, you're going to ruin your eyesight," I'd say, to no effect. For Dennis, movies were an addiction.

I think the only job he ever had was the one I got him, at the United Artists warehouse in New York. Dennis was put in charge of UA's vast trove of film: most of the original prints, and many secondary ones, for every movie UA ever made. Dennis loved that job. He stayed in that warehouse year after year, never sought a promotion and never received one. He had almost nothing to do in his working hours. That suited him fine. He spent his days writing script after dreadful script. The stories weren't even his own. He would alter the plot of a movie with John Wayne and make me the star. It was mental illness. At the end of the day, he would often smuggle out a can of film. If there were fifteen cans of sixteen-millimeter, he'd take one. No one ever noticed anything missing, since Dennis was the one who kept the inventory, and no one encroached on his domain. Only after his death did I realize how much film he'd acquired. His bathtub, the sink, the kitchen cupboards were filled with cans of film. He never sold any of it; profiteering wasn't his thing. He just wanted to own it all.

Dennis died in his mid-forties. He just keeled over during a solitary restaurant dinner in the Bronx. I had to go identify him. When I did, I just fell apart, overwhelmed with guilt. Dennis was the one who'd been palmed off to some other school in Jamaica while I attended the proper and prominent Morris-Knibb. I'd left him in my shadow, and never really looked back to be sure he was all right on his own. I'd failed him, or so I felt. Only later would I realize that in getting him that job at UA, I'd done perhaps the one thing I could have to give him joy.

When I called my mother to relay the news of his death, she began wailing. "Oh, God, don't tell me so . . . Ah, Jesus, why me, why me . . ." I never knew her in any greater pain than at that moment. Nothing I could say consoled her. Like all mothers, she'd felt most protective of her unsuccessful child. She'd often said that the cruelest cut my father ever inflicted was to say he didn't think Dennis was his son.

Sidney's wedding to Joanna Shimkus was, in all but one respect, rather anticlimactic. He and Joanna had known each other so long that they had two young daughters who served as flower girls for the ceremony. But Julie, who served as matron of honor, got so moved by the exchanging of vows that she declared we had to renew our own. So we tagged along with Sidney and Joanna up to Vegas for their honeymoon, got the star treatment at Caesars, and scheduled our own second wedding at a Vegas wedding chapel. In the day or two before the service, Julie shared her excitement with the wife of one of Vegas's big bosses. She went on so much about the depth and importance of the vows that the wife told her husband they had to renew their vows, too! That Vegas hotelier looked stricken at being dragged into the chapel, but apparently his wife was the one person he couldn't order around. Sidney and Joanna stood as witnesses for the four of us, and vows were duly exchanged.

Deep down, I think, Julie knew as well as I did that a second wedding wouldn't save our marriage. Somehow, at some point, love had left the room, but neither Julie nor I wanted to admit it. We were both caught up in a fierce dance of public image, dancing long after the music had stopped. We substituted politics for passion, and then confused the two. I traveled more than I had to, and that distance settled in between us, letting us lead more separate lives.

I'm sure all of my children sensed this, maybe more than we did. Certainly David and Gina, while they still lived at home, felt their father's frequent absences. I wasn't at the dinner table all that much. I didn't take them to enough baseball games or nearly enough movies and plays. I did arrange to have all four of my children join me in Vegas for summer engagements that coincided with their school vacations. We had blocks of time there, but sharing room service in suites at Caesars was not, perhaps, quite the same as eating together at home. I felt guilty about that, so I indulged them—a lot. They had the best of everything, from private schools to fancy clothes, from Lake Tahoe ski trips to Caribbean beach retreats. We'd go to Africa, but instead of going on a safari, I'd drag them along to meet with African leaders and take them on drives into the interior to a village of renowned dancers or drummers. Even when we went to the Caribbean, I packaged the adventure. But the details of their daily lives were too often relegated to other caretakers. I wanted to give the children all they wanted, all I hadn't had. In so doing, I may have deprived them of what they needed most: the grit, and the tools, to take on the world and make their own way.

Adrienne, my eldest, was the least affected by my imperfect parenting, in large part because she *was* the eldest. She'd had eight years, at least, of two parents together, and a strong enough bond with me that when Marguerite and I separated, Mrs. Byrd couldn't work that dark magic on her. As she reached adolescence, Adrienne also acquired a new, quite wonderful stepfather.

Dr. Edward Mazique was just the man Marguerite should have married in the first place, or perhaps more to the point, the son-in-law her parents wanted all along. A graduate of Atlanta's Morehouse

College—the most distinguished of the historical black colleges—and a highly credited surgeon, he'd actually met Marguerite years before, in a professional capacity, when she was pregnant with Adrienne! Marguerite had been in considerable pain, and another doctor had diagnosed appendicitis. Young Dr. Mazique had correctly diagnosed that Marguerite just had a restless baby perched on her kidney. More than a decade later, when Dr. Mazique had become the head of the National Medical Association—the black counterpart of the American Medical Association—they met again, and married, setting up a new life, with Adrienne and Shari, in Washington, D.C. Dr. Mazique and I ran together a lot; he was a gracious, urbane fellow, and also very kind to me; not long after he married Marguerite, in 1965, he and Martin ganged up to get me an honorary degree from Morehouse. So this New York high school dropout had become, in a sense, a "Morehouse man," too.

After graduating from Windsor Mountain, Adrienne had chosen to attend West Virginia State College, one of the historically black colleges, in part because one of Marguerite's brothers was on the faculty. In fact, the school had opened its doors to white students beginning in the mid-1950s, after *Brown v. Board of Education*. Over time, the college, which had been 100 percent black, became 80 percent white. Among the white students was a tall Missourian named David Biesemeyer, with German Methodist roots. He fell in love with Adrienne, and she with him. Marguerite was furious. "Why did you let her end up with that white man?" she railed at her brother the professor. It was a nasty streak in the Byrd family that I'd noticed early on. Marguerite sent Adrienne to study at the University of the Americas in Puebla, Mexico, hoping the romance would cool, but David followed her there. Marguerite kept trying to talk them into breaking up. Not only did they ignore her; they got married.

It was my turn to be alarmed when they chose to live in West Virginia, first for Adrienne to get a master's degree in community counseling from Marshall University (David had already earned a law degree), then for the two of them to settle in a small town and start a family there. To me, West Virginia was a state with its own racist tradition, of the hillbilly variety. But I was as backward in my concern as Marguerite was in hers. When I visited the young couple, I heard southern accents from their friends and neighbors that made me anxious. I was waiting for the mountain men of *Deliverance* to storm the house. To my joy, those accents came wrapped in warmth. I kept waiting for the venom to appear, but it never did; the people of that little town loved Adrienne and David, and their mixed-race marriage didn't raise an eyebrow.

The name "Belafonte" didn't stir much interest, either. When Adrienne went to these people's tables, and shared meals with them, she didn't tell stories about her father. She had her own political activism to talk about, both local and global. Along with helping in her community, she was doing humanitarian work in South Africa, participating in Habitat for Humanity building projects. As for David, he became an overseer for the United Mine Workers' pension fund. When Julie and I came to visit as grandparents, we saw young Rachel Blue and Brian growing up without any of the baggage—or the sense of entitlement—of having a Belafonte in the family. More than that, I came to see that the life Adrienne and David had made for themselves was a perfect coming to fruition of one of the goals of the civil rights movement: leading a peaceful, biracial existence in a formerly segregated state.

Shari had a more complicated legacy to absorb. She was the one born in 1954, as my marriage to Marguerite was falling apart. She had Mrs. Byrd whispering in her ear, poisoning her opinion of me and the rest of life, coaxing her back to her mother's apartment on Fifth Avenue and 108th Street with ice cream and candy, TV and treats. If not for Peter Neubauer, my analyst, I might have taken some action that would have earned me an ill-fitting striped suit in Sing Sing. "Your turn will come," he would tell me. "Never abandon her, never let Shari have the opportunity to say you weren't there for her."

I did as he suggested, and Shari survived the early tugs-of-war. She went to Hampshire College, then took a degree in theater production from Carnegie-Mellon University. There she started dating a fellow student named Bob Harper. Four days after they graduated, the two got married. Once again Marguerite was apoplectic. Bob Harper was white! My only concern was that Bob's father was one General Harper, former head of acquisitions for the Pentagon, now vice president of Raytheon, the top military contractor. This wasn't the kind of family that movement people married into. But the wedding came off well. Amusingly, General Harper and I, political opposites though we were, had written virtually the same speech for the occasion.

It had escaped no one's attention that Shari was exquisitely beautiful. I was impressed by how little she traded on her looks; her ambition was to get into movie production, not in front of the camera, but behind it. The newlyweds moved to L.A., and Shari started working in a first-rung job in the animation department of Hanna-Barbera. Bob, who'd had hopes of working in the film business when he met her, happily landed a junior position on the business side of Twentieth Century–Fox. Almost immediately, though, Shari was discovered by Nina Blanchard, who ran a well-known modeling agency in L.A. Nina sent Shari to New York to try out for a Calvin Klein commercial to be shot by Richard Avedon. Avedon not only chose her for the commercial; he put her on the cover of *Vogue*. Soon enough, Shari was gracing the covers of every other stylish magazine in the United States and Europe. In the Shari era—the mid-to-late eighties—you couldn't pass a newsstand without seeing her face: more than three hundred covers in all.

In 1983, when the producers of a new television series called *Hotel* offered her a regular part, I was delighted, but worried, too. Shari wasn't an actress; she hadn't done any of the work she needed to build an acting career. She'd just been handed this role, as a cover model with a famous surname, and told to be herself.

Shari bridled when I warned her how cruel the industry could be, how vulnerable and innocent she was, how her name might work against her as much as it worked for her. I watched her get caught up in this seduction, and I knew that she could easily become one of the victims of that culture, her values infected by those she so emulated. "Why don't you have more faith in me?" Shari would say. "Why don't you believe I can overcome that?" I would tell her that my concern had nothing to do with my belief in her, but with how deeply treacherous Hollywood could be. I had spent a lot of life living with the deceits and manipulation of an industry whose only real preoccupation was not with any greater humanity, despite its pretenses, but with the bottom line. I could not stand by and watch Shari with her high hopes walk into this venomous playground without at least having counseled her.

The series went on for a while, and Shari threw herself into Hollywood social circles. Then one day I got a call from Bob Harper. He was distraught: Shari had left him for another man. Shari called moments later to say it was true; she'd fallen for a fellow actor named Sam Behrens, once a Wrangler jeans model, lately a recurring character on the TV drama *General Hospital*.

Like Bob, Sam was white.

The pattern was unmistakable. By now, all four of my children had married white partners. I thought about that a lot. I knew I'd never told any of my children to marry white *or* black. Yet there was no escaping the formative role that race played in our family. Adrienne and Shari had two black parents; David and Gina were products of a biracial marriage. That fact alone had deep reverberations for all. Marguerite had told Adrienne and Shari, in no uncertain terms, that they should marry within their race. Both did the opposite. I may not have given Adrienne and Shari any counsel, other than to tell them to do as their hearts dictated, but what I did had far more impact than anything I said: I married a white woman. As one after another of these white partners appeared, I wondered if subconsciously I'd nudged my children toward the white side of the divide.

Perhaps I was acting on the biases of my West Indian heritage and its racial system. But there was another, more positive way to look at it. In Jamaica, as throughout the islands, marrying outside the tribe brought no stigma. My white grandmother, Jane, had married my black grandfather, and no one had batted an eye. In no memory I have of her does race matter at all. I like to think that I passed on that attitude, too, and that with all four of my children, race simply wasn't a consideration in their choice of partners. If it was, that was fine, too. Then they were doing exactly what I'd been espousing in the movement all these years: bringing the races together. How, as an advocate of racial equality, could I not encourage that? But my guess is that my children were influenced far more by their environments than by race. They went to predominantly white schools; they cultivated the mostly white children of affluent parents. In the end, class distinctions were probably more determinative of their choice in mates than the skin color of either of their parents.

With David and Gina, I did have racial concerns of a different sort as they were growing up. I worried that as children of a biracial marriage, they'd encounter prejudice. Julie, recovering in the hospital after David was born, had gotten hate mail: "Congratulations on your nigger baby." But race, as far as I could tell, wasn't a problem for either of them. The real issue was growing up as the children of a famous father, with all the attendant privileges and pressures . . . and politics.

David, as my only son, probably got more handed to him, and paid a higher price for that, than any of my three daughters. Doormen snapped to attention; porters reached for his bags. He wore the best clothes, got everything he asked for; in ways large and small, David came to feel, quite understandably, some sense of entitlement. Like so many fathers of first-generation wealth, I hoped my children would benefit from all the comforts denied me when I was young. I sent them to private schools like the progressive Ethical Culture Fieldston School, where biracial children were more likely to be welcomed by their peers than at perhaps any other school in New York. Yet at eighteen, after all this grooming, David decided to put his entire future in jeopardy by dropping out of the University of Connecticut, after secretly marrying a girl who came from the Dominican Republic and whose mother ran a beauty salon in Spanish Harlem.

To David's surprise, and hurt, I took a stern line on this. I would not support the newlyweds; they were on their own. Soon enough, the harsh realities of making their way in the world without my help, coupled with a host of other problems, led them to separate. I knew David was hurt by the severity I'd shown toward him. He'd seen a hard edge to my character that he'd never known existed. It was the edge I'd needed to survive in Harlem, to find a way out, to make a success of myself when the whole world seemed to want to keep me down. I'd learned to contain it, but I'd never lost it. If all else fell apart, it was what I'd use to fight my way back again. David, I saw, had no such hard side.

Instead of returning to college, David became the second of my children to find work as a model; like Shari, he was pretty easy on the eyes. Soon he had money enough to rent his own place. At twenty-two he married again. Anna was a lovely girl, much more from his world than his first wife, very cultured and determined to succeed as an actress. David followed her out to California, which I admired; he was making quite a sacrifice for her. But modeling work was harder to find in L.A., and David soon grew discouraged.

By this point, I most yearned to see David succeed. When his marriage to Anna dissolved, I urged him to try sound engineering. As a teenager he'd taken an interest in my recording process, and I had no shortage of contacts in the field. First I put him on to Phil Ramone, the legendary producer; David started hanging out as an intern at his studio in New York. From there he went to a similar gig at Quincy Jones's studio in L.A. Eventually I hired him as a sound engineer at Belafonte Enterprises. Perhaps, I dared to hope, David was at last on track.

Gina, my last-born child, was still in school in Manhattan when David married the first time—for a brief, agonizing time, she'd kept her older brother's secret from us, at his insistence. Like David, she'd attended Ethical Culture. Julie and I were preparing to send her on to the upper school at Fieldston, too, when one day to our surprise, Gina said no—she wanted to go instead to the High School of Performing

Arts, an alternative public school. We were so impressed that she felt so strongly, not just about pursuing the arts, but about doing it in a rigorous way, and going to a public school to do it. That led her to the State University of New York's Purchase campus, where she took a degree in drama, immersing herself as much as I had at the New School, all those years ago.

Gina came back to Manhattan determined to act—in the theater, not in the movies. She started auditioning, and studied with one of the theater's grand dames, Geraldine Page. Meanwhile, most of her former classmates at Purchase had moved to L.A. and started landing small movie and television roles. For a while, Gina resisted the pull. She stayed in New York, stuck with theater, but did play a significant role on a film I produced in 1984 called *Beat Street,* an early look at hip-hop artists that generated a soundtrack album, and then a follow-up album. When at last she did move to L.A., in about 1990, Gina landed a feature role in a new television series called *The Commish.* She seemed poised for success, grounded in the theater training that Shari had eschewed, the Belafonte name perhaps only a help, not a hindrance. But there was a problem. Gina's years of Shakespeare and Ibsen, Arthur Miller and Tennessee Williams, had left her constitutionally incapable of saying cheesy lines in a mediocre TV drama. For a while, she did the part and rolled her eyes off-set. Then she quit. Not a good career choice if you want to work in television. Though I understood how she felt: I'd done the same thing, long ago, in walking away from my budding career as a pop singer because it seemed so frivolous after all my training in serious theater.

By the early 1990s all four of my children were grown and gone, if not gone so far. Adrienne was happy and settled, Shari had a new marriage and Hollywood prospects, and David and Gina were finding their ways, or so I liked to think. But why had three of my four children chosen fields where the family name was a factor? And why, when they struggled, had they looked to me for help? What had I done to keep them from developing their own hard edges, and what could I still do, now, to see that they did?

I had no idea.

18

Nelson Mandela was still in prison, but by the early 1980s, South Africa was feeling the heat of the international sanctions movement, and I was a part of that. Which was why Carl Ware contacted me.

Oddly enough, Carl looked and sounded quite a bit like Dr. King: short, stocky, round-faced, and dark-skinned, with a deep, resonant voice. His clothes were the first sign that he was a very different sort. He wore beautiful suits, and shirts with cuff links, and elegant ties, and the softest cashmere coats. He showed up at a lot of fundraising events for black political candidates, and sowed a great deal of goodwill with the checks he wrote. But the candidates—and the rest of us—knew Carl had another agenda. He was Coca-Cola's top black executive, president of its so-called Africa group. His job was to see that a lot of Coca-Cola got sold throughout the continent, including in South Africa. My job was to put enough pressure on Coke to shut its South Africa business down.

Carl and I met more than once in his spacious corner office at Coca-Cola's headquarters in Atlanta. When he removed his suit jacket—a little show of informality between us brothers—I could see from the way his chest and biceps bulged under his crisp white shirt that he pumped iron. But he stuck to the soft sell, gently making the case for why dismantling the business in South Africa would hurt more than help. Look, he'd say in his confiding way, apartheid was doomed, with or without sanctions. Change was inevitable. And when independence came, the new black government would need all the international business it could get—including that of Coca-Cola. I disagreed. The government of P. W. Botha was fiercely unyielding, and the business brought by U.S. multinationals like Coca-Cola only helped prolong it. Meanwhile, I suggested, Coca-Cola was doing no favors to South Africa's poor blacks by paying them pennies an hour to work in its South African bottling plants, then trying to induce them to spend those pennies buying Coke! So, yes, I told Carl, I would do everything in my power to see that America's consumers, starting with its college students, boycotted his products until he pulled his business out of South Africa.

As one of the high priests of Coke, Carl had use of a corporate jet, the better to hopscotch from one to another of his African markets. Being a generous guy, he often urged me to use it. I declined. Other opinion makers took him up on his kind offer. One was Archbishop Desmond Tutu. Not wise, I warned the archbishop. "When you fly with the enemy, you lose sight of what's on the ground."

"But we're going to need these companies back eventually," Tutu said. Flying with Carl, he said, would give him a chance to win him over.

"I think the one who wins," I said, "is Carl."

Long before I'd met Miriam Makeba in the late 1950s, I'd been doing what I could against apartheid: speaking out about it, working with the exiled African National Congress, raising money for and giving money to the cause. In 1977 I'd gone further, co-founding TransAfrica, the first lobbying group to address African issues. A passionate young Washington lawyer, Randall Robinson, took the lead as TransAfrica's director. Arthur Krim, the head of United Artists, was a big supporter. So was Peggy Dulany, daughter of David Rockefeller, who worked discreetly on social issues. For the first seven years, I served as co-chair with Richard Hatcher, mayor of Gary, Indiana. TransAfrica had more than a hand in creating the sanctions movement against South Africa. In the 1970s and early 1980s, TransAfrica *was* the sanctions movement.

We started with a lot of help from organized labor, not only because I had strong ties with its leaders but because a South Africa of poor black workers who labored for pennies and had no rights was a threat to American unions. They wanted to keep U.S. union jobs from being outsourced; ultimately, American labor wanted to unionize African workers, too. Labor had political clout, but, even more, it had the financial clout of its pension funds. Was a big Wall Street investment fund in which the AFL-CIO had parked billions in pension funds doing business with South Africa? Out came the labor money. In one stroke, the American Federation of State, County and Municipal Employees withdrew $70 billion from U.S. firms involved with apartheid. That kind of money made people sit up straight.

Every U.S. administration since 1948 had done business with the apartheid government. The Big Three automakers sold cars in South Africa, Johnson & Johnson sold pharmaceuticals, and, with Carl Ware's help, Coca-Cola sold a lot of soda. For that matter, the Pentagon sold a lot of weapons to South Africa. So we had all of corporate America against us, as well as the military-industrial complex. But along with labor on our side, we had students. And, as Birmingham had proven, students can be powerful. By the early 1980s, TransAfrica had set up satellite groups on college campuses all over the country. America's colleges and universities had vast endowments, and some of that endowment money found its way, directly or indirectly, to South Africa. When those students demanded that their colleges disinvest, their presidents began to listen.

Sylvia Hill, a plucky professor of criminal justice from the University of the District of Columbia, joined the board of TransAfrica and opened a whole new front in our campaign. She organized a year of daily demonstrations in front of the South African embassy in Washington. Every day for a year, beginning on November 21, 1984, students and others demonstrated, were arrested, charged, released, and demonstrated again. To lawmakers in Washington, those demonstrations were a constant reminder of their collusion with apartheid South Africa.

My own role was to use my celebrity in any way I could. Along with helping create and guide TransAfrica, I set up a foundation to help students from Africa and the Caribbean find opportunities for higher education in the United States. As with the Africa airlifts, we were educating a next generation of activists who, with luck, would help run their country one day soon. At the same time, I lobbied at the highest levels. Along with talking to corporate leaders like Carl Ware, I went several times to London to strategize with Oliver Tambo, the president-in-exile of the African National Congress. I met with Sweden's Olof Palme and Prime Minister Pierre Trudeau of Canada. We began to build these zones of international alliance.

There was just one thing I couldn't do: go to South Africa. I applied for a visa several times but was always turned down. I can't say I was surprised. I knew that the only black visitors allowed into South Africa—aside from a few corporate big shots like Carl Ware—were servants bonded to white masters. I'd learned that back in 1951, when Sidney went to South Africa to make the film of Alan Paton's novel *Cry, the Beloved Country*. The only way he could enter the country—as a co-star of the film—was as the bonded servant of his director, Zoltan Korda.

Still, I kept applying, just to see.

I was doing more for causes—and giving fewer concerts—but not all my doings were altruistic. Even as I was orchestrating sanctions against South Africa in the early 1980s, I was nursing visions of a killing in Caribbean real estate, and I knew just the partner to take on: Roger Moore, a.k.a. James Bond.

Roger and I had met through our mutual addiction. He loved gambling too much, and so did I. We stood at many a blackjack table together in the south of France, but where we really cut loose was Aruba. Roger at the time was married to an Italian actress named Luisa Mattioli, whose rolling Italian accent I can hear still: "*Rrrroger, darrrrrling . . .*" We spent Christmases there together, they with their children, Julie and I with ours, and when we weren't losing in the casino, Roger and I were casing sandy coves on the nearby island of Bonaire.

Our Pied Piper was an Aruban named Maurice Neme, who seemed to have a lot of sway with the local government. He took us out to the tiny, uninhabited islet of Klein Bonaire, off Bonaire's west coast, a gathering place for flamingos, and told us that with his connections, we could buy it and turn it into the next big Caribbean resort. With Maurice registered as our local agent, I handed over a $45,000 down payment on the islet's insider price of $450,000. Roger, whose gambling losses were equal to mine, put in a more modest amount. Maurice had plans drawn up for what he'd taken to calling the "Largest Private Island in the World": more than three thousand residential lots, a shopping center, hotels, yacht clubs, a heliport, and more, even a bridge to Bonaire.

Up in New York, I spread the plans out on my dining room table and marveled: Here I was, a poor boy from the islands, building my own island paradise. So excited was I by Maurice's progress reports that I decided to fly down and see for myself. The local flora and fauna of Klein Bonaire were just as before, the sandy coves untouched. Only my money appeared to have undergone a change: It was so fully invested that I couldn't find it!

I bought Maurice's reassurances that time. But when I came back and found nothing more had been done, I told him we had to talk. When Maurice started making excuses, I called a couple of friends who had a way with these matters, and they paid Maurice a visit. Shortly afterward, my money reappeared, as did Roger's. That was the end of our island paradise—though in retrospect, it was all for the best. Certainly Maurice Neme must have thought so: On the eve of the new millennium, the government of Bonaire bought Klein Bonaire from him for $9 million. More important, the purchase established it as a preserve in perpetuity. The flamingos will keep their home, and the local flora and fauna will stay as they are. So will the coral reefs, whose fragile state we were naïve about when we drew up our plans.

I still had island fantasies. I just moved them from Bonaire to Jamaica, prompted by Prime Minister Michael Manley, who spent an evening bemoaning to me his island's financial straits. Jamaica had done a lot to develop its bauxite industry, but was still a tiny player on the world economic stage. Maybe as a native son of sorts I could think of some new Jamaican enterprise to get behind. I told Manley I could. Ever since my boyhood days on the island, I'd been fascinated by New Seville, a hunk of land on the northern coast, so named by the Spanish in 1509 after Christopher Columbus shipwrecked on the southern coast. While waiting for his ships to be repaired, Columbus wrote the tenets of slavery that would guide slave traffickers for centuries. Tens of thousands of Taino Indians on Jamaica and neighboring islands died, either from slavery or disease; the British then brought tens of thousands more slaves from Africa, unloading them right there at Ocho Rios to work the sugar trade. Nearly all those slaves began their awful voyages from somewhere near the Niger River, which snaked through most of West Africa. One of the sources of the Niger, as Sékou Touré had taught me, was the Djoliba. I proposed having a ten-day annual Djoliba festival in Seville, for all the countries of the slave trade's diaspora: Africa, Cuba, Brazil, Haiti, Jamaica, and more. We'd re-create one of Columbus's ships and celebrate our international alliance as the descendants of slaves. There would be musical acts from all those countries, and endless native food. I'd be enriching the culture and economy of my parents' ancestral home. Not only that, we'd make a profit! When Manley said yes, I got Ted Turner to agree to come in as a partner and, with some of his senior staff, we started gearing up.

None of it came to pass.

Why? As part of the deal, Manley's government had to upgrade the roads from Kingston to Montego Bay and Seville, to put in new infrastructure, accommodations—all the necessities for hosting a gathering of thousands. Manley's untimely death from cancer brought progress to a halt, and neither his government, nor that of his successor, P. J. Patterson, managed to deliver on Manley's—and my—dream.

Great name, Djoliba, but maybe it was time to give it a rest.

I was in Europe, on tour, when my sister, Shirley, called to say our mother had vanished. Shirley and our brother, Raymond, the children my mother had had with her second husband, Bill Wright, had grown suspicious when their calls to her little apartment on 143rd Street and Convent Avenue went unanswered. When they'd determined that she wasn't lying hurt or dead in the apartment, they called the police. The police had no record of a Melvine Wright. Shirley and Raymond feared the worst, and so did I.

For some time after my mother left Bill Wright in L.A. and settled into her Harlem walk-up, I'd tried to move her into a larger apartment. We'd gone around with brokers, looked at dozens of prospects, but my mother found something wrong with every one of them. I had to acknowledge that my mother, in her deep depression and ever-worsening self-pity, simply wanted to keep feeling bad, in the humblest possible abode, with a bathroom down the hall.

Years had passed. All that time, I sent money. That, she accepted; after all, she had no other source of income. Occasionally we would meet for grim restaurant dinners that left me as depressed as she. I'd made one last effort to make her happy. I told her I'd buy her a house in Jamaica, right in her home parish of St. Ann. It would be in her name, and it would come with a groundskeeper and two other staff people who would live in cottages in the back. I'd give her a car and driver, too, and a thousand dollars a month, a small fortune in Jamaica. "And you can share the place with your sister Claire," I added, reminding her of the sibling in her large, scattered family whom she'd always liked the most. "Me? Live with Claire?" she exclaimed. "Have you gone crazy? Live with *that*?"

The last time I'd seen her, I was furious with her. My grandmother Jane was near death, at the age of one hundred, in Jamaica. I'd taken Julie and the children down to find her bedridden in the same hillside cottage where I'd spent my happiest childhood years. Straining to speak, Jane had implored me, "Harry, let me see my Millie one more time. I just want to look at her face, Harry. Just do that for me." I'd promised her I would. But when I'd relayed Jane's plea, my mother had balked. "That's a lot of responsibility," she'd said. "And I have nothing appropriate to wear."

We were at a restaurant, so I tried to contain myself. "What you're going to wear is the least of it," I hissed.

"No, but I have so much to do these next weeks . . ."

Finally, in the car headed up to her apartment, I lost my temper. "Your mother may not live to see another week, let alone another year, and you won't grant her her dying wish?"

"What are you accusing me of?" Millie snapped back.

"I'm accusing you of being the most selfish person I've ever known."

"You know what these people did to me? Why should I rush out to see any of them? For what?" She started denouncing everyone in her life, from parents to siblings to husbands to children. Finally, as the car came to a stop in front of her building, she said, "I don't need none of you as long as I got Jesus."

That rocked me for a minute. Then I said, with a bitter laugh, "If Jesus had you to live with for a week, he'd be begging for mercy."

She glared at me, slid out, slammed the door, and marched up the front steps of her building. And that was the last time I saw her.

When two days turned to four and then six, without a police sighting of Millie, Raymond, in desperation, went from one city hospital to the next with a photograph of her. Finally at one hospital, an orderly recognized her. She'd come in with symptoms of heart failure and registered under a name none of us recognized. It was the same game she'd played long ago, when the immigration agents were on her trail. I'm not sure she'd ever stopped playing it. Or perhaps she was too proud to call me to pay her medical bills and had no way of paying them herself. Either way, she hadn't counted on dying; when she did, there was no one to claim her. What happened, Raymond asked the orderly, in cases like that? She was judged a pauper, the orderly explained, and buried in a paupers' field.

We retrieved her body—by number, not by name—and together we had her reburied in a proper coffin in Woodlawn Cemetery in Queens, in a plot adjacent to Dennis's. As painful as this was, my half brother then made it all worse. For reasons I never understood, Raymond had resented me at least since his adolescence, when I'd arranged for him to work on a kibbutz in Israel, an experience I hoped would be inspiring for him. Instead, he came back fiercely angry, denouncing the country, its people, and its politics. He had a newfound American patriotism, but with a bitter edge. When I offered to pay his college tuition, he told me he wanted nothing to do with me, and took a job with the U.S. Women's Chamber of Commerce, which perfectly fit his increasingly conservative politics. I was genuinely mystified by what had stirred this rage, but did as he wished and kept my distance—until our mother's tragic death. In its aftermath, Raymond decided that I was to blame. And he didn't just voice this sentiment in private. He went to the tabloids and persuaded a reporter to run with a story on Harry Belafonte, the selfish celebrity who let his mother be buried in a paupers' field. I've always meant to ask him where was *he* during Millie's last days, or, for that matter, her last years.

As dire as the plight of South Africa was in the fall of 1984, and as much as was being done for the sanctions movement, an even more immediate crisis faced much of the rest of the sub-Saharan continent. Almost no one outside of Africa knew it until a seven-minute BBC news story aired in the U.K. on October 24. A horrifying famine threatened to kill at least eight million people in Ethiopia; the images of skeletal, dying children were almost too painful to bear. In Ireland, a rock singer and songwriter named Bob Geldof watched the report and felt forced into action. He talked many of Britain's hottest musicians into forming a onetime charity group called Band Aid to make a fundraising single called "Do They Know It's Christmas?" The song raised millions for famine relief. When Tom Brokaw aired the same report in the United States on NBC, I had a similar reaction. Inspired by Geldof's example, I started making calls. I had no idea that what I was doing would lead to a global phenomenon. I just knew I wanted to help.

Like Geldof, I wanted to round up top musical stars and get them to collaborate. A single, an album, a concert—I wasn't sure which. I just knew that this was where my power lay, and I wanted to use it. I needed a younger generation of artists, the ones at the top of the charts right now: Michael Jackson, Lionel Richie, Kenny Rogers, and Cyndi Lauper. When I looked at the management of most of these artists, I kept seeing the same name: Ken Kragen. I remembered that Ken had been singer-songwriter Harry Chapin's manager, too. I'd met Harry quite a few times before his tragic death in a car accident in 1981, and admired his dedicated attempts to end world hunger. It wasn't some image-polishing exercise with Harry; he was the real thing. Channeling Harry's spirit, I called Kragen in Los Angeles and laid out my hopes.

Ken was polite, but noncommittal. He saw a lot of hurdles. Maybe too many. But I kept calling, and finally I flew to California to meet him. Still a bit reluctant, he called the one of his clients I most wanted onboard: singer-songwriter Lionel Richie.

Lionel said yes.

Now the pitching got a whole lot easier, and Ken started to get excited. His next call was to Kenny Rogers. Kenny said yes. Then Quincy Jones.

Quincy said yes.

Now I knew we were on our way. Quincy had all the credentials; he wouldn't just lend his name and spin a few dials in the recording studio. Quincy would take charge. He was a leader. And no one would say no if Quincy were involved. If there was any doubt of that, Quincy dispelled it by making two calls of his own: to Michael Jackson and Stevie Wonder.

Michael and Stevie said yes.

Of that core group, Michael was the hottest. After *Thriller*, the album that had finally broken my record for most weeks on the *Billboard* charts, he was the hottest artist alive. As I came to realize, he was also one of the spaciest.

That was all right. In early January 1985, Lionel and Michael began meeting on their own, struggling to come up with . . . not a song, exactly, more like an anthem that would work best when sung by a large group. Lionel came up with the opening lyrics, *"We are the world / We are the children,"* and a working melody. Later, on his own, Michael tinkered with the musical structure, added some lyrics, and came up with a nearly complete draft. On the night of January 21, 1985, the two sat together again to refine what they had.

At Kenny Rogers's recording studio on Beverly Boulevard, Lionel and Michael laid down a rough track for the dozens of singers and musicians who we hoped would record with them. We'd realized we could work off the American Music Awards, to be held in L.A. on the night of January 28. Most of the country's top stars would be there for it, and could just come over to Herb Alpert's A&M Studios in Hollywood after the show. By now we had no trouble lining up stars. *Everyone* wanted in. The challenge was getting all these public figures to keep the location a secret. If it leaked to the media, A&M would be besieged. A lot of stars would take one look at that scene from down the block and turn the other way. Somehow, we managed.

The star power walking into A&M Studios after those music awards was simply blinding: from Bob Dylan to Bruce Springsteen, Paul Simon to Kenny Rogers, Diana Ross to Billy Joel, and so many more. We'd had the luxury of choosing the world's most popular artists.

Quincy put a big sign on the recording studio door: CHECK YOUR EGO AT THE DOOR! He'd spent a lot of time in the last two weeks mixing and matching the famous voices in the room for that historic recording session. Only the best-selling artists of that outstanding group would have the solos. Everyone else would be singing backup, including me. In fact, when various stars were told they wouldn't have solos, and Quincy directed them to the backup chorus, it lessened the sting for them to see me there, too. If the guy who'd gotten this started could sing backup, so could they.

Michael Jackson wasn't spacey that night, and he wasn't childlike, either. All that talk about giraffes and merry-go-rounds on his Neverland estate? That wasn't the Michael I saw that night. He was a consummate professional, utterly focused. As others drifted in, Michael reigned supreme, even over Quincy. He didn't order anyone around. If someone sang in a way that seemed slightly off, Michael would go over to that singer on the next break and gently but firmly suggest a change in tone or breath. The stars listened because this was, after all, the song Michael had co-written. But also because he was Michael.

Security was unbelievably tight, not just to protect the stars, but to ensure that the only cameras recording this amazing event were the ones we controlled. Ken, Quincy, and I had formed a nonprofit entity, United Support of Artists for Africa (USA for Africa), through which all the money raised would be carefully allocated. We were all seasoned pros, and we knew all the income streams to be exploited here.

Outside the recording room, family members mingled in a joyous party that went on much of the night. Inside, the mood was euphoric—a kind of happiness that came only from putting self aside and harnessing all our collective talents for a higher purpose. I hadn't envisioned this when I made that first call to Ken Kragen. I'd just known something had to be done. The way Quincy put it to the room, during a recording break, was that I was the "bearer of the dream." With that, everyone in the room broke into the most riotous, ragtag version of the "Banana Boat Song." I heard "Day-O" sung as gospel, country-western, R&B—you name it. It was hilariously festive, and very humbling. Looking out over that crowd, at all the warmth and love and commitment in the room, I was overwhelmed.

Anyone old enough to remember 1985 knows that "We Are the World" made music history. The single was huge. The album, with bonus tracks from several of the artists, not only sold well but won a Grammy. Pictures and CDs sold, T-shirts sold, posters, books . . . By the summer, USA for Africa had taken in $10.8 million from the recording, and another $45 million from merchandise sold around the world. Eventually, the song's sales totaled well over $100 million. All this money—from the music to the merchandise—would go to famine relief. Assuming, that is, that we could control it carefully enough.

I hadn't anticipated "We Are the World" would be a full-time job for me after the song was out on the market. In fact, my job had just begun. We hired experts in relief work and logistics, made the command decision not to parcel out money to other, established groups, and embarked on a global effort to get the goods we needed. After all the publicity focused on famine in Africa, many countries had sent emergency food supplies. We came to see that the greatest contribution we could make at that particular moment was to bring planeloads of lifesaving drugs and other medical supplies, tents, pumps to dig wells, and more such essential nonfood goods. We started bargaining with international pharmaceutical companies to get these drugs at the lowest possible prices. USA for Africa was registered in California, and at every step, state and federal overseers had us under their magnifying glasses, looking for unpaid taxes or bogus deductions. So along with supply contractors, we had a crack team of accountants and business managers, too.

One day in June 1985, I boarded a commercial jet in New York bound for Belgium—the first step in our journey. With me were Julie, Ken Kragen, and two prominent doctors, Irwin Redlener and Lloyd Greig, as well as Michael Jackson's brother Marlon. Oh—and a pack of print and TV news journalists who had sworn they would focus their reporting on the relief effort and famine, not dwell on the tyrants in Ethiopia and Sudan. We'd had trouble persuading those governments to let us in at all. The last thing we needed was to alienate them. More of their people would die if we did.

Two chartered Flying Tigers 747 cargo jets were waiting for us in Belgium, loaded with the pharmaceutical supplies and other goods we'd pulled together. We transferred to those planes and flew on to Khartoum. There to meet us, with a big grin, was Mohamed Amin, the remarkable Kenyan cameraman whose shocking footage of the famine camps had awakened the world and launched our campaign. One of eight children born to a railway engineer in Kenya, Amin had overcome abject poverty to cover most of Africa's tragic dramas of the late sixties and seventies, from Tom Mboya's assassination to the handover of Kenya by the British to Jomo Kenyatta. His recent film *African Calvary* had dramatized the impact of famine all over the continent, particularly in Kenya, yet the outside world had ignored it. Finally he'd collaborated with BBC television reporter Michael Buerk and gotten that seven-minute clip shown on British television. He was the real hero of our story.

From the airport we were driven directly to the presidential palace, where Sudan's newest band of leaders had just set up residence. Sudan's strongman, Jaafar Nimeiri, had been pushed out of power weeks before by his defense minister, General Abdel Rahman Swar al-Dahab. We joined the general and his colleagues for dinner beneath white flags with red crescents. Al-Dahab went to great lengths to persuade us that he was a transitional leader—as soon as elections were held, he would step aside—and in fact, he did just that the next year. But he seemed unbothered that uncountable numbers of his countrymen were starving in camps outside the capital while he dined on fragrant grilled lamb and couscous. Nor did he have any qualms about warehousing sacks of grain, intended to relieve suffering in southern Sudan, in Khartoum's port. The south, after all, was controlled by the rebels in Sudan's ongoing civil war.

Since we were bringing medical supplies, not food, and perhaps since our every move was being recorded by television cameras, we were granted extraordinary access. First we went to a camp outside the capital, where tens of thousands of people lay in desperate straits. Nothing could have prepared us for this degree of horrible need. Mothers giving their children dry breasts to suck, mothers carrying dead children to an open pit, mothers and fathers sitting over these pits mourning the loved ones they'd just put in. Many graves were marked white with lime, to indicate cholera or some other highly infectious disease. The smell of death and disease was unlike any other, overwhelming and unforgettable. For weeks we'd ridden such a high from the triumph of "We Are the World." Now we were plunged to the deepest low. This suffering was too vast.

The next day we headed south in a convoy of trucks. I remember the parched earth, with not a speck of green as far as the eye could see, and the endless military checkpoints, where mostly teenage soldiers, with AK-47's, solemnly checked our papers of passage. We were going from clan to clan; at each successive checkpoint, the danger of being turned back—or detained, or worse—was very real.

The southernmost camps were even more horrifying, if that were possible. After some hours of wandering stunned past emaciated figures and little green plastic lean-tos that housed whole families with nothing but the canvas coverings over their heads and the rags they wore, I staggered back toward the supply trucks, where our doctors had set up a tent and were administering to a long line of the needy. The line went on and on; I couldn't see the end of it. Clearly, the doctors would run out of supplies long before they ran out of patients. "How can you handle that emotionally?" I asked one of the doctors that night over dinner. "Knowing that you'll never have enough to meet the needs of the people?"

The doctor, an Australian, had a ready answer. "I used to look at a crisis in all its magnitude," he said. "I never do that anymore. I look at what's in front of me. I'll never save everyone, or even very many, but the one in front of me—I may save that one, and the one behind him. You do what you can do. The important thing is that you do it."

Those words stayed with me as we flew on to Kenya. Jomo Kenyatta had died in 1978, though his dreams of national unity had expired long before. Theoretically, Kenya was a democracy, wealthier than its neighbors, and in the capital of Nairobi, we saw well-dressed citizens striding off to work. But in the outlying areas, to which Mohamed Amin led us, the people were as hard hit by the famine as anywhere else. There, Kenya was even more monochromatic than Sudan: no green leaves, no green fields, no birds or flowing rivers, just carcasses and corpses.

Our next stop was the heart of darkness, Ethiopia, where some of the worst suffering was occurring. In Addis Ababa, its capital, we met the country's notorious Mengistu Haile Mariam, responsible for the deaths of tens of thousands of Ethiopians, many of them children. Mengistu denied having smothered the ailing Haile Selassie—my mother's hero, whose face I so well remembered from movie theater newsreels. He even denied instituting a reign of terror made famous for the "wasted bullet" tax: Families whose members were shot to death would have to pay for the bullet used.

In person, Mengistu was a little Napoleon bedecked with medals, holding court in a palace of Polish marble. He talked of all the good he was doing for his people, having somehow forgotten how many of them were starving nearby. He seemed very much at ease with himself, and in truth he was a cultivated man with an easy charm, but you could tell who was boss, and by the way he spoke to his henchmen, that he was not to be trifled with. I had to suppress my deep desire to challenge much of what he was so smugly espousing. I had no choice. We needed his permission to fly helicopters to the northern province of Tigre, where much of Ethiopia's worst suffering was occurring. Since this area was rebel-held in Ethiopia's ongoing civil war, Mengistu hadn't even allowed the Red Cross to go there. No breach of diplomacy was as extreme as that between the United States and Ethiopia. Mengistu would not allow *any* contact between the United States and his government. Apparently, because of my earlier negotiations with his representatives at the United Nations in New York and my plea to let this band of artists have access to the peoples of Ethiopia for our humanitarian mission, he waived his restrictions.

We flew to Tigre on three helicopters provided by Mengistu. The landscape was strikingly monotonous—plateaus in every direction. The lead helicopter got lost, and we all had to land in a remote village, atop one of those plateaus. The children peeped out from their mothers' skirts, saucer-eyed, as if we'd come from outer space. We left them small sacks of grain, and when we were back on course, we swooped low over the plateaus and identified more villages that would benefit from food drops by cargo planes.

Near the end of that day, when we'd reached the camp in Tigre and handed out our supplies, I met a flock of nuns—in their black habits and white head scarves, they really looked like birds—and struck up a conversation with them. They were as Irish as could be, and flabbergasted to have this day in the camps end by meeting me. We sat around a campfire, and I fell in love with the whole lot of them. They weren't visiting, like we were. This was their life, helping the world's most desperate people survive, or more often, to die with comfort; more than one million Ethiopians would die from this famine before it was through. What sustained them, even more than their innate good cheer, was their faith. I still had such conflicted feelings about the Church, such anger at those Catholic nuns who'd rapped my knuckles long ago. But these ladies, these activist nuns, were a very different breed, and I felt blessed—there was no other word for it—at being in their company.

"Harry," one of the nuns said softly as the fire was ebbing, "will you do us a favor?"

"Anything," I said.

"Will ya sing 'Danny Boy' fer us? Nobody sings 'Danny Boy' like you do."

I sang alone at first, then the nuns joined in, and we sang more songs, until the fire was just embers in the Ethiopian night.

Critics—and there were more than a few among the journalists who covered our campaign—would say "We Are the World" was naïve at best, a speck in a sea of suffering. They would note that we'd worked with the repressive governments of Sudan and Ethiopia, which kept food relief from the rebel-held areas, hoping to literally starve the opposition to death. To me these criticisms seemed shortsighted and cynical. Our aid saved lives—lots of lives. And as that Australian doctor had said, you saved the lives you could. That in itself justified the effort. But it did more. "We Are the World" had brought to America the spirit of helping famine relief that Bob Geldof had ignited in Britain. Now the organizers on both sides of the Atlantic combined efforts for the next step: Live Aid, the largest famine-relief live concert, held on July 13, 1985.

Live Aid was the most ambitious live broadcast in history. Some two billion viewers around the world listened as the daylong concert unfolded on two continents simultaneously: at Wembley Stadium in London, and at John F. Kennedy Stadium in Philadelphia. I had an engagement I couldn't break that evening in Atlantic City, singing at the Golden Nugget. But the owner, Steve Wynn, was kind enough to put a helicopter at my disposal; as soon as the show was over, I flew over to Philadelphia. I arrived just in time for the finale of "We Are the World," joining dozens of musicians on that stage, led by Lionel Richie, Joan Baez, Bob Dylan, Neil Young, Mick Jagger, Keith Richards, Ronnie Wood, and many others. The stars on Wembley's stage sang with us, and millions more around the world joined in. That moment was as inspiring as the recording of the song in L.A. six months before. Financially, Live Aid was even more successful; between pledges made and merchandise sold, it raised more than $275 million.

Among the many lives changed by this amazing year was Ken Kragan's. Live Aid had barely ended before Ken began plotting his next move. This time I was the one to be a little hesitant. "You want to do what?" I'd heard right: Ken wanted to organize a human chain from New York to California, millions of people holding hands in an unbroken chain across the country, humble and famous alike, for fifteen minutes of solidarity that would raise millions more exclusively to fight hunger and homelessness in the United States—if, as hoped, each participant contributed ten dollars. Through USA for Africa, Ken hired a staff of four hundred and began working tirelessly toward his "Hands Across America" date: May 25, 1986. One of the greatest obstructionists we had to turn around was President Reagan, whose administration scoffed when we first proposed that the human chain go right through the White House. Yet by May, when we had recruited more than five million Americans to participate, most of them of voting age, and lined up major media for the event, Reagan had a change of heart.

On the day itself, I was stationed near the start of the chain, at the George Washington Bridge in Manhattan, not far from Brooke Shields. Yoko Ono and Liza Minnelli were somewhere in that New York chain as well. Bill and Hillary Clinton joined the chain in Arkansas. Nuns in Pittsburgh held hands with Hells Angels. In rural New Mexico, ranchers filled in gaps in the human chain by lining up cattle, horn to hoof. There were, no doubt, a few gaps remaining, but enough people did participate to span the country, at least mathematically. Hands Across America would be called a "noble failure," because it cleared only $3 million after its $17 million in costs, instead of the roughly $50 million that should have come in after costs if every participant had paid $10. Perhaps. But I'd emphasize "noble." Nothing like Hands Across America had ever been imagined, much less carried out. It did raise money for local U.S. charities fighting hunger and homelessness. And it passed into history as a unique demonstration of the best of the American spirit: the willingness to help those in need. I feel we're too inward, now, too self-absorbed, to create such a moment ever again.

There would be more massive fundraising efforts before this trend ebbed—Farm Aid, for one. For its own part, USA for Africa would spend the next several years giving its millions away, mostly to small African NGOs, where block grants of $50,000 could build and sustain child-care centers, women's health centers, training schools, and more. Its work done by the early 1990s, USA for Africa would lie dormant, though still ticking, until late 2010, when it would issue a twenty-fifth anniversary *We Are the World* album of new music by a new generation of artists. People are still starving in Africa, and hunger stalks far too many homes in America. The work is unfinished; sadly, the will to do it has diminished.

Our work would go on without Mohamed Amin, the Kenyan cameraman whose shocking footage had led to all that followed. For a while after the mid-eighties famine, his luck held. He was one of the first cameramen into Baghdad after the invasion of Kuwait in 1990; he covered the Ethiopian civil war that brought down Mengistu the next year. But it was in that conflict that he lost his left arm—and nearly his right as well—in an ammunition dump explosion. No one thought he would work again, but Amin designed a prosthesis that doubled as a tripod and enabled him to snap pictures with his recovered right hand. Then one day in 1996, hijackers boarded the flight he was taking from Ethiopia to Nairobi. Amin tried to reason with the hijackers, pointing out that the plane didn't have enough fuel to reach Zanzibar, where they wanted to go. The hijackers didn't believe him; the plane went down, and Amin was among those who died.

Through all these fundraising records and concerts, I never lost sight of the sanctions movement against South Africa's apartheid government, and the campaign to free Nelson Mandela. In May 1986, all the pressure put by those of us at TransAfrica on U.S. corporations, politicians, artists, and athletes, and all those daily demonstrations at the South African embassies, led to an historic triumph: the Comprehensive Anti-Apartheid Act. Introduced in Congress that month, it became the first foreign policy bill of the twentieth century to survive a presidential veto. Reagan struck it down in October, arguing that the sanctions it made official would hurt the people it meant to help. By large margins, the House and Senate disagreed. The bill banned all new U.S. trade and investment in South Africa and all commercial air travel between South Africa and the United States, and put pressure on companies like my nemesis Coca-Cola to withdraw from the country. To undo those sanctions, South Africa would have to eliminate apartheid—and free Nelson Mandela. Almost overnight, South Africa plunged into a deep recession, and for apartheid, the endgame began.

I had a plan of my own to help put more pressure on South Africa to free Mandela. I wanted to produce a TV miniseries on his life and have it broadcast all over the world. I even had the perfect actor to play Mandela: Sidney! But therein began a difficult journey that would lead to our second big break.

Getting Sidney to say he'd play Mandela was the easy part. Securing rights to Mandela's story—from Mandela himself—posed a larger challenge. I still couldn't go to South Africa, much less visit Mandela at Robben Island prison. I dealt instead with Mandela's lawyer, one Ismail Ayob, of Indian origin, a somewhat mysterious character whom Mandela would eventually successfully sue for profiteering from the use of his name and mishandling his family trusts. Twice I wrote letters to Mandela, sent them through Ayob, and heard nothing back. The third time, I got a signed agreement back from Mandela through Ayob. For his rights Mandela wanted no money for himself; any profits should be given to the foundation being formed in his name at that time.

I thought the hardest part was done. I couldn't have been more wrong. Again through Ayob, I then went to Winnie Mandela, Nelson's wife, and got her to grant us her rights as well. She, unlike Nelson, wanted money. We were instructed to send it to one of the nonprofits she oversaw, and so we did, though with misgivings. Winnie, by any measure, was a hero. She'd taken the heat, stared the police down, endured house arrest, and never wavered from attacking the state. No matter how much she was jailed (sometimes in solitary confinement) and humiliated, she held her head high. But the stress from all this, while her husband languished in jail year after year, perhaps never to be released, had taken its toll. Understandably, she saw the prospect of a big payday as her due. I just wondered how much of a guarantee our money was buying. As it turned out, I was right to worry. Winnie liked the terms of our deal so much that she sold her rights twice. I woke up one day to read in the trades that Bill Cosby's wife, Camille, had just acquired them, too.

For my project, which NBC had taken under its wing, I had commitments not only from Sidney but from Jane Fonda and Marlon Brando. (Jane would play Helen Joseph, the white South African dissident; Marlon would play P. W. Botha, the country's prime minister through most of the 1980s.) For Sidney, Jane, and Marlon to do television was almost unprecedented; they were willing to make that sacrifice, as three of the world's top film stars, to get Mandela's story out around the world. Plus I had Fay Kanin, half of a legendary screenwriting team with her husband, Michael, to write the script. Everyone understood the opportunity that existed here to do something of real importance. Everyone except the Cosbys.

I called Bill in a spirit of camaraderie to say we had an issue I was sure he'd agree with me on, and sent him copies of the exclusive rights letters from Nelson and Winnie Mandela. Both predated Camille's letter from Winnie. To my astonishment, Bill called me back to say Camille would be proceeding with her project anyway. This jeopardized my legal assurance to NBC that we had exclusive rights from the Mandela family. Camille's claim would clearly undermine that fact. NBC threatened to withdraw. I was caught in a no-win dilemma because *The Cosby Show* was on NBC, and the network was not going to risk upsetting its biggest star. Cosby said that Camille's focus on Winnie made it a different story, and that if I disagreed, the lawyers could work it out. "Take your best shot," Bill said.

So I did. I knew Bill had some of Hollywood's best lawyers, but I went all out and hired Judge Simon H. Rifkind, a founding partner of Paul, Weiss, Rifkind, one of the world's top litigation firms. Judge Rifkind found the case quite compelling, and conveyed to Bill's lawyers that he would take a special interest in it because he felt it could establish a legal precedent. At that point, Bill backed off. But our friendship was never the same.

Not long after, I heard that TransAfrica had named Bill to its board. I was incensed. *The Cosby Show* was a top-rated show in South Africa, meaning that Cosby was profiting from apartheid. What were they thinking? When TransAfrica's directors refused to reconsider, I resigned. I wouldn't return until years later, when the actor Danny Glover, a close friend, became chairman and redirected the organization.

The executive at NBC assigned to shepherd the Mandela script was a guy with the perhaps unfortunate surname of White. I knew he was salivating at the commercial prospects of a television miniseries with three of the world's top movie stars. And yet the politics of the story made him nervous. Very nervous. From his comments on Fay's first draft, it was clear he felt we should represent all sides—show white South Africans as earnest good guys who just happened to have a little prejudice problem—and thus produce a miniseries on apartheid that miraculously offended no one. To help me and Fay Kanin reach this ecumenical state of mind, he called me in to meet an academic from the Heritage Foundation, the right-wing think tank. I walked into a conference room to find the academic flanked by lawyers, executives, and secretaries, all there to record our conversation and so show due diligence in accord with the network's "standards and practices" guidelines. The academic gave his opening remarks in a patient and patronizing voice. His message, boiled down, was: *Diplomacy good, sanctions bad.* I nodded respectfully, then gave him a reply that undercut everything he'd said. I hadn't just come to this issue. I had my facts down cold. It was like chess, and before he knew it, he was on a major retreat. I was furious at being put through this indignity by Standards and Practices, and the Heritage Foundation, and all these corporate lawyers.

The miniseries was on—greenlit, moving toward production—until the day in early 1989 when Winnie Mandela was implicated by one of her personal bodyguards in the grisly murder of a fourteen-year-old boy and the vicious beating of three other boys. This happened just as NBC was about to assign Fay Kanin's approved script to a director. I pleaded with Steve White to let us follow Winnie's trial and simply write the verdict into our script. Whichever way it turned out, that would be our ending. After all, this was history! Our job wasn't to change it or lop off a slice to fit some narrative arc. Our job was to tell it as it was. And here we had three of the world's best actors to tell it. Was NBC going to walk away from a miniseries with those stars? After a lot of hand-wringing with his bosses, Mr. White inched back in from the ledge. As promised, we gave the full, final, multipart script to Sidney.

Sidney didn't like it.

It just wasn't up to his usual standard, he said. He was sorry, but he would have to pass. For reasons I don't know or can't truly understand, Sidney never gave me or Fay Kanin the chance to make a case for our script. I was devastated. With his withdrawal, NBC's interest evaporated. And that, in turn, made Marlon and Jane waver. They didn't formally back out, but the signs were all too clear. The miniseries sputtered along for a while, as dying projects do, but I knew better than to invest any more hope and heart in it. It was over.

The real sting came some weeks later, when I picked up one of the trades to read that the cable station Showtime had signed Sidney to play Nelson Mandela in a TV movie focusing on Mandela's relationship with F. W. de Klerk, the South African leader. Michael Caine was playing de Klerk. I felt that for our friendship, this was a radical breach.

393

There was no place for us to go except maybe where we went—away from each other.

I write these words now in sadness, not anger. As a young man fresh out of the navy, I had no close friends until I met Sidney at the American Negro Theatre. No one has the space that Sidney has in my life, or that I do in his. Finding our way through a labyrinth of social history, we had shared so much.

Sidney didn't throw himself into the movement as I did. Not everyone can be who you want him or her to be. The truth is that Sidney did what he wanted to do. As *the* first black movie star, he took on that mantle with dignity and power and extreme grace, and set a legacy for all the black actors who came after him. That's a lot for one lifetime.

With the U.S. government backing sanctions, and South Africa reeling from them, those of us who'd fought apartheid for so long began daring to think, by 1988, that change might finally come. A keen sense of anticipation filled London's Wembley Stadium on June 11, as another lineup of major music stars took to the stage, this time for Nelson Mandela's seventieth birthday, with a chorus heard around the world: *Free Nelson Mandela.* I opened the show with a greeting, and introduced Sting. The concert reached 600 million viewers. None was in South Africa, for coverage of the concert was banned there, but everyone in the country, from P. W. Botha to Mandela, knew it was being held, and in some intangible but real way, it added to worldwide pressure on the apartheid government.

I made my own musical contribution to the anti-apartheid movement that year: *Paradise in Gazankulu,* a studio album of original anti-apartheid songs. I still couldn't go to South Africa myself, but I could reach out to lots of South African musicians, get them to lay down tracks in local recording studios, and smuggle the tapes out to me. For whatever it's worth, I started that process some time before Paul Simon came out with his *Graceland* album in mid-1986. We were aware of each other's efforts; we were talking to many of the same musicians. In fact, Paul came to me, wanting my opinion about his plan to go to South Africa and record his album there. After all, he was white; he could do that. The problem was that he'd be stepping across the sanctions line by spending money there. I encouraged him to go first to Oliver Tambo and the ANC in London; they could give him a pass, considering that he'd be working with black musicians. But for some reason Paul didn't want to deal with the ANC or any other group. So he went to South Africa and made the album on his own terms. But when he released it in the U.K., the ANC came down on him hard. He had to do some serious rethinking and concluded that his best move would be to put together a world tour, not just of the musicians he'd used on the album, but of every South African musician of note he could hire—including Miriam Makeba, Hugh Masekela, and Ladysmith Black Mambazo. He loaded his space! Only then, with the *Graceland* tour, did the heat die down for him.

On my album, which was to be more political than Paul's, I started working with a wonderful songwriter named Jake Holmes, whom I'd used from time to time. Jake was a tall, lanky guy who looked a lot like Henry Fonda. I'd met him through my musical director Bob Friedman and liked the way we worked together. So I sent him and my pianist Richard Cummings to South Africa to be my eyes and ears. I directed them to meet with the musicians I wanted to work with—from Brenda Fassie to Laurence Matshiza—and lay down as many tracks as they could in Johannesburg. I cleared my plans first with Oliver Tambo and the ANC.

Jake was white, Richard was black, but the rules had loosened a bit: Richard didn't have to go as Jake's bonded servant. Neither had any problem getting tourist visas. (I was black *and* an open critic of the South African government; that made me a marked man.) Hiring black South African musicians and making recordings with them—of anti-apartheid songs—was a whole other matter. Jake and Richard had to skulk around like spies. They started by meeting with South African writers Nadine Gordimer and Athol Fugard, using their observations as inspiration for lyrics as the songs came together. That led to clandestine recording sessions with a changing lineup of South African musicians. Eventually someone ratted them out, and they were forced to leave. But the musicians they'd worked with smuggled the tracks out themselves to us in New York, and we then put them together. When it came out in 1988, *Paradise in Gazankulu* got glowing reviews, although it hardly sold like *Graceland*.

It was the last studio album I made.

The next year, the Kennedy Center included me as one of its honorees. Other awards followed: the NAACP's Thurgood Marshall Lifetime

Achievement Award in 1993, the National Medal of Arts bestowed at a White House ceremony by President Clinton, eventually a Grammy Lifetime Achievement Award. You know you're getting old when you find yourself on that "lifetime achievement" circuit. Then again, I guess it's better to grow older and get them than just grow older. To me, the far greater award came in 1990, the payoff for all our years of protest against apartheid: the release of Nelson Mandela.

In the months leading up to Mandela's release on February 11, 1990, all sorts of backroom maneuvering occurred, not just in Johannesburg but in England, where a series of top-secret talks between white and black South Africans took place at a grand, secluded country estate. Change seemed so inevitable that in early 1990 the ANC asked the Wembley concert organizers to stage a follow-up at which Mandela might appear. The concert came off as planned, on April 16—and there was Mandela, also as planned, frail but exuberant, coming out to a hero's welcome. Two months later, he landed in New York for the start of an eight-city, twelve-day tour that was, as one reporter put it, "instant history." I remember every detail of that trip, because the person put in charge of coordinating that visit, entrusted with the daunting responsibility of planning Mandela's whole itinerary and making sure everything went off without a hitch, was me.

In late 1989, I'd gotten a call from Lindiwe Mabuza, a South African–born professor and poet, radio journalist, and activist whose many years with the ANC had led to her current position as the ANC's chief representative to the United States, working directly for Oliver Tambo in London. "Madiba will be coming to the United States soon after his release from prison," she told me, using Mandela's African name. "Oliver wants you to be in charge."

"What do you mean, 'in charge'?" I asked warily.

"We'd like you to be in charge of his itinerary," Lindiwe explained. "You make the choices, we'll plan accordingly."

I called Oliver Tambo in London. "We have to talk," I said. "This is not my bag."

But after two days in London with Oliver, I found myself signing on.

It wasn't like "What I say goes." Oliver and the ANC had ultimate authority. But they did defer to me on all the issues of nuance and protocol: which U.S. politicians Mandela should meet (or not), which labor leaders, and which opinion makers. In Washington I started drawing up lists with TransAfrica. I'd recovered enough from my pique with the group to be working with it, and maybe I was a bit softened by the news that TransAfrica had decided to award me its first Nelson Mandela Courage Award at a star-studded ceremony with everyone from Sidney, who presented the award to me, to singer Lou Rawls, actor James Garner—and Bill Cosby. Time had passed, and if Sidney and Bill and I hadn't forgotten our grievances, we could all be gracious, anyway.

For the Mandela visit, I hooked up through TransAfrica with Roger Wilkins, a college professor and journalist whose uncle was Roy Wilkins of the NAACP. Roger would be my partner in planning all this.

"Who else is leading this parade?" he asked me.

I said, "We're it."

Once Mandela's visit became official, Roger and I found ourselves fielding calls from some powerful institutions, including the White House. First we heard from the White House staffers for protocol; they were very polite. President George H. W. Bush's private security guys were a bit less cozy. Up they came to visit us, without the sunglasses and the earphones with the little curlicue cords. They had known that Roger and I had already blocked out much of Mandela's itinerary and wanted to discuss security priorities. After hearing the details, they drew up a list of non-negotiable conditions. The security guys wanted Mandela in no open spaces. So no rallies, no ticker-tape parades. Basically, they wanted him to ride everywhere in a bulletproof car. And no public appearances at night. I said, "Mandela is not coming to America to be kept a secret—to move about incognito. He wants to express his appreciation to the American people and to move openly among the citizens of our country."

The security guards bristled, pointing out that such a visit was not quite as simple as I had imagined. There were serious security problems, and if we did not submit to their guidelines, they would not be responsible for Mandela's safety. What they wanted was for him to shake hands with a few superstars in closed-door ceremonies and then to leave the country. At the end of a long exchange, I told them that their conditions were unacceptable and that if they wanted to withdraw, we would take up the slack.

Through their embassy in London, the White House took this up with Oliver Tambo, who listened politely and then said, "We know we will be guided by Mr. Belafonte." Oliver was asked if he realized that Mandela's security would be compromised; his life would be in jeopardy. "I've discussed this with Harry, and we are working on it," he said.

And I was. The Secret Service had told me that the militant Jewish Defense League, among other groups, had come to regard Mandela with great disdain. In an interview, Mandela had compared the struggle of Palestinians to that of black South Africans, and publicly endorsed Yasir Arafat, chairman of the Palestine Liberation Organization. That had set off alarms throughout the whole Jewish community, from Jerusalem to Washington. I put in a call to Stanley Sheinbaum, a wise friend and passionate activist whose marriage to Betty Warner, daughter of Warner studio chief Harry Warner, had enabled him to push his causes with a lot of capital: defending Daniel Ellsberg, leaker of the Pentagon Papers, for one; promoting the American Civil Liberties Union, for another. I asked Stanley to help me reach out to the leaders of top Jewish organizations in the United States, and ask if I could speak to them personally. I did. Every one of them gave me the same story: Mandela's on the Palestinian side, Arafat is his friend. Not only that, he's friendly to Qaddafi and Castro—all enemies of Israel. "Everything you've just said about Nelson Mandela is misguided," I told them. "I think you owe it to yourself and every Jew in America to get your facts straight."

I proposed that six Jewish American leaders meet with Mandela in a neutral place—Switzerland—and have a no-holds-barred talk. The ground rule was that there be no handlers along, no PR spinners. Mandela would come with one assistant, mostly to help him with his bags, and these six leaders would meet him on their own. They agreed, and the meeting took place in Geneva. For two and a half hours, Mandela answered their questions and stated his views. When the group emerged, Henry Siegman, executive director of the American Jewish Congress, told journalists that Mandela had exceeded the group's "fondest expectations." He rejected all forms of anti-Semitism, he recognized Israel's right to exist within secure borders, and basically he dazzled his skeptics.

Finally the itinerary was fixed. Every moment of each of those twelve days was blocked out. Mandela would speak at the United Nations. He would meet President Bush in Washington and address a joint session of Congress. In Atlanta, he would lay a wreath at Martin's crypt. In Miami and Detroit, he'd speak to vast union audiences. In California, another parade, another rally, more receptions, and then home.

But first, when he touched down in New York, he would be greeted by Governor Mario Cuomo and a crowd of dignitaries, and walk the obligatory red carpet. I was there, by the red carpet, standing near the governor, when Mandela, still frail from abdominal surgery, walked gingerly down the steps of his jet's passenger ramp. As the crowd cheered and applauded, he approached us, this man I revered, whom I had fought so hard to see freed, but whom I had never met. He scanned the beaming faces, and then saw mine, and lit up. "Ah, Harry boy," he exclaimed delightedly. "How are you?"

After protocol at the airport, we had Mandela go directly to one of the most underserved schools in the city—the Boys and Girls High School in Brooklyn. This unbelievable appearance deeply moved the students and the principal of the school. Mandela thought it poetic that this was his first stop. And it was there that I first felt the extraordinary energy he radiated to all who heard him—an energy so much greater than his physical condition would ever seem to allow. From there it was on to a ticker-tape parade in Manhattan that New Yorkers would never forget, with Mandela riding in an open-topped car, waving to delirious crowds.

I had a lot of private moments with Nelson Mandela over those next eleven days, especially in transit. I'd had to line up a jet, which required raising money. We rented one, and at the Mandelas' insistence—Nelson and Winnie both—Julie and I rode with them every leg of the way. Julie sat with Winnie on those flights, and I sat with Nelson, doing my best to satisfy his insatiable curiosity about Martin and his tactics at every stage of the civil rights movement. Nelson's interest was not just personal; it was political. The whole catechism for apartheid was based on segregation in the United States. The United States had turned it into law, just as South Africa, following our example, had done a few generations later. How Martin had strategized to dismantle those laws provided a blueprint for Nelson to do the same in South Africa.

In those eleven days, I watched saints become devils and devils become saints. Everyone from the President on down wanted to touch Mandela's garment, and no one wanted to take no for an answer. One of the most insistent was Marion Barry, mayor of Washington, D.C., who unfortunately was under indictment for smoking crack cocaine and was soon to go to federal prison for six months. Marion, whom I'd known since his early days as a SNCCer, insisted on meeting Mandela in front of the press. I said no, but when Mandela spoke at the

Washington Convention Center, Marion pushed his way backstage before the speech. He was one room away from Mandela, with a whole posse of press photographers ready to snap pictures of the two shaking hands, when I got an urgent tap on the shoulder from one of Mandela's assistants. "Madiba wants to see you."

"I'm having a problem with the ex-mayor," Mandela said to me. "Will you fix it?"

I went over to Marion and pulled him aside. "This is not in anyone's best interests but yours," I said. "And you are not going to do this to Mandela. No private moment, no press moment, no statement to the press."

Marion glowered at me. I knew exactly what he was thinking. I assured him that there was no authority other than mine.

Marion's face crumpled, but he nodded. I had worked with Marion in our movement for a number of years. His courage and intelligence, like those of so many of the young people of his day, were exemplary. He took a lot of risks, and I admired him for it. His commitment to the movement led him to become mayor of Washington, D.C., but during his tenure he became careless, seduced by power. He crossed to the wrong side of the law and was paying a terrible price for that. I would have done anything to help my friend in this moment of trouble, but not if it involved using Mandela.

Mandela went out on the stage to deafening roars, followed by several officials, who took the chairs awaiting them. One of them was Marion. I watched him walk onto the stage, headed toward Mandela, but then, still out of picture-frame range, turn toward one of the chairs. I breathed a huge sigh of relief. Any possible embarrassment was averted.

From my many days on the plane with Mandela, what came through most vividly for me was his sense of purpose. He knew exactly who he was; he knew exactly what he had to do; and the onslaught of press and giddy crowds and maneuvering politicians in no way unnerved this man who'd just emerged from twenty-seven years of prison. I would have been blinking at daylight if I were in his shoes, stunned by freedom, incapable of addressing a crowd, much less a country. Not Mandela. He didn't need to rise above the fray. He was already there.

Our last stop was Oakland, California. Never had the Oakland Coliseum been so full; never had such love and exhilaration filled that space. I rode with Nelson and Winnie in the stretch limousine that took them from there to the airport, along with Julie, who'd become

Winnie's companion for much of the trip, and Roger Wilkins. When the Mandelas finally took off, their plane waggled its wings over the still-packed Oakland Coliseum. The crowd went wild all over again.

As I watched the plane fly off, I felt enormous, profound relief; nothing bad had happened! But also such a flood of affection and admiration. We had parted with a powerful hug, and Nelson's last words to me were "See you soon." I hoped I would, but maybe I wouldn't. Perhaps I'd just had my last glimpse of this astonishing man. I could see that Roger Wilkins felt the same way. One of the most fascinating and dramatic times in our lives had just come to an end.

19

Mandela was free, and the pillars of apartheid were coming down—but not overnight, and not all at once. The newly legitimate African National Congress would have to negotiate for four years with the ruling National party before free elections were held. And while those elections would lead to the ANC taking power—and Mandela becoming president—not all change was for the better. I saw that up close with Carl Ware. All through the 1980s, he and Coca-Cola had hung tough, refusing to dismantle the company's South African bottling plants, ignoring the sanctions movement altogether. Meanwhile, archrival Pepsi-Cola *had* pulled out of the apartheid market in response to our entreaties. So what happened? Once in power, the ANC gave national contracts to the company that was up and running: Coca-Cola. Pepsi, the multinational that had made a moral decision in order to help South Africa's blacks, was shut out. Carl Ware, by staying coldly pragmatic and apolitical, handed his bosses a big business coup.

South Africa's needs were still profound. So were those of nearly every other country in Africa. I couldn't ignore those needs, not even if I wanted to; I had a new, formal obligation to help. Back in 1987, I'd succeeded the late comedian Danny Kaye as goodwill ambassador for UNICEF. As with my Peace Corps mission, this new posting drew me mostly to Africa. I started by organizing a forum with UNICEF's director, Jim Grant, in Dakar, Senegal, called "Artists and Intellectuals for Children," that brought together all of Africa's leading artists and thinkers to focus on children's issues: hunger, polio, malaria, measles,

HIV/AIDS, and more. From that gathering came everything from countrywide immunization programs for children to sexual education to help prevent women from contracting HIV/AIDS and passing it on. For me, it led to visits with leaders of nearly all the sub-Saharan countries. On these trips, one or more of UNICEF's other celebrity board members was usually with me, among them actors Roger Moore, Audrey Hepburn, Liv Ullmann, and Peter Ustinov, and director Richard Attenborough. All were fun, but none more so than my erstwhile Bonaire business partner Roger Moore.

With Audrey Hepburn we went on a mission to Senegal. She'd worked for UNICEF since the 1950s, but in the late 1980s and early 1990s, she traveled constantly as a goodwill ambassador, not just to Africa but all over the world, overseeing vaccination programs, bringing water systems to remote villages, visiting displacement camps and famine sites. No one, not even Princess Diana or Grace Kelly, had her shimmering radiance. What made her all the more dazzling was that she'd go without hesitation into the most impoverished places. Hungry children would be sorting through mountains of garbage and waste for scraps of food, fighting with mangy dogs, and emitting a low, constant moan of extreme hunger. It was in that moment of great degradation that Audrey would go over to one of these desperate children, pick him up, and bring him over to one of the large enamel basins used both for bathing and for washing dishes and clothes. She would set the child in fresh water and clean him while she soothed him with her gentle voice. She never succumbed to sentimentality in these situations; she just focused on getting the job done. I don't think any of us other goodwill ambassadors inspired the love and gratitude that she did just with her extraordinary presence and compassion. There was something deep in her that I never saw in anyone else. She was searching for an answer; I wondered what the question was, because she wasn't just cleaning these children as a response to a social crisis. It was so spiritual, the way she did it, that she had to have been on some quest for meaning. I found myself envying her, because if what she was looking for could lead her to do the work she was doing with such abandonment, the quest was meaning itself. By about 1992, I sensed she was ill. I saw her tiring easily, getting frail, being more selective about the trips she went on. And then suddenly, she was gone, dead from cancer in January 1993. She was sixty-three years old.

. . .

That same month, I sang at William Jefferson Clinton's inaugural ball. I had a unique perspective: I was the only performer on the roster who had participated in John F. Kennedy's inaugural three decades before. Clinton was nearly as young as Kennedy had been then, and in his own way as charismatic, but I was under no illusions. I'd made some critical campaign appearances for him all over the country, but mostly in the Deep South, where he needed every black vote he could get, and I'd spent time in planes with him, offering my vision for what had to be done to advance civil rights. But as he filled out his circle of advisers, I felt that Clinton would be far more centrist than Jack Kennedy, certainly more than Bobby Kennedy.

It was a different time, a less idealistic time, for all of the new president's rhetoric. When I called him, as I did about Haiti and the administration's early failure to support deposed president Jean-Bertrand Aristide, he returned those calls, and we had a spirited debate. But no one in the Clinton White House reached out, as President Kennedy had, to enlist help in forming a new civil rights agenda.

That was all right with me. I had my own portfolio with UNICEF. Of all those trips, the one that haunted me most came the following year, when I went with Nigel Fisher to Rwanda.

Fisher was—and is—a courageous and indomitable figure, a long-time envoy for UNICEF in the world's most war-torn places. When I joined him on a fact-finding trip to Rwanda in the late summer of 1994, the one-hundred-day genocide was just winding down. No one could imagine how many had died: some eight hundred thousand, it would turn out, mainly Tutsis killed by Hutus. I thought I'd seen carnage in Ethiopia and Sudan, but the famine of 1984–85 was, at least, a work of nature, if one made worse by human cruelty. Nature played no part in Rwanda. Human fear and hatred and prejudice were solely to blame. I'd never doubted the existence of evil; I'd seen it all too often in the American South. But the scale of atrocities in Rwanda was overwhelming. "The horror," says Joseph Conrad's character Kurtz with his dying breath in *Heart of Darkness*. "The horror." And that's what it was.

Lieutenant-General Roméo Antonius Dallaire, whom we met upon arriving, had seen more of that horror than most. As commander of the U.N.'s peacekeeping force in Rwanda beginning the previous fall, he had sensed that the country's civil strife was entering a dangerous new phase, and pleaded in vain to be allowed to seize a planeload of weapons and ammunition going to the Hutu army. When the genocide began, Dallaire had had to stand by, his forces too meager to put up any fight, his pleas for reinforcements refused by U.N. Undersecretary General Kofi Annan and the U.N. Security Council. His inability to act left him deeply anguished; later he would suffer from deep depression and attempt suicide. When we met him, the pain and horror of his experience were written all over his face as he bared his feelings to us. He was a broken man.

Almost more disturbing was the young UNICEF staffer, Marcel Rudasingwa, who became our mission guide. He was a Tutsi who'd been in Italy at a UNICEF conference when the genocide began. The Hutus had murdered all his children, five of them. Yet Marcel had steadfastly committed himself to helping his countrymen, steadfastly ministering to their pain and somehow pushing his own aside. Watching him, I wondered what deep faith sustained him. Whatever it was, I envied it. I would have simply collapsed. Certainly I wouldn't have been ready to lead our delegation, as he was, in search of orphaned children, getting them to centers where they could be cared for and perhaps found by relatives.

"Can you really do this?" I asked him gently.

"My wife and I will bring more children in the world," he told me simply. "Meanwhile, we must help the ones who survived."

Most, but not all, of the bodies had been cleared from the roads and villages by the time Nigel and I arrived. But so much remained to be done. Our group went to the building UNICEF had used as its local headquarters. At the gate, our military escort stopped us. For a moment we stood in silence, looking at something. "What is it?" I said at last. Nigel pointed: The gate and entrance were booby-trapped. Had we walked in, we would have been killed.

While the military cordoned off the area and set about gingerly defusing the bombs, Nigel located a bank building that would serve as temporary headquarters. To his fury, the building's owner started haggling with him over the rent. The city was all but abandoned; no one else would rent the building; who did this owner think he was? But the owner, sensing a windfall, held firm. Nigel, who does not recognize the word *retreat*, outnegotiated the owner; we paid for nothing but his space, and we removed all the dead bodies. Then we took occupancy until our main building could be secured.

We pushed into the interior, only to be stopped at checkpoints commanded by teenage boys from the Rwandan Patriotic Front (RPF) with AK-47's. Some looked to be as young as fourteen; their guns were almost bigger than they were. "Report to Major Rose," we kept hearing. "You need Major Rose for safe passage." Finally we got to a Spanish-style hacienda where, we were told, Major Rose presided. When we walked in, we were stunned; Major Rose was a woman, all of thirty-three, extraordinarily beautiful, with coal-black eyes and high cheekbones, who might have just posed for the cover of *Vogue*. And yet her young male soldiers snapped to attention with crisp salutes. Clearly she'd done something to deserve this respect, but we thought better than to ask what it was.

We treated a lot of children on our ten-day trip. Often we came upon groups of orphans huddled together, and so we put them up on our truck beds and got them to safe havens. We also went over the border into the Congo, where the retreating genocidal Hutu army had been given safe haven by Congo's tyrant Mobutu, but forced to remain on a barren stretch of black volcanic rock called Goma. Families had fled here, too, and were trying to set up camps on this razor-sharp volcanic rock. The whole area, for miles in every direction, had become a no-man's-land in which man, somehow, would have to find a way to survive. We saw so many orphans there, too, and brought as many as we could back to Rwanda, to field hospitals and orphanage centers. The faces of those orphans—I've never forgotten them. We filmed everything we did, and took lots of notes, and all this reporting found its way to the international agencies trying to make sense of what had happened. But I came home unconvinced that there *was* any sense to be made of all this. For more than four decades my activism had been underpinned by the conviction that change could come, that the world *could* be a better place.

After Rwanda, I wasn't so sure.

I spent a lot of time with actors on those African trips, but I was far away, in every sense, from any acting work myself. Mostly I felt fine about that. I didn't want to waste time reading mediocre scripts that always avoided hard truths. I also kept from pinning my hopes to the rare script of substance that made it through Hollywood's hoops, only to die when it finally appeared. I could live without more of those heartbreaks. Certainly I could go without making another crowd-pleaser like *Uptown Saturday Night*. But in the roughly two decades since then, I'd never quite shaken the hope of acting again in a role that had purpose and meaning. All that New School training, all that fierce ambition instilled in us by Erwin Piscator to do theater that lit up the world—I'd never entirely let those dreams go.

Then along came Robert Altman, the legendary director who'd made film history with M*A*S*H, McCabe & Mrs. Miller, Nashville, and so many others. Altman was a staunch supporter of the civil rights movement. We were a mutual admiration society. I loved his films, and Altman appreciated my work as an activist; he once told Vanity Fair that I was the person he most admired. I stayed as a guest of Bob and his wife Kathryn in their large Paris apartment. It was an apartment that had a very long hall. One night, I remember, Bob was in his bedroom at one end of the hall watching the winter Olympics. From the guest bedroom where I was staying, at the other end of the hall, I had a long, unobstructed view of Bob's television set. And I had the remote control. When I saw one of the top skiers fly into the air, I pointed and clicked. "What the hell!" Bob swore from down the hall as the TV switched to another station. He leaped up from his bed and changed the channel back. Up came the next event, and the next dramatic moment. Click. "Goddamn it!" And so it went, with the channels changing and Bob cursing French television until I couldn't hold my laughter any longer. He finally realized that I was the culprit, and from that time on, wherever we went together, he made it his business to hide the remote control.

Bob had given me a cameo role as myself in his brilliant Hollywood satire The Player, in 1992. We hadn't met at that point; he just thought I'd be right for the movie. Two years later he gave me another in Prêt-à-Porter, his send-up of the fashion industry. And then in 1995, he offered me a meatier part, one that I wasn't at all sure I could play, in a film about Prohibition gangsters set in 1930s Kansas City, against a backdrop of searing jazz.

In our social get-togethers, Bob and I inevitably talked about films we wanted to make. We were roughly the same age, and had grown up listening to the same radio shows; we shared a fascination with The Amos 'n' Andy Show, still awed that white actors had played its black characters with such preciseness. Bob wanted to make a film about them, and the complex social and racial implications of white performers in blackface. He even had a title for it, Cork, after the burnt cork that white performers in minstrel shows, and later in vaudeville, used to blacken their faces. For Bob, Amos 'n' Andy was a metaphor for a culture of masks that he—and I—saw as a pervasive aspect of American society. Everyone wears masks, from their first "Good morning" to their last "Good night." The masks of racial attitudes are perhaps the most blatant—hiding, as they do, the underlying truths of racism—but Bob was fascinated by all masks, and saw *Cork* as the way to convey those cultural realities. Bob and I both felt that if America could honestly resolve the contradictions of race, with *Cork* as a contribution to that dialogue, we could go on to confront those other masks. He never got to that one, but he did get to *Kansas City*.

Bob was a native son, and the jazz he'd grown up with in Kansas City was basically the same music I'd grown up with in Harlem. The settings were similar, too. Kansas City was white, but it had its Harlem equivalents in numbers runners, racketeers, jazz clubs, bordellos, and, until 1933, speakeasies. Like Harlem, it also had its share of black gangsters. In one long evening talk at my apartment, I shared with Bob my memories of Uncle Lenny, and the swath he'd cut through his Harlem turf, running his numbers game, paying off the beat cops, and cold-cocking any who got too greedy. I loved Uncle Lenny, but I knew how tough he could be, how cruel and immoral, to keep his operation going. I thought I was helping Bob shape a character that an actor like Morgan Freeman or Danny Glover would play. I was astounded when Bob asked if I wanted to take on the role myself.

"Are you nuts?" I said. My concern was that the depth of the character's complexity, if not portrayed in a truly believable fashion, would be a problem for the audience. My persona was the exact opposite of the character Bob had written, and I was concerned that the audience would be distracted.

I expressed my concerns to Bob, and in his own cool style he said, "Belafonte, tell me something. Who started this rumor that you were an actor?"

I glared back. "Okay," I said. "This one's on you." But when shooting began, I realized I *could* play mean. I just had to summon that old hard streak, the one that had pulled me out of poverty.

The story was entertaining in itself—a gun moll kidnapping the wife of a powerful politician to free her own husband from the clutches of a big-time gangster (me!). But the music was even better. Bob had found some of the greatest living jazz musicians and cast them as the jazz kings of that earlier age, not just to speak a few lines but to riff. Here were modern-day counterparts of Count Basie, Coleman Hawkins, Jay McShann, and my personal angel from the Royal Roost days, Lester Young. In one scene, Bob had them engage in a "cutting contest" of competing solos. To hear Joshua Redman wail with Lester's signature style filled me with love and regret. I could close my eyes and hear Lester say again, "Hey, Harry, how're your feelings?"

When it came out in August 1996, *Kansas City* got a lot of applause. Maybe not as much as Altman's greatest films, but enough. Critic Roger Ebert, for one, admired Altman's "originality and invention" in *Kansas City*, and praised the jazz scenes as "terrific." He even liked my performance. And so did others. To my joy, I won the New York Film Critics Circle Award for that year's Best Supporting Actor. At the ceremony, Paul Newman was the one who gave it to me. He knew, from our Actors Studio days, exactly how long I'd hoped for validation like this. To this day, I'm as proud of that film critics' award as I am of all my gold records.

I still gave concerts, dozens a year, but as I came up on seventy, I had a harder and harder time summoning the desire to sing the standards my audiences wanted to hear. I couldn't cut them from my repertoire; that wouldn't be fair. But maybe I could reinvent them.

My first thought was to dip into reggae. I'd picked up genres from around the world; why not embrace the music homegrown in Jamaica? Along with its beauty and power, reggae took on social issues. Wasn't all that perfect for me? It wasn't. I had boundless admiration for Bob Marley, but I saw no way to bring a stamp of my own to what he did. You either did reggae the way Marley did, or you didn't do it at all. So I never did perform or record a reggae song. I just knew to leave it alone.

I did connect with Chris Blackwell, the music producer who'd founded Island Records at the age of twenty-two and single-handedly brought reggae to the world stage. Chris, it turned out, was a fan of mine from his early days; he'd named his record company after "Island in the Sun." He agreed that I should leave reggae alone, but he urged me to draw up a new ensemble of "world music" players, not just for my concert tours but for a new record label that would intermingle African and American black music, cross-pollinating the two. We called our new enterprise—what else?—the Djoliba Project.

We never did get the record label up and running, but I formed an amazing new band of mostly African musicians. We rehearsed intensely for months, and then made our debut in a concert at the

State University of New York's Purchase campus in March 1997. The concert was broadcast on public television as "An Evening with Harry Belafonte and Friends," and turned into an album for Chris's Island Records. All my standards were in the lineup, but reinvigorated by these wonderful players and their pan-African sounds. It was a good way to enter my eighth decade. With that as our springboard, we spent much of the next three years touring the world.

About the only place we didn't go on that tour was Vegas. My Vegas days were behind me now. I'd had a great run, but at some point, the crowd had changed and the fun had left the room. Instead of high-rolling cattlemen gambling fortunes away because they knew they'd soon have more, I saw families that had come in desperation, the kids bedding down in station wagons in the parking lot while their parents tried to stave off destitution at the slot machines. Somewhere along the way, I'd stopped being a high roller myself. It hadn't happened overnight. It had taken a lot of conversations, over many years, with Peter Neubauer, probing why I seemed compelled to stir the very fires I most feared would consume me: the sudden loss of all my money, the sickening slide into poverty again. Unlike the cattlemen, I didn't have money to burn, so if I went on long enough, I'd go through it all—it was just a matter of time. One week in Vegas I avoided the tables completely, and then as I played the Strip less and less, it became easier and easier to put gambling, in all its once-tantalizing varieties, aside. Life was better without it.

One day in October 2000, Julie and I walked into the Bryant Park Grill, right behind New York's main public library on Fifth Avenue, for a joyous event: David was getting married for the third time, and yes, the third time seemed the charm.

Both of my West Coast children were there—Shari and Gina—along with Adrienne, up from West Virginia. Friends filled the festive room with its lovely park view, and former New York mayor David Dinkins officiated. As I watched the simple ceremony begin, I got very choked up. Here were all my children together in one room—a rare occasion now—thrilled to see one another, wishing one another well, gathered at what felt, to me at least, a real milestone for the whole Belafonte clan. In their own very different ways, all four were happy. But at least three of them—Shari, David, and Gina—had had their share of frustrations, and still nursed unfulfilled hopes. Life hadn't turned out quite as they expected.

Ever since her television series *Hotel* had ended in 1988, Shari had struggled to find acting work. Her training was in theater production, not acting, and perhaps that showed. Or perhaps Hollywood's casting agents had just turned to the next wave of twenty-something beauties for the latest eye-candy roles. Shari fell back on putting packages together; this actor would commit to the script she'd found if those other actors, and that director, signed on. I was constantly being asked to be one of those elements, and with pain I would have to say no. Then would come the recriminations: Why hadn't I ever helped her in her career? Why hadn't I ever asked her to be in a movie with me? I pointed out that I turned down other such packages, too, that my rejection of those, and Shari's own packages, was just based on the quality of what I saw.

Weeks before David's wedding, Shari had truly startled the rest of us. Maybe that was the point. After gracing some three hundred fashion and beauty magazine covers in the 1970s and early 1980s, she'd just appeared on the cover of one I never would have expected: *Playboy*. If she'd asked my permission, I would not have granted it. But of course she was far too old for that. As the magazine noted, she was, in fact, forty-six, an impressively advanced age at which to bare her physique to the world. Having last seen her nude when she was about eight years old, I was gratified to see her so healthy and fit and clearly unconcerned by what anyone might "think." My regret was more complex. Fame had become Shari's fix long ago, and the harder it became to score, the more determined her pursuit of it. *Playboy* had given her a little buzz of attention. But now that that issue was off the stands, I didn't think she'd be any happier for having done it.

Gina, my other West Coast daughter, had struggled to find acting roles without much success. Her work on the television series *The Commish* in the early 1990s had soured her on the business, or at least on commercial acting. Her search for a new line of work had led her back to me. After working as my on-set acting coach for *White Man's Burden*, an independent film I'd starred in with John Travolta, she'd done the same for me on *Kansas City*, and I was deeply grateful for her help; my New York Film Critics' award surely owed something to her. She'd also married a bodybuilder, Scott McCray, who decided that *he* wanted to be an actor, and landed a few television roles. Gina and Scott had a lovely daughter, Maria, born in November 1996, and by the time Maria was three, they'd decided *she* would be the actor in the family. Now they were shuttling Maria to children's drama classes and auditions for television commercials. Their own acting dreams might not have come to pass, but they had a new dream, and it seemed to have galvanized them.

As for the groom, for some years after the end of his second marriage, to Anna, David had worked for Belafonte Enterprises. He'd become an excellent sound engineer, not just in the studio, but on the road; when I toured, he came with me and not only oversaw the sound engineering for each concert venue but became our tour manager. He was still under my wing, but not, I hoped, for long. Then David met Malena Knopf Mathiesen, a beautiful Danish fashion model some years his junior. Malena, like Anna, was ambitious; she hosted a celebrity profile program on Danish television, and was popular enough to have it called *The Malena Mathiesen Special.* Her parents were both classical musicians. David and Malena were marrying five years after they'd met. As a wedding present, I'd just given them the apartment in which they'd been living, the apartment owned by Belafonte Enterprises where David had lived ever since his return from Los Angeles. I admired how devoted David clearly was to Malena.

Of my four children, only Adrienne, my oldest, remained unaffected, in the fall of 2000, by show business and its sorrows. With wry affection, Adrienne dubbed her three siblings "the show business crowd." She'd stayed in rural West Virginia with her growing family, and started a private family counseling practice focused on children. With her daughter, Rachel Blue, she'd also started a volunteer program for Americans to help with social needs in South Africa and the Caribbean. They focused the Anir Foundation on housing, education, HIV/AIDS education and prevention, and other health issues related to women and their families. By the fall of 2000, they were coordinating projects with President Jimmy Carter's Habitat for Humanity. Soon Rachel Blue would take the first of many trips to South Africa to build Habitat housing. I loved all my children with all my heart, but I couldn't help feeling a special surge of pride in what Adrienne had accomplished, and in how much she and her daughter gave back, of their time and resources, to causes I cared so much about myself.

When the vows were exchanged and the drinking began, I found myself watching all four of my children interact with their partners, and with one another. I saw a lot of love and mutual respect. All four couples seemed happy—an achievement in itself. Moreover, none of my children was doing anything hypocritical, and all four did their part to make our larger family work. When any one of them was sick, or had a setback, the others were on the case, doing whatever was needed until the situation was corrected.

As I sat there, taking that all in, I remembered the sad day two years before, when Marguerite died. Her second husband, Dr. Mazique, had predeceased her, the victim at too young an age of a heart attack. Marguerite's death was unexpected, too; she'd gone to a Valentine's Day dance, had a lovely time, and then, upon returning home, suffered a pulmonary embolism. I was out of the country at the time. Everyone was caught off guard. Yet almost immediately, Adrienne was on the scene, after driving from West Virginia to D.C. Shari was on the first plane from L.A.; Gina and David were on the phone with me and their siblings, helping with the funeral arrangements; and all four came to the funeral, where David served as a pallbearer. The family, in short, pulled together without a moment's hesitation.

That meant a lot.

In 2001 I was seventy-four, but I was still doing everything and trying to balance it all. I still toured; I was out on the road up to one hundred days a year. I tended to play college campuses rather than Vegas now—though I did still play Caesars—because in those venues I could try out new African and Latin music, natural outgrowths from *Paradise in Gazankulu*. I couldn't imagine surpassing it—which meant, to me, that it was a good album to go out on. And so I did. I would release a collection or two after that, but no more new music. I'd done all I could, as best as I could. It was time to let that ball fall.

To my surprise, and delight, an album I'd started planning back in 1961 did get produced at last, in the fall of 2001, but it wasn't an album of my music. At least, not exactly. It was a gathering of songs from black culture. The idea was to track black history through its music, starting with African folk songs and work songs sung by African-American slaves to songs sung in the fields and on the chain gangs, songs of resistance and hope and despair. I would take that history right up from slavery to the Underground Railroad and the black church to the great migration of African-Americans to the industrialized American cities. I'd started recording some of the songs myself, but I'd also gotten wonderful musicians like Sonny Terry and Brownie

McGhee, Joe Williams and Gloria Lynne to lend their talents. RCA had gotten excited about it, in part because of a partnership it had with *Reader's Digest*. RCA would produce the album, and *Reader's Digest* would publish a book to go with it. But the partnership fell apart, and so did the project—until, in the late 1990s, an energetic music executive at BMG, Alex Miller, took on the job of sifting through RCA's archives, and came upon a shelf of dusty recordings: my project, all but forgotten. After both RCA and *Reader's Digest* had abandoned it, the rights had reverted to me. With a happy go-ahead from me, Alex Miller and my son, David, remastered all the songs and worked up a gorgeous boxed set, replete with a glossy book, wonderful liner notes, and artwork by Charles White. We called it *The Long Road to Freedom: An Anthology of Black Music*, and when we sent out copies to the press, the response was rapturous.

On the day of the launch, I had an early-morning live interview with Katie Couric on NBC's *Today* show. Originally, my itinerary had called for me to go on to the giant J&R Music World store down by City Hall, but the television interview was over by 8:30 a.m., and the store didn't open until 10:00 a.m., so the publicists for BMG scheduled a stop in between: a breakfast appearance at Windows on the World, the restaurant atop the World Trade Center. I was in the NBC dressing room, getting my makeup rubbed off, and chatting with Katie, who'd come back for a moment to say good-bye, when out of the corner of my eye I saw something odd on a television screen: a plane going into the World Trade Center. My first thought was that it looked like the trailer for some new adventure flick. But then we saw there were two planes, and that both towers were imploding. In just thirty more minutes I would have been in that restaurant.

The Long Road to Freedom won three Grammy nominations the next year. But any commercial hopes we had for it were smothered, of course, by 9/11. The world had more important things to worry about that fall than boxed albums, as fine as they might be.

I was, perhaps, in the minority of Americans who watched President Bush's statements and speeches after 9/11 and found them uninspiring at best. I'd followed his administration's opening gambits, both at home and abroad, with anger and dismay. This swaggering president, who had so little to swagger about, seemed to take a perverse pleasure in neutering the agencies that civilize our country, from the Environmental Protection Agency to the U.S. Department of Justice, whose civil rights division was literally turned on its head; instead of stopping southern states from disenfranchising black voters, it was now helping them do it. Tax cuts for the rich, a dizzying slide from surplus to deficit, corporate lobbyists and Wall Street bankers feeding at the trough—all this from a man whose presidency, as far as I was concerned, was illegitimate in the first place. But so far, I'd bitten my tongue. Until the morning in October 2002 when a radio host in California asked me to comment on Bush's Secretary of State, Colin Powell.

I was still giving concerts when the elements seemed right, and had agreed to give one in San Diego, through a promoter who always did his best to ensure that the concerts he set up for me were sellouts. This time he called two days in advance to say, apologetically, that about four hundred tickets remained unsold in the four-thousand-seat theater he'd booked. If I just gave an early-morning interview to a popular San Diego radio-show host, I would surely sell those remaining seats. "Just keep mentioning the concert," the promoter advised. What, I asked, would the host and I discuss? "Light stuff," the promoter said. "His listeners are all driving to work; they just want a little patter to get them through the rush hour."

At the San Diego hotel where I checked in the night before the concert, I asked for a 7:30 a.m. wake-up call, half an hour before the host was due to call in on that line. The wake-up never came. Instead, I was awakened at 8:00 a.m. by the radio host's call. "Good morning, Mr. Belafonte. It's a great day in San Diego, how are you beginning it?"

I'd barely had time to mutter a groggy good-morning when the host asked his next question: "How do you think Colin Powell is doing?"

I was caught completely off guard. This was hardly the light banter the promoter had promised, but not one ever to duck a question, I replied, "He serves his master well."

"Serves his master well?" the radio host chortled. "What do you mean by that?"

"In the days of slavery," I explained, "there were those slaves who lived on the plantation, in shacks out back, and those who lived in the master's house. You got the privilege of living in the house if you served the master well."

Now I was fully awake. The urbane black Secretary of State hadn't yet given the speech that would put his seal of approval on the half-truths and lies about Saddam Hussein's "weapons of mass destruction." Still, he'd done plenty already to help the Bush administration ramp up for war with Iraq in retaliation for 9/11, even though Iraq had played no part in the attacks. "Colin Powell's committed to come into the house of the master," I added. "When Colin Powell dares to suggest something other than what the master wants to hear, he will be turned back out to pasture."

Before I was done, I managed to rap the administration's other prominent black as well. "I'd like to see both [Powell] and [National Security Adviser] Condoleezza Rice show some moral backbone, show some courage," I said, "show some commitment to principles that are far higher than those being espoused by their boss."

By the time I opened my concert that night, my comments were national news. I felt I had no reason to regret them, certainly no reason to apologize to Powell and Rice, but I got some blowback from unexpected quarters. "Harry knocked a brother," Quincy Jones said disapprovingly on one interview show, as if no black should ever criticize any other black. Other black commentators harped on what a fine, upstanding fellow Colin Powell was, a war hero; how could I insult him that way? I was ready for the debate—I had a lot to say about Bush administration flunkies willing to sign off on sending young men and women to war on the basis of no hard evidence at all—and I knew just where to deliver my remarks. Ken Sunshine, a deft and much-admired public relations director, represented me (and still does). He called Larry King and asked if King would have me on his show the next night.

The show started with a lot of positive footage about my role in the civil rights movement and other social causes. That was good. Larry and I then talked for a while about Colin Powell, I said my piece, and finally I took calls. The last one was the hardest, but also the one I'd been waiting for. "Hello, Mr. Belafonte. . . . I'm the mother of a twenty-three-year-old boy that was killed on— Tower One because he was an American citizen. . . . I feel that you're talking first as a black man, as an American secondly, and that's what saddens me and I think it would sadden all of us—the three thousand families whose people were mowed down because we were Americans trying to live the American dream. My boy was killed because he went to work."

I expressed my heartfelt sorrow for this woman's terrible loss and for the U.S. servicemen she also invoked. "I sit and I grieve with each and every American who lost some loved one on 9/11," I told her. "And

I also sit and grieve with every American mother who lost some son to the Ku Klux Klan. Tyranny is not exclusive in the experience of Americans just to 9/11. A lot of people have known terror and terrorism. It's a sad thing. And I'm not first black and then American. I've always been and will be first American and then whatever I happen to be, like the mosaic that makes up this country.

"And I'm sorry if what I have said and the way in which I interpret our policy offends you to the degree you think I am ignorant of and willing to dismiss the death and pain that our nation feels. As a matter of fact, quite the contrary. It is precisely the pain that I know that this nation feels that I dread seeing us go through more of it, to lose more sons, more daughters, because we are being ill advised on how to deal with the ills of the nation. . . . And I hope we can find policies and thinkers and people who will come to their senses and lead us out of this abyss."

Separately, Larry King had Colin Powell on his show to get his take on all this. Powell said he didn't mind my attacking his politics, "[but] to use a slave reference, I think, is unfortunate and is a throwback to another time and another place that I wish Harry had thought twice about using." I'd often heard remarks such as the one Powell used about "a throwback to another time," and such references were unfortunate. I am always saddened that, among blacks in particular, such views could be embraced, especially by the educated. For me, it is precisely the absence of debate on all the ramifications of slavery and the unwillingness to be thrown back "to another time" that has caused the issue of slavery to be an embarrassment for some and a trivial matter to be avoided at all costs for others. When Powell said what he did, I thought, Shame on you.

Condoleezza Rice, asked for her reaction by another journalist, said, "Everybody should be able to debate views, but I don't need Harry Belafonte to tell me what it means to be black."

To which I say, nine years later: Who was right and who was wrong about Iraq? About the satellite images showing supposed mobile factories for chemical weapons? About the supposed bunkers of munitions workers? About the stockpiled weapons of mass destruction? And is it too much to suggest that Powell and Rice, in their eagerness to please their president, did indeed make the moral compromises that house Negroes made in the days of slavery? That had they followed a higher moral calling, they might have helped prevent that war?

By the time I next toured Europe, America had invaded and occupied Iraq. I'd always spoken my mind on issues of the day that upset me, both onstage and in press interviews, and I didn't stop now. I called the war in Iraq a mistake, compounded by the mistake, as I saw it, of not pursuing the real malefactors of 9/11 in Afghanistan. In Germany, I made a point of praising the government and its people for being one of the first U.S. allies to refuse to send troops to the coalition in Iraq. I even debated representatives of the U.S. government on German television.

One night in Hamburg, a group of young Afro-Germans came backstage to see me. My message had resonated with them; in fact, they were rappers putting out their own version of "racist experiences" in their communities, songs that pertained to their plight. Their group was called Brothers Keepers: Adé Bantu from Nigeria, Tyron Ricketts from Jamaica, and Frank Dele Tibor, nicknamed "Quiet Storm."

Germany, they explained over coffee, had absorbed its first blacks after World War I, when France imported black French Senegalese troops to help oversee the Rhineland. Hitler had promised to destroy France and rid the German landscape of these savages; by 1937, the Gestapo was rounding up African-German blacks and either forcibly sterilizing them or simply making them disappear. By 1939, assimilated African-German blacks were as openly persecuted as Jews. More than half a century later, Germany's resurgent right wing was targeting blacks again. Even in mainstream German society, blacks were ghettoized.

What I heard that night was the voice of the country's underclass, oppressed but uncowed, a voice I'd never heard because I never even knew it existed. I began to understand how many Afro-German citizens there were. Some were actually the sons and daughters of black American G.I.'s based in Germany during the Cold War, and African diplomats, who'd since married white German women.

I decided, then and there, to make a documentary about these and other rappers, expressing their own frustrations in various countries—including the rap underground I'd found in Cuba. Seven years later, I'm still working on it, still gathering footage for the project I've come to call *Another Night in the Free World*. Through these rappers, I want to dramatize the social injustices that exist in the world's most developed countries—to comfort the afflicted and afflict the comfortable, as that great social activist Mother Jones so famously put it.

My hope, when I added *Another Night in the Free World* to my fairly full plate of social causes, was to sing along on some of the raps, perhaps even add my own. I was eager to see what I could do—I hadn't noticed any rules against septuagenarians in rap music—and I liked to think if I was part of the package, the film's prospects might only improve. But by 2004, I had to confront a painful truth: My voice was nearly gone. I spoke in a hoarse rasp now. When I sang, my vocal cords, so stiff and scarred, couldn't push my voice where I meant it to go. I'd undergone surgery and waited for the voice I remembered to return. But for all that New York's best throat surgeons attempted, it hadn't come back.

So my new German friends would have to rap without me. More important, my European concerts of 2004 became my last. In Hamburg I sang before a capacity crowd of more than ten thousand, whose response led me back to my first performance in Berlin in the Tatania Palace in 1958. My prediction that the new Germany would become a different society from the one we had known during the Second World War had come to fruition. The Germans were by far my strongest and most loyal audience, and now, on this night, I wondered how many of my listeners had been with me that night at the pre–Berlin Wall performance almost fifty years earlier. Not many, I told myself. But their sons and daughters carried the flame, and one could not ask for more. That audience, one I had come to love, gave me a farewell I shall never forget. They didn't know it was my good-bye. I never made a public declaration that it was over. Still haven't. Often I'm asked, "Do you miss it?," and my reply is, "Not more than I have to."

I made the same farewell in Vienna, then Paris, then flew back for two final concerts in the United States. One was at the Greek Theatre in L.A. Simply by chance, my very last public performance was a benefit concert in Atlanta for their local opera company, a booking to which I'd committed some time before. I did my best, and came out for two, maybe three encores with the crowd on its feet. But finally it was time to say good-bye.

From those last concerts, I understood, with a sense of revelation, what it was I'd done. More than half a century ago, I had brought a young actor's skills and ambition to the small wood stage of the Village Vanguard, and found a way to use them as a singer. Audiences came to see me as much as to hear me. I was a performer delivering lines set to music, with every nuance of every song blocked out, like an actor hitting his marks. The audiences appreciated the pacing. They saw how the lighting enhanced my act—not a mere spotlight, but colors constantly changing as the music's moods changed. In a culture of replication, where each new star inspired copycats, no one had ever tried to imitate me, because mine was—literally—a hard act to follow, complicated on every level, and because at root it was an actor's performance. Singers, at least the singers I knew, didn't want to take that on. The fact was, I'd had no choice: I was good as a singer, but I wasn't the best, and I'd known that from the start. I'd had to rely on my acting, and in the end, I could make a case that I was the greatest actor in the world: I'd convinced everyone I could sing.

I remained a goodwill ambassador for UNICEF through President George W. Bush's first term, and traveled a lot for the organization. I went to South Africa to promote understanding on HIV/AIDS—a subject that needed a lot of understanding, given that South Africa's new president at the time, Thabo Mbeki, believed, among other misguided theories, that AIDS was the result of poverty, not blood-to-blood viral transmission. I went to Kenya and Senegal to promote public education, especially for girls, and to raise awareness there, too, of the facts of HIV/AIDS. UNICEF's executive director was Carol Bellamy, a staunch Democrat and former New York state senator, who had been appointed by President Clinton, and she was doing such an outstanding job—she'd actually doubled UNICEF's resources from $800 million to $1.8 billion—that she could hardly be broomed out, at least not in Bush's first term. And while she stayed, so did I.

That changed with the start of Bush's second term. Bellamy was replaced by Ann M. Veneman, formerly Bush's Secretary of Agriculture. Veneman came in with a fully partisan Republican agenda, and one of the first items on her to-do list involved me.

At an early staff meeting, I was later told, Veneman went down the list of goodwill ambassadors one by one. When she got to me, she said, according to my source, "How do we get rid of him?"

No one replied.

I'm told she asked the question again because she thought perhaps she hadn't been understood. "How do we get rid of him?"

"You don't," came a solitary, brave reply.

Veneman bristled.

"Unless you have very good cause," this staffer explained, "you'll have a lot of answering to do in a lot of countries. Belafonte has a long history in the developing world and is held in very high esteem in places where we do a lot of work."

I don't know what, if any, further inquiries Veneman made about me. I just know that she stopped trying to nudge me out. The agency did stop sending me on international missions; I could only interpret that as pique on Veneman's part. But it couldn't stop me from accepting other countries' requests to have me visit: South Africa for one, Norway for another, Germany and Sweden, too.

With President Obama's election in 2008, Veneman was replaced by Anthony Lake, National Security Adviser under President Clinton. Once again I was deemed to be useful. In July 2010, I helped launch an international documentary project called Envision, partly sponsored by the United Nations, that plans to stage an annual festival of documentaries focusing on global children's issues. It's no secret that documentaries are where a lot of the world's most important journalism is being done now, and I'm very excited by Envision's potential. The very word defines, better than any other, what's guided me all these years. All of us see the world as it exists; fewer envision what it might look like if made to change; and fewer still try to put together the people and ideas that make change happen. Paul Robeson was one; Martin Luther King, Jr., was one; Bobby Kennedy became one. And, of course, Nelson Mandela. I had just enough vision to see that they *were* visionaries, and to do what I could to help.

The irony about envisioning is that it's always prompted by a grave injustice right there in plain sight. Emmett Till. Rosa Parks. Walter Gadsden. To a list far longer than that, a new name was added on March 14, 2005: Ja'eisha Scott.

I was in a Washington, D.C., hotel room when a horrifying story on the television news pinned me to my seat. Five-year-old Ja'eisha, a black kindergarten student at a public school in St. Petersburg, Florida, became unruly enough to be sent to the assistant principal's office. Because the school had installed video cameras as part of a self-improvement exercise for teachers, what happened next was caught on tape. The assistant principal did try to calm Ja'eisha down by talking to her for some time, but the girl remained highly agitated. Finally the assistant principal called the police. When Ja'eisha refused to heed the three white officers who arrived, they pinned her arms behind her back with plastic ties as she screamed, "No, no," handcuffed her ankles together, carried her forcibly out of the school, and kept her bound in their police car—for hours. How could this happen in America? I wanted to know. How could a five-year-old child be handcuffed and detained like a violent adult criminal?

My first call was to Connie Rice, a cousin of Condoleezza Rice but a fundamentally different person from the Bush administration's newly named Secretary of State. Connie was a poverty lawyer in southern California, often representing members of the Bloods and the Crips. She'd brought class-action suits to take on race and sex discrimination; she'd worked with Police Commissioner Bill Bratton to investigate massive police corruption in the L.A. Police Department. I'd met her back in 1993 when the NAACP gave me its Thurgood Marshall award; Connie was regional director of the NAACP's Legal Defense and Educational Fund. Was Ja'eisha Scott an isolated case? I asked her. Connie told me no: It was a new code of social behavior, in a country that looked increasingly like a police state. Hundreds of children under ten years of age had been treated that way, she said. Child incarceration was an appalling reality.

With Connie's help, I convened what I called "The Gathering of the Elders" in Atlanta: distinguished civil rights activists, public policy pioneers, writers of conscience. Marian Wright Edelman, founder of the Children's Defense Fund, was a sponsor. So was Andy Young. Among the elders were Professor Cornel West, my onetime colleague from the American Negro Theatre Ruby Dee, and many of the old-guard movement figures—Jesse Jackson, John Lewis, Louis Farrakhan, and Oren Lyons of the Seneca and Onondaga peoples. I listened to various speakers say their piece, and as the day and a half of our scheduled talks wore on, I grew more and more despairing. These leaders were too dug into their own particular institutions and power bases. Any suggestion that we try to build something new was greeted with blank stares. They, more than half a century ago, were the youth who had turned America around. They'd taken to the streets and stopped the machine and seized the power to force change. I felt that now they were trapped by their pasts; they just couldn't see the relevance of what I was asking them to consider. I needed today's young and disenfranchised. And if child incarceration was my new focus, I had to look where those children were—in jail. All too often, I suspected, that's where I'd find their older siblings and parents, too.

With Connie Rice's help, I started visiting prisons in southern California. The young men and women I met reminded me of SNCC volunteers—fierce and fearless—only tougher. I talked to a woman who'd been locked up for years on a third-strike violation: stealing three sweat suits. Maybe the judge had appreciated that she'd stolen the sweat suits in order to sell them to buy food for her children. But the judge had no power to reduce her sentence; the state legislature had overridden him by establishing mandatory sentencing rules: third strike and she was out, sentenced to twenty-five years to life. Where were this woman's children? Left to the whims of the world, and facing prospects for incarceration themselves by their early teens.

I talked to some brilliant minds in those prisons: minds wasted in a country that hurried to lock them up at the slightest pretext, because these young people were inner-city black, and Hispanic, and sometimes Asian, too. Then I learned how many of these prisons were privately run, for-profit companies—the more prisoners they locked up, the higher their profits—and my blood really started to boil.

I decided to hold a series of gatherings around the country for hardcore youths either just out of prison or all too likely to go back in. Most would be gang members. Gangs, after all, were the great recruiters of inner-city youth; by the age of twelve, a boy or girl in South Central L.A. either joined a gang and started breaking the law or risked being killed for not joining. Connie helped put out the word, and I paid everyone's way to Epes, Alabama, a backcountry settlement of former black sharecroppers one hundred miles from the nearest distractions. It now served as a base for the Federation of Southern Cooperatives, dedicated to helping black farmers keep their land. After we bunked down, we gathered in the main farmhouse.

"Okay, Mr. B.," one of them said, "we're here. What's the agenda?"

"The agenda," I said, "is to find the agenda."

"What does that mean?"

"Well, look at us," I said. "Look how we're suffocating inside the box." I fed them all these statistics about youth and incarceration: that one out of every three black males in their twenties is in prison on any given day in this country; that the last thirty years have seen a 500 percent increase in America's prison population, to 2.3 million, more than any other country in the world; that 60 percent of that population are racial and ethnic minorities; that 800,000 are black males. If they were going to change those statistics, I told my new friends, they would have to mobilize, and learn how to fight—not with knives and guns, but with the principles and practices of nonviolence that Martin had learned from Mahatma Gandhi, and I'd learned from Martin.

A few months later I held a second gathering, this one in Santa Cruz, California. This time most of the participants were Mexican and Native American, largely from gangs. I invited a number of blacks as well, most of them gang members, too. I made the two groups describe themselves to each other, and start noticing what they had in common. Turned out they had a lot in common. Why, then, were they killing each other? Why couldn't they appreciate the power they'd have if they teamed up against their mutual oppressor, the American justice system, and used the tools of nonviolence to make it change? That led to a treaty between southern California's Latinos and blacks. The treaty was forged by two truly remarkable young men—Nane Alejándrez, leader of the northern California Latino movement Barrios Unidos, and Bo Taylor from the Los Angeles group Unity One. Both of these men had been deeply involved in the gang world, had served time in the armed forces, and, upon leaving the service, dedicated their lives to gang reform. It was through that work that Connie Rice brought them an ally: of all people, Sheriff Leroy D. Baca of Los Angeles County.

In gatherings that followed, I kept putting together different pairings: Native Americans and Hispanics, blacks and Asians, blacks and whites. Just as SNCC had done nearly half a century before, we targeted communities, made them our bases, reached out to other groups, and made the network grow. Today The Gathering for Justice is a national movement. Like SNCC, it's not a membership organization. Each person in its hierarchy has a constituency, and at any moment those leaders mobilize thousands and thousands of grassroots members to engage in campaigns of teaching and practicing nonviolent activism. One campaign, in 2009, took on the high incidence of violence at a Chicago school called North Lawndale College Prep. The school's one hundred fights a year were part of a larger crisis; more people were killed in the streets of Chicago that year than U.S. soldiers were killed in Iraq and Afghanistan combined. After a newly formed cadre of "Peace Warriors" at the school were trained in nonviolence, the school achieved a record 150 days of peace, and North Lawndale earned a prestigious Heroes in the Hood award.

I talk a lot these days with The Gathering's young leaders around the country. They are, without exception, eloquent and poised, charismatic and committed. I hear them and I wonder: Were we that impressive? Dr. King at twenty-four, and me at twenty-six? Julian Bond and John Lewis at seventeen? The truth is: yes, because we had to be. Just as these youth have to be now.

I'd thrown myself into The Gathering, and *Another Night in the Free World*. At the same time, a Canadian producer named Michael Cohl had come to me to propose financing a documentary about my life, to be called *Sing Your Song*. I was flattered by the pitch, but I had another reason for signing on: Marlon's death in 2004. I wasn't entirely surprised that he went when he did; he was eighty and in poor health. What shocked me was all the stories he'd taken with him to his grave, stories that his memoir all but ignored. He'd taken a lot of history with him—not just of Broadway and Hollywood but of the civil rights movement, all his passionate efforts on behalf of blacks and Native Americans—and now that history was gone. I knew I had a history worth recalling. I also knew that a lot of my contemporaries who had their own stories of the movement to tell weren't getting any younger. If, in my documentary film, I could interview them as well, I could be onboard for that. Cohl agreed, though neither he nor I had any idea the filming would consume six years.

For starters, a film crew and my producer daughter Gina followed me up to the Harlem apartment on West 156th Street where Marguerite and I lived when Adrienne was a baby, tracing my unlikely path. We sifted through archives for footage of those early rallies for peace, of Paul Robeson, of the Montgomery bus boycott and a young Martin Luther King, Jr., of SNCCers on their voter registration drives, of Birmingham and the March on Washington and Jay Richard Kennedy interviewing civil rights leaders later that day, of Selma and Black Panthers and the assassinations of Bobby and Martin. Gina and I interviewed the survivors: Sidney and Coretta and John Lewis and Julian Bond, and so many more. Seeing all that footage, and all those interviews, was like seeing my entire life unspool. What would I have changed? I had some thoughts on that, but they weren't worth the time it took to think them. For better or worse, this was my life. My quest. My song.

All these projects—*Another Night in the Free World*, The Gathering for Justice, and now *Sing Your Song*—charged me up and put me on the path to finding an answer to that fundamental question: What next?

That, I realized, was the same question I'd been asking about my marriage. After forty-eight years, Julie and I were played out. I hadn't made a move yet, but I knew I would. I just couldn't abide this husk of a marriage anymore. What next?

On that one, happily, I knew the answer.

20

At David's wedding on that New York fall day in 2000, I'd looked around the room and marveled at how happy all of my children were with their partners. For all our emotional complexities, we were a family better off than most. Until my gaze landed on Julie. And then I was reminded that of all the couples that made up our family, we were the exception.

I was not easy to live with. I so often flared with anger; I had an ego that was easily bruised and led to scenes I regretted. I still nursed grievances long past when I should have let them go. I traveled too much, and when tensions arose, I traveled more, which only made things worse. If I went to Paris or London to give a concert, Julie might come with me, happy to indulge in the pampering we got at fine hotels. But she wouldn't come to the Atlantas or Wichitas, if she could avoid them. Observing that, I began visiting such places more often, until I found myself booking a lot more out-of-the-way concert venues than my popularity could sustain.

The pantomime we'd put on had lasted for years, and although to the public it might have looked real, at night in that vast West End Avenue apartment, with the children grown and gone, we struggled to be civil, and too often didn't succeed. I could set my watch to the sound of the ice going into Julie's glass for the first drink of the evening. When she drank, I drank, too. The best part of the ritual was the toasting; for me, the pleasure diminished from there. In the later stages of our marriage, my continuing participation in the drinking game robbed me of any rights to complain about the consequences. Instead of helping Julie drink less, I was the enabler. Nightly, I saw the fog of inebriation settle over us, and hated being enveloped by it. If there was another way to get through an evening at home, I didn't know what it was. Inevitably we'd fall to arguing, and then retreat to our separate wings, bitter and befuddled. The more we played out those roles, the more I sought distraction—in gambling, sympathetic women, and all the concerts and social causes I could handle. I got to a point where I no longer knew what I wanted; the search itself exhausted me. Until one day I felt a warm and sympathetic glow from a place I least expected it: a woman I'd met long before, not as a date or a dalliance, just as a fellow activist with mutual friends.

I'd known Pamela Frank casually since a memorable night in September 1982, when Julie and I went to cheer on our old friend Diahann Carroll as she stepped into the lead role of the play *Agnes of God* for one week while its star, Elizabeth Ashley, was on vacation. (For Diahann, that week led to a run of her own in the play the following spring.) The play's director, Michael Lindsay-Hogg, was there, too, along with his very attractive date. Afterward we all ended up at Sardi's restaurant. Michael's date, I learned, was a photographer, a divorcée with two children, active in various civil rights causes. I guessed Pam to be quite a few years younger than I was, which in 1982 meant she was in her late thirties. Since she was spoken for, and I was married, I simply regarded her as a very attractive dinner companion. She did make an impression, however, with the story she told me that night.

"We've met before, you know," Pam said. "Back when I was in college."

That's the kind of line, coming from a beautiful woman, that makes a guy with my kind of record pay attention. I leaned toward her so that this bit of public disclosure would be confined to no greater perimeter than my eardrum.

"Really?"

Pam explained that as a student at Syracuse University, she'd gone down to the Bahamas on a spring break with her girlfriends. (One of them, I later found out, was her closest friend, Neilia Hunter, who would go on to marry a young man she'd met on that trip—Joe Biden. Pam never quite got over the fact that Neilia died six years later in a tragic automobile accident, just as Biden's political star began to rise.) Pam went on to explain that while there, the girls had met actor Sean Connery, who was making the James Bond movie *Thunderball*. Connery had invited them to stay and be extras. Neilia had preferred to fly back in time for the start of classes, but Pam and some of the other girls had stayed on to be in the film. Arriving alone at the tiny Nassau airport for her flight home, Pam found herself waiting in a line behind me. (I was on my way to a smaller island in the Bahamian chain to spend the week with Sidney.) She'd asked if she could take my picture with her tiny Minox—those little spylike cameras that were all the rage at the time. After a brief chat, I'd agreed.

"Was that . . . it?" I asked her at Sardi's.

She flashed me a mischievous smile. "No."

"Oh," I said. Now she really had my attention. "Then what?"

Some time later, Pam explained, her father had called her to report that a flood had ruined everything stored in the family garage, including boxes of negatives from all the pictures Pam had taken. By then, Pam had become a professional photographer. She had covered Broadway shows, shot album covers, book jackets, and political campaigns. She also had her own studio on Madison Avenue, specializing in family portraits and pictures of children. Out of the thousands of negatives she'd had in those boxes, only a few had survived.

"And . . . ?" I asked.

"Those were the pictures of you."

That was the whole story.

Four years after that Sardi's dinner, a powerful South African play called *Asinamali!* came to Lincoln Center. Pam, who had become very active in the anti-apartheid movement and taken a lot of photographs to publicize the situation in South Africa, was the play's official photographer. So impressed was she with the play that she called me and a number of others to come see it as prospective backers. I ended up helping underwrite its passage to Broadway, along with Miriam Makeba, Paul Simon, and others. I found myself taking more notice of her. I started calling her to take pictures for various "Free South Africa" fundraisers. That kept us in touch. We attended screening parties Bob and Kathryn Altman gave for many of Bob's films; Pam knew the Altmans, too. The more I saw of her, the easier I found it to be around her. The more I shared my feelings with her, the less anguished I felt. One day I took her to lunch at the Carlyle. That led to more lunches, and then to dinner, and finally dinner led to breakfast.

A lot of intimations of mortality at that time had had me asking myself, more urgently, why I was still in my marriage. At sixty-nine I had been diagnosed with prostate cancer. Like most men who get it these days, I'd undergone an operation that eradicated it completely, though not without a lot of pain and soul-searching. Sidney, in fact, had been diagnosed not long before me with the same problem, and had the operation just weeks before I did. This business of parallels in our lives was getting ridiculous. At least he'd survived the operation, I thought, as I went in for mine! (As I became more knowledgeable about the disease, I was stunned to learn that black men as a group were by far the likeliest victims of prostate cancer. In the black culture, rectal exams conjure up associations with homosexuality, so black men, who must struggle culturally with what is perceived as a stigma, shun them. It's surely not the sole reason for this troubling statistic, but homophobia greatly pushes the odds. When I recovered, I volunteered to be an advocate for the American Cancer Society, and for a long while, pictures of me and Shari, taken by Francesco Scavullo, flooded New York City's subways and buses with a blunt message to black men: Being skittish about rectal exams for prostate cancer is a good way to end up dead.) Still, how much time did I have left, really, and how was I spending it? In my sessions with Peter Neubauer, we talked about the sense I had that I was always running from something, and never fast enough.

One night in 2004 I came back to the apartment from a round of errands in advance of yet another road trip. Julie had called dinner for 6:30; I got home at 7:00. The libations, I saw, had been flowing freely: Julie was glassy-eyed and angry. Angry for my half-hour lateness? I wondered. Or at our whole life together? After a few choice words about my tardiness, she declared, "If you decide to ever eat tonight, your dinner's in the oven. I'm going to bed."

This was hardly the first time I'd been late for dinner. So why was this scene, which had played itself out so many times before, circling the room like a vampire looking for blood? Something was different.

I felt angry and trapped, but then I'd always felt that way. Trapped by my mother, by poverty, by being my brother's keeper at the age of five, by my father and what he did, by living in Jamaica on a plantation, by having a nomadic childhood, by dropping out of school and having to work at dead-end jobs, by feeling a failure and then, when I did succeed, never trusting my victories. Trapped, too, by the responsibility I felt for the global poor; trapped by the ignorant right-wing politics that made the plight of the poor so much worse. And now I was in my *seventies*! Maybe I'd never stop feeling suffocated by all that. But I sure didn't need to keep fighting for air in an airless marriage.

"It's over," I told Julie.

"What's over?" she said.

"Our life together is over."

She sneered. "Again?"

That really threw me. She was right: I'd stepped away in frustration before but never left, bound as I was by guilt and all the other binding agents of marriage and parenthood. This time felt different. I might be at an age—seventy-seven—when almost no man breaks the domestic pattern of his life and leaves his wife. But this was it. This *was* what I had to do. Julie didn't know it yet, although I'm sure she sensed it. Our life *was* over. Whatever divorce would bring—*whatever*—I was ready to take it on, no matter the cost.

For some years now, Julie and I had basically led separate lives in our vast, U-shaped apartment, with a whole wing for each of us. Now we went further, shutting the folding doors of the connecting living room. Since each side had originally been a separate apartment with its own elevator line, we didn't need to see each other at all. I started making the requisite calls to lawyers and financial managers. They warned me that the cost of untangling forty-seven years of marriage would be considerable. As they started to explain the details of the process, there was no question it was going to exact a great emotional toll, beginning with our having to sell the apartment.

That was difficult. For me, and Julie, too, those twenty-one rooms still echoed with our children's laughter, parties and weddings, and the voices of an era—John F. Kennedy, Martin, Sidney, SNCCers, Black Panthers, and so many others. Only half jokingly, Clarence Jones, Martin's lawyer, had declared the apartment should be registered as an historic site, open for the public to see where Martin and his kitchen cabinet had met so many times to plan the movement's next goals.

Put up for sale in August 2005, the apartment was bought by Abigail Disney, Walt's niece. We had a home in St. Maarten, too, on a beach with a truly beautiful view of the sea. I had bought it from my friend Chris Blackwell. I loved that place. But we'd made so few visits there with the children and friends, because drinking had turned many a beautiful sunset into a blurred horizon of disappointment. I'd imagined retiring there eventually. But that wasn't to be. It, too, was put up for sale.

I knew I'd stay on the Upper West Side of Manhattan. The neighborhood was as much my home as the apartment, with its crowded markets and Jewish delicatessens and Chinese-Cuban and Italian restaurants, its jumble of students and pensioners, actors and eccentrics.

Pam and I found a newly renovated space in a grand old building barely a stone's throw from where I'd lived for nearly fifty years. The new space was modest, but joyous—perfect for the rhythms of this new life of ours. Julie found a new place nearby, too; the neighborhood was as much her home as mine. Sometimes these days I see her walking her dog on Broadway, and on occasion we stop and chat. The legal wrangling is behind us; we have grandchildren to discuss; life goes on.

In the wake of my divorce, I still had more comforts than most people on the planet. But no Town Car sits idling outside my door. I've rediscovered the New York City transportation system, the buses and subways, where I have found delight in studying all those faces, with so many gradations of skin tone. The classes seem more mixed than when I last rode those creaky cars with any daily regularity: the young Wall Street workers, the tired secretaries with their iPods, the happy students from public and private schools, the young and the old swaying together. Sometimes I tote up, in my mind, how much money I gave over the years to the movement and other causes. How would my life be now if I had it all back? More hedonistically comfortable, perhaps . . . but not better. At the very end, what consolations do we have or really need? Surely not vast sums of money smothering our generosity toward the needy and the poor.

In my late seventies, I was slowing down, but when the right political cause tugged at me, I still jumped in. And in my choice of causes, I remained not just liberal but an unabashed lefty. I was still drawn to idealistic left-wing leaders, or at least left-wing leaders who seemed to embody the true ideals of socialism. And so it was hardly surprising to my family and friends that in early 2006 I led a delegation to meet with Venezuela's fiery socialist president, Hugo Chávez.

To me, Chávez seemed far more complex than the swaggering lout he was portrayed as in the Western media, even *The New York Times*. In the wake of Hurricane Katrina the previous summer, Chávez had personally offered to help with disaster relief. Venezuela had had more than its share of natural calamities, and had learned some valuable lessons. Yet President Bush had given Chávez the back of his hand—an unstatesmanlike gesture, to say the least. Chávez had also just declared that he would make Venezuelan heating oil available at cut-rate prices to needy New Englanders for the coming winter, after President Bush had ignored their pleas for help as oil prices rose. (Joseph Patrick Kennedy II, Bobby's oldest son, had stepped in and embraced the offer as head of a regional nonprofit called Citizens Energy.)

I knew how controversial Chávez was. But since coming to power in 1999, he had achieved something that Bush seemed to have no interest in doing in America: He'd cut the ranks of his country's unemployed in half. And for that, Chávez was a lot more popular in Venezuela than Bush was in the United States. I suspected that, as with every left-wing leader who became a target of U.S. foreign policy, there was another side to his story, and I wanted to hear it. I also had a proposition for him.

Along with condemning Chávez, the U.S. government had been doing all it could to eradicate Venezuela's coca fields, to stanch the northward flow of cocaine. Chávez had asked why the United States couldn't instead put its money into training Venezuelan farmers to cultivate another profitable crop. That caught my fancy. I started thinking about what the best alternative crop might be, and how Venezuela and the United States might both benefit from harvesting and trading it. I sought out Ralph Paige and leaders of the Federation of Southern Cooperatives in Epes, Alabama—the group representing thousands of black farmers in the Deep South who had on several occasions come to me for help. To my friends in Epes, the answer was obvious: coffee. For various reasons, Brazil and Colombia dominated the South American coffee business. What if we helped Venezuela expand its own coffee industry by providing a new U.S. distribution network for it? And what if that U.S. network could be set up and overseen by some of America's toughest but most economically challenged citizens: former members of the Bloods and the Crips and other inner-city youth groups?

Father Greg Boyle, a legendary white Irish Catholic priest, who for decades has worked with L.A.'s gangs, had made me see the potential here. He'd started a Homeboy Bakery in downtown L.A., a Homeboy Café, and a Homeboy silk-screening retail business. *Homeboy*. I liked the name. Why not sell Homeboy coffee—piping hot or fresh-ground—at the partly Venezuelan-owned chain of Citgo gas stations, starting in L.A. and then extending around the country?

I had no interest in being a commodities broker, or a wheeler-dealer in international affairs. But as an activist and artist, I had a Rolodex that cut across classes and professions, and that frankly reached up into many a presidential office. I knew that when sovereign states fail to communicate, and issues of human rights are ignored as a result, an outsider can sometimes intervene and make things happen. That's all I hoped to do here. So I reached out to Chávez through intermediaries, and back came an invitation to come see him.

The delegation I took down in January 2006 included actor Danny Glover, talk-show host Tavis Smiley, professor Cornel West, Bo Taylor, a former gang leader, Nane Alejándrez of Barrios Unidos, and others. It was an eclectic group, and whatever we experienced would not be lost for want of eyes and ears.

The barrel-shaped president came bounding out of his office into a large and rather elegant conference room where we had been directed to wait. As he greeted us, I was taken with the focus that Chávez gave each of the fifteen members of our delegation. His was more than just a social performance. It had purpose. I sensed how tightly coiled he was, bristling with energy, ready to deal with anything we put before him. Yet at the same time he radiated a sunny charm and fierce curiosity. He steered his group of cabinet members, staff, professors, and policy-makers to sit opposite us at the long oval table. As for Chávez himself, he sat directly across from me.

As he spoke, Chávez would reach for one or another of the books before him, find the citation he sought, and read aloud with a translator at his side. As with Fidel, there was no subject that he didn't attack with ferocious enthusiasm—and none that he lacked an opinion on. Certainly he had a strong grasp of Latin American history and of the fine distinctions in law between Venezuela and its neighbors.

That meeting went on all day. It went on for *nine hours*. Chávez was there the whole time. He showed enormous interest in our coffee idea, and turned routinely to delegate one aspect or another of it to one of his colleagues. Video cameras recorded it all. We'd brought a camera crew of our own; a Venezuelan television crew was there beside us. This marathon session was followed by a Sunday excursion with the president, as he led us into the rural interior for his weekly meet and greet, this time with an awestruck community of farmers. All over the country, Venezuelans watched their president on television having impromptu exchanges on-air with farmers, women, intellectuals, local officials, students, athletes, and artists who performed at given intervals. In a most spontaneous way, Chávez asked me to say a word to the Venezuelan people—not only to the thousands gathered before us but to the millions watching on TV. I realized this was an opportunity that I should treat carefully. I needed to be succinct, and easily translatable, especially for the international journalists. Mostly, I needed to speak from my deeper self, which I did.

"We're here to tell you that not hundreds, not thousands, but millions of the American people support your revolution," I said. As for President Bush, I added that he was "the greatest tyrant, the greatest terrorist in the world." I went on to encourage the Venezuelan people to stay on course and seize their chance to shape a truly equitable society.

Our group left very encouraged by the fervor with which Chávez endorsed our coffee project. Back home, we drew up our plans in detail, with all we'd learned on our trip. In the next weeks, delegates from Venezuela came to California, and delegates from our group went to Caracas. Young leaders from both sides debated issues of common interest. We even went so far as to visit each other's prison systems in the quest for more humane forms of rehabilitation. Then suddenly, from our new Venezuelan colleagues, there was silence. Our phone calls went unreturned; deadlines were missed; the whole project shuddered to a halt. We read in the papers that Venezuela was caught in an economic downspin. But why would that kill a project that could only help hard-hit farmers?

As far as I could tell, we'd been used. Apparently, for Venezuela, the power of those television images showing the distinguished American delegation in dialogue with its president had been worth all those hours of Chávez's time. I don't doubt that the U.S. State Department may have done its own part to quash the project; the Bush administration was hardly apt to view a business alliance between a left-wing American entertainer and the socialist president of Venezuela with much warmth and respect.

After some fifty years of working with developing countries, I've found that a lot of good can be done by private citizens working back channels for public good. But these ventures stand a greater chance of success when the volunteers are white and from Wall Street than black and from Main Street.

I really did think—still do—that George W. Bush was a terrorist. My only mistake was in calling him the greatest terrorist in the world, since I had not met them all. His launching a war against Iraq without cause, and with treacherous intent, resulting in the needless deaths of thousands of American servicemen and -women and tens of thousands of Iraqi citizens, the majority of them civilians, qualified him for the title, as far as I was concerned. Those thousands of innocent lives lost were, to the Bush administration, just "collateral damage," a phrase that I find infuriating. To me, collateral damage is just a brazen attempt to find moral grounds for crimes against humanity.

Just days after my return from Venezuela, Coretta Scott King was dead, at seventy-eight, the result of various health problems, including respiratory issues, multiple strokes, and ovarian cancer. That sad news stirred up a lot of mixed feelings in me.

My bonds with Coretta and her children had loosened over the years. I was, by choice, no longer a director of the King Center, and while the children still referred to me as Uncle Harry in our infrequent catch-up phone calls, I didn't see them much. But my history with the family was deep and long, and so I wasn't surprised to be asked to speak at Coretta's memorial service. I was, however, *very* surprised, a few days later, to get a call from Mrs. King's secretary advising me that I would not be speaking. Not only that, I got the feeling it would be better if I did not come at all.

When I'd recovered from my shock, I called Martin III to ask what had gone down. He was full of apologies. "Oh, Uncle Harry, there's such confusion down here." He meant in Lithonia, Georgia, where the funeral service was to take place. "Nothing is being coordinated right—I'm so sorry about this." He spoke as if the whole event were out of his control. It wasn't. I knew that.

For some years now, Bernice, Martin's youngest child, had tacked to the far right politically. She'd spoken out publicly in support of President Bush and his war in Iraq. She was also vehemently anti-gay, which made her a comrade-in-arms with a born-again Baptist preacher, Eddie Long, who ran a black megachurch called New Birth Missionary Baptist, where Coretta's funeral was to take place. Long had taken Bernice into his fold, and introduced her to colleagues like Jerry Falwell. Bitterness, politics, and evangelical fervor got all mixed together in this group, and right-wing conservative family values ruled. Only they didn't always prevail: In September 2010, the very Reverend Eddie Long would be the target of lawsuits accusing him of multiple instances of sexual abuse of young males in his congregation.

In early 2006, I was the one swimming in moral turpitude, as far as Bernice was concerned. My recent comments about Hugo Chávez and George W. Bush had made the national news. I had little doubt that they'd angered Bernice and her born-again ilk. When I learned that the President had just agreed to attend the service, all my suspicions were confirmed. Forced to choose between one of their father's close friends and a president their father would have abhorred, the children had had no trouble reaching their decision.

Why, some must have wondered, was the service being held at the Reverend Long's church in the first place? Why not at Ebenezer Baptist, the start of Martin and Coretta's historic journey? Reverend Long was one of the evangelical right's most revered black figures, the recipient of millions of dollars in contributions from that quarter, and a lot of that money found its way to Republican campaign coffers. Bush's decision to come to the funeral was for them a win-win. It elevated the Reverend Long and his church to even greater national prominence. I have to suspect that it also inspired him and the Christian right to channel a little more lucre to the gay-bashing Republican party.

Word of my disinvitation got out before the service, and among the people I heard from were Jesse Jackson and Al Sharpton. "Just go in with us," they said. "And if they cause any fuss, we'll take it to the next level"—by which they meant the press. I told them I appreciated their support. But hurtful as this was, I said, it was impossible for me to imagine confronting Martin's children, especially around the occasion of Coretta's death. After further exchange, we concluded that in the spirit of the movement, we should be trying to heal, not put further distance between each other.

I didn't say a public word on this. I watched the service on television, saw President and Mrs. Bush sitting solemnly along with former Presidents Bill Clinton, George H. W. Bush, and Jimmy Carter, and heard the Reverend Joseph Lowery, a close associate of Martin's for years in the Southern Christian Leadership Conference, steal the show with his fiery rhetoric and blunt statement that no weapons of mass destruction had been found in Iraq. I was especially moved by the writer Maya Angelou, who was most gracious in her reference to my absence. She was standing on that stage, she declared, for all the millions of people Coretta had inspired—millions who could not be there. One of those, she said, was me.

I was sorry not to be there, but not that sorry. The children had grown up to be the people they were. I was who I was. In a sense they were right: In our current space, we really had nothing much to say to each other. The fact saddens me. Even more so since Yolanda, the firstborn, suddenly passed away, leaving behind a promise we had made to each other that we would come together again.

. . .

My frayed relations with Martin's family are upsetting, but not overly so. Things that might have really undone me in the past no longer do. In large measure I give Pam credit for that. I am too happy in my new life with her to dwell on misfortune. With Pam, I feel all the love and trust I always struggled to find and sustain. I know that a lot of complex psychological knots have come undone. I often ask: "So why, after all these years, does love feel so easy?"

Peter Neubauer, my therapist of so many years, was naturally curious to meet the woman who'd turned me around at last, so I brought her with me to his office one day. As soon as he saw Pam, he smiled broadly and gave her a hug. In an instant, he could feel all the warmth and empathy she radiated. He'd taken to telling me that I was his oldest patient—not in age, but in the number of years I'd worked with him. Over the decades, our therapy had evolved into an intellectual bond. I think he felt that although my psychiatric journey was not quite complete, I'd come very far, from someone with so much bitterness and anger to a man nearly as happy as I could become. Pam was the proof; it was only by working through so many of my issues with Peter that I had been able to respond, as an open, loving person, to the love that Pam had to give. Only then, in the deepest way, could I trust another human being.

The role Peter played in my life is hard to overstate. I'd spoken with him nearly every week, often more than once, for half a century. He knew me better than anyone else did, even Julie or Pam. Our exchange was so lively and intimate, with no holds barred. Often I'd tell him he was looking at something a certain way because he was white, or Jewish, or both. We'd debate that, sometimes in anger, at least on my part, but then the process moved on. Between a white analyst and a black patient, race is always part of the dialogue. But only part—we went much deeper than that. With almost every challenge I faced—whether emotional, with my family and friends, or artistic—I would wait to talk with Peter before making a critical decision. And even now, when sudden flare-ups occur, I still ask, even in my anger: What would Peter say about this? But Peter was more than a decade older than I, and suddenly, to my shock, at the age of ninety-four, he was dying.

The last time I saw Peter wasn't a session; it was a farewell visit I made to his apartment in February 2008. He was sick, and as a doctor—a great doctor—he understood exactly the kind of disintegration his body was experiencing. He'd lost his freedom of movement, and his intellect was no longer keen. He told me that without his work, he no longer had a reason to live. He'd enjoyed our therapeutic relationship enormously, he said; he'd watched me learn how to deal so much better with life, especially with the women in my life, with my children, with the ghosts of my parents and past. As I listened to him, I began to understand. I was on my own at last.

He died just days later.

The timing was a fluke, but it felt symbolic: Pam and I had already set a date for our wedding just weeks later. To avoid having to choose which friends to invite and which to leave off the list, with all the attendant hurt feelings, we made it a family-only affair. Including grandchildren, nieces, nephews, and in-laws, the total came to a not-inconsiderable thirty people. Neither of us wanted a religious wedding, and so, like David, we chose a New York restaurant as our venue. For us it was Terrace in the Sky, up near Columbia University, with its panoramic skyline views. The date was April 12, 2008, a bit anticlimactic, since Pam and I had been living together for some time, but a profoundly joyous occasion, nonetheless. Former Mayor David Dinkins had done such a good job at David's wedding that we had him officiate at ours, too. Besides, Dave is one of my closest friends. He will say at the drop of a hat that it was I who, at the critical moment, pushed him to run for mayor of New York. I am still not quite sure if he considers that advice a blessing or a curse.

This time, when I took in the whole assembled clan, I could say that *all* of our marriages were happy. And happily, all of my children were still with the same partners they'd had at David's wedding. As for David himself, he and Malena had had two beautiful children, Sarafina and Amadeus, the latter of whom was just eight months old at our wedding.

This was not to say that the "West Coast crowd," as Adrienne put it, had not struggled professionally in the last eight years. Shari and Sam were still putting "packages" together. For many years, Shari had tried to lure me into working together with her. Nothing had made sense to me until Sam, in what was more a shot in the dark than a serious overture, asked me to play a role in his film *Last Supper*. Shari was producing it, Sam was directing it, and I, if I agreed, would play the lead: a vampire. Neither Shari nor Sam believed I'd sign on for this one, but I did. I can't say I agreed because I wanted to play a vampire; I simply wasn't going to say no again. In fact, not long before, I'd promised myself that if ever Shari pitched me another of her projects, I would say yes without the slightest hesitation. So I signed on, and they clapped a mask on me, and hung me from a harness on pulleys—hour after hour, day after day. It was one part *The Silence of the Lambs*, one part *Spider-Man: Turn Off the Dark*. I had to wonder if this was Shari's revenge. The shooting is finished, but the film is still on the editing table.

Gina and Scott, also in L.A., are still auditioning for roles, though Gina has spent the last several years working on *Sing Your Song*, the documentary about my years in the civil rights movement. As its West Coast producer, she conducted many of the interviews herself and often made something happen that I would have found awkward to pursue myself: interviewing Sidney, for example. Her diligence also helped us interview some of my colleagues who shortly afterward passed away. At the same time, Gina is a hands-on mother with Maria, steering her to school plays and drama classes that may yet lead her to become an actress herself. The lure of acting is still strong in my family, perhaps a bit too strong. For all of its frustrations, Shari and Gina are still determinedly engaged.

Of all my children, David is the one who tried something entirely new. He started an arts-oriented company, Belafonte Arts and Media. Like anyone else in the financial world, he struggled during the downturns. And so, as I write these words, David and I are working on a cultural adventure called Bread and Roses for Local 1199 of the Service Employees International Union (SEIU). Its mission is to encourage the union's more than two million members to express themselves and their cultures through the arts: to write and record their songs, start choral groups, produce plays, write prose and poetry. We want the real stories of union workers put to words and music, to have them heard by the rest of the country. They will have their own record label. It's been a long time since working people had that kind of public platform. Not since Woody Guthrie and the Great Depression, the time of the great American cultural renaissance spawned by President Roosevelt and his Works Progress Administration programs, has there been a time when artists were so encouraged by an institution to use art for social expression.

The union actually set up its Bread and Roses program more than forty years ago at its New York headquarters, right in the heart of the theater district in midtown Manhattan.

This undertaking with David completely absorbs me. Each day that I walk into the building on the way to my office, I am immersed in a diaspora of African workers. There is much to smile about or even laugh at as they, along with their Latino and Asian counterparts, launch into their early-day storytelling in the elevator. I am greatly inspired by the strength and resolve of these workers. They clean our hospitals, they care for the ill and disabled, they empty our urinals and change our sheets and raise their children. They in many ways do all the things my mother did. I see and understand their circumstances and struggle. I embrace their dignity. Our mission with Bread and Roses is to hold a mirror up to them, and honor their work and aspirations. In this time of cruel and tragic acts against the workers of America by the power elite, I'm called back to a time when Woody wrote:

> As I went walking I saw a sign there
> And on the sign it said "No Trespassing."
> But on the other side it didn't say nothing,
> That side was made for you and me. . . .
> In the squares of the city,
> In the shadow of a steeple,
> By the relief office, I'd seen my people.
> As they stood there hungry,
> I stood there asking,
> Is this land made for you and me?

With rank-and-file artists coming to embrace our efforts and put their workplace issues into story and song, the question before us is: How can we protect the rights that Americans have struggled to achieve for a hundred years, and are now in grave danger of losing? Artists are truly empowered, as they were generations before, with the gift to make a difference. We are the engines of inspiration, and if we use this gift, then we validate Paul Robeson's belief that artists are the gate-keepers of truth and the true documentarians of history. I expect that the rest of my life will be spent in this pursuit.

About my own life, I have no complaints. But I do have grave concerns about race and poverty in this country, about what the movement has left undone and how little of a movement remains to do it.

To some degree, those needs have been papered over, for amazingly enough, we have a black president. Few if any of us in the early civil rights days would have imagined that would come to pass in our lifetimes—or ever. It's an astonishing show of progress in American attitudes about race, and if lots of other factors were at play, from Barack Obama's eloquence on the stump to his brilliant use of the Internet to reach voters, from Republican missteps to the economy's meltdown—if, in other words, race wasn't the largest factor—then that's even more remarkable. Perhaps in my children's lifetimes, or at least in *their* children's, a presidential candidate's skin color—and gender—may not matter to voters at all.

Yet the problems faced by most Americans of color seem as dire and entrenched as they were half a century ago. And as I write this, our President has yet to acknowledge that this fact is of any concern to him, let alone offer a blueprint of solutions that would inspire our citizens to participate and make the sacrifices to ensure the health of the nation.

In the politicians I've admired, I've sensed an underlying spiritual essence. Bobby Kennedy could be coldly pragmatic, but when confronted by desperate poverty, he couldn't turn away; he had to speak about what he'd seen with passion and clarity, and when I heard him, I knew he was speaking from that place Martin Luther King knew existed and told us to find—his moral center. Bobby spoke from the heart. There is no substitute for that.

For all of his smoothness and intellect, Barack Obama seems to lack a fundamental empathy with the dispossessed, be they white or black. Frankly, I would have thought the first black president would work especially hard to alleviate the plight of inner-city black Americans. I appreciate the passing of the stimulus package. I understand that a national health insurance bill helps us all. But why, I have kept wondering, hasn't he used his power to bring more humanity to a justice system that imprisons one out of every three black males in America, giving us the largest prison population in the world? I would like for him to say more forcefully that racial problems exist. Show some heart, put some skin in the game. By tacking to the political center, disassociating himself from the left, he has all but abandoned the poor. And who else, after all, speaks for the poor *but* the left?

For the poor of America, a very bad time is about to get worse. Our black president seems to be holding his tongue because he is, after all, pragmatic. But here's something I know, after more than half a century in the movement: The poor will not just curl up and die, much as the new political majority wishes they would. When your belly is empty, you do whatever it is you need to do to stop those hunger pains. You march, or you steal, or you pick up a gun.

In his book *Black Reconstruction in America*, W.E.B. Du Bois predicted that race would be the overarching issue of the twentieth century. I think he was right, especially if one adds in the genocide of World War II by a deluded "superior race" intent on ridding the world of "inferior" Jews (and blacks). I have little doubt that race is going to dominate the twenty-first century, too, not just at home but around the world.

I do acknowledge that in America we've made a lot of progress on race. The same country that could elect its first black president in 2008 no longer seems to openly tolerate racial slurs and racial humor. To the extent that a middle class still exists in this country, blacks are part of it. Mixed-race marriages are blurring the lines of race more than ever—just as southern racists feared they would—and as a result, to some extent, race is less and less of a factor in the workplace. All that is good. My frustration is: Where are the inheritors? Where are the new, young activists, shaking up the social order? They're in Egypt, in Tunisia, in other more blatantly oppressive societies. But not here.

Here we have two tiers: the very rich, and everyone else. And the next generation, instead of tearing that system down, aspires to reach the top tier. How smooth is the machine that continues to oppress—so smooth that it co-opts those who might resist it, and saps their anger, and magnifies their greed until those squeezed hardest by that two-tier system have nothing to lose, and *their* anger spills into the streets.

Martin Luther King once said that anger was a necessary ingredient for change. And I subscribe to that completely. I was angry when I met him. Anger had helped protect me. Martin understood my anger and saw its value. But our cause showed me how to redirect it and to make it productive.

Of late, something has come into my life that daily touches me: two small creatures from some faraway celestial body. Pam calls them her grandchildren, Mateo and Olive. I call them miracles to be celebrated and visited—and revisited. The eleven children who are the extensions of my gene pool—Adrienne, Shari, David, and Gina; their children, Rachel, Brian, Maria, Sarafina, and Amadeus; and the first two great-grandchildren, Isabella and Gabriel—all came into my world at varying stages of what has been my journey. I watch these children latch on to the world around them, propelled by the seductions of modern technology, and I both worry for them and envy them. Worry, because those high-tech tools seem to force us apart more than pull us together. Envy, because whatever this new world offers should, in many ways, lead us to the greater heights we struggle to attain.

I believe that my time was a remarkable one. I am aware that we now live in a world overrun by cruelty and destruction, and as our earth disintegrates and our spirits numb, we lose moral purpose and creative vision. But still I must believe, as I always have, that our best times lie ahead, and that in the final analysis, along the way we shall be comforted by one another.

That is my song.

ACKNOWLEDGMENTS

With my appreciation of literature and great admiration for writers, I'd always hoped I could master language and maybe one day be a storyteller. Sensing an inadequacy for the task, I never really contemplated the idea of writing a book. But a combination of circumstance and desire overcame my insecurity, the consequence of which is this work.

It was difficult. It took me to places that exhausted me, frustrated me, troubled me. But in the end I was rewarded by the challenge.

I cannot say enough about Michael Shnayerson and what he brought into my space, guiding me through the minefields of storytelling. His enviable gift of craft created the frame within which this story was shaped. His focus kept me disciplined, and his challenges and questions always improved the result. I am both grateful for and rewarded by our journey.

There are many who could take credit for the fact that this book exists. I often was encouraged, more forcefully by some than by others, to document my life's journey. To all of these people, I feel indebtedness: Stony Cooks; Carlos Santana; Jake Holmes, whose gift turned many of our thoughts into poetry; Taylor Branch; Julian Bond; Ira Gilbert; Richard Rosenberg, the *gribenes* of my life; Jay Cooper; Cy and Shirley Rossman; John Lewis; David Dinkins; Bill Lynch; my boss George Gresham and everybody at 1199; Jack and Mary Willis; Philip Rotter; Kenneth and Maria Cole, whose generosity of spirit soothes many anxious moments; Christina Malach; Jeff Roth of *The New York Times* for exhuming old clippings of my early career. Michael Fuchs . . . thanks for the pool, the vista, and the dogs! My gratitude to Peter Gethers, my very capable and encouraging editor at Knopf. And to the numerous others who nudged me along the way.

. . .

ACKNOWLEDGMENTS

Mario Cuomo was my boss when, for seven years, I served as chairperson of the New York State Martin Luther King, Jr. Commission. In the decades since, we have locked steps in our pursuit of justice. Above all, though, he is my friend, and I am mindful that his was the final word that committed me to the task of putting pen to paper. Thanks for the push.

For my friends in The Gathering for Justice, The Brotherhood/Sister Sol, the Burns Institute, Barrios Unidos, Unity One, and all the missionaries of resistance who with their youth have invigorated me, with their minds have kept me endlessly attuned and alert, and with their passion for justice have stirred my spirits constantly. They continue to do so. Thanks for inspiring so much in this book.

For Harold Melvin, who insists on keeping me honest with his irreverence. To Esther Newberg, whose stewardship steered me to a safe port. Her advice was critical. For Mike Remer, who wisely counseled that suing the enemy doesn't always guarantee justice and could be a sure way to abject poverty. He kept the ship afloat in the midst of J. Edgar Hoover's consistent effort to sink it. And for Abe Briloff, whose moral clarity, strength of conviction, and caring attention made me keep my eye on the sparrow. To Chris Blackwell, my fellow Jamaican, who affords me many wondrous moments in my favorite place in the world—his home on Jamaica's north coast. Thanks for your kindness. For Orin Lyons, who has daily deepened my trust in fellow beings. His wisdom, always shared with me, continues to guide me. Connie Rice: No movement person has more sway over me than she. When choices are put before us that could have dire consequences if miscalculated, she brings intellect and courage to the decision-making process that enables us to consistently triumph on the side of justice. Her will inspires me. And to Danny Glover. When he stepped into the autumn of my life and offered me his unconditional friendship, he filled a space that had been vacant for a long time. He calmed the loss of Paul Robeson and added joy for the walk ahead. For Nane Alejándrez, who embodies the courage of every noble warrior I have ever stood with; his generosity toward humanity moves the heart to reach for greater truths. Thanks for the time we spend in the prisons of California and for Cinco de Mayo. And I thank you for what you have brought to the struggle. In memory of Bo Taylor, who, in his death, left our mission without any doubt that honor was indispensable. We learned that our service to the cause should never waver from the examples of truth and courage that he displayed. That was his gift to us. Sorry he isn't here for the dance. I am forever grateful that Shirley Cooks is my sister. How proud she makes me feel. Her quiet dignity commands respect from those she encounters, and her contribution in the service of our country is invaluable. She shares with me the peaks and valleys of our sibling history and validates the journey. To Lauren Coakley-Vincent for her sanity and for keeping me on track in a life that is filled with persistent demands and impossible schedules. I'm glad you do it. I just don't know how. Perhaps most indispensable of all, Dr. David Miller, Dr. Reese Pritchett, and Maria Spinelli—I thank you for continued life and breath. Michael Cohl and Lori McGoran: So much was started on your turf. You understood the undertaking and knew that moments would come when I would need space. You made it available by sharing your homes, Yankee games, and so much more along the way. Your generosity always arrived when I needed it most. Thanks.

Lindsey, Sarah, Bill, Elise, Roy, Sue, and Dede, thanks to Pam, are now members of my extended family. I thank them for the many moments they helped me steal when the guards at the gate weren't watching. Their love and thoughtfulness helped me scale the walls.

And to you dear Pamela,

Many of the things that I have done over the last years would not have happened had it not been for you. This book is one of them.

As fully as I had lived life, until I met you I had not visited that inner place you helped reveal. I wanted to tell a story, not just about my life, but about encounters experienced during my journey that might in some way enhance an understanding of the times. In our many conversations, you helped me understand the story I had to tell, and kept urging me to tell it. This book has taken up a great deal of time in your life, and your willingness to stay with me throughout the process has brought the whole thing to fruition. Thank you for all that you have given to bring this moment to pass. Your patience, your caring, your attentiveness to intent all helped to secure the confidence I needed to dare the venture. This work is very much your doing, and I thank you for the joy of it, thank you for helping me stay the course. Thank you for being.

Love you. Harry

INDEX

INDEX

INDEX

INDEX

Underground Railroad, 412
UNICEF, HB as goodwill ambassador of, 341–2, 401–5, 419–20
United Artists (UA), 176, 206–7, 364–5, 374
United Automobile Workers (UAW), 262, 276, 305
United Fruit Company (UFC), 16, 32–3, 34
United Nations (UN), 195, 213, 229, 286, 303, 386, 403–4, 420
United Negro Improvement Association (UNIA), 43
United Steelworkers, 262
United Support of Artists for Africa (USA for Africa), 382–3, 388–9
Universal Pictures, 133
Uptown Saturday Night (film), 351–2, 405–8
Utah, University of, 130

Vandiver, Ernest, Jr., 217
Variety, 102
vaudeville, 57, 179, 211
Vaughan, Sarah, 93, 203
Veneman, Ann M., 419–20
Venezuela, 431–4
Venice Film Festival, 201–2
Vienna, University of, 175
Vietnam War, 267–8, 288, 319–20, 323–4, 337–8, 356
Village Vanguard, 92, 94–5, 98–102, 107, 112, 113, 138, 179, 202–5, 418
Vogue, 369, 405
voter registration drives, 3, 4, 235–6, 253–4, 288–9, 307–8
Voting Rights Act (1965), 304, 307–8, 339, 343
Vroman, Mary Elizabeth, 102

Waldorf-Astoria Hotel, 153, 154, 180
    Empire Room of, 139, 140, 143, 156, 185
    Starlight Roof of, 139–40
Wales, 63, 94
Walker, Drake, 349
Walker, James, 15
Walking with the Wind (Lewis), 294
Wallace, George, 256, 271, 300, 304

Wallace, Henry, 70, 77, 83, 94, 97
Ware, Carl, 373–6, 401
Warren, Robert Penn, 66
Warso, Arnie, 353
Washington, D.C., 51–2, 95–6
    Adams Private Hospital in, 84
    Constitution Hall in, 152
    Lincoln Memorial in, 172, 276, 278–9
    segregation in, 51–2, 55, 71, 84
    Union Station in, 55, 278
    Washington Mall in, 336–7
    Washington Monument in, 189, 279
Washington, Dinah, 250
Wasserman, Lew, 132–3, 138
Waters, Ethel, 139
Waugh, Alec, 163
Waugh, Evelyn, 163
Weapons Station Earle, 54–5
"We Are the World," 158, 381–3, 385, 387, 389
Weavers, The, 96, 106, 156
Wechsler, James, 255
Weiss, Cora, 195
Wells, Robert, 130
West, Cornel, 421, 433
West Africa, 16, 377
Western Union, 5
West Indians, 12–30
    accents of, 13, 18, 58, 59
    American blacks vs., 13–14, 47–52
    Caribbean cooking of, 16, 17–18, 33–4
    caste system among, 23, 39–41, 60
    gradual independence gained by, 14
    music of, 100–1
    pride and ambition of, 14, 30
West Indies, University of, 41
West Virginia State College, 367
What's My Line?, 141
"Whispering," 85
Whitaker, Rogers E. M., 99, 203
White, Charlie, 171
White, Josh, 73, 94, 98, 111, 120
White, Loray, 182–3
White House, 227, 252, 280, 388, 395
    Oval Office of, 228, 272, 273
    Rose Garden of, 272–3

PHOTO CREDITS

A NOTE ON THE TYPE

The text of this book was set in a typeface called Aldus, designed by the celebrated typographer Hermann Zapf in 1952–53. Based on the classical proportion of the popular Palantino type family, Aldus was originally adapted for Linotype composition as a slightly lighter version that would read better in smaller sizes.

Hermann Zapf was born in Nuremberg, Germany, in 1918. He has created many other well-known typefaces including Comenius, Hunt Roman, Marconi, Melior, Michelangelo, Optima, Saphir, Zapf Book, and Zapf Chancery.

Typeset by Scribe,
Phildelphia, Pennsylvania
Designed by Virginia Tan